Educational Technology for Teaching and Learning

Educational Technology for Teaching and Learning

Third Edition

Timothy J. Newby
Purdue University

Donald A. Stepich
Boise State University

James D. Lehman
Purdue University

James D. Russell
Purdue University

PEARSON

Merrill
Prentice Hall

Upper Saddle River, New Jersey
Columbus, Ohio

Library of Congress Cataloging-in-Publication Data

Educational technology for teaching and learning/Timothy J. Newby . . . [et al.]—3rd ed.
    p. cm.
    Rev. ed. of: Instructional technology for teaching and learning/Timothy Newby . . . [et al.]. 2nd ed. c2000.
    Includes bibliographical references and index.
    ISBN 0-13-046714-6
    1. Instructional systems—Design. 2. Educational technology—Planning. 3. Computer-assisted instruction. I. Newby, Timothy J. II. Instructional technology for teaching and learning.

LB1028.38.1587 2006
371.33—dc22   2005041454

Vice President and Executive Publisher: Jeffery W. Johnston
Executive Editor: Debra A. Stollenwerk
Assistant Development Editor: Elisa Rogers
Editorial Assistant: Mary Morrill
Production Editor: Alexandrina Benedicto Wolf
Production Coordination: Carlisle Publishers Services
Design Coordinator: Diane C. Lorenzo
Cover Designer: Ali Mohrman
Cover Image: Corbis
Photo Coordinator: Maria Vonada
Production Manager: Pamela D. Bennett
Director of Marketing: Ann Castel Davis
Marketing Manager: Darcy Betts Prybella
Marketing Coordinator: Brian Mounts

This book was set in New Century Schoolbook by Carlisle Communications, Ltd. It was printed and bound by Banta Book Group. The cover was printed by Coral Graphic Services, Inc.

Photo Credits: Peter Skinner/Photo Researchers, Inc., pp. 3, 42, 139; Geri Engberg/Geri Engberg Photography, p. 4; Anthony Magnacca/Merrill, pp. 10 (all), 103, 104, 155, 193, 257, 266; Carl D. Walsh/Aurora & Quanta Productions Inc., pp. 24, 287; Science Photo Library/Photo Researchers, Inc., p. 26; © The Stock Market/Charles Gupton, p. 36 (left); Scott Cunningham/Merrill, pp. 36 (right), 63, 105, 122, 125, 129 (top), 132, 162, 171, 179, 214 (bottom), 292; Timothy J. Newby, p. 43; SanDisk Corporation, p. 45; © Dorling Kindersley, p. 51; Tom & Dee Ann McCarthy/Index Stock Imagery/PictureQuest, p. 69; Bill Tarpenning/USDA, p. 71; Tony Freeman/PhotoEdit, p. 75; Michael Newman/PhotoEdit, p. 78; Tom Stillo/Omni-Photo Communications, Inc., p. 86; Bonnie Kamin/PhotoEdit, pp. 87, 228; David McLain/Aurora & Quanta Productions Inc., p. 101; ADAMSMITH/Getty Images, Inc. – Taxi, p. 102; Tom Watson/Merrill, p. 108; © ZEFA/Masterfile, p. 118; Dennis MacDonald/PhotoEdit, p. 119; Cindy Charles/PhotoEdit, p. 126; Davis Barber/PhotoEdit, p. 129 (center); Robert Brenner/PhotoEdit, p. 140; Patrick White/Merrill, p. 161; © ViewSonic Corporation 2000–2005, p. 174; AP Wide World Photos, p. 185; John A. Rizzo/Getty Images, Inc. – Photodisc, p. 186; Frank La Bua/PH College, p. 211; Michael Littlejohn/PH College, p. 212; John Underwood, Center for Instructional Services, Purdue University, p. 214 (top); Polycom, Inc., pp. 215, 222; © David Young-Wolff/PhotoEdit, p. 223; Laura Bolesta/Merrill, p. 233; Andy Crawford © Dorling Kindersley, p. 234; Laima Druskis/PH College, p. 246; National Park Service, p. 258; Ryan McVay/Getty Images, Inc. – Photodisc, p. 278; Jon Spaull © Dorling Kindersley, p. 279; Corbis/Bettmann, pp. 281, 282; IBM Archives, p. 283; © 2005 SMART Technologies Inc., used with permission, p. 289; Russ Lappa/Prentice Hall School Division, p. 290 (left); Georgia Tech Communications, p. 290 (right); Stockbyte, p. 293.

Pearson Education Ltd.   Pearson Education Australia Pty. Limited
Pearson Education Singapore Pte. Ltd.   Pearson Education North Asia Ltd.
Pearson Education Canada, Ltd.   Pearson Educación de Mexico, S.A. de C.V.
Pearson Education—Japan   Pearson Education Malaysia Pte. Ltd.

10 9 8 7 6 5 4 3 2 1
ISBN: 0-13-046714-6

PREFACE

VISION AND GOALS OF THE TEXT

The vision of this textbook has always been to **provide the foundations** for **enhanced learning experiences** through the **meaningful integration of technology.** Our first goal is to provide a solid foundation to help you understand the research and background that support the selection, integration, and implementation of specific techniques and technologies. This foundation provides the supporting structure so that proper selections can be made and confidently executed.

Second, in today's information society, the enhancement of learning experiences is essential. We need to discover how we can make learning more effective and efficient, influence a wider diversity of learners, encourage transfer of learning, and perhaps even induce higher levels of learner motivation.

Our third goal is the meaningful integration of technology. This text outlines and explains not only the different types of technologies that are available but, more important, the conditional knowledge of when and why they should be used. When integrated in a meaningful way, technology can greatly facilitate the learning process. Likewise, there will be times when limited use of technology is the optimal course of action. Knowing what to use and when to use it are skills all teachers need.

After using this text, readers will:

1. Be proficient in selecting, modifying, and designing instructional materials.
2. Be able to plan instruction that addresses and solves complex learning problems for individual students.
3. Have a repertoire of instructional methods and media to select from and use those which most effectively and efficiently influence student learning.
4. Be able to use the computer to develop and manage instructional materials, and as a learning tool for students.

ORGANIZATION OF THE TEXT

The text is integrated around three components: the principles of designing instruction, the selection and use of methods and media, and the effective use of computers. To facilitate this integration, the text is designed around the PIE—*P*lan, *I*mplement, *E*valuate—model. Chapters 1–3 provide the needed background on learning, learning theories, and the computer. Chapters 4–8 help the reader discover how to **plan** effective and efficient instruction. This section provides guidance on gathering the needed information about the learner, learning goals, instructional setting (Chapter 4), and the essential elements and activities needed to create an instructional plan (Chapter 5). It introduces the most commonly used instructional methods (Chapter 6) and media (Chapter 7), as well as how to select and/or create instructional materials (Chapter 8). This section emphasizes how technology can be integrated to enhance the learning experience and influence the overall learning that occurs.

The **implementation** phase focuses on how students actually experience instructional materials and activities. Here, we discuss proper integration and implementation of the computer (Chapter 9), the Internet (Chapter 10), and various forms of distance education (Chapter 11). Each chapter emphasizes when, why, and how these technologies should be integrated to enhance learning.

Chapter 12 examines both the **evaluation** of instructional materials and the **assessment** of student performance. We examine how teachers can use evaluation to continuously improve not only the abilities and skill of their students but also the effectiveness of their instruction. The role of the computer in storing, organizing, analyzing, and managing evaluation data is discussed.

The final section focuses on the key issues confronting the field today (Chapter 13), what we have learned from the past, how it has affected what we do today, and the future direction (Chapter 14).

STRUCTURING A COURSE USING THIS TEXT

Traditionally, preservice teachers have taken separate courses in instructional planning and design, media utilization, and computing to gain needed skills and competencies. *Educational Technology for Teaching and Learning,* Third Edition, is a single, integrated source that introduces preservice and in-service teachers to the basic principles of effective instructional material planning and development; to different types of methods and media and how to best utilize them; and to the computer as a powerful tool in planning, developing, delivering, and evaluating effective instruction.

There are at least three ways courses can be structured to accomplish these goals:

▸ *Emphasize the development and use of the instructional plan.* Covering the text's chapters in sequence will accomplish this task. Begin with the general chapters on learning, educational technology, theory, and the computer as a tool to develop and execute the plan. The remaining chapters (based on the steps of the PIE model) show how one *plans, implements*, and continually *evaluates* to learn and teach effectively.

▸ *Emphasize the learning experience itself.* You may want to begin with the chapters that focus specifically on methods and media (Chapters 6 and 7) and their role in the learning process. This can be followed by how the computer, the Internet, and distance education (Chapters 3, 9, 10, and 11) can facilitate the learning experience. Finally, the chapters on designing (Chapters 4 and 5), developing (Chapter 8), and evaluating (Chapter 12)

can be addressed to help your students learn how to develop and improve such learning experiences.

▸ *Emphasize the computer as a powerful tool that can improve learning.* You might begin by looking at background materials on computer hardware (Chapter 3), followed by how and why the computer can be effectively used by both teachers and learners (Chapters 3 and 9). You may then wish to investigate the "power of the computer" and the Internet's use with distance education (Chapters 10 and 11). Coupled with a lab component, this gives extra emphasis to the computer as a key tool for students and teachers, and demonstrates its effectiveness within the classroom setting.

NEW TO THIS EDITION

Several special pedagogical features have been added.

▸ *NETS Connection: Addressing the Standards.* At several points within each chapter, this special feature facilitates your understanding of the National Educational Technology Standards. The journal activity allows you to reflectively consider how to interpret specific standards, as well as what should be considered to properly address these standards. Keeping an electronic and/or paper-based journal enables you to reflectively respond to questions and develop your thoughts and ideas on technology and its use. Moreover, you will be able to monitor your own development and understanding as you gain more experience with the technologies that are introduced, and directly link that relevant information to the standards. This helps you better understand what is expected, and how these standards can be used to inform and guide your understanding. This feature is supported by supplementary materials on the CD accompanying the text.

▸ *Technology Coordinator Corner.* Found at the end of each chapter, this feature examines technology integration from a unique perspective. Cases and scenarios involving various school technology coordinators and the problems and challenges that they face daily are presented. Situations range from a simple question asked by a teacher who is struggling with her first attempts at integrating some piece of software, to more complex issues, such as how to plan a new school that will create the optimal learning environment. This feature provides an insider's look at what must be considered to overcome challenges and successfully integrate technology.

▸ ✓ *Check It Out.* Several "✓ Check It Out" activities provide opportunities to interact, explore, discover, and apply what is discussed within the text. It allows you to examine and use several different kinds of software evaluation forms, determine how to construct one that best suits your current needs, and learn specific computer terms through a computer-assisted instruction in a drill-and-practice tutorial. Moreover, you will also experience guided instruction on how to use various types of computer applications, including video-editing software. These opportunities to interact with the presented materials will help you better understand the materials and apply them in your classroom. This feature is supported by supplementary materials on the CD accompanying the text.

▶ *Extended Example.* A specific lesson plan is developed in Chapters 4–12 and refined as the processes of planning, implementing, and evaluating instructional materials are explained. This extended example allows you to examine how plans for learning experiences evolve given increased emphases on activities, methods, media, technology integration, and evaluation.

▶ *Technology Integration.* We have highlighted when, why, and how various forms of technology can be integrated within the classroom setting. In some cases, this entails the teacher using the computer as an assistant in developing some types of instructional materials. However, in many cases it includes how the computer (or other technology) is integrated to affect the overall learning experience, such as ideas on how to integrate distance education technology for students who are unable to participate in the normal classroom setting.

OTHER FEATURES OF THIS TEXT

The following features are also found in each chapter.

▶ *Chapter-opening analogies* help set the stage for the principal content of the chapter and how it is presented and eventually understood. To prepare you for the new material, each chapter begins with an analogy that compares key principles with something more familiar to help you encode, retain, and recall the new information.

▶ *Key words and objectives* outline the sequence of the information, how it is structured, and when it will be presented. The desired learning outcomes outline what you should be able to do once you have studied the materials within the chapter. Several key words and concepts that may be new to you are found in the glossary.

▶ *Toolboxes* throughout the text present relevant, useful pieces of information. These toolboxes are categorized as Tips, Tools, and Techniques. A *Toolbox Tip* might include a short section on the care of computer hardware or use of software; a

Toolbox Tool might include a description and use of a specific tool, such as Internet search engines; and a *Toolbox Technique* might include information on how, when, and why to use analogies within a set of instructional materials.

SUPPLEMENTS AND RESOURCES FOR STUDENTS AND TEACHERS

▶ *Accompanying CD.* The accompanying CD contains various ancillary materials, many of which will be referred to within the "✓ *Check It Out*" and the "*NETS Connection*" activities in each chapter. These materials include example projects and sample instructional materials, software evaluation forms, media preview forms, computer-assisted instructional tutorials, chapters and exercises from the text *Teaching and Learning with MS Office and FrontPage,* and electronic narrative forms and exercises, among others. In addition, links to websites that are referenced in the text are found on the CD for easy access to the Internet. This icon identifies when you should access the CD.

▶ *Companion Website.* The companion website, **http://www.prenhall.com/newby,** informs users of changes in the field, and provides additional resources and materials that could not be included in the text. Professors will enjoy the use of an online syllabus builder and online course management tools. Professors and students will benefit from the Q&A database that allows students to search previously asked relevant questions, review the responses generated by the authors, ask their own questions, and have their answers posted within the database. Moreover, short videos within each chapter highlight key elements and how to understand these materials. Additional self-assessment tools, reflective activities, and related websites of interest are also accessible via this website.

▶ *Instructor's Manual.* An accompanying instructor's manual is available to professors using this text. The guide includes (a) identification of the key chapter concepts and principles, and ideas for introducing each of the main concepts; (b) strategies for teaching the chapter content; (c) ideas for assessment and feedback; (d) sample lesson outlines; and (e) reference and supplemental resources.

▶ *Computerized Test Banks.* A customizable test bank is available for both Macintosh and Windows users. To request online access to the test bank or the instructor's manual, please contact your Merrill/Prentice Hall representative.

▶ *Live Telelectures and Internet Chat Sessions*. The authors are available for live telelectures or Internet chat sessions if you so desire.

CONTACTING THE AUTHORS

We believe wholeheartedly in communication and feedback. If you have a question or suggestion, let us know. Both students and professors are encouraged to send us e-mail messages and to visit the Companion Website.

Tim Newby
E-mail: newby@purdue.edu
Telephone: (765) 494-5672 (office)

Don Stepich
E-mail: dstepich@boisestate.edu
Telephone: (208) 426-2339

Jim Lehman
E-mail: lehman@purdue.edu
Telephone: (765) 494-7935 (office)

Jim Russell
E-mail: jrussell@purdue.edu
Telephone: (765) 447-6441

ACKNOWLEDGMENTS

We would like to thank all those who have contributed to this edition. In particular, our students, colleagues, and the scores of in-service teachers who have offered examples and insights need to be given special thanks. Through their timely advice we were able to identify areas to add, adapt, and improve. Also, thanks to Debbie Stollenwerk (Executive Editor) and Elisa Rogers (Assistant Development Editor) of Merrill/Prentice Hall for their guidance, edits, and motivation.

Finally, we thank our reviewers for their ideas and suggestions: JoAnn Layford Bing, Nova Southeastern University; James B. Browning, University of North Carolina, Wilmington; Jean Camp, University of North Carolina, Greensboro; Cathy Cavanaugh, University of North Florida; Todd A. Curless, Nova Southeastern University; Deborah Dunn, Tusculum College; Dorothy P. Fuller, Black Hills State University; David Georgi, California State University, Bakersfield; Jeffrey M. Kenton, Towson University; Michael S. Page, Louisiana Tech University; Brenda Peters, College of Saint Rose; Nancy Phillips, Lynchburg College; and Donna R. Starr, Nova Southeastern University.

We hope this text will provide both preservice and in-service teachers with a solid foundation for planning, implementing, and evaluating instruction. By integrating the principles of instructional design, by selecting and utilizing relevant instructional methods and media, and by making appropriate use of the computer, the teaching-learning process can become more effective, efficient, and appealing.

Tim, Don, Jim, and Jim

EDUCATOR LEARNING CENTER: AN INVALUABLE ONLINE RESOURCE

Merrill Education and the Association for Supervision and Curriculum Development (ASCD) invite you to take advantage of a new online resource, one that provides access to the top research and proven strategies associated with ASCD and Merrill— the Educator Learning Center. At **www.educatorlearningcenter. com,** you will find resources that will enhance your students' understanding of course topics and of current educational issues, in addition to being invaluable for further research.

HOW THE EDUCATOR LEARNING CENTER WILL HELP YOUR STUDENTS BECOME BETTER TEACHERS

With the combined resources of Merrill Education and ASCD, you and your students will find a wealth of tools and materials to better prepare them for the classroom.

Research

▶ More than 600 articles from the ASCD journal *Educational Leadership* discuss everyday issues faced by practicing teachers.
▶ A direct link on the site to Research Navigator™ gives students access to many of the leading education journals, as well as extensive content detailing the research process.
▶ Excerpts from Merrill Education texts give your students insights on important topics of instructional methods, diverse populations, assessment, classroom management, technology, and refining classroom practice.

Classroom Practice

▶ Hundreds of lesson plans and teaching strategies are categorized by content area and age range.
▶ Case studies and classroom video footage provide virtual field experience for student reflection.
▶ Computer simulations and other electronic tools keep your students abreast of today's classrooms and current technologies.

LOOK INTO THE VALUE OF EDUCATOR LEARNING CENTER YOURSELF

A four-month subscription to Educator Learning Center is $25 but is **FREE** when packaged with any Merrill Education text. In order for your students to have access to this site, you must use this special value-pack ISBN number **WHEN** placing your textbook order with the bookstore: 0-13-224515-9. Your students will then receive a copy of the text packaged with a free ASCD pincode. To preview the value of this website to you and your students, please go to **www.educatorlearningcenter.com** and click on "Demo."

ABOUT THE AUTHORS

Tim Newby is Professor of Educational Technology at Purdue University. He teaches introductory courses in educational technology, as well as advanced courses in instructional design research, foundations of instructional design theory, and instructional strategies. His primary research efforts are directed toward examining the impact of learning and instructional strategies on students' learning and toward defining/investigating instructional conditions that foster and support the development of expert learners. Tim is particularly interested in the use of analogies and their impact on learning and memory. Thus, throughout this book, you will note the use of something familiar to explain something new. Tim's other life consists of coaching soccer and trying to keep up with an overly committed wife.

Don Stepich is currently Associate Professor in the Instructional and Performance Technology Department at Boise State University, where he teaches courses in instructional design, learning theory, needs assessment, and evaluation. As an instructional designer, Don is interested in the use of interactive strategies to help students learn and in the improvement of instructional materials through continuous evaluation. He is particularly interested in how individuals become experts in a professional discipline, case-based instruction, and the use of analogies in learning. In a former life Don was a professional social worker in a variety of mental health and private counseling practices. In fact, it was his counseling work that led him into education. He found that he was spending a lot of time teaching assertiveness, active listening, and communication skills, which led him back to school to study learning and instructional design.

Jim Lehman is Professor of Educational Technology and currently serves as the head of the Department of Curriculum and Instruction in the College of Education at Purdue University. He teaches classes on the educational applications of personal computers, integration and management of computers in education, interactive multimedia, and distance learning. He is a member of the university's Teaching Academy and was inducted into its Book of Great Teachers. His research interests include integration of computer technology into education, especially in the sciences, interactive multimedia design, and computer-mediated distance education. He directed a PT3 implementation project at Purdue focused on enhancing preservice teachers' preparation to use technology, and he works with colleagues in the K–12 schools on the integration of computers and related technologies. In his spare time, Jim likes to bike, garden, and do home repairs.

Jim Russell is Professor Emeritus of Educational Technology at Purdue University and Visiting Professor at Florida State University. A former high school mathematics and physics teacher, Jim still teaches courses on media utilization and instructional design. The Purdue University Teaching Academy has recognized him as a fellow and has honored him for exemplary work. Jim is also involved with Purdue's Center for Instructional Excellence, where he conducts workshops on teaching techniques for faculty and graduate assistants. His specialty areas are presentation skills and using media and technology in classrooms. When away from the university, Jim enjoys building plastic models and operating his HO-scale model railroad. His wife, Nancy, is a parish nurse; their married daughter, Jennifer, is a high school guidance counselor; and their son-in-law, Lance, works for Lilly Pharmaceuticals. Jim and Nancy's granddaughter, Lauren, is a true joy in their lives.

BRIEF CONTENTS

CONTENTS

SPECIAL FEATURES

SECTION

I

INTRODUCTION TO EDUCATIONAL TECHNOLOGY

Read Me First!

Have you opened a package containing new hardware lately? If so, you may have noticed a section entitled "READ ME FIRST," included because the authors want to tell you about the materials *before* you head off into some trial-and-error learning process. In similar fashion, we think it is important for you to know a few things about this text before you dive into the initial chapters.

First, it would be helpful to know *why* this textbook was developed. We believe that many individuals, especially those within teacher education, need to know (1) how learning experiences and especially instruction are designed, developed, and improved; (2) the types and uses of different media formats—especially the personal computer; and (3) how the design of the instruction and the media are integrated to promote student learning. Meeting these three needs requires integrating the three general areas of instructional design, instructional media, and instructional computing. Traditionally, these have been taught through individual texts and separate courses; however, teachers must apply them in an integrated fashion to have maximum impact on student learning.

Second, it is useful to know that this text is organized around a simple Plan, Implement, Evaluate (PIE) model. The main sections of the text (Sections II, III, and IV) are all based on this model. The different aspects of instructional design, media, and computing are discussed within this structure.

Third, there are a number of special features within this text designed to facilitate your learning. This text focuses on educational technology, especially on the tools that can increase the effectiveness, efficiency, transfer, impact, and appeal of instruction. We have created a "toolbox" feature, which highlights important hardware, methods, techniques, and other tips. There are Check It Out exercises to have you explore, discover, and interact with the various concepts and technologies discussed within these pages, and there is a NETS Connection feature that allows you to examine and reflect on how, when, and why the educational technology standards should be and are addressed.

Of special interest within this text is the emphasis on the integration of technology within the learner-centered classroom environment. We include various sections within each chapter to address the benefits, challenges, and solutions to integration. In addition, we have included a feature to review each chapter's content from the unique perspective of school technology coordinators. Looking through their eyes helps to keep the issues of integration interesting, practical, and on target with what actually happens in the normal school setting.

Throughout this text, we frequently ask questions, present ideas for you to ponder, and describe problems that need thoughtful analysis and synthesis in order to be adequately worked through. This is our attempt to get you involved and to help you to remember and apply the information.

IF WE WERE STUDYING THIS TEXTBOOK, WE WOULD . . .

A few years ago, one of our students asked, "If you were going to study for this exam, how would you go about it?" In response, we created a set of notes that began with the statement, *If we were studying for this exam, we would* . . . The goal was not to provide a list of specific items to memorize; rather it was to guide them so they could draw their own conclusions. These notes worked so successfully, we decided to include a similar set here. So, *if we were studying this textbook, we would . . .*

▶ *Read and reflect on the vision of the text.* As stated here (and also within the Preface and Chapter 1) the vision of this text is: "To **provide the foundations** for **enhanced learning experiences** through the **meaningful integration of technology.**" The purpose, therefore, is to help you discover and explore the key principles and foundations of educational technology that allow the effective integration of technology tools to successfully select, adapt, and create exceptional, meaningful learning experiences. Fully understanding this vision helps you to realize and prepare for where the text is headed and what you will experience. Read and ponder this vision frequently as you venture through each section of this text.

▶ *Pay close attention to the plan, implement, and evaluate model.* Whenever you approach learning (from either a teacher's or learner's perspective) you need to think about how the planning will occur, how the learning will be experienced, and how assessment measures will indicate what worked and what needs improvement.

▶ *Realize that learning is not a simple process.* There are no set prescriptions to ensure that it will consistently occur. You must be prepared to solve unique problems and to draw solutions from a repertoire of possible techniques, strategies, approaches, and media. If you see that one method or tool is not overly helpful, you must be in a position to determine what alternatives would be more effective.

▶ *Reflect on how the textbook material can be applied to your own experiences.* We have included hundreds of examples throughout the text. It is our hope that you will review what is offered and then determine how they match with your own experiences and how your experiences can expand your understanding.

▶ *Realize that this book has been designed to serve as a foundation.* It will not teach you everything. This book will give you the fundamental knowledge and skills you need for your own learning and future teaching.

▶ *Do not underestimate the power of the computer.* Unlike many media formats that are mainly used to present information, the computer can be used by both learner and teacher during the planning, the implementation, and the evaluation phases. The computer can combine a number of different methods and media formats (e.g., multimedia) to enrich and enhance learning experiences.

▶ *Learn to appreciate the power of the computer as a teaching and learning tool, but do not be overwhelmed by it.* Don't fall into the trap of thinking that the computer is the savior of education. The computer is not the most important tool in *all* learning situations. It is one of many tools that can facilitate your work. In addition, don't think that the computer is such a complex tool that you cannot master it.

▶ *Reflect and question.* Take time to reflect on what is presented in this text and, more important, how you can *use* it. When a principle is presented, imagine how, when, and why you might apply it. Use both "NETS Connection" and "✓ Check It Out" features within each chapter to help you reflect, ponder, and think beyond what is presented within the text. In all cases, think about how the information can be applied in your situation.

▶ *Ask for help.* As you reflect and question, feel free to contact us directly. Our desire is for you to be challenged by what is here, not to be frustrated or overwhelmed. If you have questions or problems or suggestions, please contact us. Our e-mail addresses, phone numbers, and mailing addresses can be found in the Preface.

▶ *Be excited about learning!* Learning should be a marvelous adventure, whether you accomplish it personally or assist in helping others experience it. As you learn about educational technology and begin to see its potential, we hope you will become as excited as we are.

OVERVIEW: SECTION I

This first section of the text, entitled "Introduction to Educational Technology," is an introduction to the field of educational technology and the supporting contributions of instructional design, media, and computing. Central to Chapter 1 is the concept of learning and how you can enhance it through the integration of technology.

In Chapter 2 we explore the theoretical foundations of teaching and learning. We look at learning from a number of different angles to enable you to consider which teaching and learning orientation might be best, given a particular topic, situation, and/or type of learner. To increase the usefulness of this theoretical background, realize that the emphasis is not simply on knowing the different perspectives of learning but on understanding how each perspective applies to real students in actual classrooms.

Finally, we have designed Chapter 3 to supply important prerequisite information about the computer and how it can be used to enhance learning. This is a powerful machine, and it is intricately involved in the design, development, implementation, and evaluation of learning experiences.

1

Introduction to Learning and Technology

KEY WORDS AND CONCEPTS

Learning
Technology
Educational Technology
Instructional design
Instructional computing
Instructional media
Cognitive overload
Transfer
Learner-centered instruction
Instruction
Instructional plan

CHAPTER OBJECTIVES

After reading and studying this chapter, you will be able to:

◗ Describe and give examples of learning and what constitutes "an enhanced learning experience."

◗ Evaluate given learning scenarios and determine how, when, and why each learning experience could be "enhanced."

◗ Describe examples of technology and Educational Technology.

◗ Describe the contributions of instructional design, instructional computing, and instructional media to Educational Technology.

◗ Describe how technology potentially can impact learning in a meaningful manner.

◗ Explain the role of the NETS standards in the technology integration process.

◗ Generate diverse examples of meaningful technology integration and highlight key elements needed in order for the integration to be effective.

WELCOME

Welcome to *Educational Technology for Teaching and Learning.* We want you to know from the opening pages that we are excited about this book's contents. Demands on teachers and their students have never been higher. At the same time, we live in a era when phenomenal tools allow for rapid access and manipulation of information. The need as well as the potential for learning is great. In this text we will explore ways to design instruction incorporating computers and related technology that can have a positive impact on learning.

In this chapter, we will share the vision of the book—where we are going and why. We will define and provide examples of learning and technology, and more important, we will begin to discuss integrating the two. In addition, we will address questions such as How can technology positively impact learning? What are the roles of teachers, learners, and technology? and What obstacles stand in the way of effective technology integration and enhanced learning?

Making a Comparison: A Construction Metaphor

To prepare for learning the new information, imagine walking through a new home that is reaching the final stages of construction. Ponder on what had to occur in order for that structure to be ready for someone to live in it. How were the initial plans developed? Where did the builder begin? What different craftsmen with their various skills, knowledge, and tools were needed in order to create the finished structure? How was the work coordinated in such a way to be completed in an effective and timely manner?

Within this text we will also be discussing a "construction" process. Instead of walls, ceilings, and floors, however, our work focuses on the development of experiences that enhance learning. Similar to the building contractor, we use specific skills and knowledge, as well as tools to accomplish the desired end results. Table 1–1

The planning and construction of a building project has many similarities with the planning and construction of effective instructional learning experiences.

compares the similarities between constructing buildings and creating learning experiences. This text will focus on what needs to be built as well as when, why, and how they are effectively used to impact learners.

In this chapter we will extend this construction metaphor, highlight the vision of where we are going and what you will learn, explain the key principles that will be the center of this text, and basically outline how we will get there.

It is important that you begin the chapter realizing the need for tools, as well as a need for how, when, and why specific tools should be used.

VISION OF THE TEXT: WHERE ARE WE GOING?

The relevance of this construction metaphor will become apparent as we look closely at the vision of the text and examine the key elements used to *construct* significant learning experiences. The text's vision (with highlighted key concepts) is:

TABLE 1–1 *Constructing Houses and Learning Experiences*

Constructing a House Requires:	Constructing Learning Experiences Requires:
Knowledge of materials, building codes, heating, plumbing, electrical principles, etc.	Knowledge of learners, learning environments, learning principles, and the content/subject matter
Access to tools such as hammers, saws, and various power equipment	Access to learning tools such as computers, the Internet, various forms of media
Skill with developing and reading blueprints, managing and coordinating the purchase and delivery of materials, as well as the proper use of various tools and techniques	Skill with planning, designing, and developing learning experiences, as well as implementing, managing, and evaluating the use of various media, methods, and instructional techniques

To provide the foundations for **enhanced learning experiences** through the **meaningful integration of technology.**

From this vision, first and foremost will be an emphasis on designing learning experiences. We will examine what is required, as well as how it is accomplished, applied, and evaluated. Moreover, the strategic selection, integration, and use of technology will provide a means to examine potential learning enhancements. In sum, our vision is for you to become an instructional expert capable of helping others learn. To begin, we examine learning itself, and the key elements of the learning process.

LEARNING

Based on the text's vision, a central focus is on human learning and how it is accomplished. Even though most of us are quite familiar with the "learning experience" and we know we have "learned" in the past, there are still key questions to address so that we are in the best position possible to truly impact what is learned.

- What exactly is learning?
- How does learning typically occur?
- Why is the study of learning important?
- How can the learning experience be enhanced?

What Exactly Is Learning?

It is relatively easy to cite examples of learning. For instance, reflect on the past few days or weeks and think about something you learned. Maybe it was something that required concerted time and effort, such as learning how to write a specific type of research paper. Or you learned something that needed less effort or time, such as the location of the closest parking facility for your new night class. Or possibly your learning occurred without you consciously realizing it, such as when you learned two full verses of an obnoxious jingle from a television commercial. The time, effort, and purpose involved in each of these examples varied considerably. However, in each case, learning occurred.

Learning is a broad concept and occurs across such a variety of subjects that defining it concisely is not simple. However, here are some definitions with consistent terminology.

- "Learning is a relatively permanent *change* in behavior due to *experience.* Learning is a relatively permanent *change* in mental representations or associations as a result of *experience*" (Ormrod, 2004, p. 3).

- Learning is "an enduring *change* in behavior or in the capacity to behave in a given fashion resulting from practice or other forms of *experience*" (Schunk, 1996, p. 445).
- Learning is "a persisting *change* in performance or performance potential that results from *experience* and interaction with the world" (Driscoll, 2005, p. 1).
- "Learning refers to lasting *changes* in the learner's knowledge, where such changes are due to *experience*" (Mayer, 2003, p. 5).

Note that within each of these definitions *change* is brought about through *experience* or some form of interaction with the environment. To *learn* is to change (or have the capacity to change) one's level of ability or knowledge in a permanent way. Typically, learning is measured by the amount of change that occurs within an individual's level of knowledge, performance, or behavior. To qualify as learning, Woolfolk (1998) explains, "this change must be brought about by experience—by the interaction of a person with his or her environment. Changes simply caused by maturation, such as growing taller or turning gray, do not qualify as learning" (p. 205). So, for example, as novice construction workers begin to drive nails faster and with greater accuracy in framing a new home, we can then infer that their interaction with the environment (repeated use of the hammer on the job) has resulted in a positive change in their hammering skills. Thus, we can say that learning has occurred. Table 1–2 compares examples and nonexamples of learning. Note the need for change to occur due to experience. More than 70 years ago, Thorndike (1931) emphasized the importance of change by writing, "Man's power to change himself, that is, to learn, is perhaps the most impressive thing about him" (p. 3).

How Does Learning Typically Occur?

Learning may occur in a number of ways. For example, it may come about through: (a) direct experience (e.g., touching a hot stove and learning about the pain associated with such a touch); (b) vicarious experience (e.g., learning by watching someone else go through an experience such as touching a hot stove); (c) instructional presentation (e.g., learning through a presentation, reading, etc., to recognize, identify, and properly be wary of hot surfaces); and (d) a combination of any or all of the others.

The selection of the optimal format of learning depends on several factors. Each factor must be considered before the selection of the type of learning experience can be properly made. The factors to consider include the learner, the learning environment, and the content that is to be learned (see Chapter 4 for extended discussions on each of these factors). Learners vary greatly in their ability to understand a learning experience whether it is derived from direct, vicarious, or instructional presentation types of experiences. Developmental

TABLE 1–2 *Examples and Nonexamples That Illustrate the Accomplishment of Learning*

Examples:

- Executing a perfect kickboxing "round house kick" on command
- Reciting a J.R.R. Tolkien quote from memory
- Deriving and using an equation to solve a novel math problem
- Choosing not to drink milk that "smells funny"

Nonexamples:

- Gaining weight or growing taller (results of maturation or physiological changes)
- Demonstrating perceived heightened interpersonal skills brought on by high levels of alcohol consumption (results of drugs or alcohol that are generally of short duration)

level, learning styles, gender, ethnicity, intelligence, etc., all impact the degree to which a learner gains from a specific type of learning experience. Likewise, the learning environment will allow and restrict the type of learning experience that can be selected and used. Being able to have students have a direct experience using a flight simulator may be readily accomplished with a small group of students who live near a flight school, but large classes of hundreds of students will not have ready access to direct experience because of the numbers involved or the location of the simulator. Finally, there is some content that lends itself to be directly experienced and other content that does not. Learning about writing a research paper is content that frequently lends itself to individuals gaining direct experience; whereas, learning about different management styles within major investment corporations may be more readily accomplished through a more presentation-oriented learning experience.

Why Is the Study of Learning Important?

Learning is complex. It may occur across all types of tasks (e.g., changing a car tire, falling in love, delivering a speech, identifying cell anomalies), for all types of learners (e.g., a newborn child, a business CEO, a high school student, a 90-year-old violin player), and in various environments (e.g., in the mountains, on a production line floor, in a small group of students, sitting at a computer). Moreover, it may occur today for a specific person, in a specific location, covering a specific topic; however, tomorrow (or even later today), it may not be as readily achieved.

The study of learning focuses on identifying and describing general conditions and principles that facilitate and/or inhibit learning and determining how they can be best utilized to promote reliable learning. If learners and those who guide the learning of others (e.g., teachers/trainers/parents) understand these key principles, then the chance of facilitating the learning process may

be enhanced. Through the study of learning, we can come to identify specific theories and principles that allow us to predict certain situations that will facilitate (and what may hinder) certain learning for specific individuals.

As highlighted in the given definitions of learning, experience plays a key role. This indicates that the quality of the experience potentially enhances (or inhibits) what is actually learned. Specific activities, methods, media, techniques, technologies, etc., employed within a learning experience can be used to enhance the learning. ***Thus, the study of learning helps learners, and those who guide learning, to strategically identify, select, implement, and evaluate key elements of an experience that will ensure reliable changes in desired behavior.***

As an illustration, review the contributions of Mayer (2003). His research on the Cognitive Theory of Multimedia Learning indicates, for example, that individuals have a limited capacity to attend to and process incoming information through a single sense modality (e.g., auditory). That is, only a certain amount of information can be heard, understood, and processed efficiently by a learner at any one time. More than the restricted amount will not be retained because a form of **"cognitive overload"** may occur. However, if a second channel (e.g., visual) is utilized to convey additional information, then the limited capacity for processing new information by learners can be expanded to some degree. Through the use of multimedia, for example, the impact of the learning experience may be significantly enhanced. By studying the research of Mayer and others, we can come to see how learning experiences can be designed and structured to enhance overall learning.

Benefits, as shown in Figure 1–1, that are directly connected with the study of learning include:

▶ Increased **effectiveness.** In this case students actually learn in a better way than they would without the experience. The study of learning helps

Increased levels of:

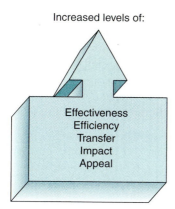

FIGURE 1–1   The study of learning can lead to increased levels of several key benefits.

to identify how to increase the encoding, retention, depth of understanding, and recall of needed information and skills.

▶ Increased **efficiency.** Here the focus is on time. Through the study of learning we can identify ways to organize and deliver learning experiences in a manner that helps students obtain the information or skills in a more rapid/timely manner.

▶ Increased **transfer.** Through the study of learning we may identify how to better generalize what is learned so that it can be utilized in different but related contexts or content areas. For example, learning how a specific problem-solving technique can be used across a wide variety of problems increases its value and usefulness to the learner.

▶ Increased **impact.** Identifying and implementing techniques that allow a greater diversity of learners to be positively influenced by the learning experience can also be achieved through the study of learning.

▶ Increased **appeal.** Identifying ways to enhance learner motivation for a specific learning experience can increase the possibility that students will devote time and energy to the learning task as well as the likelihood they will return to review and work on the material at other times. Appeal is strongly associated with learners' attitudes toward the information and their motivation for investing effort.

Plan, Implement, Evaluate (PIE): A Reliable Model to Impact Learning

The study of learning is important for both those who will be learning and those who will be guiding the learning of others because specific actions, techniques, and technologies can have an impact on the quantity and quality of what is learned. By understanding learning we can better design and develop strategic learning experiences.

Our emphasis is on what learners and teachers can do to positively impact learning. As shown in Figure 1–2, such things relate to the following:

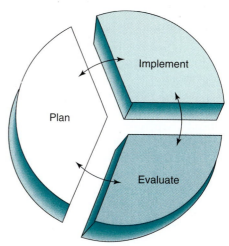

FIGURE 1–2   Plan, implement, and evaluate. The phases of learning.

▶ The *planning* required to ensure that instruction is developed and sequenced in a manner that the learner can effectively process

▶ *Implementing* the instruction

▶ *Evaluating* both the instruction and the student's resultant learning

This emphasis can be compared to the approach of an expert home builder. The expert is noted for planning, for understanding the strengths and weaknesses of various tools and materials given different situations and expected outcomes, and for reflecting on and evaluating the effectiveness of the tools throughout the entire design and construction process. Throughout this text, we place a similar emphasis on *planning, implementing,* and *evaluating.*

In planning, the focus is on what students are to learn, as well as how, when, and why it might best be accomplished. The result is an outline, lesson plan, or blueprint of the learning experience that will bring about the desired goal. This plan helps to delineate learners' *present* knowledge and abilities, as well as what their knowledge and skills *should* be, and it suggests ways to reduce the difference between the two. This plan influences the manner in which you develop and present information and the learner experiences it. Section II of this text (Chapters 4–8) focuses on planning.

Implementation focuses on putting the plan into action based on what situational constraints exist, using selected instructional materials and activities. For learners, implementation is when, where, and how they experience learning. For the teacher, implementation includes monitoring and managing the instruction, groups of learners, and individuals with special needs. Section III (Chapters 9–11) explores implementation in greater detail.

The emphasis during evaluation is on the assessment of the effectiveness of the materials. This is a time to reflect on what was accomplished, to compare that with your desired goal, to suggest changes in future planning and implementation, and to complete suggested revisions and fix-ups. Section IV (Chapter 12) focuses on evaluation.

The planning, implementing, and evaluating process (we refer to as the PIE model) helps to guide us to systematically structure our approach to developing effective instructional learning experiences. Refer again to Figure 1–2 and note that each of the stages within the model is highly interactive with each of the other stages. For example, the planning impacts both how the instruction is implemented and how it is evaluated. The implementation feeds information back to the planning for future reference and updates and also helps dictate how and when evaluations can take place. Likewise, the evaluation gives critical feedback to both how future instruction is planned, as well as how it is best implemented.

How Can the Learning Experience Be Enhanced?

Referring back to the construction analogy given earlier, one might ask the same question about how to enhance the home that is being constructed. Through various tools, the exterior, for example, could be enhanced by adding stronger, more durable materials (e.g., bricks) that may require less maintenance, adding greater levels of insulation, and perhaps increasing overall visual appeal. Likewise, the learning experience may be enhanced in various ways in order to increase effectiveness, efficiency, transfer, impact, and appeal. Let's examine the following example of how a lesson focused on multicultural education could be experienced within a normal classroom setting:

Situation A: Suppose you were teaching a class on multicultural education. For one lesson within the course

you design a discussion on the unique differences between rural versus inner-city classroom structure and students. To facilitate the discussion you have the students read the textbook chapters that cover the content and you have them explore some readings from various sources you have selected. Finally, you give them key questions to reflectively think about prior to coming to the class.

Now review the following situation involving the same lesson that has been adapted in a number of ways.

Situation B: Suppose you were teaching the same class as described in Situation A. However in this case, before the discussion you also have your students join an Internet listserv focused on issues confronted within the inner-city schools and have them monitor the discussions of current teachers in those situations. In addition, you make arrangements for your class to be linked via a two-way interactive video so that they can monitor visually and aurally a class of students at both an inner-city and rural school location. Your class then discusses a comparison between the two locations.

Reflect on the following questions:

▶ What are the key differences between how the information was experienced in the first learning situation versus that of the latter?

▶ What could potentially be the key differences in the quality of the discussion that the students have within your course from those that participated in the second situation versus those that participated in the first?

▶ What are some benefits and challenges of each of these situations for both the student and the instructor?

Check It Out

PIE Model

Imagine that you find yourself in the following situation. You have been asked to help students in a high school biology class learn about the impact of commercial fishing on the seal population in Alaska's Maritime National Wildlife Refuge during the last 30 years. From the *perspective of the teacher,* review the questions in the first column of Table 1–3 and see if they help you to grasp what needs to be considered when such an experience is being planned, implemented, and evaluated.

Once you have reviewed this task from the perspective of the teacher, do it again, but in this case take it from the potential *learner/student perspective.* Review the questions in the second column of Table 1–3 and see how the different elements of the PIE model also should be considered by students as they approach a learning task.

Finally, after reviewing the other two perspectives, review the final column of questions. Think of ways in which *technology* could be used to facilitate that which is required of students and teachers during each of the PIE stages. We will discuss technology in greater detail later in this chapter, but these questions help to set the stage for the role of technology within the teaching/learning process.

TABLE 1–3 *Instructional Process: What Questions Should You Ask?*

	The Teacher	The Learner	Educational Technology
Plan	• What task must the students be able to do, and how can I determine when it has been accomplished? • What do the students already know that will assist in learning this task? • What resources, facilities, and equipment are available and accessible? • What information should be included in the instructional materials or activities? • What is the most effective, efficient, and appealing manner in which the to-be-learned task can be acquired by the students? • In what order should the learning activities be sequenced? • What is the best medium to assist students in learning the new information? • What can be done to help this learning be transferred to other similar situations? • Are there relevant instructional materials (or parts thereof) that already exist? Which materials will need some adaptation? Which materials will need to be created? • Based on need and practicality, what methods and media should I include or have students include within the instruction?	• What is the goal of this task (i.e., What am I supposed to learn?)? • What will I need to learn this task (e.g., learning strategies, assistance from others, time, effort)? • In what ways can my previous learning experiences help? • What obstacles and problems could hinder me from learning this task? • How will my motivation and effort in this task be generated and maintained (e.g., Am I good at this kind of task? Do I like this kind of work?)? • How should I attempt this task in order to effectively learn the materials while maintaining my motivation and overcoming presented obstacles (e.g., Does this type of activity require a great deal of concentration?)?	• In what ways can educational technology effectively impact how a student addresses a learning task? • In what ways can instructional process technologies (e.g., methods, techniques) and high-tech and other media technologies effectively impact how a teacher designs and creates instructional materials? • How can students and/or teachers improve learner attention and topic motivation through the use of instructional technology? • How can instructional technology improve the efficiency of student learning and/or teacher preparation?
Implement	• How will the instructional experience and activities be managed? • How will groups of learners as well as individuals with special needs be managed during their learning experience? • During the learning process, how will my students' attention and motivation be maintained?	• How do I assemble or create what is needed to carry out the plan? • How do I begin and follow the planned learning strategies? • Is this going the way I planned? • Do I understand what I am doing? • What outside materials or resources should be added? • What should I look for in order to tell if learning is occurring? • How can I tell if my task motivation is being maintained?	• In what ways can instructional technology assist and impact the manner in which the student experiences the instruction? • In what ways can teacher efficiency during the delivery of instruction be increased through the use of educational technology?
Evaluate	• Was the quality and quantity of learning at the needed level? • What did I do when the selected tactics and learning strategies didn't work? • What obstacles were encountered, and what strategies were or were not effective in overcoming those problems? • What have I learned from this experience that could be used at other times for different tasks? • What improvements could I make for future learning tasks?	• How can I determine to what degree the students have learned the material? • What types of remediation or enrichment activities may be necessary for my students? • In what ways can these instructional materials and activities be improved for repeated or adapted use? • How will needed changes throughout the learning experience be monitored? • How will student self-evaluation and regulation be learned and encouraged?	• How can technology be used to determine the degree of student learning that has occurred? • How can technology be used to generate teacher and student feedback? • In what ways can technology be used to measure the effectiveness, efficiency, and appeal of the implemented instructional materials?

Teachers take on several roles as they plan, implement, and evaluate instructional learning experiences.

Although the quality of the learning experience can be enhanced in a number of ways (e.g., quality of the text information, how the questions are asked within the discussion, use of attention-getting devices to focus the learner's attention) based on the vision of this text, we will concentrate on how to enhance the learning experience through the meaningful integration of various technologies both for the learner and for the individual who will be creating the learning experience. Throughout this text, we will highlight the use of these various technology tools, methods, and media and how they impact the design, development, delivery, and evaluation of the learning experience.

The Teacher as Instructional Expert

An integral part in most educational settings, and particularly within learner-centered instruction, is the teacher.

Although classroom instructors frequently serve a variety of roles from administrator to surrogate parent, the most important function is that which Woolfolk (1990) refers to as the "instructional expert." In this capacity teachers are actively involved in several aspects of the instructional learning process. The instructional expert's involvement can range from little actual interaction with students (e.g., when devoting time and effort to developing learning activities) to a high amount of group or individual interaction (e.g., when presenting new materials to students in a lecture or discussion format).

Over the years the functions of teachers as instructional experts have remained relatively constant. Whether direct or indirect, good or bad, teachers heavily influence what students experience and subsequently learn in the classroom. Even in situations where students have more control (e.g., a discovery/exploratory environment, individualized instruction), the teacher selects

Check It Out

Identifying Learning

Table 1–4 highlights several scenarios that may involve learning. Read through each of the scenarios and then do the following:

▶ Categorize each individual scenario as an example or nonexample of learning. Describe your rationale.
▶ For the identified examples of learning, describe how, when, and why each experience could be enhanced.

TABLE 1–4 *Examples and Nonexamples of Learning*

1. At the county fair, Jordan has been asked to demonstrate how to tie a sheep bend knot in order to safely secure his calf to a post. If completed successfully, is this a demonstration of something Jordan has learned?
   ☐ example
   ☐ nonexample

2. Jared is asked to demonstrate how to reduce his hay fever by taking a new hay fever tablet. If Jared takes the pill and shortly thereafter his hay fever abates, has learning been demonstrated?
   ☐ example
   ☐ nonexample

3. Janette desires for her teeth to be whitened by her dentist. In order to do that, he creates a mold of her mouth, and shows her how to apply the bleaching agent to the mold and hold it in her mouth for 30 minutes twice a day for 10 days. If her teeth become lighter in shade, does this indicate that learning has occurred?
   ☐ example
   ☐ nonexample

4. Lacy has decided to get into better physical shape so she joins an after-school aerobics class at her local gym. At first, she thought she would never be able to successfully follow the instructor as she worked through the routine. However, after a few days, Lacy was successfully completing the main steps involved in the aerobics routine. Is this a demonstration that learning has occurred?
   ☐ example
   ☐ nonexample

5. Richard discovered that he was able to estimate the cost of new carpet in his bedroom by applying several simple math equations he had been studying at school. Is this a demonstration that learning has occurred?
   ☐ example
   ☐ nonexample

or arranges the activities and gives guidance and clarification. Because of this critical role, *this text will focus on what you as an instructional expert should know and do so that your students can learn.*

Using the plan, implement, and evaluate model, the expertise of the teacher is shown to be needed in each of these areas. During planning, teachers identify students' instructional needs by identifying existing gaps

TOOLBOX
TOOLS
TIPS
TECHNIQUES

Toolbox: Tools, Tips, and Techniques

As you venture through this text, note that we have inserted special short features called "Toolboxes." Just as a cabinetmaker's toolbox holds valuable things that allow him to successfully complete his job, our toolboxes contain items that will play a role in your success as both teacher and learner.

Similar to the builder's toolbox, the ones in this text contain a variety of items. Each one of these will be designated as a "tool," a "tip," or a "technique." Toolboxes appear strategically throughout the text because of our desire for you to immediately see their value and worth. Instead of giving you a long list of tools in an appendix, for example, our goal was to locate individual toolboxes where their need was apparent and where we could illustrate an example of its use. In that manner, you can read about the tool, tip, or technique in the inserted toolbox on the same page that you can see its value and potential usefulness.

The **TOOL** toolbox will generally focus on hardware or software that you will find helpful in specific situations. We might, for example, discuss scanners, digital cameras, or graphic software that could help as you develop instructional materials.

The **TIP** toolbox will be devoted to giving you insight on things that the authors and others have learned through experience that warn you of potential problems and help you accomplish your job in a more professional and efficient manner. Examples include "How to use visuals in instructional materials" and "Care of computer systems."

The **TECHNIQUE** toolbox will be devoted to different types of instructional techniques that have been shown effective in improving learning, for example, mnemonics, analogies, reflection, and debriefings.

We could not, of course, include everything you will need for all learning situations. We had to be very selective. This is our way of helping you begin to develop a toolbox of your own. Some of these items you may find you need and use daily; others you may use only on a very limited basis. It is important for you to understand that this is just a beginning. Throughout this text and as you venture on through your career, you will continue to add relevant tools, tips, and techniques to your learning toolbox.

between current and desired levels of skills and knowledge and then select instructional methods and strategies to meet those needs. Other considerations at this time include the type of learners they are dealing with and the teacher's own personal style of teaching. The principal result is a plan or blueprint of instruction, which includes learning content, which strategies and activities to use, when to use them, and how to structure them. Throughout this process teachers need to be familiar with the tools of technology that can assist the planning of the learning experience.

After teachers assemble or produce needed instructional materials, they then become a "director of learning activities" (Ausubel, Novak, & Hanesian, 1978). This may require the teacher to personally disseminate information through some form of expository lecture, inquiry discussion, or demonstration; to serve as manager of other learning vehicles (e.g., video presentation, small-group discussion); or to become a guide/coach who encourages and helps students experience learning on their own. The primary outcome is that the student experiences the instruction. Likewise, knowledge of technology tools can be utilized to facilitate how the instructional experience is delivered and how the learners come to experience the learning activities.

The final role for the instructional expert is that of **evaluator** of student learning, as well as the overall learning experience. Teachers traditionally have done this by examining how well students completed the lesson and by determining if they have attained the desired level of performance. Increasing attention is now being focused on providing continuous evaluation throughout all stages of learning (Stiggins, 2005). Evaluation should also be a time to reflect on successes achieved and problems encountered. The evaluation's result is a description of the strengths and weaknesses of the program, which teachers may then use for instructional improvement. Knowledge and use of technology during this process may aid in the manner in which evaluative information is gathered, analyzed, and reported. Teachers may come to find that technology can be used to examine closely what works and what doesn't within the learning experience, as well as assess how well students are gaining the desired knowledge and skills.

For most teachers, planning, implementing, and evaluating instruction are all ongoing processes. On any given day a teacher may plan and develop several future lessons, monitor current topics to ensure that they are being properly addressed, and reflect on completed lessons and the results they produced.

The Learning Environment: Shifts Toward Learner-Centered Instruction

For a moment, think about the "traditional" classroom setting. For most, this will conjure up thoughts of a room with rows of desks and chairs. The traditional view of teaching and learning is one in which the teacher stands and delivers the content, while students sit and receive.

This view places the control of all learning in the hands of the teacher. It assumes only a slight diversity in the manner in which most students assimilate information. For some types of learning, mostly those dealing with basic rote skills, this traditional approach has proven quite efficient.

In today's world, however, demands on the learner have increased substantially. Where once it may have been sufficient to learn rote responses within given working environments, now the real world demands individuals use high-order reasoning skills to solve complex problems. Access and accountability for solving complex problems are no longer left to the few; all individuals, whether they are working on an assembly line or in a corporate think tank, need problem-solving skills. As stated by Driscoll (2005), no longer should learners be viewed as "empty vessels waiting to be filled, but rather active organisms seeking meaning" (p. 387). Learners must now be viewed as proactive participants in learning, actively seeking ways to analyze, question, interpret, and understand their ever-changing environment.

From another viewpoint, think about the average classroom from 90 years ago and the demands placed on the classroom teacher. The majority of students, and teachers as well, came from homogeneous backgrounds (e.g., grew up in the same town, raised in two-parent families, one parent was home to raise the children, less mobility). Today, the diversity among class members is much greater. With that diversity comes the challenge of different learning styles, greater differences in background experiences, varied home life settings, and so on. Classrooms of today are much more diversified, leading to more complex learning problems for teachers and students alike.

A Need to Shift to Learner-Centered Instruction

Today we live in an age of lightning-fast information transfer. Technology has allowed individuals to obtain, assemble, analyze, and communicate information in more detail and at a much faster pace than ever before possible. One consequence of this is the ever-increasing demand on education to help all learners acquire higher-level skills that allow them to more readily analyze, make decisions, and solve complex "real-world" problems. According to Bruer (1993), learners must rise above the rote, factual level to begin to think critically and creatively. These increased demands dictate changes in the way teachers interact with students; moreover, these changes must be grounded in an understanding of how a diverse population of individuals learns.

Throughout this text, we give examples of many techniques, methods, and technologies for helping learners acquire new knowledge. We understand that at times you will engage your students in lower-level, rote learning, and as needed we describe techniques to help learners acquire factual information. (For example, we highlight the use of mnemonics or specific drill and practice techniques for basic-level learning.) In such cases, the teacher-centered "traditional" view of teaching may prove most efficient and effective.

Of particular importance, however, will be teaching the higher-order skills and the manner in which students acquire them. A major emphasis must be on problem solving and transfer. We emphasize the use of such methods as simulations, discovery, problem solving, and cooperative groups for learners to experience and solve real-world problems. In these cases, you will note a shift in the manner in which the learning experience is planned and carried out. Instead of the traditional teacher's total control and manipulation, the importance of the learner's role in planning, implementation, and self-evaluation will be emphasized. Learners engaged in **learner-centered instruction** proactively engage with various sources of potential information (e.g., the teacher, technology, parents, media) to gain insights into a problem and its possible solutions. The teacher's role shifts to one of guide and facilitator who assists learners in achieving their learning goals.

Table 1–5 highlights several key changes in the roles of the teacher and the learners within a learner-centered environment. As you reflect on these changing roles, imagine the impact they have on the manner in which you plan and carry out instruction. We want to emphasize that because of the diversity in both learners and information, a single approach to all instruction will not always work: A number of different methods and media exist for designing and developing learning experiences, and the roles of learner and teacher shift based on the situation, the content, and the special needs of the individuals involved.

TECHNOLOGY

Technology has been referred to as "the systematic application of scientific or other organized knowledge to practical tasks" (Galbraith, 1967, p. 12). In other words, it is "the application of science to industry" (Mehlinger & Powers, 2002, p. 10). Note the emphasis on *application* within these definitions.

Technology is the manner in which research is applied to solve practical problems. As depicted in Figure 1–3, technology performs a bridging function between research and theoretical explorations provided by

TABLE 1–5 *Key Role Changes in a Learner-Centered Environment*

For the STUDENT

A Shift From:	A Shift To:
Passively waiting for the teacher to give directions and information	Actively searching for needed information and learning experiences, determining what is needed, and seeking ways to attain it
Always being in the role of the learner	Participating at times as the expert/knowledge provider
Always following given procedures	Desiring to explore, discover, and create unique solutions to learning problems
Viewing the teacher as the one who has all of the answers	Viewing the teacher as a resource, model, and helper who will encourage exploration and attempts to find unique solutions to problems

For the TEACHER

A Shift From:	A Shift To:
Always being viewed as the content expert and source for all of the answers	Participating at times as one who may not know it all but desires to learn
Being viewed as the primary source of information who continually directs it to students	Being viewed as a support, collaborator, and coach for students as they learn to gather and evaluate information for themselves
Always asking the questions and controlling the focus of student learning	Actively coaching students to develop and pose their own questions and explore their own alternative ways of finding answers
Directing students through preset step-by-step exercises so that all achieve similar conclusions	Actively encouraging individuals to use their personal knowledge and skills to create unique solutions to problems

FIGURE 1–3 The bridge of
technology between research
and practical problems.

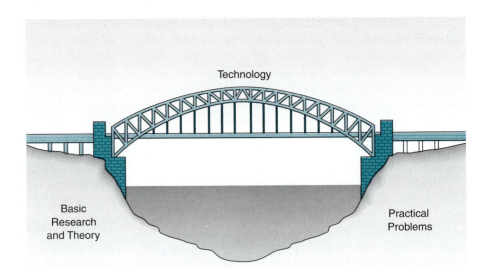

Technology

Basic
Research
and Theory

Practical
Problems

TOOLBOX TOOLS

Toolbox Tool: The Technology Standards

Standards are tools for guidance and measurement. They are developed to help determine needed levels of skill proficiency as well as a comparison stick to measure the quality of skill attainment. Most professions have well-established standards they use to make judgments about current performance. For example, medical doctors must meet or exceed specific standards in order to practice their profession. Standards help to ensure that individuals have the competencies necessary to complete critical tasks.

Within Educational Technology, standards have been developed for both students and teachers. These standards are known as the National Educational Technology Standards (NETS) and they have been developed in conjunction with the International Society for Technology in Education (ISTE). Within the ISTE website (**http://www.iste.org**) the National Educational Technology Standards are listed and discussed. Moreover, examples and scenarios of their use are presented. In the Teacher Resource A of this text we have listed the NETS and performance indicators for all teachers.

NETS CONNECTION: ADDRESSING THE STANDARDS

Throughout this text we will be highlighting the relationship between one's ability to perform at the proficiency level outlined by the technology standards and one's ability at effectively enhancing the learning experience through the integration of technology. To help facilitate your understanding of the standards and how they can be used to guide your perception of technology and learning, we have included an additional feature within this text known as "*NETS Connection: Addressing the Standards.*" This feature will be based on a journal writing activity that we encourage you to actively use and develop through the use of this text. In each case, this activity will highlight one or more relevant standards and guide you to reflectively consider how to interpret the standard, as well as what should be considered in order for it to be properly addressed. To help you succeed in addressing the standards, we have also placed each of these "NETS Connections" on the text's accompanying CD. The electronic version allows immediate access to compare all standards, as well as easy word processing forms for your thoughts and responses.

By keeping an electronic and/or paper-based journal, you will be able to reflectively respond to questions asked and develop your thoughts and ideas about technology and its use. Moreover, you will be able to monitor your own development and understanding as you gain more experience with the technologies that will be introduced. In each case, you will be able to directly link that relevant information to a respective standard. This is designed to help you better understand what is expected, as well as how these standards can be used to inform and guide your level of understanding.

TABLE 1–6 *Examples of Problems and Application Tools Used within Various Industries*

Various Industries	Sample Practical Problems	Resultant Application Tools
Communications	Need for relatively easy and inexpensive communication between individuals across wide distances	Cell phones, Internet, video conferencing equipment
Publishing	Desire to deliver various forms of media in a cost-efficient and timely manner	Printing presses, digital pictures, online publications
Sports	Need to protect players in contact sports	Lightweight, flexible, protective jackets, braces, helmets, face guards, etc.
Medicine	Need to better diagnose internal disease and injury	X-ray, MRI, and CAT scans

science on the one side and the real-world problems faced by industry and other practitioners on the other.

The space industry offers a good example. Numerous practical problems have been encountered as humans have traveled in space (e.g., How does one breathe in a place devoid of oxygen?). To solve such problems, contributions from physics, materials science, and other fields of research had to be translated to practical application. In many cases the results were tangible products such as the space shuttle, space suits, and advanced telecommunications capabilities. In other situations, the resultant tools and products have taken not-so-tangible forms such as enhanced safety procedures, formulas for reentry projections, and backup contingency plans. In each instance, scientific knowledge was reviewed and applied to answer specific practical problems. Table 1–6 highlights several other examples of practical problems faced by various industries and the resultant applications tools.

In each instance, technology served as the application bridge between the scientific research/knowledge and the practical problems.

In most cases, some type of tangible tool is produced to allow this application to occur. For a construction worker a hammer may be a useful application tool; however, the builder also accesses and uses other tools (e.g., blueprints, management processes, safety procedures) that may be less tangible, but just as important, for solving the practical problem of building a structure.

Why Is the Study of Technology Important?

Technology offers solutions to problems. Those solutions, however, don't just magically appear. Through study we are able to refine what and how applications are determined and implemented. This helps us identify the alternatives, select the best option, and evaluate and readjust as needed.

For example, a builder is often faced with decisions about the exterior siding for a building. Although it is critical to know various kinds of exterior coverings

(vinyl siding, brick, wood, stucco), it is more important to know how the building is going to be used, what the desired look is to be, how the temperatures within the region typically vary, the moisture content for the region, the cost of the materials, the availability of craftspeople to install a selected covering, and the like. Obtaining such information first allows the builder to make the optimal exterior siding selection for that particular situation.

Similarly, studying technology is not just identifying different pieces of hardware. It is understanding what is available, when and why it should be used, how it is effectively adapted, integrated, evaluated, and adjusted.

What Exactly Is Educational Technology?

Just as technology has been used to address practical problems in communication, medicine, sports, and so on. it has also been used to address practical problems involved in human learning. Formally stated, **Educational Technology** is the "application of technological processes and tools which can be used to solve problems of instruction and learning" (Seels & Richey, 1994, p. 4). As depicted in Figure 1–4 it serves as the bridge between those who conduct research on human learning (e.g., psychologists, linguists) and those students and teachers who face practical learning challenges. Resultant application tools include principles, processes, and products that teachers and students use to enhance learning.

Educational Technology utilizes application tools to accomplish the overall goal of constructing and delivering optimal learning experiences.

How Is Educational Technology Utilized?

Consider the following situations:

▶ A small high school desires to offer an advanced chemistry class for several capable students; however, a qualified teacher is not available.

▶ Two middle school teachers (one from the English department and one from social studies) desire to

Addressing the Standards

NETS Connection

In part, the National Educational Technology Standards (NETS) I (Technology Operations and Concepts) and III (Teaching, Learning, and the Curriculum) for teachers emphasize the need *to be able to identify and understand the potential benefits of technology for the learner.* Reflect on those standards (see Teacher Resource A for a full listing) and then complete the following journal entry. Do the best you can at this point; however, as you progress through this chapter and the remaining chapters in the book, continually adapt what you have written:

▶ Create two lists, one that includes the different types of technology that may be used to impact learning and another that includes the different types of learning that one may encounter (e.g., rote memorization, physical/motor skill development, complex problem solving).

▶ Reflect on the two lists and then reflectively suggest ways in which the various forms of technology may be used to effectively enhance the various forms of learning.

Note: This NETS Connection can be accessed and completed on the text's accompanying CD (**Chapter info and activities>>>Chapter 1>>> NETS Connection**).

---

create a combined unit on explorers of North America.

▶ An art teacher at the elementary school level wants students to study insects and create their own bug art.

To utilize the tools of Educational Technology in such situations, the following should be considered:

a. How should the learning experience be constructed?
b. How should it be delivered/experienced?

Within this text we will expand on each of these questions. Using research on human learning, for example, various techniques, methods, strategies, and activities (e.g., organization and structure of the materials, the use of analogies, cooperative learning groups, tutorials,

discovery learning, and discussions) will be examined and integrated with the content to create an optimal learning experience. Moreover, how the experience is planned, implemented, and evaluated will be examined in detail. In addition, various tools in the forms of computers, distance learning equipment, the Internet, and other forms of media will be examined in order to determine how the learning event should be received and experienced by each learner.

Note that as we proceed through the text, we will emphasize the use of various tools that can facilitate the development and delivery of learning experiences. However, we will also emphasize the reasons for the use of those tools. That is, similar to the builder, we don't want you to just learn about a specific tool (e.g., the hammer, saw) but also to understand how it is used to create a

---

FIGURE 1–4 The bridge of technology between learning research and practical learning problems.

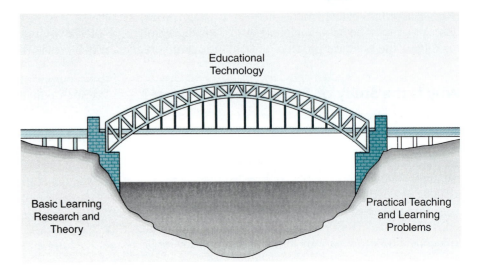

Educational Technology

Basic Learning Research and Theory

Practical Teaching and Learning Problems

usable structure. The computer is a very important tool for those developing and delivering instructional materials; however, it isn't the whole story. You must also come to understand how the learning experience is designed in a manner that makes it effective for the individual learners. Together, the integration of the tools within the context of developing and delivering the learning experience will create the most beneficial result.

What Is the Meaningful Integration of Technology?

The meaningful integration of technology is knowing when, why, and how specific tools should be used to facilitate overall learning. It requires both the ability to plan and select the optimal application tools, as well as the knowledge and skill to implement and evaluate their effectiveness.

It is more than just presenting a tool such as a computer to a learner and saying, "Go forth and learn!" It requires knowledge of the learner, the content to be learned, as well as an understanding of how the tool can be used to help the learner accomplish the learning goals.

Humans are noted for the use of tools in attempts to make their lives better in some way. Within education, examples of integration can take many forms. For instance:

▶ A preschool teacher who helps her students grasp the concept of small living organisms may incorporate the use of a magnifying glass or a

microscope in order to accomplish the learning goals.
▶ Teachers in art and language may find their learning goals better served by having students reflect and write about examining the paintings and sculptures from the world's past masters after they have visited (virtually) several of the world's most prestigious art galleries.
▶ A head nurse may find that her new nurse trainees may begin to analyze and critique newborn babies with higher levels of proficiency following the review of a CD-ROM that highlights key new baby evaluation procedures and how to detect abnormalities.

How Is the Meaningful Integration of Technology Accomplished?

Technology as the application of tools is used continuously throughout our lives. However, meaningful integration within education requires the use of tools that have been strategically selected and implemented to directly impact the achievement of specific learning goals.

With the goal of enhancing a learning experience in a meaningful manner, technology integration follows a three-step process: (a) planning the integration, (b) implementing the integration, and (c) evaluating the integration. Each phase has specific questions that need to be addressed in order to accomplish a successful integration and ultimately enhance learning. Table 1–7 highlights each phase of the integration process and supplies

---

Addressing the Standards

NETS Connection

In part, the National Educational Technology Standards (NETS) III (Teaching, Learning, and the Curriculum) and IV (Assessment and Evaluation) for teachers emphasize *the need to observe and experience the use of technology as it is being used within one's own field of study.* Reflect on those standards (see Teacher Resource A for a full listing), then record your thoughts and ideas after completing the following:

▶ Focus on your selected field of study (e.g., math, English, elementary education) and reflect on the importance of technology within that specific field (e.g., when is technology relevant and when is it not?).
▶ Experience some instructional materials from your specific field of study (e.g., attend a presentation/lecture, examine a textbook, view a video, examine relevant web pages).
▶ Evaluate the use of the technology you experienced within the learning experience. Write your thoughts about the impact of the technology and include ways in which you think technology could have been used to enhance the learning of this specific subject matter.
▶ Remember this activity and as you go through this text, refer back to your writings and adapt/append them to reflect new information and thoughts that you learn.

Note: This NETS Connection can be accessed and completed on the text's accompanying CD (**Chapter info and activities >>> Chapter 1 >>> NETS Connection**).

Check It Out

Technology Integration

Return to Table 1–4 and select one or two examples of learning and determine how technology could be integrated to enhance overall learning. Highlight key elements needed for technology integration to be effective.

Once you have completed that activity, explore the InTime website (http://www.intime.uni.edu/) on the Internet. You may also access this website via the text's accompanying CD (**Chapter info and activities >>> Chapter 1>>> InTime Video Source**). This is a fascinating website that allows you to access online video vignettes of PreK–12 teachers as they demonstrate the different ways they have come to integrate technology within their classrooms. Select a content area and/or grade level of personal interest and explore the examples that are provided. Begin to imagine how you could use these examples to increase the technology integration within your teaching.

TABLE 1–7 *The Technology Integration Process*

Planning for Integration

Planning is the process of determining the optimal technology to produce an enhanced learning experience based on the specific *content, learners,* and learning *environment.* This is the phase that determines what elements of the instructional experience should/could be enhanced.

Key questions to consider:

• What are the goals of the current learning experience?

• What is the content that learners will need to learn?

• Who are the target learners and what background knowledge and experiences should they have prior to the learning experience?

• Are the learners motivated to learn this content?

• How could learner motivation be increased and/or maintained?

• What are the possible ways the learning could be experienced by the learners?

• Where and under what conditions could the learning experience occur?

Implementing for Integration

Implementing focuses on the selection and use of one or more types of technology that enhance the manner in which learning occurs.

Key questions to consider:

• Based on information about the learners, content, and learning environment, what are the potential types of technology most applicable to this learning situation?

• What are the benefits and costs from selecting and using each of these potential technologies?

• What are the steps and sequence involved in the integration of technology within this specific learning experience?

• Who will implement and monitor the use of the technologies within the target learning experience?

Evaluating the Integration

Evaluation is the process to determine the effectiveness of the technology integration and to identify better ways for future implementations.

Key questions to consider:

• To what degree did the implemented technology enhance the learning experience?

• What procedures should be followed to evaluate the impact of the enhanced learning experience?

• What types of feedback information would help us to optimize use of technology and what was learned?

• What key obstacles to integration need to be addressed/overcome?

several key questions to be considered during each phase. Throughout the remaining chapters of this text (especially within Chapter 8), we will be addressing these phases and their corresponding key questions.

THE ROLE OF INSTRUCTION

Instruction is "the deliberate arrangement of learning conditions to promote the attainment of some intended goal" (Driscoll, 2005, pp. 352–353). In this text, the role of instruction is to use instructional technologies in ways that maximize students' learning. The extent to which these technologies enhance teaching and learning is determined by the degree to which you properly select individual teaching and learning tools and learn to use them interdependently.

In many cases individuals take one course to learn how to design and develop instructional materials, another course to learn about different forms of media and how to use them properly, and still another to learn how to use the computer in the classroom. Although such a disjointed approach may give students a solid background in all three individual areas of study, it may limit their ability to see how each area may expand the effectiveness of the others. We feel that such an approach, while better than not having any courses, can be improved by emphasizing the relationships among these areas. It is only through an integrated approach that teachers can identify and solve the more difficult problems of human learning. Through such an integrated approach teachers may readily see how computers can contribute to designing the instructional plan and developing the instructional materials, how the design directs the media selection, and, likewise, how using the media affects students' interpretation and acceptance of the designed instructional message. Although you could study instructional design, media, and computing independently, viewing them as an interrelated whole magnifies their potential for teacher and student alike.

Instructional Design

Instructional design is the process of translating principles of learning and instruction into plans for instructional materials and activities (Smith & Ragan, 1999, p. 2). The emphasis is on creating a plan for developing instructional materials and activities that increase an individual's learning. Reigeluth (1983) compared this task with that of an architect. The architect produces a blueprint or plan that effectively integrates the needs of those who will purchase and use the facility, the environment in which it will exist, the costs involved, the appropriate materials, and other design specifications for functionality, safety, and aesthetics. Similarly, instructional experts incorporate learning principles into plans

for instructional materials and activities based on analyses of the learners, the situation, and the task or content to be learned.

Although a builder may attempt to build a structure without using the architect's plans or blueprints, he may encounter problems he could have avoided by using a plan—walls may be in the wrong location, electrical outlets forgotten or misplaced, or improper materials purchased. As with any plan, the major benefit of an instructional plan is the guidance it gives. This does not mean that all instruction should be designed based on a single set of plans (like a subdivision of one-style homes), but rather that specific principles can be used to solve different instructional problems and to produce unique solutions in a variety of situations.

Power of the Plan

The overall **instructional plan** plays a critical role in directing the selection and use of all other tools within the learning environment. Just as the building contractor uses a plan to determine what materials and construction tools to select and use, so too the teacher and learners should use an instructional plan to determine the methods, techniques, and media they will use. Additionally, the plan helps to determine how and when to present specific sets of information and when additional information is required.

Even though a plan gives teachers direction, it should not be perceived as a rigid structure that dictates regimented, systematic procedures. Whenever learning is required, different types of learners, tasks, and situations all interact, requiring flexibility. The plan provides a means to review alternative possible solutions to instructional problems, assess their potential, and then confidently select the best. If and when those alternatives do not produce desired levels of learning, the plan can be revised and additional alternatives selected. Robinson (1981) notes that expert fishermen usually outperform those of lesser ability, not because they know the best bait for a given fish on a specific day, but because they also know the second- and third-best alternatives. Similarly, the power of the instructional plan is that it suggests alternatives and a means whereby they can be investigated and evaluated before investing time and money in developing the final products.

Aspects of instructional design include:

▶ **the overall instructional plan**—what to include and how to arrange the components
▶ **various analysis techniques and methods** that help determine both learners' current skill levels and those needed to accomplish the task
▶ **a repertoire of methods, techniques, and activities** that can be used to increase student learning (Table 1–8)

TABLE 1–8 *Types of Instructional Tools: Methods, Techniques, and Activities*

Instructional Methods	Instructional Techniques	Instructional Activities
Cooperative learning	Focusing questions	Motivation activities
Discovery	Highlighting	Orientation activities
Problem solving	Analogies	Information activities
Instructional games	Mnemonics	Application activities
Simulation	Imagery	Evaluation activities
Discussion	Concept maps	
Drill and practice	Embedded questions	
Tutorial	Feedback	
Demonstration	Case studies	
Presentation	Role-playing	

▶ **strategies for sequencing instructional media and materials** so that learners get the proper amount of information when needed

▶ **an emphasis on evaluation** to ensure that the instructional materials and procedures resulted in students achieving the desired goals

This text explains how to design instruction so that learners and teachers all may benefit. Table 1–8 lists instructional tools that aid in instructional design. These include instructional methods, techniques, and activities teachers may use to create and augment successful instructional materials. We discuss these technologies in greater detail throughout the text.

Specific chapters have been devoted to the discussion of instructional methods (Chapter 6) and instructional activities (Chapter 5). Instructional techniques are integrated throughout Section II within the various Toolbox: Technique features.

Instructional Media

A **medium** "refers to anything that carries information between a source and a receiver" (Smaldino, Russell, Heinich, & Molenda, 2005, p. 9). In addition, Smaldino et al. (2005) explain, if those messages contain information with an instructional purpose, they are considered **instructional media**. In one case the selected instructional medium may be videotape, in another it may be audiotape, in still another it may be computer software, or even a diagram. Each instructional medium represents a means of connecting learners, the teacher, and the instruction. Table 1–9 lists several forms of media, each with its own set of unique attributes. Important questions involving the manner in which learners experience information include the following:

▶ What forms of media are available?

▶ What impact do the different media formats have on learning?

▶ Under what conditions can this potential impact be altered?

▶ How are various media formats most effectively used?

When investigating the answers to these and similar questions, research in the areas of perception, cognition, communication, and instructional theory comes to the forefront. For every learner and teacher, the central concerns are how information is structured and what happens once individuals have perceived and experienced it. Research shows that various forms of media and their respective selection and utilization processes directly impact what learners perceive and how they retain and recall information (Kozma, 1991).

Instructional media for teachers and learners can be used to:

▶ present materials in a manner learners can readily assimilate (e.g., a video can clearly illustrate how cells divide in the early stages of reproduction)

▶ deliver materials independently of the teacher, thus allowing students some control over how much of the material they will experience and when (e.g., students can rewind or fast-forward portions of a video- or audiotape to match their own learning needs)

▶ allow learners to experience materials through various senses (e.g., seeing projected visuals, reading textual materials, and hearing a verbal description of the same content)

▶ provide learners with repeated and varied experiences with subject matter to help them construct their own understanding and meaning

▶ gain and maintain learners' attention on the subject matter

▶ motivate students toward a goal

▶ present information in a manner that individual learners otherwise could not experience (e.g.,

TABLE 1–9   *Types of Media with Attributes and Examples*

Instructional Media	Key Attributes	Example
Real objects and models	Actual item or three-dimensional representation	A living animal A plastic model of the human eye
Text	Written words	Biology textbook Written material from an electronic encyclopedia
Video	Moving pictures	Instructional video on the procedures to insert memory chips in a computer Video on how to seek shelter during a tornado Audio CD of an inspirational speech
Audio	Sound	Audiotape of directions for completing a process
Graphics (visuals, slides, overhead transparencies)	Pictures, line drawings, maps	Projected overhead transparency of the state of South Carolina Map of the organizational structure of a school corporation
Multimedia	Combination of various media forms	Computer program on comparative culture that incorporates pictures, textual descriptions, native music, and short videos of individuals speaking different languages

events can be speeded up or slowed down, objects can be decreased in size [e.g., the universe] or increased in size [e.g., an atom])
- accommodate varying sizes of audiences

Power of the Learning Experience

Review the list of media formats presented in Table 1–9. Teachers can use all of these to help students learn. The question is, "Why do we need all of the different types of media?" For example, isn't an overhead projector an effective medium for delivering information to students? Why then are videos, computer software, textbooks, and so on also used? The answer lies with the learning experience itself. Various levels of content, types of learners, and learning situations dictate that some media formats are at times better suited or more feasible than other formats.

Each medium has its own set of unique characteristics, and how people interact with a message is shaped by the medium's particular attributes. For that reason, it is important to understand what each medium can contribute to the learning experience. For example, readers make use of the stable quality of information presented in the traditional textbook. When they encounter a difficult passage, learners can slow down, reread portions, skip back and forth, refer to pictures or diagrams, and so on. As learners struggle to create meaning from information in a textbook, their interaction with the *book* is dependent, to a great extent, on the characteristics of that medium.

Throughout this text we will emphasize the importance of correctly selecting and utilizing these various forms of media. *It is critical to keep in mind that no matter how good the medium, learning will be hindered*

if the message is poorly designed. Learning also will be obstructed if the message is well designed but delivered in such a fashion that the learner can't understand or interpret it correctly. The power of the learning experience very much depends on the learners' experiences. The media format dictates how the instruction will be delivered and how learners will subsequently experience it. Clearly, media play a critical role in the overall learning process.

Instructional Computing

The computer has made a tremendous impact throughout our society, and that impact has been particularly strong within the field of education. **Instructional computing** is defined as the use of the computer in the analysis, design, development, delivery, and evaluation of instruction. The computer's power within education is due to its versatility as both a production and a presentation tool. Although it is a form of media and should be considered as such, the computer's capability to be *both* a presentation and production tool sets it apart from other media formats (e.g., text, videos). For example, in a single day a classroom computer may be used to write a creative short story about a character from the Wild West, monitor on the Internet the current shape and velocity of a tropical storm off the coast of Florida, store scores from the last social studies assignment, and look up information on Nelson Mandela and listen to parts of his major speeches. These examples illustrate the power of the computer in teaching and learning.

Because of its current impact and tremendous potential, it is imperative that classroom teachers understand the power of the computer and how they can use and adapt it for learning. Throughout this text, we devote sections to explaining how you may use the computer, when and why it is a valuable asset, and how to integrate it in the classroom to ensure the maximum effect on your teaching and on your students' learning.

Instructional computing for teachers and learners can be used to:

▶ enhance the quality of instructional materials using the electronic capabilities of the computer

▶ reduce the time required to design, produce, and reproduce instructional materials

▶ increase the overall effectiveness of instructional materials through enhanced presentations

▶ combine graphics, video, audio, and textual forms of media into single, integrated instructional presentations

▶ store and quickly access huge amounts of information and data

▶ communicate with others at both near and distant locations

▶ function as a learner, in which the student programs the computer to complete a task or to solve a problem

▶ function as an instructional expert, in which the computer makes decisions about levels of student learning, suggests media and learning experiences to students, and then selects and presents those media and experiences

Power of the Machine

The real power of the computer is in its versatility. At times it becomes an assistant, helping to manage classroom and instructional development efforts. At other times, it can become the actual way through which students experience the instructional activities and learn content. In still other cases, it becomes the means by which students attempt to solve complex problems. This versatility, coupled with its power to store, access, and manipulate huge amounts of information, is why so much attention has been devoted to computers in education.

TECHNOLOGY COORDINATOR'S CORNER

In order for you to begin to see how the information provided within the chapters of this text can be used in the real classroom setting, we will include in each chapter a short section based on the perspective of a school technology coordinator. In this section we will highlight situations and problems commonly encountered by the coordinator and how those challenges were addressed.

These problems will be presented to the coordinator by teachers with varying degrees of technology expertise who are dealing with a wide variety of students and content. You will read stories of success, frustration, excitement, and apprehension. Some teachers will provide insightful ideas that need further exploration and expansion; while others will need encouragement and help to find the proper direction for their efforts.

Each chapter's *Technology Coordinator's Corner* will integrate and illustrate the application of the key information from within that specific chapter. At times simple, straightforward answers will be readily apparent. At other times there may be several potentially relevant responses. In some cases, little help will be offered by the tech coordinator. All of these situations were designed to help you see the relevance of the material found within the chapter pages.

SUMMARY

In this chapter we have introduced several initial key concepts. We defined *learning* as a change, or potential to change one's level of skill or knowledge, and it is of central concern for both students and teachers. We emphasized that the design and use of effective, efficient, and appealing instruction can enhance learning.

Learning is difficult to measure and to consistently achieve because of the inherent differences in learners, content, and contexts. Facilitating learning requires an active knowledge of a variety of tools and techniques plus an understanding of how, when, and why they should be appropriately used. Educational technology includes tangible tools (high-tech hardware such as computers, and instructional media such as overhead transparencies and videotapes) as well as other technologies (methods, techniques, and activities) for planning, implementing, and evaluating effective learning experiences.

Learners, teachers, and instruction all play key roles in the learning process. Furthermore, each of these roles shifts as the instructional focus changes from planning, to implementing, and to evaluating instruction.

SUGGESTED RESOURCES

CD Resources

To increase retention and transfer of this information, review the *Reflective Questions and Activities* located in the Chapter 1 section **(Chapter info and activities>>> Chapter 1>>> Reflective Questions and Activities)** of the text's accompanying CD.

In addition, the CD allows direct access to relevant Internet websites, NETS Connection exercises, and direct e-mail access to the text's authors.

Website Resources

Access the text's website **(www.prenhall.com/ newby)**, navigate to Chapter 1, and review Question and Answer section for relevant questions that have been generated by students and answered by the authors. You may also submit your own questions directly to the authors. In addition, you can access presentations by the authors about this chapter and gain insights directly from them about the topics that have been presented.

Print Resources

Bruer, J. T. (1993) *Schools for thought: A science of learning in the classroom.* Cambridge, MA: The MIT Press.

Driscoll, M. P. (2005). *Psychology of learning for instruction* (3rd ed.). Boston: Allyn & Bacon. (Chapter 1)

Jonassen, D. H., Peck, K. L., & Wilson, B. G. (1999). *Learning with technology: A constructivist approach.* Upper Saddle River, NJ: Merrill/Prentice Hall. (Chapter 1)

Seels, B. B., & Richey, R. C. (1994). *Instructional technology: The definition and domains of the field.* Washington, DC: Association for Educational Communications and Technology. (Chapter 1)

Smith, P. L., & Ragan, T. J. (1999). *Instructional design.* Upper Saddle River, NJ: Merrill/Prentice Hall.

Woolfolk, A. E. (2003). *Educational psychology.* Boston: Allyn & Bacon.

2

Theory into Application

KEY WORDS AND CONCEPTS

Theory
Learning theory
Antecedent
Behavior
Consequence
Attention
Encoding
Retrieval

CHAPTER OBJECTIVES

After reading and studying this chapter, you will be able to:

▶ Explain theory and describe its practical value.
▶ Discuss the role of the instructional expert from three theoretical perspectives on learning.
▶ Discuss the role of technology from three theoretical perspectives on learning.

This chapter focuses on the concept of learning. In Chapter 1 we defined learning and discussed how understanding it will make us all better learners and better teachers. In this chapter we discuss learning from three different perspectives: behavioral, information processing, and constructivist. We take a practical approach, describing applications of each learning theory.

INTRODUCTION

The students in Ms. Moreno's sixth grade Spanish class are working at computer terminals on a vocabulary lesson. The computer presents students with increasingly difficult sentences in Spanish. Each sentence contains a blank space and students are asked to enter a Spanish word or phrase that fits into the sentence, such as the following:

¿ _____ te llamas?
¿ _____ viva Maria?
¿ _____ Ud. De Mexico, senora?

After students respond, the computer gives them feedback about the appropriateness of their chosen word or phrase. The computer allows for a number of "correct" responses for each sentence. When the response is correct, students move on to the next sentence. When the response is incorrect, the computer gives them a hint regarding how to translate the sentence and asks again for a response. If the response is again incorrect, the computer translates the sentence and provides several appropriate responses.

Down the hall, the students in Mr. Patrick's sixth grade Spanish class are corresponding with pen pals in Barcelona, Spain. The students work in small groups to write a letter describing current events, the history of their city, or some other topics of common interest. The letter is then sent, via e-mail, to a group of students in Barcelona, who respond with a letter about the same topic. The students must then translate the letter from the Spanish students and send a reply. Because the students in Barcelona are learning English, the students correspond in Spanish for a month, in English for the following month, and so on.

Is one of these classes better than the other? No. But they are taking a very different approach to the instruction, based, in large part, on different views of how students learn and how technology can be used to support that learning. Recall from Chapter 1 that **learning** refers to a change in an individual's level of knowledge, performance, or behavior resulting from interaction with his or her environment. **Instruction** refers to the deliberate arrangement of learning conditions to maximize learning. **Instructional technology** refers to the application of scientific knowledge about human learning to the practical tasks of teaching and learning. **Instructional expert** refers to an individual who uses

his or her knowledge of instructional technology to plan, implement, and evaluate instructional activities.

This chapter will combine those concepts, using learning theory as the glue that holds them together. There are four essential points to keep in mind throughout the chapter:

▶ The purpose of teaching is learning.
▶ The teacher's primary role in learning is that of instructional expert.
▶ Instructional technology can be used to help carry out that role.
▶ Learning theory should inform the use of instructional technology.

THE VALUE OF THEORY

A **theory** is an organized set of principles explaining events that take place in the environment (Gredler, 2001). Theories evolve from observations. As observations about causes and their effects accumulate, a theory attempts to explain those observations. Based on that explanation, the theory makes predictions, or hypotheses, in the form of "If *x,* then *y*" statements that can be tested, resulting in more observations, which lead to additional predictions, and so on (see Figure 2–1).

As an example, the theory of immunity was Edward Jenner's (see Figure 2–2) attempt to explain why milkmaids in early nineteenth-century England were less likely to catch smallpox than were most other people (Asimov, 1984). Jenner noticed that the milkmaids were *more* likely to catch cowpox, a similar but relatively minor disease. He hypothesized that individuals exposed to cowpox develop a natural protection against the disease that also protects them from smallpox. To test his theory, Jenner injected a young boy with cowpox.

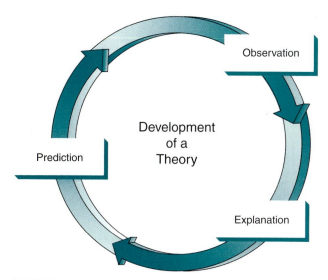

FIGURE 2–1 Development of a theory.

FIGURE 2–2   Edward Jenner's experiments confirmed a theory of immunity.

of teaching can be translated into practical guidelines. For the remainder of this chapter we describe theories that inform instructional practice and discuss practical guidelines derived from them.

Before we begin, however, we have two caveats. First, we haven't tried to include all of the theories that inform teaching practice. We focus on learning theory. Although motivational theory, communication theory, and others are important, we believe learning theory is critical because the way we teach is governed by what we know about how people learn. Second, our purpose here is *not* to provide a definitive statement of any theory. We want to outline some key features of several learning theories, and emphasize how they inform instructional practice. Thus, we will describe each theory in terms of four central questions: (1) What is learning? (2) What is the learning process? (3) What is the role of the instructional expert? and (4) What role can technology play?

LEARNING THEORY

A **learning theory** is an organized set of principles explaining how individuals learn, that is, how they acquire new knowledge and/or abilities. But we can't describe learning theory as a single entity. Learning has been studied for hundreds (perhaps thousands) of years, and many theories have been proposed to explain it (see Driscoll, 2005; Gredler, 2001). Of these theories, we have selected three broad theoretical perspectives: behavioral, information processing, and constructivist.

These perspectives represent major trends or themes in the way learning is conceptualized and inform practice in different ways. They have different views on what learning is, how it occurs, how the instructional expert can facilitate learning, and what role technology can play. The perspectives are described briefly in Table 2–1 and in more detail in the following sections.

It is important to note that we present these perspectives in roughly historical order rather than in order of importance. Each perspective is alive and well today and has both theoreticians and practitioners as adherents.

Behavioral Perspective

Behaviorism began in the early part of the twentieth century with the argument that "the subject matter of human psychology is the behavior *or activities of the human being*" (Watson, 1924, p. 3, italics in the original), rather than the mental phenomena, such as consciousness, that had been the subject of study during the latter part of the nineteenth century. In education, behaviorism is most closely associated with the work of B. F. Skinner. In contrast to other forms of behaviorism (such as Pavlov's classical conditioning), Skinner focused on the

Two months later he injected the same boy with small-pox. The boy did not get sick, which confirmed Jenner's theory.

That's what a theory is. But the question is, *What is the practical value of theory?* Effective professional practice requires more than knowing what tools and techniques are available and how to use them. The hallmark of professional practice is the ability to select and use tools and techniques to devise a solution that meets the demands of a particular situation. This requires the flexibility and adaptability that come from understanding at the level of theoretical principle rather than at the more superficial level of technique.

Theory informs practice in every profession. For example, thanks to Edward Jenner, physicians now routinely provide vaccinations as protection against infectious diseases such as diphtheria, measles, and the flu. The relevant principle from biology is that the body naturally develops immunity to many of the diseases it encounters.

Similarly, theory informs practice in the classroom. For example, students in a Spanish class will often practice their conversational skills together. Their progress may be slow because of their inability to give one another good feedback. The relevant principle from learning theory is that students learn best when they have frequent practice followed by *immediate* and *accurate* feedback. An instructional expert can implement this principle in live practice in the classroom or build it into a multimedia CD-ROM that encourages students to practice frequently and gives them feedback for each practice.

In summary, theory is not simply a collection of abstractions that aren't relevant to the real world. Theory has *practical* value for teachers. As with other professions, the principles that form the theoretical foundation

TABLE 2–1   *Comparing the Three Theoretical Perspectives of Learning*

	Behavioral Perspective	Information Processing Perspective	Constructivist Perspective
What is learning?	A change in the probability of a behavior occurring	A change in knowledge stored in memory	A change in meaning constructed from experience
What is the learning process?	Antecedent → behavior → consequence	Attention → encoding → retrieval of information from memory	Continuous process of experience and reflection, often done in a group
What is the teacher's primary role?	Arrange external contingencies	Arrange conditions to support memory processes	Model and guide
What can the teacher do to carry out that role?	• State objectives • Guide student behavior with cues • Arrange reinforcing consequences to immediately follow students' behavior	• Organize new information • Link new information to existing knowledge • Use a variety of attention, encoding, and retrieval cues	• Provide opportunities to solve realistic and meaningful problems and to reflect on those experience • Provide group learning activities • Model and guide the process of constructing knowledge within the context of mutual problem solving
What role can technology play?	Organize different kinds of materials (text, audio, video) and exercises into an instructional "program"	Help students organize new information, link it to their existing knowledge, and encode it into memory	Facilitate collaborative communication among students, instructors, and other experts Provide a variety of complex, realistic, and safe problem-solving environments
What is the student's primary responsibility?	Respond to cues	Actively synthesize information	Explore like a scientist

voluntary, deliberate behaviors that he believed made up most of an individual's behavioral repertoire. These behaviors, which he termed "operants" because they are the individual's way of operating on, or influencing, the environment, are affected by what follows them, as well as what precedes them. Understanding this type of behavior, therefore, involves understanding all of the environmental events surrounding it. Skinner developed his theory during the 1930s and began applying it to an increasingly broad array of human problems, including education, during the 1950s. He believed that, by applying behavioral principles, "the school system of any large American city could be so redesigned, at little or no additional cost, that students would come to school and apply themselves to their work with a minimum of punitive coercion and, with very rare exceptions, learn

to read with reasonable ease, express themselves well in speech and writing, and solve a fair range of mathematical problems" (Skinner, 1984, p. 948).

What Is the Behaviorist Definition of Learning?

Learning has been defined in various ways. But, as we point out in Chapter 1, a central idea in those definitions is *change*. In considering these theoretical perspectives, the question becomes—change in what? A primary assumption of the behaviorist perspective is that we must focus on the *behavior* of the learner and that, like other behaviors, learning is largely determined by the external environment. Within the behavioral perspective, learning is described as a change in the probability that a person will behave in a particular way in a particular situation (Ertmer & Newby, 1993).

What Is the Behaviorist Learning Process?

An A → B → C model can be used to explain how behaviorists view the learning process. The environment presents an **antecedent** (A) that prompts a **behavior** (B) that is followed by some **consequence** (C) that then determines whether the behavior will occur again (Woolfolk, 1995). Learning is said to have occurred when students consistently behave in the desired way in response to the specific antecedent, that is, when A consistently results in B.

Students learn without instruction, but instruction provides "special contingencies which expedite learning" (Skinner, 1968, p. 64). These contingencies are the antecedents and consequences that influence individuals' behaviors. To shape a behavior, teachers gradually and carefully adjust the environmental contingencies to encourage students to behave in ways that are progressively closer to the goal. For example, when learning to parallel park a car, a driving instructor may begin by asking students to park in a space that is much longer than a car. Gradually, the instructor will reduce the size of the space until students can park in a space that is only slightly longer than a car. According to Skinner (1968), well-designed instruction allows teachers to concentrate on those aspects of the learning situation that are "uniquely human": diagnosing learning needs and providing encouragement, support, and guidance.

What Is the Role of the Instructional Expert in Behaviorism?

This A → B → C framework emphasizes the influence of the external environment on learning. Instruction, then, refers to the environmental conditions presented to the students. Within the behavioral perspective, the primary responsibility of the instructional expert is to arrange these environmental conditions (antecedents and consequences) in a way that will help the students learn. This can be done by:

1. Stating instructional objectives as specific learner behaviors (B) that, when successfully performed, will indicate that learning has occurred. This involves identifying the goal and breaking that goal down into a set of simpler behaviors that can be combined to form the desired behavior.
2. Using cues (A) to guide students to the goal. Initially providing a cue will help ensure students' success by guiding them to the desired behavior. The cue can be gradually withdrawn to make sure the behavior is linked to the appropriate antecedent.
3. Using consequences (C) to reinforce desired behavior. Using consequences effectively involves two tasks. The first is to select reinforcers. Unfortunately, this is not always easy. Reinforcement is defined solely in terms of its

effects on a student's behavior and, as a result, can often be determined only after the fact. In addition, different things reinforce different students and, to make matters even more complicated, the same student may be reinforced by different things at different times. Common reinforcers include praise, tangible rewards (good grades, certificates, etc.), and time spent on enjoyable activities. The second task is to arrange the selected consequences so that they reinforce the desired behavior. Timing is critical. To be effective, the consequences should immediately follow the behavior they are meant to reinforce. Otherwise, it may reinforce an unintended behavior that doesn't help students progress toward the goal.

What Role Can Technology Play in Behaviorism?

Technology can be used to create an effective instructional "program." An instructional program is made up of a logical sequence of units, often called "frames." Each frame includes information along with a question, problem, or exercise that calls for a response. Students receive immediate feedback for their responses and move through the program at their own pace. The knowledge needed to move from one frame to the next is purposely kept small in order to increase the frequency of correct responses and, therefore, the frequency of reinforcement. Before the advent of the digital computer, instructional programs were built into programmed learning textbooks and mechanical teaching machines. But modern computers allow the development of instructional programs that are much more flexible and powerful. This is because computers allow us to:

▸ Incorporate different kinds of materials. Frames can include audio and video as well as text and pictures.
▸ Incorporate different kinds of exercises. Short simulations can be included along with more traditional questions.
▸ Monitor each student's progress. Information can be stored in the computer and retrieved at any time.
▸ Provide feedback that is immediate and geared to the student's response. They allow branching based on a student's response and can incorporate remedial information, if necessary.
▸ Set up the instruction so the students can start and stop whenever they like.

Note that a very simple version of integrating technology from a behavioral perspective would contain each of these key elements. For example, each of you will probably have some experience with the low-level flash-card-type technology. As shown in Figure 2–3, one

FIGURE 2–3 Electronic flash cards used to study physics concepts.
Source: Reprinted with permission from The FlashcardExchange.

side of the flash card shows some type of antecedent (in this case, a term from physics). When using the cards, this side of the card is presented to the student and then, after making a response, the student can turn over the card and see the answer. This is very simple technology—but it easily illustrates the idea behind presenting an antecedent (A) to the learner, which is followed by a behavioral response (B) from the learner, which is followed by a consequence (C).

These same simple principles are also reflected in most computer-assisted instructional programs. For example, review the screen of the math program shown in Figure 2–4. Note the stimulus that is presented (equation on the submarine captain's table), the required behavioral response by the learner (identify the correct answer on one of the fish and click it with the mouse), and then the immediate feedback that is supplied. In addition, this program can increase its power by adding a number of sophisticated features. For example, performance levels of the learner can be electronically monitored and as mastery of simple problems is achieved, more challenging problems can be automatically introduced. Conversely, if continual mistakes are made with a certain

type of problem, additional review problems can be interjected by the program. If the individual needs to stop work for a period of time, the computer program can remember where the student was and return him/her to that location immediately upon return. Even more sophisticated computer assistance can be shown in programs that monitor the types of mistakes that are being made and give tailored feedback to help a student overcome a specific learning difficulty. An element might also be added allowing the software to monitor when a specific type of problem has been mastered and automatically introduce problems at the next level of difficulty. However, it also periodically reintroduces the "mastered" problems in order to help the learner maintain high levels of retention. Additionally, motivational incentives can be added (scoring elements that give students additional levels of achievement to obtain, rewards, etc.) that help the learner invest greater amounts of effort and maintain attention to the task for longer periods of time.

Using the computer's power, these types of sophisticated drill and practice elements can be added to other tutorial, simulation, and problem-solving programs so

FIGURE 2–4   A screen from Stickybear Math Splash, a popular drill and practice computer program.
Source: Stickybear's Math Splash, Optimum Resources, Inc.

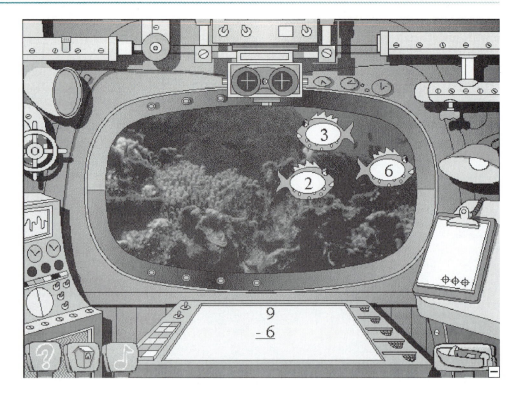

that learners can be taught independently, in a self-paced learning fashion that may include all types of needed enrichment and/or remediation activities. Behavioral principles illustrated within the simple flash-card-type drill and practice activity have become quite powerful when teamed with the power of the computer.

Information Processing Perspective

Behaviorism developed as a reaction to the study of mental phenomena, such as consciousness, that had characterized nineteenth-century psychology. In a similar way, cognitive psychology developed as a reaction to behaviorism. Cognitive psychology "was officially recognized around 1956" (Gardner, 1985, p. 28), in large

part because of a growing dissatisfaction with behaviorism's inability to adequately explain complex behaviors such as language acquisition. For example, at a 1948 symposium on "Cerebral Mechanisms in Behavior," Karl Lashley argued that when people use language their behavior is so rapid and continuous that it could not possibly be controlled by external prompts alone, as behaviorism would suggest (Gardner, 1985). Their behavior must be organized and planned in advance, using processes that occur internally in the mind. Lashley used language as his primary example, but he argued that most human behavior is similarly complex and governed by mental processes.

The perceived limitations of behaviorism led to a search for new ways of explaining human learning. At

Check It Out

Behaviorism Comparative Organizer (CO)

This Check It Out will require the use of information from the text's accompanying CD-ROM. Access that CD and then do the following:

1. Go to this textbook's accompanying CD and locate and print the Behaviorism Comparative Organizer (**Chapter info and activities >>> Chapter 2 >>> Behaviorism perspective**).
2. Read the example case that is found accompanying the CO (**Chapter info and activities >>> Chapter 2 >>> Behaviorism case**).
3. Using the CO, identify what learning needed to occur and what strategies and techniques could be used to facilitate learning based on the behavioral perspective outlined in the CO.
4. In what ways could technology be used within the realm of this theoretical perspective to enhance the learning as described within the case?

the same time, rapid technological advances led to the development of the high-speed computer as a mechanism for swiftly manipulating large amounts of information. As these two trends came together, one result was the development of the information processing view of human cognition, using the computer as a model for the way humans think. While this view isn't the only one that has developed from cognitive psychology (see Driscoll, 2005, for descriptions of other cognitive theories of learning), it has been a prominent view that has influenced instructional practice. The information processing perspective suggests that, like a computer, the mind takes information in, organizes it, stores it for later use, and retrieves it from memory. With the growth of cognitive psychology the focus was again on the mind, as it had been before the advent of behaviorism. However, using computer models and other laboratory methods (e.g., reaction-time tests), cognitive scientists were now able to quantify mental functions with much more scientific rigor than before.

What Is the Information Processing Definition of Learning?

The behavioral perspective emphasizes the influence of the *external* environment. In contrast, the information processing perspective has an *internal* focus. Learning is described as a change in knowledge stored in memory. The central principle is that most behavior, including learning, is governed by internal memory rather than external circumstances. Understanding learning, therefore, requires understanding how memory works.

What Is the Information Processing Learning Process?

Human memory is active rather than passive. That is, it doesn't simply receive information. It actively synthesizes and organizes information, integrating it with knowledge already stored in memory. As shown in Figure 2–5, this involves three processes: attention, encoding, and retrieval (Driscoll, 2005). **Attention** refers to the process of taking in some information from the environment while ignoring other information. **Encoding** refers to the process of translating information into some meaningful, memorable form. **Retrieval** refers to the process of recalling information for a particular purpose. Learning is said to have occurred when individuals encode information in a way that allows them to easily recall that information from memory and effectively use it in a particular situation.

As a way of understanding how these memory processes work, imagine a library receiving new books and subsequently making them accessible to its patrons (Stepich & Newby, 1988). A library continually receives information about new books and selects some of those books for addition to its collection (attention). New books

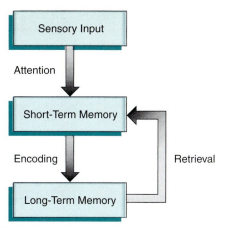

FIGURE 2–5   Role of attention, encoding, and retrieval in human memory.

that are selected are cataloged using a classification scheme such as the Dewey Decimal System (encoding). This places the new books into coherent categories and allows related books to appear on the shelves near one another. It also provides a search cue (a catalog number) to help someone find the books later. To locate a particular book in the library, an individual begins with the search cue and searches the shelves for the desired book, perhaps at the same time scanning the shelves for other relevant books (retrieval).

Memory works in a similar way. Humans are constantly bombarded with information from the environment and select only some of it to remember (attention). New information is considered in light of what is already known and integrated into existing knowledge whenever possible (encoding). This creates a coherent organization that makes new information more meaningful and allows related information to be linked together. It also provides a "search cue" that makes it easier to find information at a later time. In order to recall information from memory, an individual begins with the search cue and searches memory for the desired information, perhaps at the same time scanning memory for other relevant information (retrieval).

There is, of course, at least one significant difference between memory and a library. A library keeps physical objects (books) in specific places (shelves). In contrast, the facts and ideas that make up memory aren't physical objects, and we can't yet pinpoint where in the brain specific memories reside. However, the processes of attention, encoding, and retrieval are similar.

What Is the Role of the Instructional Expert in Information Processing?

The emphasis of the information processing perspective is on students' cognitive processes and on the critical role memory plays in helping them translate new information into a form that they can remember and use. Instruction, then, involves a deliberate effort to help students make this translation. Within the information processing perspective, the primary responsibility of the instructional expert is to create conditions that will support these cognitive processes. This involves:

▶ Organizing new information. Because humans actively seek order in information as a way of making sense of it, new information will be easier to encode if it is organized in some explicit way.

▶ Carefully linking new information to existing knowledge. This linking makes information more meaningful and, thus, more easily learned.

▶ Using various memory aids (such as highlighting, mnemonics, analogies, and imagery)—techniques designed to help students attend to important information, encode that information into a memorable form, and retrieve that information when needed.

What Role Can Technology Play in Information Processing?

Again, the behavioral perspective focuses heavily on getting passive learners to respond in appropriate ways through the environment providing structured cues and associated contingencies. From the information processing perspective the view is of a much more active learner who continually seeks ways to better organize and assimilate new information with that which is already known and experienced by the learner. From this perspective, technology can be useful by providing means to facilitate the organization, chunking, linking, assimilation, and accommodation of new information within memory. For example, software that is used to help chunk large amounts of information and perhaps put it into some readily usable outline would be useful to the learner. Inspiration is a type of software that allows individuals to quickly brainstorm ideas, organize one's thoughts in a visual manner, and show relationships between key elements. Figure 2–6 shows a small concept map that was created using this software to help the learner recognize the key elements within the targeted concept.

Another example would be how individuals learn to gather and use information from the Web. The Web at times can become overwhelming because of all the information that one can access. Software, such as that included as part of the WISE science project at the University of California at Berkeley (Williams & Linn, 2002), guides students through basic information pages that give the overall content, but then also facilitate information processing by providing tools that offer hints on how to organize, places to make journal entries for

FIGURE 2–6   Example of a concept map (controlling bleeding) created with brainstorming software (e.g., Inspiration).

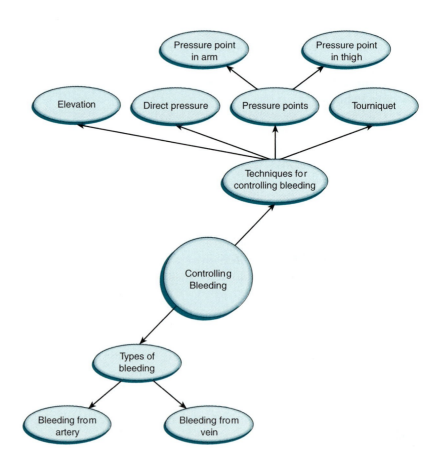

FIGURE 2–7   A screen showing how the WISE website guides students as they gather and process information.
Reprinted with permission from University of California, Berkeley.

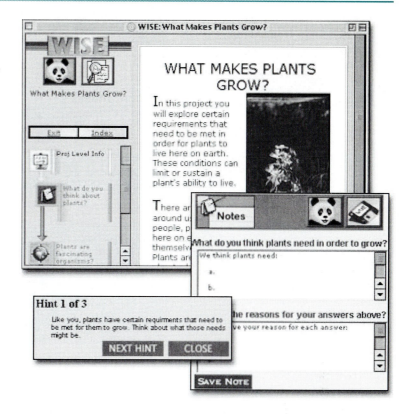

student reflections, and other tools to facilitate discussions between students, the visualization of data, and how to assess the information they have gathered. Each of these tools has been designed to help the learner organize and process information (see Figure 2–7).

There are other technology tools that are also closely aligned with this perspective. For example, tools that help a student visualize data (e.g., charts in a spreadsheet program) or help a student see information in a different or perhaps more relevant way (e.g., tables created within a word processing program). As an example, review Table 2–1 on page 27. This contains a wealth of comparison information about the three different learning theory perspectives. Use of a word

processing function that allows for such a table to be constructed facilitates the learning of those creating the table, as well as helping structure it in a fashion that may be readily encoded by those using the table to acquire and assimilate/process the presented information. As the technology has allowed for easier development, revision, and publishing of such table features, there has been a significant increase in its use.

Multimedia programs that incorporate audio, textual, as well as pictorial information are also programs that help learners more readily recognize meaningful prior learning and how the new information relates. A multimedia software program (see Figure 2–8) about the history of the civil rights movement, for example, may

Check It Out

Information Processing Comparative Organizer (CO)

This Check It Out will require the use of information from the text's accompanying CD-ROM. Access that CD and then do the following:

1. Go to this textbook's accompanying CD and locate and print the Information Processing Comparative Organizer (**Chapter info and activities >>> Chapter 2 >>> Information processing perspective**).
2. Read the example case that is found accompanying the CD (**Chapter info and activities >>> Chapter 2 >>> Information processing case**).
3. Using the CO, identify what learning needed to occur and what strategies and techniques could be used to facilitate learning based on the information processing perspective outlined in the CO.
4. In what ways could technology be used within the realm of this theoretical perspective to enhance the learning as described within the case?

FIGURE 2–8   Use of multimedia software to facilitate learning from multiple sources such as visuals, audio, and text materials.
Reprinted with permission from ABC-CLIO.

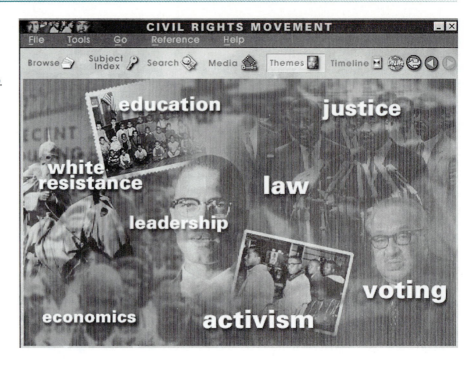

include pictures of relevant individuals, sound clips from important speeches, video clips of key events and news stories, and music and sounds from the era. Allowing students to "experience" the civil rights movement from a number of different perspectives should allow them to make needed connections.

One note should be made. A technology tool may include elements of the behaviorist perspective, along with the information processing perspective. For example, the civil rights multimedia experience may include a tutorial or drill and practice piece that incorporates an antecedent that prompts a behavior that is followed by a consequence. This kind of combination of elements is often seen within various types of educational software.

Constructivist Perspective

Constructivism is a relatively recent term used to represent a collection of theories, including (among others) generative learning (Wittrock, 1990), discovery learning (Bruner, 1961), and situated learning (Brown, Collins, & Duguid, 1989). The common thread among these theories is the idea that individuals actively construct knowledge by working to solve realistic problems, usually in collaboration with others (Duffy, Lowyck, & Jonassen, 1993).

While the label is relatively recent, the ideas that make up constructivism have been around for a long time. As early as 1897, for example, Dewey argued that "education must be conceived as a continuous reconstruction of experience" (1897, p. 91) that occurs through "the stimulation of the child's powers by the demand of

the social situations in which he finds himself" (1897, p. 84). In the middle of the twentieth century, the idea that knowledge is constructed through social collaboration can be found in the theories of Piaget, Bruner, and Vygotsky (Driscoll, 2005).

What Is the Constructivist Definition of Learning?

The constructivist perspective describes learning as a change in meaning constructed from experience. On the surface this seems the same as the information processing definition of learning. But there is a critical difference in the way the two perspectives define knowledge (Jonassen, 1991). The information processing perspective defines knowledge as an *objective representation* of experience, whereas the constructivist perspective defines it as a *subjective interpretation* of experience.

An analogy will help to illustrate this critical difference. In the information processing perspective, the mind is like a mirror, accurately reflecting the objects and events in our experience. The assumption is that knowledge is objective and can be described as separate from the knower. In other words, regardless of whose mirror is used, the picture in the mirror is essentially the same. Learning, then, refers to the *acquisition* of new representations. In the constructivist perspective, on the other hand, the mind is like a lens. When we look through our lens, some aspects of our experience are in sharp focus, some are fuzzy, and some can't be seen at all. The assumption in the constructivist perspective is that knowledge cannot be separated from the knower. In other words, the picture we see is determined by the lens we use. Learning, then, refers to the construction of new interpretations.

Thus, knowledge construction is a process of thinking about and interpreting experience. And because each individual has a unique set of experiences, seen through a unique lens, each individual constructs a unique body of knowledge. Learning is said to have occurred when our knowledge is changed in a way that allows us to interpret our experience in a more complete, complex, or refined way, that is, when our lens allows us to see something that we couldn't see before or to see things in sharper focus.

What Is the Constructivist Learning Process?

A basic premise underlying constructivism is that knowledge is constructed as learners try to make sense of their experiences. Learning, then, is a continuous process of experience and reflection in which learners create, test, and refine mental models that will synthesize their experience. Mental models are dynamic. As a learner's experience grows, his/her mental models become richer, meaning that they incorporate a wider range of experience. In addition, mental models do not necessarily correspond to any objective, external reality. What is important is that a mental model is useful and viable, that is, that it represents the individual learner's existing experience in a way that makes sense to him/her at the time.

There is some debate about exactly how this knowledge construction occurs (Phillips, 1995). Some constructivist theories (sometimes referred to as radical constructivism) focus on the individual learner, suggesting that constructing knowledge is a matter of individual interpretation. Other theories (sometimes referred to as social constructivism) focus on social interaction among individuals, suggesting that constructing knowledge is a matter of dialog leading to a shared interpretation. In general, however, this is a matter of degree and most constructivist theories incorporate both individual and social perspectives.

What Is the Role of the Instructional Expert in Constructivism?

According the constructivist perspective, learning is determined by the complex interplay among students' existing knowledge, the social context, and the problem to be solved. Instruction, then, refers to providing students with a collaborative situation in which they have both the means and the opportunity to construct "new and situationally-specific understandings by assembling prior knowledge from diverse sources" (Ertmer & Newby, 1993, p. 63). From a constructivist perspective, the primary responsibility of the instructional expert is to create and maintain a learning environment that has two essential characteristics: learning in context and collaboration.

Learning in Context.   According to the constructivist perspective, knowledge is like a muscle: it grows when it is used. Therefore, constructivist instruction asks students to put their knowledge to work within the context of solving realistic and meaningful problems. The idea is that when they work to apply their knowledge to a specific problem, students will naturally explore their knowledge and this will, in turn, lead to the continual refinement of that knowledge. However, not all problems are equally effective. To be effective, a problem should:

▶ Be seen by students as relevant and interesting.
▶ Be realistically complex.
▶ Require students to use their knowledge.

Collaboration.   From the constructivist perspective, students learn through interaction with others. This collaboration has two basic aspects. The first involves relationships among students. Students work together as peers, applying their combined knowledge to the solution of the problem. The resulting dialog provides students with ongoing opportunities to explore alternative interpretations and to test and refine their understanding. The second aspect of collaboration involves the role of the teacher. Constructivist instruction has been likened to an apprenticeship in which teachers participate *with* students in solving meaningful and realistic problems (Collins, Brown, & Holum, 1991; Rogoff, 1990). This doesn't mean that the teacher knows "the answer" to the problem. In fact, the problem may be just as new to the teacher as it is to the students. However, teachers are probably more familiar with the processes of solving problems and constructing knowledge. Teachers, therefore, serve as models and guides, showing students how to reflect on their evolving knowledge and providing direction when they are having difficulty. Learning is shared. Teachers are likely to learn as much as students. Responsibility for instruction is also shared. As much as possible, students determine their own learning needs, set their own goals, and monitor their own progress. The amount of guidance teachers provide depends on students' knowledge level and experience.

What Role Can Technology Play in Constructivism?

With the advancement of technology, we have moved from an industrial to a more informational age (see Reigeluth, 1999, Chapter 1). Technology has allowed us to gain greater access to more types of information than ever before. As this shift has developed, a need has been created for individuals who can more readily process information and make decisions based on that information. Instead of a focus on memorizing standard procedures, our world now requires us to access information, analyze it, and synthesize it in order to create novel solutions to problems that are often "ill-defined" (problems that don't have clear, easy solutions). With the access to more information has come a greater demand for higher-level problem solving by a greater number of individuals. Technology has created an environment in which more (higher levels of learning and problem solving) is expected from the learner.

Not only has the advancement of technology generated new types of demands on learners, but in many ways it has also begun to be used as a means to teach and educate learners to accomplish those higher-order tasks. Let's take a look at several ways that technology has been used to accentuate key constructivistic elements.

First, a key element within this perspective is *social interaction.* Technology now allows for groups of students to interact with each other face-to-face, as well as across great distances. For example, recently a course at Purdue University was taught by preservice teachers observing and participating in a class of fifth-grade students at a school that had a high number of non-English-speaking students. This was a very good experience for the preservice teachers to see how such a class was organized and how the teachers worked with the various students. However, the preservice teachers were located 70 miles away from the classroom they were observing. Through the use of two-way live video and audio technology, connections were established and students in both classes could see, ask questions, and exchange ideas with those in the other class (Phillion, Johnson, & Lehman, 2004). Instead of just reading about the benefits and challenges of such a classroom situation, as shown in Figure 2–9, this technology allowed the students to experience what it was like to actually be there and exchange ideas on what works and what needs to be refined.

Other forms of communication (e.g., e-mail, instant messaging) have also opened up new ways of having students interact at a greater level than ever before.

Students, for example, have greater access to content experts and can gain from their insights and thoughts. For example, e-mail exchanges between students and subject matter experts such as scientists, authors, politicians, sports stars, etc., are now readily accomplished. The technology has made it relatively easy and fast to gain access to individuals who previously would not have had the time or means to respond and offer their expertise. In addition, this same technology allows for ready access to one's classroom teacher and to fellow students. Social interaction within small-group exercises can also be enhanced as students can discuss and share ideas even when they are not in the same location.

Second, the constructivistic perspective views the learner as *actively creating meaning* from what is encountered in the environment. Active participation is a key to learning. The use of technology has facilitated this participation in a number of ways. For example, hypermedia software allows students to actively create projects. Instead of just reading about the Serengeti plains in Africa, students can create multimedia programs about this part of the world. Use of the Internet to explore current research, photos, and videos can help students not only learn about it but also retain what they learn. Students learn about the Serengeti and about planning a project, working cooperatively with others, developing skills with various forms of software, presenting information in a way that others can understand, and so on (see Figure 2–10).

The construction of meaning can also be enhanced through learners interacting with models and working within apprenticeships. Technology has allowed students more ready access to models of specific types of behaviors and skills. Think about how the high school art teacher may be able to work closely within a summer apprenticeship program with a master sculptor—even though the master may be in another part of the

FIGURE 2–9 Synchronous interchange between students at two different locations via distance education technology.

FIGURE 2–10 Learners using software to create projects and increase personal meaning.

Check It Out

Constructivism Comparative Organizer (CO)

This Check it Out will require the use of information from the text's accompanying CD-ROM. Access that CD and then do the following:

1. Go to this textbook's accompanying CD and locate and print the Information Processing Comparative Organizer (**Chapter info and activities** >>> **Chapter 2** >>> **Constructivism perspective**).
2. Read the example case that is found accompanying the **CO** (**Chapter info and activities** >>> **Chapter 2** >>> **Constructivism case**).
3. Using the CO, identify what learning needed to occur and what strategies and techniques could be used to facilitate learning based on the constructivism perspective outlined in the CO.
4. In what ways could technology be used within the realm of this theoretical perspective to enhance the learning as described within the case?

world. Through technology, the learner can monitor and observe the master's techniques, attempt various new skills, and ask for direct feedback on her creations. It may not be a perfect substitution for actually having the master in the same studio, but it will provide a greater degree of learning than if no contact was possible.

Finally, from the constructivistic perspective, meaningful learning occurs within an environment that resembles the real world, which is often a very ***complex environment.*** Finding such a complex environment that is conducive to the needs of the learner is often difficult, if not impossible. For example, training firefighters about the complex nature of fighting high-rise fires is difficult unless one is actually working on such a fire. Teaching student drivers to react appropriately to small

children running in front of them as they drive down a suburban street is also difficult and dangerous to achieve in a planned learning environment. Technology has been introduced to meet such learning needs. Simulations have been helpful in creating similar complex environments that may be more convenient, reliable, and less dangerous for the participants. Advanced flight simulators, for example, allow pilots to be repeatedly exposed to all types of mechanical, weather, or passenger-related problems, without incurring the severe cost of time, money, and health risks that could be imposed in a real-world environment. In the classroom environment, many types of instructional simulations have been developed for students to learn about such topics as solving problems of drug abuse, prejudice, the

Addressing the Standards

NETS Connection

In part, the National Educational Technology Standard (NETS) III (Teaching, Learning, and the Curriculum) for teachers emphasizes *the use of technology to help students develop higher-order and complex thinking skills that include problem solving, critical thinking, and informed decision making.* Consider how the development of higher-order skills ties in directly with this chapter's discussions of the various theories of learning. For example, what are some of the practical applications and strategies that have developed based on these various theoretical perspectives and research? Review NETS III (see Teacher Resource A for a full listing), then complete the following:

▶ Based on the different theoretical perspectives reviewed in this chapter, create a list of the key elements you would expect within an educational experience that would increase student development of complex/critical thinking and problem solving.
▶ Review software that simulates a complex, real environment and that presents problems for students to experience. You may need to visit the school or city library and/or media centers to obtain access.
▶ Imagine using this software in an actual classroom. Would student problem-solving and critical thinking skills be developed in some way? What would be the benefits and challenges of using this type of software?
▶ Record in your journal the elements within a simulation (or similar type software) that are needed to ensure higher-order and complex thinking skills will be addressed and developed.

FIGURE 2–11 Screen shots showing how technology can be used to present students with complex problems. *Reprinted with permission from Tom Snyder Productions, www.tomsnyder.com*

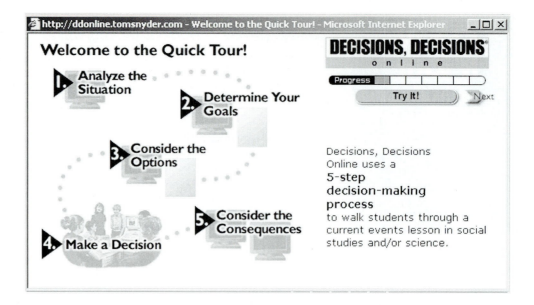

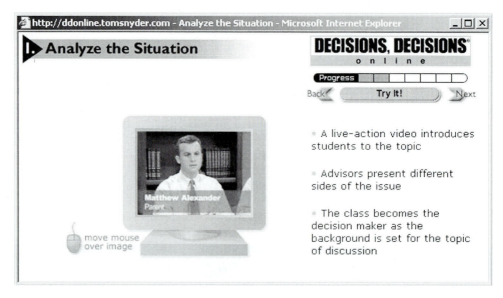

environment, as well as what it would be like to be a participant in such events as the Revolutionary War, the gold rush of 1849, or even to be a New York City resident on 9/11/2001. An example is "Decisions, Decisions Online" from Tom Snyder Productions (see Figure 2–11). This software asks students to work together, following a five-step process, to find a solution to a complex social issue, such as Internet censorship, television violence, or cloning. Throughout the process, the software provides live-action video access to advisors who help to explain the issues and the implications of the solution the students have chosen. Using technology in this way leads to greater levels of meaningful learning, allowing students to acquire knowledge and experience that previously took years in the real world to acquire.

SELECTING THEORETICAL PRINCIPLES

Learning theory has been defined as an attempt to explain how people acquire new knowledge and skills. We have presented three perspectives on learning and, because these three perspectives view learning in distinctly different ways, you might ask, *Which theory is best?* While this is a natural question, we believe it isn't the right one to ask. It is similar to asking, *Which food is best?* The inevitable answer is that no one food is best. We should eat a variety of foods, because each one contributes something to good nutrition. Similarly, we believe that teachers should understand a variety of theoretical perspectives because each perspective contributes something to good instruction.

Check It Out

Learning Theory and Lesson Plans

Access a lesson plan from the Lessons Plans Page (http://www.lessonplanspage.com). Within that site, for example, explore the high school biology section and link to a lesson plan that deals with how animals adapt to their environment. Or explore a high school language arts class lesson plan that focuses on helping students understand how literature and history influence one another.

1. Which theoretical perspective do you think is most prominent within the lesson plan that you've chosen? That is, do you think the lesson plan is using a primarily behaviorist, information processing, or constructivist approach to help the students learn?
2. What do you see within that plan that leads you to that conclusion? Be as specific as possible. What principles from that theoretical perspective do you see being used? What is being done to implement those principles?
3. Think about how you might incorporate more of the other two theoretical perspectives within the lesson plan that you've chosen. Be as specific as possible. What theoretical principles would you want to implement and what would you do to implement those principles?
4. Think about how you might incorporate more of the other two theoretical perspectives within the lesson plan that you've chosen. Be as specific as possible. What theoretical principles would you want to implement and what would you do to implement those principles?

Principles from the different theories can be applied to virtually any learning situation. For example, reinforcement (from the behavioral perspective), organized information (from the information processing perspective), and learning from one another (from the constructivist perspective) are principles that will be useful in virtually every instructional situation. At the same time, however, some theories fit some learning situations better than others. Ertmer and Newby (1993) suggest that this fit depends on two critical factors: students' knowledge level and the amount of thought and reflection required by the learning task. As Figure 2–12 shows, students with little content knowledge are likely to benefit most from learning strategies based on the behavioral perspective. As students' knowledge grows, the emphasis may shift to the information processing perspective and then the constructivist perspective. In the same way, learning tasks requiring little thought and reflection

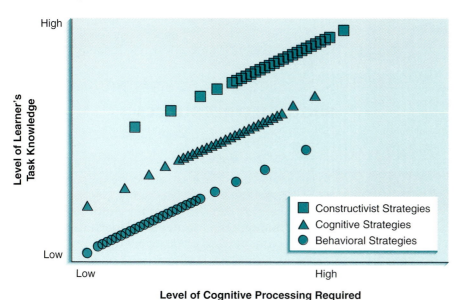

FIGURE 2–12 A heuristic guide for selecting principles from the three theoretical perspectives on learning. *Note: Copyright 1993 by the Learning Systems Institute, Florida State University, Suite 4600 University Center, Bldg. C. Tallahassee, FL 32306-2540. Reprinted by permission from* Performance Improvement Quarterly.

TECHNOLOGY COORDINATOR'S CORNER

Lexy Bowman was getting increasingly bored as she sat in the media center reviewing advertisements for newly released software. As her mind wandered, she began to listen in on a nearby conversation between a couple of student teachers who were currently in the middle of their teaching assignment at the high school. Both were in the media center looking for materials for an upcoming unit they were teaching in their government classes. They were worried that it was going to be difficult to get high school students interested in the traditional legislative process. Having them actually learn the key concepts and the steps of the process was going to be even more challenging.

Lexy listened for a while and then offered a few suggestions that the young teachers might want to consider. Above all else, she suggested, the students needed to become active participants in the learning process. One suggestion might be to use an available software simulation that allowed small groups of students to take on different insiders' roles within the U.S. government (e.g., a senator's aide, a researcher for a specific lobbying group, a presidential cabinet member) and then experience what is required to promote a good idea into a law. Learning about procedures, negotiations, and compromise are outcomes that often result from this experience. Past students have reported that these case studies helped them to appreciate the complexity involved in the whole legislative process.

A second idea was to have the students identify a local problem and get involved with the city government to try to promote a solution. Reducing property damage caused by skate boarders and inline skaters might be one possibility the students could find personally relevant and of interest. Groups could be formed to research what other cities have done to curb the problem, the city counsel representative with whom they would discuss this problem, how to develop and present a proposal for a solution, and so on. Lexy offered to assist the classes with the use of technology such as the Internet sites to access relevant information, brainstorming and flowcharting software to formulate ideas on what could be done and how to proceed, and other software needed to write proposals, make the formal contacts, create awareness in the community, and create and deliver presentations about their solutions. Lexy acknowledged that such a plan would take additional time and effort to implement, but the benefits for the students in what they recall later and how they use and transfer that information to other complex real-world problems should make this time well spent.

(e.g., memorizing facts, following a rote procedure) are also likely to benefit most from behavioral learning strategies. As the amount of thought required by the learning task increases (e.g., finding unique solutions to

"old" problems, inductive reasoning, creative thinking), the emphasis may shift to the information processing and then the constructivist perspective.

The shift from behavioral to information processing to constructivist strategies involves an important shift in the extent to which the students direct their own learning. With behavioral strategies, responsibility lies almost entirely with the teacher. Students learn by responding to cues the teacher builds into the environment. In contrast, with constructivist strategies, teacher and students share responsibility for directing learning. Students learn by collaborating with one another and with the teacher to solve mutually determined problems. Information processing strategies occupy a middle ground. Teachers may present the cognitive supports that facilitate effective information processing or students may develop these supports for their own use.

SUMMARY

As a teacher, your primary role, that of instructional expert, is based on a theoretical foundation. In every profession, including teaching, theory informs practice. This means that theory offers a set of consistent principles teachers may use to create solutions to a variety of unique problems. As in other professions, understanding theory allows teachers to select the tools and techniques that will work best with specific students and learning goals, apply those principles in a coherent manner, and adapt instruction as students' needs change.

Instructional practice is built on a diverse theoretical foundation, with learning theory as the critical cornerstone. In this chapter, we have described three broad categories of learning theory—behavioral, information processing, and constructivist—in terms of their central principles, their applications to your role of instructional expert, and the part technology can play in carrying out that role. Just as different foods contribute to good nutrition, different learning theories contribute to good instruction.

SUGGESTED RESOURCES

CD Resources

To increase retention and transfer of this information, review the *Reflective Questions and Activities* located in the Chapter 2 section (**Chapter info and activities>>>Chapter 2>>> Reflective Questions and Activities**) of the text's accompanying CD.

In addition, the CD allows direct access to relevant comparative organizers, case studies, Internet websites, NETS Connection exercises, and direct e-mail access to the text's authors.

Website Resources

Access the text's website **(www.prenhall.com/newby)**, navigate to Chapter 2, and review the Question and Answer section for relevant questions that have been generated by students and answered by the authors. You may also submit your own questions directly to the authors. In addition, you can access presentations by the authors about this chapter and gain insights directly from them about the topics that have been presented.

Print Resources

Driscoll, M. P. (2005). *Psychology of learning for instruction* (3rd ed.). Boston: Allyn & Bacon.

Ertmer, P. A., & Newby, T. J. (1993). Behaviorism, cognitivism, constructivism: Comparing critical features from an instructional design perspective. *Performance Improvement Quarterly, 6*(4), 50–72.

Electronic Resources

http://tip.psychology.org/
Kearsley, G. Explorations in Learning & Instruction: The Theory into Practice Database. Retrieved November 25, 2004.

http://www.myecoach.com/idtimeline/ learningtheory.html
A database of descriptions of over 50 learning and instructional theories. Learning Theory. Retrieved November 16, 2004.

http://wwwkihd.gmu.edu/immersion/ knowledgebase
Learning Theories and Instructional Strategies Matrix. Retrieved November 16, 2004.

http://www.infed.org/biblio/b-learn. htm
Smith, M. K. (1999). Learning theory. *The encyclopedia of informal education.* Retrieved November 16, 2004.

http://carolyn.ilcarroll.net/LearnThrySite.html
Study Aids for Visual Learners. Retrieved November 16, 2004.

3

Computers and Computer Tools for Teaching and Learning

CHAPTER OBJECTIVES

After reading and studying this chapter, you will be able to:

▶ Identify and describe the functions of the main hardware components of a computer system (processor, internal memory, mass storage, input and output devices).

▶ Define software, and identify an example of systems software and applications software.

▶ Discuss factors to consider when evaluating computer systems.

▶ Describe basic troubleshooting techniques to use to resolve routine computer hardware and software problems that can occur in the classroom.

▶ Describe ways to maintain a healthy environment for using computers.

▶ Describe educational applications in which the computer can be used as a teacher, a learner, or an assistant.

- Describe each of the major categories of software tools discussed in this chapter (word processor, graphics, presentation software, database, spreadsheet, telecommunication tools).
- Describe two or three examples of teacher and/or student uses of each of the major computer tools discussed in this chapter.
- Describe how assistive technology can be used to assist students with special physical needs.

In Chapters 1 and 2, we introduced you to educational technology, and we presented fundamental concepts of learning and the theories that help us to understand it. In this chapter, we introduce the computer, a multifaceted tool that can be of benefit to you and your students in many different ways. Common computer tools that you can use to design, develop, and evaluate instruction are described. In Chapter 4, we will move on to look at the instructional planning process.

INTRODUCTION

An acquaintance of ours is an expert model builder. She constructs all sorts of models: plastic replicas of product packaging (e.g., the bottle for a new perfume), model buildings to illustrate architectural plans, and various other creations from plaster, fiberglass, and just about any other material you can think of. Not long ago, she was asked to create models of an alien city of the future that were to be used in a science fiction movie. Like most expert artisans, she uses a variety of tools to make her models. She has one special tool, however, that she uses more than the others. It is called a rotary multitool.

A rotary multitool is a device, sort of like a drill, that spins a shaft at very high speeds. The user can attach a variety of different implements to the end of the shaft, such as drill bits; circular disks to cut wood, metal, and other materials; or sanding and grinding attachments to mold the contours of wood, plaster, or fiberglass surfaces. In short, the multitool, as its name implies, does a lot of different things.

What our friend likes so much about the multitool is its versatility. Rather than needing a lot of different tools, she can use one tool to perform different model-making tasks, simply by changing its attachment to one appropriate for the job at hand. With this one versatile tool, she can accomplish many of her aims.

The computer is a multitool for teaching and learning. It is a machine that can help with many different teaching and learning tasks. Rather than having separate tools for common tasks such as writing, drawing, filing, and developing multimedia, in the computer you have one tool that can do them all. Just by changing the software, like changing the attachment on a multitool, the computer can do many different things. In this chapter, we take a closer look at this remarkably versatile educational tool.

A computer, like the multitool shown here, is a machine that can be used for many different tasks.

UNDERSTANDING COMPUTER SYSTEMS

The computer's capabilities are defined, enabled, and constrained by the **hardware** (physical components) and software that comprise a particular computer system. The hardware sets absolute limits on what the computer can do. With only a monochrome display screen, for example, a computer cannot display multicolor images. **Software** is the term for the programs or instructions that tell the computer what to do. The software unlocks the capabilities of the hardware. A computer is capable of performing an amazing variety of tasks, but each task requires appropriate software.

In popular terms, the word *computer* refers to a machine that processes information according to a set of instructions. A **personal computer,** also known as a *PC* or *microcomputer,* is intended for use by an individual, and since PCs proliferated in the 1970s and 1980s, they have become the focus of most of the computing industry. When we use the term *computer* in this book, we almost always refer to a personal computer. We emphasize the personal computer because it is such a useful tool for teaching and learning. When most people picture a computer, they envision elements such as a keyboard, a box with a disk drive, and a display screen. This is actually a computer system, a collection of components that includes the computer and all of the devices used with the computer to realize or extend its capabilities. Figure 3–1 shows diagrammatic and pictorial representations of a personal computer system. Let's take a closer look at its components.

Hardware

The hardware components of a computer system perform the basic functions that make everything work. See Table 3–1 for a summary of the functions of the basic

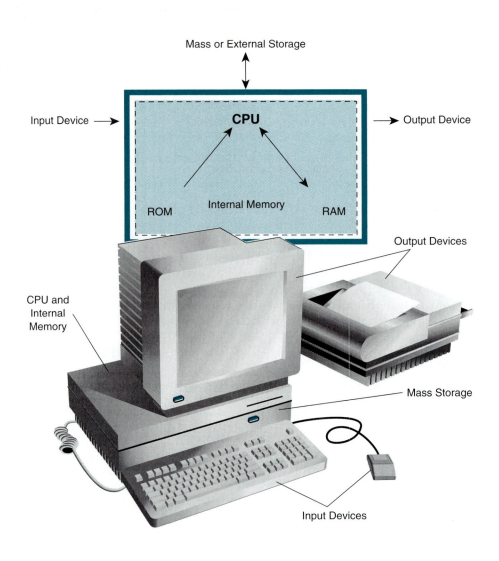

FIGURE 3–1 Diagrammatic and pictorial representation of a typical computer system. (*Note:* The dashed box represents the computer proper in the computer system.)

Mass or External Storage

Input Device →

CPU

→ Output Device

ROM   Internal Memory   RAM

Output Devices

CPU and Internal Memory

Mass Storage

Input Devices

TABLE 3–1   *Computer System Components and Their Functions*

Hardware Component	Function	Examples
Processor	Acts as the "brain" of the machine; controls the functions of the rest of the system and manipulates information in various ways.	Pentium G5 Athlon
Internal or Main Memory	Stores instructions (programs) and information where they can be readily accessed by the processor. The computer's working memory is where your programs and data are stored when you work with the computer.	RAM, DRAM
Input Devices	Put information into the computer.	Keyboard, Mouse, Microphone
Output Devices	Get information from the computer.	Display (CRT or LCD), Printer (ink-jet or laser) Speakers
Mass or External Storage	Stores information over long periods of time; acts as a "library" of readily accessible software and personal work that can be copied into working memory when needed.	Hard disk, Floppy disk, CD-ROM/DVD-ROM

components. A brief discussion of these components follows.

The **processor** runs the show. In most personal computers, the processor is a single computer chip, a little square of silicon with millions of microscopic electronic circuits etched onto it. Different computers are distinguished from one another, in part, by the particular processor each uses. The processor works with digital data, the bits and bytes that represent the various kinds of information (e.g., text, graphics, audio, video) that we use.

Input devices allow us to put information into the computer; they include the keyboard, mouse, and microphone. Output devices allow us to get information from the computer; they include the speakers, display, and printer. An input or output device communicates with the computer through an electronic go-between called an interface or port; the **USB** (universal serial bus) port is a standard that supports many input/output devices today.

Output devices include the computer display, printer, and audio speakers. Computer displays are one of two main types: a television-like display called a **CRT** or monitor, or a flat panel display usually based on **LCD** (liquid crystal display) technology. Flat panel displays, long used in laptop computers, are now popular in desktop systems as well. Displays are distinguished from one another by size, resolution, and color capability. Two types of printers are common in personal computer systems: ink-jet and laser printers. **Ink-jet printers,** so-named because they shoot tiny electrically charged droplets of ink onto the page, are widely used in home and school computer systems. They yield very good print quality and most support color printing at moderate cost. **Laser printers** use a combination of laser and photocopying technology to produce excellent print quality, at densities of 600 dots per inch or more. They are widely used in schools and businesses but can be expensive to buy and operate.

There are other types of input and output devices as well as devices that can serve both functions. **Modems,** for example, are both input and output devices that permit personal computers to communicate with other computers via phone lines.

Information inside the computer is stored in the internal or main **memory.** RAM (random access memory) is your personal workspace inside the computer. When you do word processing, your computer copies the word processing software from disk into a section of RAM. The document that you write with your word processor occupies another block of RAM as you compose it. The power of RAM is its flexibility to be used for different purposes at different times as need dictates. The capacity of RAM is usually described in terms of the kilobytes or megabytes of storage. A single page of text requires about 2 kilobytes (KB), or about 2000 bytes, of storage.

Digital video files, on the other hand, often require many megabytes of RAM.

Mass storage (also called *external storage*) refers to devices that maintain a "library" of readily accessible software and personal work and bring it into working memory when needed. Large storage requirements are met by the computer's **hard disk,** which has a high storage capacity of gigabytes (GB) or billions of bytes. The operating system and commonly used software are kept on the computer's hard disk for ready access. Many computers today rely on floppy disks (or diskettes) to meet small-scale, portable storage needs. The **floppy disk** is a flexible magnetic storage medium; most computers use 3.5" floppy disks that hold 1.44 megabytes (MB) of data. Some computer manufacturers are doing away with floppy disk drives on their computer systems because the small storage capacity of floppy disks makes them of limited value in modern computer systems.

Some devices are available to meet intermediate (between floppy and hard disk) mass storage needs. The Iomega Zip disk, for example, works like a floppy disk but stores from 100 to 750 MB depending on the particular model. A newer form of intermediate storage is the USB **flash drive** or jump drive. This miniature device relies on a special type of memory called flash memory that does not lose its contents when power is cut off; a flash drive plugs directly into a computer's USB port and acts like an extra drive on the computer. Flash drives typically store 64 MB to 2 GB of data and can be transported from one computer to another to meet portable intermediate storage needs.

Optical storage technologies also address storage needs. Most computers come with a CD-ROM or DVD-ROM drive. A single **CD-ROM,** a relative of the audio CD, can store 650 MB of data. Many software programs are now distributed on CD-ROM. **DVD** is a newer standard for digital information storage and delivery that is beginning to replace CD-ROM. First-generation DVD-ROM disks can store up to 4.7 GB of information. While

A flash drive is a small device that plugs into the computer's USB port and allows data to be stored and transported from one computer to another.

CD-ROM and DVD-ROM are prerecorded media, CD-R/RW and its DVD cousins are recordable versions that allow for archiving of data. These are popular options for storing and transporting personal computer data.

Software

It is important to recognize that software is also an essential component of any computer system. Software, within the limitations set by the capabilities of the hardware, determines what the computer can do. Like the music (software) you play on a stereo system (hardware), it is the software that gives the hardware real meaning. In a computer system, software takes the form of computer programs, sets of instructions to the computer's CPU that tell it how to perform a particular task, such as processing text or presenting a computer-based lesson. Most programs are loaded from disk into the machine's RAM for use as needed. There are two basic categories of software: systems software and applications software.

Systems software is the basic operating software that tells the computer how to perform its fundamental functions. The main systems software is called the **operating system (OS).** The OS acts as the master control program for the computer. Key components of the OS are loaded from disk into RAM when the computer starts up; other components are accessed from disk as needed. Different computers use different operating systems. The most widely used operating systems in education today are Microsoft's Windows, the latest version of which is Windows XP, and Apple's MacOS, the latest version of which is called OS X. Both Windows and MacOS use a graphical user interface (GUD), a system that relies on graphical symbols instead of text commands to control common machine functions such as copying files and working with disks. See Figure 3–2.

Applications software includes programs designed to perform specific functions for the user, from processing text to doing calculations to presenting a lesson on the computer. Thus, applications software includes common computer productivity tools (word processors, databases, etc.) as well as educational software. Although applications software interacts frequently with the OS, it is through the applications software that most of the real work gets done. The most commonly used applications are discussed later in this chapter.

Computer Operation

When your computer operates, it carries out a complex set of actions that involves interplay among the various components of the system and you. Suppose that you wish to use your word processing software to compose a lesson plan. When you sit down at your computer and turn it on, the computer's basic startup information is retrieved from built-in memory. On most computers, a brief check of all systems is conducted to make sure everything is operating properly. Your operating system is then loaded into RAM, where it assumes control of your computer.

To begin your word processing session, you probably use your mouse to click on the icon (pictorial representation) for the software. This input passes to the processor and on to the OS, which acts on it by instructing the computer to copy the word processing program from your computer's hard disk into working memory. The word processing program then assumes control of your interactions with it.

As you begin to type, each keystroke sends a signal to the processor. The word processing software working with the OS keeps the information in RAM and

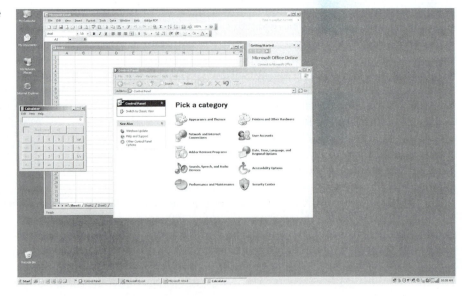

FIGURE 3–2   Windows XP, shown here with several open windows, is the latest version of the popular operating system software from Microsoft that controls the basic functions of most personal computers today.
Reprinted with permission from Microsoft Corporation.

displays the contents of your document on the computer's display. When you finish, you select the print option from the word processor. The OS handles sending a copy of your document to your printer, and the hard copy emerges. Finally, you save a copy of your document to a diskette for later reference or editing. Again, the computer system, operating system software, and word processing software work in concert to carry out the desired action. The whole process involves a complicated interplay of many different components. Fortunately, most of the time this process works so well that we never even notice it is happening.

COMPUTER SYSTEM EVALUATION AND ACQUISITION

Now that you know something about the components of a computer system, what should you consider when evaluating a computer system for possible purchase? Today, the education marketplace is dominated by two main

groups of computers: (1) those designed to run the Windows operating system using Intel and compatible processors, often called "Wintel" machines for short, manufactured by companies including Dell, Gateway, HP, IBM, and others; and (2) Apple Macintosh computers, designed around processors made by Motorola, that run the MacOS operating system. Both groups of computers are popular in education, although the Windows platform is far and away the most widely used in homes and the workplace.

See Table 3–2 for factors you should consider when selecting computer system hardware. Not surprisingly, it is important to consider each component that makes up the computer system. To select a personal computer system, carefully investigate these factors. Compare competing brands. Talk to users if you can. Visit vendors and tryout the machines. In the end, make your decision based on how well you believe a particular computer system will meet your specific needs.

TABLE 3–2 *Computer System Evaluation Considerations*

Factor	Issues/Considerations
Software Availability	• What do you want to be able to do with the computer system? Identify software that can meet your needs, and acquire a computer system that can operate the software. • Both Wintel and Macintosh computers feature easy to use operating systems, but some people prefer the way one operates over the other. • Many popular applications are available for both platforms, but some applications may be available for only one or the other. If a key application you need is available only for one platform, that may be an overriding consideration.
Processor	• How much processing power do you need? Generally, newer processors are capable of more processing power and faster operations than their predecessors, although there are exceptions. • When all else is equal, look for faster processing speeds (more megahertz). Faster processor speeds contribute to faster overall performance. • When comparing different processors where design differences can confound simple comparisons, examine the results of benchmarking tests, well-defined sets of processing tasks used by testing labs to rate the performance of different processors.
Internal Memory	• How much memory will you need for basic operations? Newer operating systems generally need at least 256 to 512 MB for basic operations. • Special applications, such as multimedia development or digital video editing, may benefit from significantly more memory than needed for the basics.
Keyboard and Mouse	• How important are input devices to you? A full-sized keyboard with 101 keys, special function keys, numeric pad, and cursor-control keys can simplify the use of many software applications. Pay special attention to laptop keyboards where limited space can restrict layout and functions. • Wintel system mice have two buttons, while single button mice are standard on Macintosh computers. Do you have a preference for one or the other? • The standard mouse uses a roller ball that can become dirty and require periodic cleaning; the newer optical mouse has no moving parts and hence does not have to be cleaned.
Display	• Will you need a lot of "screen real estate"? Display size is measured diagonally like televisions. Most desktop personal computer systems feature displays of 15 to 21 inches. Laptop computer displays range from 10 to 17 inches. • Consider screen resolution, which refers to how many dots or pixels (picture elements) can fit onto the screen. Most displays today support 1024 by 768 pixels or better. • Color capability is another display factor. So-called true color, capable of millions of hues, requires 24 to 32 bits of color information for each pixel. Computers must have adequate display memory to support true color at the highest resolutions.
Sound	• Is sound important? Digital sound capability is standard on most computers today, but quality can vary. • A good sound card and high-quality speakers are needed to support high-fidelity sound.
Printer	• What kind of printer will you need? Ink-jet or laser is one choice. Ink-jet printers are less expensive and offer color capability, but ink cartridges are costly. Laser printers are more expensive, most lack color, but they offer excellent performance for the cost. • Other printer factors include speed (pages printed per minute), resolution (dots printed per inch), paper-handling capability, and ability to operate on a network.
Mass Storage	• How much and what kind of mass storage will you require? A hard disk is an essential feature of all PCs. Capacity and speed of access to data distinguish different models. A fast hard drive can greatly enhance overall system speed. • For most systems, a CD-ROM or DVD drive is a key mass storage option. For archiving data and making music or video CDs, a CD or DVD recorder, often called a "burner," is another popular option. • Most Wintel machines include a floppy disk drive, but Apple has eliminated this small-scale storage option from Macintosh computers.

TABLE 3–2   *Continued*

Interfaces	• Does the computer have built-in Internet connectivity capability, such as a wired Ethernet port and a modem port for dial-up access? For laptop computers, especially, does it have wireless Internet connectivity capability?
	• What ports are available for connecting peripherals? USB ports are now nearly universal on personal computers, but the number of available ports varies. If you hope to work with digital video, you may also want to look for an IEEE-1394 (also called Firewire or iLink) port; it is commonly used to connect digital video camcorders.
System Expandability	• Expansion slots permit components to be added to the system. How many expansion slots does the computer have? Are all available, or are some used by existing components?
	• Increasing memory is a common system upgrade. Will the system support additional memory without modification? Can you add memory without removing existing memory?
	• Some computers are designed to accept newer processors to upgrade performance. Is this an option?
Warranty and Service	• How long is the warranty and what does it cover? Look for the most comprehensive coverage.
	• If service is needed, what are your options? Usually, service options include on-site service (service personnel come to your location), carry-in service (you must take the computer to the vendor's store), and ship-back service (you must ship the computer back to the vendor).
Cost	• What are you willing to spend? Today's computer systems can range anywhere from a few hundred dollars to more than $5000.
	• A good basic computer system for school use can generally be purchased for between about $1000 to $2000.

TROUBLESHOOTING COMPUTER PROBLEMS

Computer systems are complex devices, and problems are not uncommon. So, it is important to be able to troubleshoot basic computer problems to keep going on your cyberspace travels. Computer troubleshooting is not an easy task, especially for beginners. There are many possible causes of problems—hardware, software, network, user error—and interactions among the various components can complicate matters. For example, suppose that you try to print a document from an application, but nothing happens. There are many possible causes of such a problem. Your ink-jet printer's ink cartridge might be empty or your printer cable might have come loose (hardware problems). Your printer may not be selected within the operating system or your printer software may not work properly with the application (software problems). If you use the printer on a network, your network connection to the printer might be "down," meaning not functioning (a network problem). You may have accidentally clicked Cancel instead of OK in the print dialog box (user error). How can you sort out the problem?

While you may not be able to solve all the problems that you encounter, it is possible to develop some basic troubleshooting proficiency, so that minor problems do not become major obstacles. Here are some fundamental troubleshooting guidelines and tips. Table 3–3 summarizes these steps.

Identify the problem. While this may seem obvious, the first step is just to identify the problem as specifically as possible.

▶ What is the extent of the problem? For example, have you lost all computer function, or is the problem something more limited in scope such as an inability to print from an application?

▶ Under what circumstances does the problem occur? Does the problem occur all of the time, only in specific applications, or only at specific times?

▶ Can you repeat the problem or is it something that occurs intermittently? Repeatable problems tend to be more easily identified. Intermittent problems may result from a difficult-to-observe combination of conditions.

Look for possible causes.

▶ Begin by checking the obvious. If you've apparently lost all computer function, is the computer still plugged in and the power switch turned on? If you are unable to print, is the printer still connected, receiving power, and switched on?

▶ Read your computer documentation. Make certain that you are using the computer and applications correctly.

▶ Consider whether you have made any changes to your computer system recently. Problems with computers often arise as a result of changes in one part of the system that affect other parts of the system. For example, if you recently installed

TABLE 3–3   *Computer Troubleshooting Summary*

Steps	Actions
Identify the problem	• Determine the extent of the problem. • Under what circumstances does the problem occur? • Can you repeat the problem or does it occur intermittently?
Look for possible causes	• Check the obvious—plug, connections, power. • Read your computer documentation. • Have you made any changes to your computer system recently? • Use diagnostic software to check for problems.
Use a process of elimination	• Localize the problem: What works? What does NOT work? • Check the control panels in your system. • Substitute a working component for one that you suspect to be faulty. • Check one thing at a time.
Resolve the problem or seek assistance	• If you can identify the specific problem, try to correct it. • If you cannot identify the specific problem, or it is beyond your ability to resolve, then seek assistance.
Take preventative measures	• Install anti-virus software, and regularly update virus definitions. • Regularly use software to check for and correct file/disk errors. • Make and keep an emergency startup disk for your computer. • Keep your system up-to-date.

a new piece of software, it might have changed your system (e.g., installed new printer software or changed control panel settings) in ways that affect other applications.

▶ Use diagnostic software to check for problems. For example, use virus protection software to scan for a virus. Viruses, often accidentally downloaded from e-mail or other online sources, can wreak havoc with your system. Use a utility (e.g., Windows *Scandisk,* Apple's *Disk First Aid,* or Semantec's *Norton Utilities*) to check for problems with your files/disks. Disk errors can lead to many problems.

Use a process of elimination to identify the specific problem.

▶ Localize the problem by determining what *does* work as well as what *does not* work. For example, if you are having trouble printing from an application, try to print from another application. If you can print from another application, then the problem is not a generalized printing problem. If you are unable to receive e-mail, check to see if you can access a website. If you can access a website, the problem is not a general network connection problem.

▶ Check the control panels in your system to make certain that all of the settings are correct.

▶ If you suspect a problem with a particular component, substitute a known working component. For example, if you are having trouble with your printer, replace it with one known to be working. If the problem persists, the printer is not at fault. If the problem is resolved, then the printer was faulty.

▶ Check one thing at a time. When trying to identify a problem, be systematic about checking first one thing and then another. If you change more than one thing, it may obscure the source of the problem and make it harder to find a genuine solution.

Resolve the problem or seek assistance.

▶ If you are able to identify the specific problem, try to correct it by making any necessary changes.

▶ If you are unable to identify the specific problem or you determine that the problem is beyond your ability to resolve, then seek assistance. Ask friends or associates if they have had a similar problem and know how to correct it. If all else fails, call for professional assistance. In a school setting, contact your technical support staff. For a home computer, contact an authorized service center or the telephone support line for your computer brand.

Take preventative measures to avoid future problems.

▶ Make sure that you install anti-virus software, and keep it up-to-date by regularly updating your virus definitions.

▶ Regularly use software to check for and correct file/disk errors. Defragment your hard disk periodically using software designed for that purpose (e.g., *Windows Defrag* or *Norton Utilities Speed Disk*). Over time, files on your hard disk

can become split into pieces or fragments, and defragmenting consolidates the pieces to make your computer operate more efficiently.

▶ Make and keep an emergency start-up disk for your computer to use in the event of serious system failure. (Macintosh users can boot from the system CD-ROM in an emergency.)

▶ Keep your system up-to-date. Regularly check for and install operating system upgrades (especially critical or security-related upgrades) and the latest

Toolbox Tips: Healthy Use of Computers

In recent years, it has become clear that improper placement and/or use of a computer can pose a threat to your health. To minimize your risks, follow the guidelines below.

▶ Repetitive stress injuries, such as carpal tunnel syndrome, have become increasingly common among those who use computers extensively. Proper application of **ergonomics**, the study of the physical interaction of human with machines, can help to limit problems. Adjustable office furniture is a big help. The keyboard should be placed at the proper height for typing, usually about 27 to 29 inches from the floor, so that your elbows are at a 90° angle when typing. The mouse should be next to the keyboard at the same height or slightly higher. When typing, your wrists should be level; if necessary, use wrist rests for support. Your chair should be comfortable and provide good support for your back. Keep your posture straight but relaxed and your feet flat on the floor. Finally, take regular breaks from computer work to stretch and rest.

▶ CRT-type computer monitors can emit radiation that might pose a health risk. (Flat panel displays do not have this problem.) While monitors are shielded to reduce emissions and the extent of the danger is unclear, it is wise to be cautious. It is recommended that you sit at least 28 inches from the front of the monitor; maintain a distance of at least 48 inches from the sides or rear of the monitor, which may emit more radiation.

▶ Lengthy viewing of computer displays can cause eyestrain, headaches, and vision problems. The computer display should be placed at eye level. Reduce ambient lighting in the room if it is bright. Minimize glare off the screen by positioning the computer display away from direct sunlight and lighting fixtures. Anti-glare coatings or screens can be used if repositioning is not enough to reduce glare. Text should be easily viewable when you are seated the proper distance from the screen. Adjust the font size in your application to make it easily readable, if necessary. If you wear eyeglasses or contact lenses, consider getting a special prescription for computer work. Finally, take regular breaks to allow your eyes to rest.

Proper computer placement and ergonomics will help you to stay comfortable and healthy when using the computer.

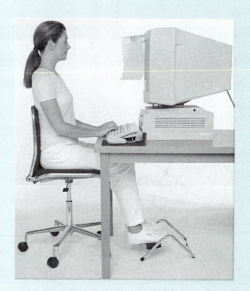

drivers for your peripherals. Manufacturers usually release updates on their websites that fix known problems. Before installing new applications or upgrading existing applications, check the system requirements to make certain that they will work with your system.

COMPUTER AS TEACHER, LEARNER, AND ASSISTANT

The computer is a powerful machine with a number of different uses in education. This diversity is reflected in a popular categorization scheme developed by Robert Taylor (1980). Taylor's "tutor, tool, tutee model" divides the educational applications of computers into three broad categories: computer as teacher, computer as learner, and computer as assistant. Each category is summarized in Table 3–4.

Computers can be used to present instruction directly to students. In this mode, the computer engages in activities traditionally associated with human teachers or tutors. It presents instruction, provides instructional activities or situations, quizzes or otherwise requires interaction from learners, evaluates learner responses, provides feedback, and determines appropriate follow-up activities. As teaching machines, computers can be highly interactive, individualized, and infinitely patient. Applications that utilize the computer for teaching are usually labeled computer-based instruction (CBI), computer-assisted instruction (CAI), or computer-assisted learning (CAL). There are a number of common categories of computer-based instruction: drill and practice, tutorial, simulation, instructional game, and problem solving. We will discuss these in more detail in Chapter 9.

When the computer functions as the learner, or in what Taylor (1980) called "tutee" mode, the traditional roles of computer and learner are reversed. The computer becomes the learner; the student becomes the teacher. The goal is for the student to "teach" the computer to perform some task or to teach others some content through computer-based materials. To achieve this goal, the student must learn how to perform the task and then must direct the computer to perform the task or present the content to others. This requires logical thinking and problem-solving skills, and, as a result, many experts believe that this is one of the most valuable ways to use a computer in education. Activities of this sort may involve traditional computer languages such as Logo, BASIC, and C; when using a programming language, students must program the computer to perform a task (e.g., sum a set of numbers, draw a geometric figure on the computer's display screen). Students may also use multimedia/hypermedia authoring tools such as *HyperStudio, eZedia,* and *Director,* or web page authoring tools such as Microsoft *FrontPage* and Macromedia *Dreamweaver,* in this mode. When using authoring tools, the goal is for the student to create interactive presentations of content (e.g., tutorials, hypermedia programs) that others can use to learn about the content themselves. Thus, the student teaches others by developing computer-based materials. We will look in more detail at the computer as a learner in Chapters 9 and 10.

As an assistant, the computer aids the teacher or learner in performing routine work tasks. It can function as a typewriter, a filing system, a financial worksheet, an artist's canvas, a drafting table, and much more. Software programs (commonly called applications) for these uses include word processors, graphics packages, presentation software, databases, spreadsheets, and telecommunications programs. Teachers often employ computers as labor-saving devices to produce instructional materials (e.g., printed matter, graphics, presentations) and manage their instruction (e.g., to maintain records and calculate student grades). Of course, learners can also employ the computer as an assistant. Students can use

---

Addressing the Standards

NETS Connection

In part, the National Educational Technology Standard VI (Social, Ethical, Legal, and Human Issues) for teachers emphasizes that one should *identify and discuss health and safety issues related to technology being used in the school setting.* Read that standard, study its performance indicators (see Teacher Resource A on page 297 for a full listing), and then complete the following:

▶ Brainstorm a list of physical health issues that may be caused by the use of technology in a school setting. Research where you could go for information on how to avoid such problems.

▶ In addition, create a journal entry where you describe other potential issues of health and safety (e.g., mental, emotional, physical safety) that should be considered when one spends ever increasing amounts of time working on computers or using other (e.g., TV, video) technologies. Are there resources that one can find and use that may help individuals who have become overly excessive users of the technology (e.g., http://www.computeraddiction.com/)?

TABLE 3–4   *Computer as Teacher, Learner, and Assistant*

Computer's Role	Description	Examples
Teacher	The computer, functioning like a human teacher or tutor, presents instruction, provides instructional materials or activities, quizzes or otherwise requires interaction from learners, evaluates learner responses, and provides feedback. As a teaching machine, the computer can be highly interactive, individualized, and infinitely patient.	• computer-assisted instruction (CAI) • computer-based instruction (CBI) • computer-assisted learning (CAL)
Learner	The computer is "taught" to do something by the student, who takes on the role of the teacher. To achieve this aim, the student must learn the relevant content or procedure and also learn how to get the computer to perform the procedure or present the content to others. This requires organization, logical thinking, and problem-solving skills.	• computer programming • hypermedia authoring • web page development
Assistant	The computer aids the teacher or learner in performing routine tasks such as writing, calculating, filing, or presenting information. Teachers may employ computers as labor-saving devices to produce instructional materials and manage their instruction. Learners may also employ the computer to help with their schoolwork.	• word processors • graphics packages • presentation software • spreadsheets • databases

the computer to produce materials (e.g., term papers, presentations) and can use software tools in ways that help them learn (e.g., for research and calculations). In this chapter, we introduce the computer as an assistant so that you have an understanding of available applications that can help you as you learn to plan and design instruction in the coming chapters. We will look in more detail at applications of the computer as a teacher and as a learner when we discuss integrating computers into learning experiences for students in Chapter 9.

COMPUTER TOOLS

In the role of assistant, the computer is an aid in performing routine work tasks. When computers are used in the workplace, they are most often used as a tool to assist the worker. Secretaries prepare documents using word processors, businesspeople store customer records in databases, accountants use spreadsheets to calculate balance sheets, graphic artists use drawing programs, and so on. So, it makes sense that teachers and students use computers in schools in the same ways that they are used in the workplace. Students can use computers as assistants when doing schoolwork. Teachers can use the same tools to prepare instructional materials. We introduce these tools here so that as you continue in this text and begin to learn how to plan for the effective integration of technology in your own teaching, you will be

aware of the key computer tools that are available to help you with the task of planning instruction and preparing educational materials and learning experiences for your students. What follows are descriptions of some of the most common computer applications for assisting teachers and learners as well as examples of how teachers and students can use them.

Word Processors

Word processors are the most widely used computer personal productivity tools. A **word processor** is a computer application that allows you to enter, edit, revise, format, store, retrieve, and print text. Word processors today also permit you to include graphic and tabular materials along with text. Today, many word processors have features (e.g., columnar display of text, integrated handling of graphics) once found only in programs designed to support publishing. Nearly all word processors have spelling checkers. Some work "on the fly" as you enter text, and some do basic grammatical checking (e.g., subject-verb agreement).

Popular word processors for personal computers include Microsoft *Word* and Corel *WordPerfect* as well as those in integrated packages such as *AppleWorks*. There are also particularly easy-to-use word processors designed specifically for school use, such as *Bank Street Writer*. See Figure 3–3.

Word Processor Uses for Teachers and Students

Teachers' Uses	Students' Uses
• Preparing lesson plans, handouts, worksheets, and other instructional materials • Recording ideas during in-class brainstorming sessions • Creating quizzes, tests, and other forms of evaluation • Writing letters, permission slips, newsletters, and other forms of communication with parents, students, and administrators	• Writing papers and other assigned written work • Performing prewriting activities such as brainstorming, note taking, and idea collection • Typing handwritten notes to reinforce learning or when studying for an exam

Graphics Tools

While word processors are primarily tools for manipulating text, graphics tools handle pictorial information. Any computerized pictorial representation of information—drawing, chart, graph, animated figure, or photographic reproduction—is called a **graphic.** On a computer screen, graphic images are composed of many tiny dots, much like photographs in a newspaper. Each screen dot is referred to as a picture element, or **pixel** for short. There are many different graphics file formats (that is, ways of storing graphic information in a computer file). Some of the most common graphic file formats are shown in Table 3–5.

Computer-based graphic tools can create or manipulate images, generate graphs/charts, and so forth. For creating or manipulating images, most graphics applications let you use the mouse as a pencil, paintbrush, color fill bucket, or eraser. You can draw perfect lines, circles, and polygons, as well as curves and irregular shapes. You can move or rotate portions of graphics as well as cut, copy, and paste them. You can select and control colors, and fill shapes with colors and/or patterns. Advanced graphics applications let you apply special effects such as blurring, textures, and the illusion of embossing. Popular graphics packages include Adobe *Photoshop* and *Illustrator,* Corel *PhotoPaint* and *Draw,* Macromedia *Freehand* and *Fireworks,* and Microsoft *Paint.* Graphics packages oriented for elementary students' use include Brøderbund's *Kid Pix* and Knowledge Adventure's *Kid Works.* See Figure 3–4.

Presentation Software

Presentation software is designed for producing and displaying computer text and images, usually for presentation to a group. It replaces the functions typically

FIGURE 3–3   A screen from Microsoft Word showing features including text formatting, a two-column layout, and an embedded graphic.
Reprinted with permission from Microsoft Corporation.

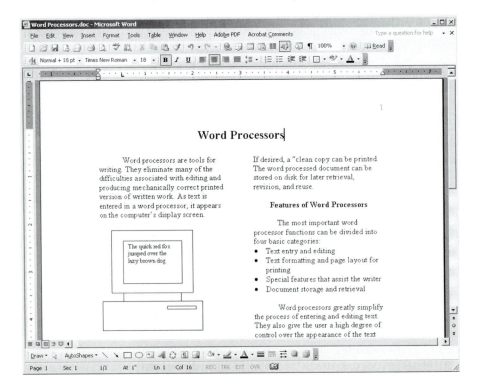

TABLE 3–5 *Common Graphic File Formats*

Graphic Format	Description
BMP—Windows Bitmap	The standard Windows bit-mapped (raster) graphic format.
GIF—Graphic Interchange Format	A format originally developed for CompuServe that stores images with up to 256 colors. It is widely used on the Web for icons, clip art, and other limited color images. It also supports a form of animation that is popular on the Web.
JPG or JPEG—Joint Photographic Experts Group	A format widely used for photographic images on the Web. It can support images with millions of colors and offers varying levels of compression to reduce storage size.
PICT—Macintosh graphic	The standard Apple Macintosh graphic format capable of storing both bit-mapped and object-oriented (draw) images.
PNG—portable network graphics	A Web image format designed as a replacement to the proprietary GIF format. It supports up to millions of colors and better compression than GIF.
TIF or TIFF—Tagged Image File Format	A widely supported format for bit-mapped images that is often used with images in printed materials. Scanners often store scanned images in this format.

FIGURE 3–4 A screen from Adobe Photoshop, a popular program for editing digital photos and creating graphic images.
Reprinted with permission from Adobe Systems, Inc.

Graphic Tool Uses for Teachers and Students

Teachers' Uses	Students' Uses
• Creating images for handouts, worksheets, and other instructional materials for student use	• Making drawings for mini-books, reports, and other illustrated material
• Creating signs or other graphical material for classroom display	• Creating a graph of data collected in the science laboratory
• Maintaining graphical information (e.g., pictures of students) in a class database	• Producing major school works such as the school newspaper or yearbook
• Designing and producing a class newsletter to send home to parents	

Presentation Software Uses for Teachers and Students

Teachers' Uses	Students' Uses
• Supporting lectures or other presentations in the classroom, at professional meetings, or in other settings	• Making in-class presentations
• Displaying information at events such as parent open house nights; most presentation packages support timed or auto-run features that allow slide shows to run unattended	• Developing multimedia reports or projects
• Recording the results of brainstorming or other development activities in the classroom	• Preparing textual information, pictures, or other material that can be printed, transferred to photographic slides, or converted for placement on the Web
• Preparing notes, pictures, or other material that can be printed, transferred to photographic slides, or converted for placement on the Web	

associated with traditional media presentation tools such as slides and overhead transparencies. Most presentation software is built around a slide concept, with pre-designed templates for slides, special effects to transition from one slide to another, ability to sort and order slides, and ability to add multimedia elements to slides. Like other computer-based tools, it offers advantages over its traditional counterparts. Information is easily entered, edited, and presented. There is no need to set up or fumble with traditional media and equipment such as slides and slide carousels. With a presentation package, it is easy to produce very professional looking presentations complete with multimedia elements. Popular presentation packages include Microsoft *PowerPoint,* Adobe *Persuasion,* Lotus *Freelance Graphics,* and Corel *WordPerfect Presentations.* See Figure 3–5.

Computer Databases

A **database** is nothing more than a collection of information. We are familiar with many examples of databases that are *not* computerized: a telephone book, a recipe file, a collection of old magazines. Computer databases offer significant advantages compared to their non-computer counterparts: They can hold huge amounts of information, you can readily search through that information by category, and it is relatively easy to set up and manipulate computer databases.

Most computer databases are structured in similar fashion. Suppose you want to computerize your name and address book. See Figure 3–6. Each entry in the address book corresponds to an individual. Within each entry are various items of information: name, address,

FIGURE 3–5   A screen from Microsoft *PowerPoint* showing multimedia elements including bulleted text, clip art, sound, and an action button.
Reprinted with permission from Microsoft Corporation.

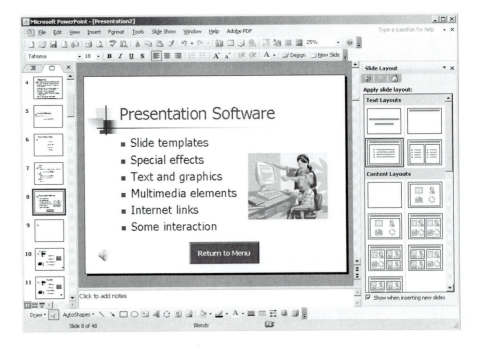

Database Uses for Teachers and Students

Teachers' Uses	Students' Uses
• Creating and maintaining basic information about students in classes	• Locating information in prepared databases such as the school's electronic card catalog or a database of U.S. presidents
• Developing bibliographic files of books and/or articles that support the curriculum	• Developing problem-solving and higher-order thinking skills by investigating the answers to complex questions through searching databases
• Keeping records of media and materials available in the classroom or resource center	• Developing original databases as class projects to research various topics (e.g., U.S. states, class members' pets, dinosaurs, elements of the periodic table)
• Building a collection of test or quiz questions referenced by topic, book chapter, objective, and possibly other identifiers, such as level of Bloom's taxonomy	
• Storing compilations of teaching methods, strategies, and lesson plans	

FIGURE 3–6 Components of a computer database.

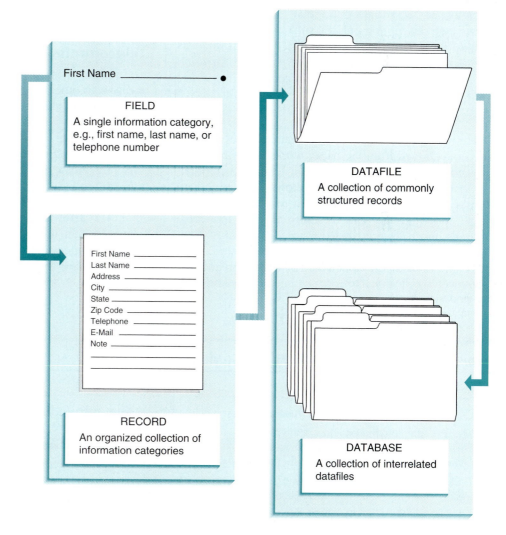

First Name _____ ●

FIELD
A single information category, e.g., first name, last name, or telephone number

DATAFILE
A collection of commonly structured records

First Name _____
Last Name _____
Address _____
City _____
State _____
Zip Code _____
Telephone _____
E-Mail _____
Note _____
_____
_____

RECORD
An organized collection of information categories

DATABASE
A collection of interrelated datafiles

telephone number, e-mail address, and so on. In computer terminology, each individual category of information that is recorded is called a **field.** So there might be a name field, a street address field, a city field, a telephone number field, and so on. The whole collection of fields that corresponds to one individual is called a **record.** Each record contains the same collection of fields. All of the records are collected into a **datafile.** The datafile corresponds to the entire address book. In simple cases the database consists of only a single datafile. So-called flat file databases work with only a single datafile at a time. In other cases the database is a collection of datafiles that are interrelated in some way. See Figure 3–8. For example, you might cross-reference your name-and-address file with your recipe file to make sure that you prepare a different dish the next time you have certain friends over for dinner. **Relational databases** allow multiple datafiles to be accessed and interrelated. Popular flat filers include the database components of integrated products such as Microsoft *Works* and *AppleWorks.* In addition, popular computer spreadsheets (see description below), such as Microsoft *Excel,* include basic flat filer functionality. Programs such as Microsoft *Access, dBASE, FileMaker Pro,* and *Paradox* fall into the relational database category.

Electronic Spreadsheets

Electronic **spreadsheets** are general-purpose calculating tools derived from the paper worksheets once used by accountants. A spreadsheet is like a large piece of paper that has been marked off into rows and columns to form a grid. Each intersection of a row and column, a single block in the grid, is called a **cell.** Individual columns and rows are labeled for reference; most commonly columns are lettered and rows are numbered. Thus, each cell can be uniquely identified by its column and row reference. A cell normally contains one of three types of information: a number, text, or a formula. Numbers are the basic stuff that spreadsheets work with. Text may be used to label parts of the spreadsheet or as part of a database (see discussion above). **Formulas** are mathematical expressions that direct the spreadsheet to perform various kinds of calculations or operations on the data entered in the cells. Formulas work on values in the spreadsheet by referring to the cells where the values are located. See Figure 3–7.

Most spreadsheet programs contain a wide variety of built-in mathematical functions (e.g., basic statistics, trigonometric functions, common financial functions) to facilitate calculations. They support data entry, editing, formatting, and printing. Most spreadsheets support graphing of data. As noted above, some spreadsheets also include basic database functionality. Popular spreadsheets include Microsoft *Excel,* Lotus *1-2-3,* and Quattro *Pro.* In addition, spreadsheets are found in integrated packages such as Microsoft *Works* and *AppleWorks.* The *Cruncher* is a spreadsheet program designed especially for school use.

Telecommunications Tools

Telecommunications tools permit computers to communicate with other computers to share information. Today, we live in an era of global computer interconnectivity that brings a whole world of information to the personal computer user through computer networking and telecommunication. By accessing the Internet, you can instantly locate up-to-date information, communicate with others, and otherwise explore the far corners of cyberspace.

The **Internet** is the vast collection of computer networks that links millions of computers and tens of millions of people worldwide. Computers on the Internet are linked together by a maze of interconnections sort of like a spider's web. This web is composed of

---

Spreadsheet Uses for Teachers and Students

Teachers' Uses	Students' Uses
• Creating a gradebook to maintain students' grades • Keeping other information about students (e.g., a physical education teacher might maintain student performance in various exercises or sporting activities) • Tracking costs of classroom materials (e.g., a chemistry teacher could maintain information about the costs of chemicals used in laboratory exercises) • Demonstrating complex calculations to a class (e.g., a business teacher might build loan amortization tables varying by interest rate as a class illustration)	• Maintaining financial records of a student organization (e.g., tracking candy sales by members of the pep band) • Setting up and maintaining a personal budget • Entering and analyzing data from science experiments • Performing "what if?" simulation or hypothesis-testing activities (e.g., What would happen to my monthly cost of operating a car if an accident doubled my insurance rates?)

FIGURE 3–7 A sample worksheet in Microsoft *Excel* for calculating students' grades. Cell H2, which is highlighted, includes a formula to calculate a student's overall percentile.
Reprinted with permission from Microsoft Corporation.

	A	B	C	D	E	F	G	H	I
1	Name	Quiz 1	Quiz 2	Quiz 3	Quiz 4	Exam 1	Final	Overall	
2	Ahn, Justin	22	19	24	25	86	90	89.20	
3	Buffington, Peggy	25	24	25	25	98	94	97.30	
4	Chang, Mei-Mei	24	21	25	25	90	91	92.80	
5	Dell, Dennis	21	19	24	22	88	86	86.40	
6	Doe, Jane	15	16	20	20	75	83	75.40	
7	Glickman, Nita	18	19	20	20	83	87	81.20	
8	Ihrke, Barbara	20	22	20	22	91	89	86.90	
9	Lin, Ella	18	23	21	20	82	78	80.80	
10	Mandell, Susan	23	23	22	22	93	88	90.00	
11	Ross, Bill	22	20	20	24	84	84	85.00	
12	Ward, Aggie	19	21	18	22	77	81	79.70	
13									
14	Class Average	20.64	20.64	21.73	22.45	86.09	86.45	85.88	

Cell H2 formula: =SUM(B2:E2)*0.5+F2*0.2+G2*0.3

Learning to Use Popular Productivity Applications

Microsoft's *Office* suite of applications is one of the most popular collections of productivity software for both teachers and students. To learn to use these applications, including *Word, Excel,* and *PowerPoint,* complete the level 1 and level 2 activities in Chapters 2 through 5 of the book:

Newby, T. J. (2004). *Teaching and learning with Microsoft Office and FrontPage: Basic building blocks for computer integration.* Upper Saddle River, NJ: Merrill/Prentice-Hall.

Note: These activities have also been placed on this text's accompanying CD-ROM. Launch the CD and click on the following links: **Chapter info and activities >>> Chapter 3 >>> word processing** *(or Spreadsheet, Database, or Presentation software learning activities). Read and study the materials and work through the various "Workout" exercises.*

---

many separately administered computer networks with many different kinds of computers linked together by means of a common communications *protocol* (a set of common rules) known as **TCP/IP** (Transmission Control Protocol/Internet Protocol). Every computer on the Internet has a unique address, actually a number, called its *IP address.* Home users usually connect to the Internet by using a **modem** to dial up an **Internet service provider (ISP)** such as America Online, MSN, or another service. Some home users have faster, always-on connections that use special modems to connect to a cable TV network or a telephone digital subscriber line (DSL). Most schools have dedicated connections to the Internet through high-speed telephone lines such as T1 lines that can support many users simultaneously.

The Internet provides teachers and students with unprecedented access to up-to-date information and resources, and it supports new forms of communication, such as electronic mail, instant messaging, Internet-based telephony, and video conferencing. The three most common educational functions of telecommunication tools today are communication, information retrieval, and information publishing. We briefly consider each here. We will discuss the Internet and its educational applications in more detail in Chapter 10.

Communication in the form of **electronic mail (e-mail)** is the most widespread application of computer telecommunications. E-mail is analogous to postal mail but much faster and more versatile. It allows messages to be sent from individuals to other individuals or from individuals to groups. An e-mail message travels from the sending computer to the receiving computer, usually in less than a minute, and it is stored in the receiver's electronic mailbox until he or she is ready to access it. Once the message has been received, it can be stored, printed, replied to, or forwarded to someone else. Popular programs for composing, sending, and receiving e-mail include Microsoft *Outlook* and *Outlook Express,* Qualcomm *Eudora,* and Netscape *Messenger* as well as the e-mail functions built into services such as America Online and MSN. Free, Web-based e-mail accounts are available through services such as *Yahoo! Mail* and *MSN Hotmail.*

Today, another popular form of communication with others is **instant messaging** (IM). Instant messaging allows two users on the Internet to type messages back and forth to one another in real time, sort of like having a telephone conversation in print. Common instant messaging programs include *AOL Instant Messenger* (AIM), *MSN Messenger, Yahoo! Messenger,* and *ICQ.*

Information retrieval is one of the most important uses of the Internet especially for education. The **World Wide Web** (WWW or just the Web) consists of millions of sites of information displayed in hypermedia format; it supports formatted text, graphics, animations, and even audio and video. Through the Web, one can electronically visit the White House, tour exhibits from the Library of Congress, see the latest pictures from NASA's Hubble Telescope, and find information on just about any topic imaginable. A software program used for accessing the Web is known as a **browser.** Browsers allow users to navigate the Web, bookmark favorite sites, control how Web pages are displayed, and manage the behind-the-scenes interactions that take place when retrieving Web information. Popular Web browsers include Microsoft *Internet Explorer,* Netscape *Navigator,* Apple *Safari,* Mozilla *Firefox,* and *Opera.* See Figure 3–8.

Increasingly, the Web is also being seen as a place where organizations and individuals can display information for others to view and/or retrieve. So, many schools have created their own websites, which teachers and students can use for display of projects as well as for dissemination of information about the school. Web pages are written in Hypertext Markup Language (HTML), which is plain text with embedded labels called tags that tell browsers how to display the information. While HTML can be created using any text editor, software packages that support the development of web pages without the need to write HTML code include Microsoft *FrontPage,* Macromedia *Dreamweaver,* and Netscape *Composer.*

Other Tools

The computer tools listed above are among the most popular and widely used. However, this list just begins to scratch the surface of what is available to teachers and learners for doing work of all kinds. For example, when one needs a finer degree of control over text and graphic layout than is available in typical word processors, teachers and students can turn to desktop publishing programs. Examples include Microsoft *Publisher,* Adobe *Pagemaker* and *InDesign,* and Quark *XPress.* There are

FIGURE 3–8 A screen from Mozilla *Firefox,* a new Web browser, showing the Library of Congress website (http://www.loc.gov).
Reprinted with permission from The Mozilla Organization.

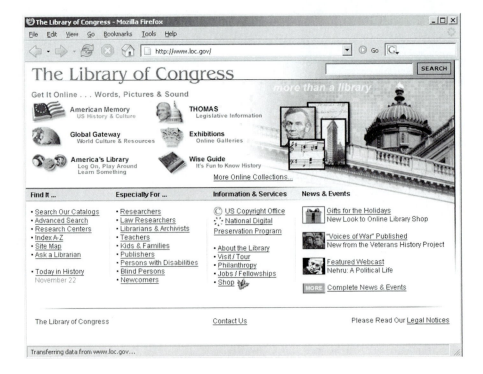

Telecommunication Tool Uses for Teachers and Students

Teachers' Uses	Students' Uses
• Accessing online databases of teaching methods, strategies, and instructional plans • Gathering up-to-date content from the Internet to plan and carry out lessons • E-mailing other teachers in similar positions to exchange ideas and reduce teacher isolation • Setting up a classroom home page to let students, parents, and community members know about class activities, children's homework assignments, upcoming field trips, and so on	• Accessing up-to-date information on the Internet to research a paper, prepare a speech, or write a report. • Using e-mail for pen-pal exchanges with students at other locations to learn more about other places and cultures or to practice a foreign language • Sharing data or exchanging work with students at other locations • Publishing class projects, with appropriate permissions, on the World Wide Web for access by other students, parents, and members of the community

FIGURE 3–9   A screen from Apple *iMovie*, software for editing digital movies.
Reprinted with permission from Apple Computer, Inc.

also many other graphics tools besides general drawing and painting programs. For example, to create graphic organizers, such as concept maps and flowcharts, one can turn to software such as *Inspiration* and the elementary-friendly version called *Kidspiration*. For technical drawing, there are programs such as *AutoCAD* and *TurboCAD*. Digital video is now becoming common in many schools, and there are a number of software packages available for capturing and editing digital video including Apple's *iMovie*, Adobe *Premiere*, Ulead's *VideoStudio*, and Windows *Movie Maker* among many others. See Figure 3–9. Digital audio can likewise be created and edited using

programs such as *Acid, Cakewalk*, and *Sound Forge*. Our point here is just to emphasize that the computer truly is the multitool of education. Computer applications exist to support almost any kind of work or production of media that one can imagine, and there will be new applications developed in the future that will allow us to do even more with our computers. Throughout the book, we will mention other computer tools of interest to the topics being discussed. However, always keep in mind that the list of computer tools will continue to grow and expand, and in the future you are likely to be limited in the classroom only by your own imagination.

NETS Connection

Several of the National Educational Technology Standards (e.g., I [Technology Operations and Concepts], III [Teaching, Learning, and the Curriculum]), IV [Assessment and Evaluation], and V [Productivity and Professional Practice]) for teachers emphasize the need *to use technology tools to increase the level of academic learning by students, as well as to augment personal productivity.* Reflect on those standards (see Teacher Resource A on page 297 for a full listing) and then complete the following:

▶ Within this chapter, go back and review each of the ways in which the various applications software was suggested to be used by both teachers and students. Underline several of those that you have personally used in a similar fashion.

▶ Contemplate on one specific project that you completed where you were pleased with what was learned and how the final product turned out.

▶ In your journal, describe the impact of technology on the completion of that project. Also consider how the outcome may have differed if specific software and hardware would not have been accessible to you.

Assistive Technology

Assistive technology is a special category of computer as assistant; it refers to any equipment or software that is used to maintain or improve the functional capabilities of individuals with disabilities. When planning instruction for students with special needs, it is important to make available appropriate assistive technology. Computers can empower students, and access to the technology can be provided in various ways. For example, you may easily accommodate a student in a wheelchair by using an adjustable-height computer table in a computer laboratory. Various forms of adaptive technology are available to assist students with particular disabilities.

For visually impaired learners, for example, there are numerous solutions available. With mild visual impairment, simply enlarging fonts on the computer can provide access. You can use special software to magnify on-screen text even further. Optical character recognition (OCR) systems can convert print materials into electronic form for computer accessibility. For individuals with significant visual impairment, speech synthesizers can convert text on the computer screen into spoken language. In addition, Braille printers are available for personal computers. There are even special software packages that allow visually impaired individuals to access the often nonlinear and graphically oriented World Wide Web (although they work best when web page developers design their pages to be easily accessible).

A variety of special computer input solutions are available for physically challenged learners. Alternative keyboards, for example with oversize keys, are available for individuals who lack fine motor control. Accessibility options are built into modern computer operating systems; for example, Microsoft Windows has a feature called StickyKeys that makes it possible for a user with motor difficulty to more easily use shift and control keys. When StickyKeys are activated, pressing the shift key twice activates it, so that the user does not have to be able to simultaneously depress shift and another key to type a capital letter. Also, the keyboard can be used as an alternative to the mouse for selecting information. In addition, speech recognition systems allow spoken input of text as well as voice control of the computer. For individuals with significant motor impairment, there are adaptive hardware and software systems that provide computer input through any kind of simple switch (e.g., finger movement, head movement, puff switch). Depending upon the particular system, the switch can be used to do such things as select an option within the computer operating system (e.g., pick an application to open), select options from within an application program, and select letters or even whole words for input.

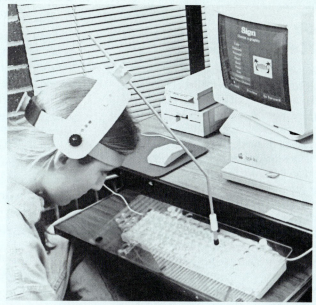

Student using adaptive hardware to work with a computer.

Many assistive technologies are available today that offer a range of options to meet specific students' needs. If you have a student who might benefit from assistive technologies, talk to your school's special education teacher. Availability of these technologies can make a world of difference to a student with special needs!

Addressing the Standards

NETS Connection

A section of the National Educational Technology Standards (NETS) VI (Social, Ethical, Legal, and Human Issues) for teachers emphasizes the need to *meet the special needs and challenges of students by recognizing and employing the use of assistive technologies.* Read and ponder this standard (see Teacher Resource A on page 297 for a full listing) and then complete the following:

▶ Create a journal entry where you insert a two-column table. On one side list several types of special needs of students that teachers in your field may encounter. In the other column, brainstorm and list several types of technologies that may be used to assist students with those special needs.

▶ Go to a website that offers case studies of individuals with special needs and how the use of technology has impacted their lives. A Web search using such terms as "Assistive Technology case studies" should provide you with several sites to explore. One particular site that may be of interest is: http://www.microsoft.com/enable/casestudy/videos.aspx.

▶ After viewing the websites, reconsider the list that you generated. Should your list be adapted in some way? What additional things could be added and/or adapted in your list?

▶ How is it possible for a teacher to stay current with all of the potential technology changes that could be used to impact students (with and without special needs)? Brainstorm and record in your journal ways that the technology may be used to help in this regard (e.g., use of the Internet, development of a database for technology advances or assistive tech resources).

TECHNOLOGY COORDINATOR'S CORNER

Mary Jordan is a veteran teacher at Spring Valley Elementary School. Over the summer, the school replaced all of the aging computers in the building with brand new machines equipped with the latest edition of Microsoft *Office*. In addition to a lab, each classroom now has several computers including one dedicated to the teacher's use. Just before the beginning of the school year, the school held an in-service workshop to orient the teachers to the new computers and the available software applications. Mary attended the workshop along with the other teachers in her building. The district's technology coordinator, Bob Jones, conducted the workshop and introduced the teachers to the current edition of Microsoft *Office* and how the teachers could use the suite of applications to do their work.

After the workshop, Mary approached Bob and expressed the personal concerns she was feeling about the new computers. While happy that the district was providing new computers, she was anxious about the changeover to new equipment and software. She had reached a certain level of comfort with the old computers and software, but she felt overwhelmed by what she had to learn about the new computers and the *Office* suite. Like many teachers, she complained that she didn't have the time to learn how to use the computers.

Bob counseled Mary how to approach the use of the new computers. He suggested taking it one step at a time. He recommended that Mary start with the basics, such as using *Word* to prepare handouts and other materials for her students. He also recommended *PowerPoint*, another application that most teachers found pretty easy to use. After getting comfortable with those, he suggested that Mary try *Excel* for organizing information. He counseled that she take her time and add new software to her repertoire gradually. He urged her to not be afraid to try new things, to use the help built into the applications to learn how to do new things, and, of course, to ask another teacher or him for help if needed. He noted that teachers do not need to know everything to get started.

Bob also suggested using students as helpers in the classroom. The teacher doesn't always have to be the expert when it comes to technology. Students and teachers can be co-learners. Students often pick up technology very quickly, and they may enjoy the chance to share their computer expertise with others. A classroom strategy that can facilitate this approach is having small groups of students work together on a project, such as using *PowerPoint* to prepare reports. When the students work together in a group, they help one another learn to use the software and take some of the burden off the teacher.

Bob noted that a spirit of adventure and openness is the best attitude to have when working with computers. As you learn and grow, you will become more comfortable with the technology, and you will find more and more ways that the computers and software can be of benefit both to you and to your students.

SUMMARY

In this chapter, we examined computer systems and computer tools for teaching and learning. Computer systems consist of several components including the CPU, internal memory, mass storage, input and output devices. These components work together to allow us to perform useful tasks with the computer. When evaluating computer systems for possible acquisition, one should consider these components in light of the desired uses of the system. In order to maintain a healthy working environment, one should follow some basic rules about the positioning and use of computer components. Finally, follow some basic guidelines to troubleshoot problems with computer systems.

The computer can be used in education in three basic ways: as a teacher, as a learner, and as an assistant. In the role of an assistant, commonly used computer tools include word processors, graphics tools, presentation packages, databases, spreadsheets, and computer telecommunications tools among others. We described common features of each type of software and presented typical applications for both teachers and learners. In addition, we described assistive technology, a special class of hardware and software designed to assist individuals with disabilities to use computers and computer applications.

We hope that this chapter has given you many ideas about how you might begin to use the computer for your own productivity (i.e., to design, develop, and evaluate instruction) and as a tool in your own classroom. Keep in mind that the computer with appropriate software is just a tool, albeit a very versatile one. Like the rotary multitool described in the beginning of the chapter, the computer can do a lot of different things. However, it is not appropriate for everything. Just as the multitool does a poor job of hammering a nail, the computer is not particularly effective in many learning situations ranging from helping students learn handwriting to assisting with some types of complex reasoning and problem solving. While the computer can do a lot, it isn't right for everything. In teaching and learning, as in model building, it is important to know when and how to use available tools appropriately. As we look closely throughout this text at the best ways to plan and implement instruction to help your students learn, we will highlight ways that computers can be useful tools for you and for your students.

SUGGESTED RESOURCES

CD Resources

To increase retention and transfer of this information, review the *Reflective Questions and Activities* located in the Chapter 3 section (**Chapter info and activities**>>>

Chapter 3>>> Reflective Questions and Activities) of the text's accompanying CD.

In addition, you can access relevant tutorials, Internet websites, NETS Connection exercises, and direct e-mail access to the text's authors.

Website Resources

Access the text's website **(www.prenhall.com/newby)**, navigate to Chapter 3, and review the Question and Answer section for relevant questions that have been generated by students and answered by the authors. You may also submit your own questions directly to the authors. In addition, you can access presentations by the authors about this chapter and gain insights directly from them about the topics that have been presented.

Print Resources

Newby, T. J. (2004). *Teaching and learning with Microsoft Office and FrontPage: Basic building blocks for computer integration.* Upper Saddle River, NJ: Merrill/Prentice-Hall.

Shelly, G. B., Cashman, T. J., & Gunter, R. (2002). *Teachers discovering computers, integrating technology in the classroom* (2nd ed.). Boston, MA: Thompson Learning.

Smaldino, S. E., Russell, J. D., Heinich, R., & Molenda, M. (2005). *Instructional technology and media for learning* (8th ed.) Upper Saddle River, NJ: Merrill/Prentice-Hall.

Taylor, R. (1980). *The computer in the school: Tutor, tool, and tutee.* New York: Teachers College Press.

White, R., & Downs, T. (2003). *How computers work* (7th ed.). Indianapolis, IN: Que Publishing.

Electronic Resources

http://www.abledata.com/
(AbleData information about assistive technology)

http://www.actden.com/
(Digital Education Network online tutorials for popular software)

http://dir.yahoo.com/Computers and Internet/
(Yahoo computers and the Internet directory)

**http://www.howstuffworks.com/category.htm?
  cat=Comp**
(How stuff works: computers)

http://www.factmonster.com/jpka/A0774696.html
(Fact Monster: how computers work)

http://www.healthycomputing.com
(Healthy Computing)

http://www.microsoft.com/learning/default.asp
(Microsoft Learning site)

II

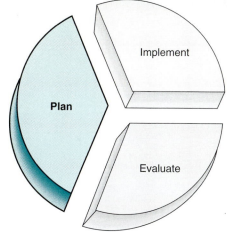

PLANNING THE TECHNOLOGY-ENHANCED LEARNING EXPERIENCE

Webster's *New World Dictionary* defines a *plan* as "any detailed method, formulated beforehand, for doing or making something." Planning is a natural part of life. We plan in order to exercise some influence over future events and to increase the likelihood that things will turn out the way we want. Although a plan doesn't guarantee success, not having a plan often ensures failure. Plans can take various forms:

▶ A recipe helps us to make sure the food we are preparing includes the necessary ingredients and cooks for the right amount of time.

▶ An itinerary helps us to make sure our vacation trip includes all the things we want to see and do, given our limited amount of time.

▶ A budget helps us to make sure our income both covers our expenses and also allows us some spending money.

▶ A grocery list helps us to make sure we purchase the necessary items when we go shopping.

This section is about planning for instruction and learning. Our purpose is twofold: to convince you that effective planning is a vital part of effective instruction, and to provide you with some practical guidelines for effective planning.

This is the first part of the PIE model described in Chapter 1. Your instructional plan directs what takes place during the implementation and evaluation stages of instruction. Once you have a plan for your instruction, you can move on to implement the instruction outlined in the plan. Once you have implemented your instruction, you can evaluate its effectiveness in helping your students learn. Planning instruction is made up of three parts:

1. *Developing the plan.* This involves (see Chapter 4) identifying the important characteristics of your learners, specifying your intended objectives for the instruction, and specifying the relevant features of the learning environment. In addition, developing instructional activities that will ensure learning is discussed within Chapter 5.

2. *Identifying methods and media.* A variety of instructional methods (Chapter 6) and media (Chapter 7) exist that can impact how learners experience the learning situation. With the variety of content, as well as differences in learners and the practical constraints of time and budget, it is imperative that you become aware of the different methods and media available. We discuss these options, the advantages and limitations of each, and how one goes about selecting the most appropriate option.

3. *Selecting, adapting, and/or producing instructional materials.* We explore in Chapter 8 the process of assembling and/or developing the instructional materials you will need to carry out your plan. We address the practical aspects and issues (e.g., copyright) related to preparing instructional materials within your time and budget constraints.

In this exciting section of the book we encourage creativity, problem solving, and reflection. For many, the art of teaching is embedded in planning and developing what students will experience and how they will learn from those experiences. This section focuses on how you can create learning experiences that will ensure your students' success.

4

Technology and Instructional Situations: Understanding Learners, Learning Objectives, and Learning Environments

CHAPTER OBJECTIVES

After reading and studying this chapter, you will be able to:

▸ Outline a process for instructional planning.
▸ Identify the important characteristics of a group of students and how those characteristics may influence your use of instructional technology.
▸ Describe how diversity can be used as an asset in instructional planning.
▸ Specify the objectives for a lesson of your choice.
▸ Identify the relevant characteristics of a learning environment.

INTRODUCTION

In the next several chapters, we will describe the components of the instructional planning process, with each chapter describing a different component of the process. To begin, we'd like to introduce you to a teacher. Kevin Spencer teaches social studies in a suburban elementary school. He's been a teacher for eight years and has taught at his present school for seven years, after working as a substitute for a year. Kevin enjoys working with the students and the students seem to like him. He knows his subject and is good at creating lessons that get the students working with one another and that include a variety of "fun" activities.

When Kevin was in college, instructional technology was still relatively new. But he's seen some of his younger colleagues do some very exciting things in their classes, using technology to motivate their students and help them learn. Instructional technology has become better and easier to use, and Kevin has come to the conclusion that this would be a good time for him to incorporate more technology into his teaching. His plan is to begin with his sixth-grade social studies class.

We will return to Kevin at the end of the chapter. But first, we will provide an overview of the instructional planning process and describe the first three components of that process: students, objectives, and learning environment. These three components are considered the foundation for instructional planning. Instruction usually involves helping particular students accomplish particular learning objectives within a particular learning environment. So, information about students, objectives, and learning environment will allow the teacher to develop a plan that is matched to the particular situation in which s/he is working.

OVERVIEW OF INSTRUCTIONAL PLANNING

Recall from Chapter 1 that *learning* is the process of acquiring new knowledge and skills through experience. *Instruction* is the process of helping students learn through the deliberate arrangement of information, activities, methods, and media. *Instructional design* is the process of developing plans for instruction through the practical application of theoretical principles (some of which are described in Chapter 2).

Designing instruction is often described as a "rational" or objectives-first process (Hunter, 1982) in which the elements of the plan are put in place in a prescribed order, beginning with objectives. However, practicing teachers don't always follow an objectives-first order when they plan their instruction. They may begin by specifying objectives. But they are just as likely to begin by:

▶ Creating a practice activity
▶ Outlining the content to be covered
▶ Identifying students' existing knowledge
▶ Developing a test
▶ Selecting a relevant computer activity

Teachers are likely to follow an equally varied order in developing the remaining elements of their plans. To mirror this flexibility, we suggest that instructional planning is like assembling a jigsaw puzzle. The pieces of the puzzle must fit together to complete the picture, but the order in which the pieces are put in place isn't particularly important. As shown in Figure 4–1, we suggest a planning process made up of nine key pieces.

This "jigsaw puzzle" illustrates four important principles of instructional planning:

1. Instructional planning is a systematic process. It is a logical, methodical process in which each element of the plan is considered and carefully linked to the other elements.
2. Instructional planning is a flexible process. The order in which the elements are considered is likely to vary from one situation to the next.
3. Instructional planning is a dynamic, interactive process. Decisions made while developing one element of the plan will affect decisions about other elements. This may mean reconsidering, even changing, decisions you have already made.
4. The result of the process is a coherent plan made up of elements that work together to promote learning.

FIGURE 4–1   The pieces of the instructional planning "puzzle".

STUDENTS

We begin our discussion with students because the purpose of instruction is to help particular students learn. As shown in Figure 4–1, knowledge of your students is a key piece in the planning puzzle. As a teacher, your challenge is to help **all** students reach desired learning goals. However, developing an instructional plan will be easier if you first consider the characteristics of your students, including:

- Gender
- Socioeconomic status
- Culture and ethnicity
- Existing knowledge of the content
- Motivation
- Learning style
- Special needs
- Technology literacy

Extensive discussion of these characteristics is beyond the scope of this book. Our purpose is to briefly describe student characteristics that might affect your instructional planning. More information can be found by referring to the resources listed at the end of the chapter.

Gender

When they're young, boys and girls are more similar than different. However, as they mature, some differences appear. For example, beginning at puberty (approximately 11 or 12 years of age), boys tend to be taller and have more muscular strength; boys tend to be more physically aggressive, while girls tend to be more affiliative, concerned with social relationships; and boys tend to explain their successes in terms of ability ("I'm smart") and their failures in terms of effort ("I didn't try very hard"), while girls tend to explain their successes in terms of effort ("I kept trying until I got it") and their failures in terms of ability ("I'm not very good in science") (Deaux, 1984).

These differences are partly the result of biology (boys become stronger because of increased levels of the hormone testosterone). However, they are mostly the result of **socialization**—the process by which we learn the rules, norms, and expectations of the society in which we live. In general, boys and girls are treated differently by parents, peers, teachers, and mass media. As a result, they learn that some things are appropriate for males, while others are appropriate for females. For example, boys may be reinforced for being independent, competitive, and logical. As a result, they may be drawn to school subjects such as science and to occupations such as engineer and electrician. In contrast, girls may be reinforced for being cooperative, sympathetic, and artistic. As a result, they may be drawn to school subjects such as social studies and to occupations such as librarian and nurse.

These gender-related stereotypes have been decreasing during the past 20 years, but they still exist and affect students at all grade levels. However, it's important to note that, even as they mature, few substantial differences in academic ability exist between boys and girls. As a group, their scores on IQ tests are comparable. While socialization may lead boys and girls to prefer different subject areas and different instructional methods, they have the same *ability* to *learn* in all content areas.

Socioeconomic Status

Socioeconomic status (SES) encompasses a variety of factors, including family income, parents' occupations,

---

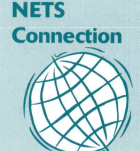

Addressing the Standards

NETS Connection

Each of the six key National Educational Technology Standards (NETS I, II, III, IV, V, VI) address, in some way, the need for teachers to *use technology to locate, collect, and evaluate information from various sources in order to facilitate planning for instruction and to ultimately address learner needs, affirm diversity, and maximize student learning.* As you begin to read through each of the following ways in which students, objectives, and learning environments could differ and offer challenges to the classroom teacher, reflect back on the technology software tools described in Chapter 3 of this text (e.g., spreadsheets, word processing, database). Through the use of your journal, ponder on the potential role of technology and note the following:

- How do teachers obtain needed, relevant information on each of their students?
- How can that information become useful and not overly burdensome or frustrating?
- How could that information be useful in planning the learning experience, during the implementation of that learning experience, and even after the learning experience has been completed? What would be the potential role of technology during each of the planning, implementation, and evaluation phases?

and the amount of formal education parents have completed. In general, the more education parents have completed, the more "professional" their occupations, and the more money they earn, the higher the family's SES. SES is worthy of our attention because it is consistently related to "success" in school, as measured by things such as standardized test scores, grades, truancy, and dropout rates (Macionis, 1997). This is largely because of the nature of the parent-child interactions that occur within families. In general, high SES parents are more likely to provide their children with a variety of educational experiences outside of school (e.g., travel, music lessons, visits to museums), be involved in their children's school and extracurricular activities, and value education and communicate that value to their children. SES may also affect the experience with technology that a student brings to school.

However, it is important to note that these are broad generalizations that aren't limited to high SES families. It can be easy to stereotype low SES parents as unable and/or unwilling to support their children's education. But this would frequently be inaccurate. Many low SES parents maintain high educational standards, actively participate in their children's school activities, take their children to museums, and encourage their children to participate in a variety of extracurricular activities. In addition, all families have "historically accumulated and culturally developed bodies of knowledge and skills essential for household or individual functioning" (Moll, Amanti, Neff, & Gonzalez, 1992). Though the content may differ, these "funds of knowledge" can be used to help children learn by connecting school experiences with home experiences. For example, children from farm families may have access to information about plants and animals that would be relevant in a science class. Children whose parents are police officers may be familiar with laws and courts in a way that would be relevant in a social studies class.

Various backgrounds and experiences engender diversity in the classroom.

The point is that understanding these varied "funds of knowledge" can be helpful in instructional planning by enabling teachers to:

1. Tap into unique learning experiences that naturally occur in the home.
2. Provide opportunities for parents to become directly involved in their children's education through their day-to-day activities.
3. Help students maintain a sense of pride in their families and the contributions they make to the community.
4. Provide diverse approaches to subject matter that enriches the learning for all students in a class.

Culture and Ethnicity

Culture refers to the attitudes, values, customs, and behavior patterns that characterize a social group (Banks, 1997). Part of culture is **ethnicity,** which refers to the way individuals identify themselves with the nation from which they or their ancestors came (deMarrais & LeCompte, 1999). Within the United States there are a number of ethnic groups, including African American, Hispanic, Asian American, Native American, and various immigrant groups, including Italian, Polish, Israeli, Indian, and many others.

For the most part, schools in the United States are based on a white, middle-class, American majority culture. Students from different cultural backgrounds are likely to experience a "cultural mismatch" (Ormrod, 1995), in which important discrepancies appear between their home culture and the school culture. This may result in confusion about what to expect or what is expected of them, which may, in turn, result in reduced achievement for these students. Teachers sometimes contribute to this cultural mismatch through the natural human tendency to view student behaviors through their own cultural windows. The resulting misinterpretations may lead teachers to conclude that minority students lack ability and/or motivation. They may very well be wrong. Consider the following examples:

▶ During a conversation with the teacher, a student looks down rather than maintaining eye contact. The teacher interprets this to mean that the student is bored and isn't paying attention. However, the student may come from a culture in which eye contact with an adult is a sign of disrespect.
▶ A student seems to wait a long time before responding to a question. The teacher interprets this to mean that the student doesn't understand the question or know the answer. However, the student may speak a language other than English at home and need time to translate the question.

As with SES, knowing about your students' culture and ethnicity can facilitate instructional planning because it will help you understand and accommodate the attitudes, experiences, and "funds of knowledge" students bring to school. For example, cultural mismatch can be particularly prominent with some cultures. Ogbu (1992) distinguishes between ethnic groups who immigrated to the United States voluntarily (such as Irish or Vietnamese) and groups who were brought to the United States against their will (such as African Americans) or were conquered (such as Native Americans). Students from these "involuntary minorities" may form "resistance cultures" (Ogbu & Simons, 1998) in which school success is perceived as a rejection of their native culture. As a result, these students often experience low grades, disciplinary problems, and high dropout rates. To counter these effects, teachers may have to work harder to build trust with the students, provide instruction that is culturally responsive, and involve parents and members of the cultural community in the children's education.

Existing Knowledge of the Content

Existing knowledge of the content refers to what students already know when they begin a lesson. There are two related questions: Are the students ready to begin the lesson? Have they already achieved the desired goals? To understand the first question, it is important to understand the concept of **prerequisites.** As we will see in the next section, objectives define the knowledge students should have at the *end* of a lesson. Prerequisites, on the other hand, define the knowledge students should have at the *beginning* of the lesson. When students don't have the necessary prerequisites, they will, at best, have a difficult time succeeding in the lesson. Learning is cumulative, and this means two things. First, it means that virtually every lesson has prerequisites. The objectives of one lesson often form the prerequisites for the next. Second, it means that finding out what the students already know will help with instructional planning because it will allow you to create instruction that builds on that existing knowledge.

Imagine that you are planning a lesson on long division. The prerequisites for long division are subtraction and multiplication; to learn long division effectively and efficiently, students must be able to subtract and multiply. Students lacking these prerequisite skills cannot learn long division. Figure 4–2 illustrates the order in which these prerequisites lead up to long division. It

represents three students who differ in what they already know. The first student, Tom, has mastered subtraction, but not multiplication. Long division is over his head; he isn't ready yet because he doesn't have all the prerequisites. He's likely to be frustrated and lost. The second student, Becky, has all the prerequisites. She knows how to subtract and multiply but doesn't yet know how to do long division. She's ready to begin. The third student, Polly, has gone beyond the prerequisites. She knows how to subtract and multiply, and she knows how to do long division, at least in some situations. Like Tom, Polly is likely to be frustrated, but for a different reason; she's likely to be bored because the instruction is presenting something she already knows.

Motivation

Motivation refers to a "process whereby goal-directed activity is instigated and maintained" (Pintrich & Schunk, 1996). It can be distinguished from ability in that it defines what people *will* do rather than what they *can* do (Keller, 1983). Motivation is a common influence on human activities. We are motivated to pursue certain relationships, enter certain careers, go to certain places, or engage in certain activities. Motivation makes a direct contribution to learning by focusing students on certain desired learning goals and increasing the effort they expend in reaching those goals.

Motivation can be categorized as intrinsic or extrinsic. *Intrinsic* motivation is generated by aspects of the experience or task itself (such as its novelty or the challenge it presents). *Extrinsic* motivation is generated by factors unrelated to the experience or task (such as grades or recognition). Intrinsic and extrinsic motivation are often thought of as opposite ends of a single continuum. But they are actually two separate dimensions, as shown in Figure 4–3.

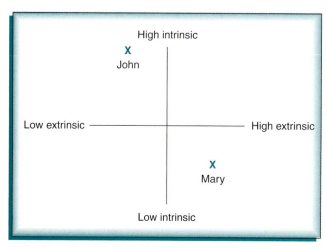

FIGURE 4–3 Intrinsic and extrinsic dimensions of motivation.

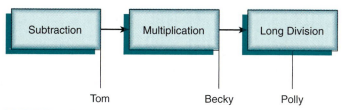

FIGURE 4–2 An example of the concept of prerequisites.

As Figure 4–3 shows, it's possible for a student to show high, medium, or low intrinsic motivation and high, medium, or low extrinsic motivation on a given activity. Motivation will also vary from student to student and from activity to activity. For example, John and Mary may participate in school debates. But John participates because he enjoys it (intrinsic motivation), while Mary participates because she thinks it will look good on college applications (extrinsic motivation). At the same time, John participates in every environmental debate he can, but is less interested in debates about social policy issues. Both intrinsic and extrinsic motivation are useful. But, in general, intrinsic motivation is more effective in learning. Students who are intrinsically motivated will work harder and learn more because of their natural interest in the material.

Knowing something about your students' motivation will help with instructional planning because it will help you add to the extrinsic and intrinsic appeal of the instruction. More specifically, it will help you determine what kinds of reinforcers (Chapter 2) might work with individual students (extrinsic motivation). It will also help you create intrinsically motivating instructional activities including (Eggen & Kauchak, 2001):

▶ Challenge—Adjusting the difficulty level of activities and providing feedback that is immediate and matched to needs of the individual student.
▶ Control—Allowing students to regulate their own learning by adjusting the pace of an activity and varying the amount and kind of assistance they receive.
▶ Curiosity—Presenting students with a variety of situations that are unique, surprising, or inconsistent with their existing ideas.
▶ Confidence—Providing students with guidance and assistance that will help them succeed, develop their confidence in their own abilities, and increase their interest in other, more difficult activities.

Learning Style

Learning style refers to students' approaches to learning, problem solving, and processing information (Snow, Corno, & Jackson, 1996). There are a number of ways to categorize learning style. One simple way to think about learning style is to consider the sensory channel a student prefers for taking in new information—visual, auditory, or kinesthetic. As shown in the following table, knowing your students' preferred sensory channels can help in planning your instruction.

Now that we've presented this information, a couple of important cautions are in order. First, the categories aren't mutually exclusive. Each student will use all three sensory channels, though one channel may be stronger or used more frequently than the others. Second, no value judgment should be made about these learning styles. For example, visual learners aren't smarter or better than auditory learners. They're simply different. In fact, these learning styles should not be used to label or categorize students (Susie is an auditory learner). Instead, they should serve as reminders:

▶ Students aren't alike. They differ from one another in the sensory channel they prefer. Perhaps as important, they differ from us. The sensory channel we prefer won't be the sensory channel that all of the students prefer.
▶ We should vary our instruction to accommodate those differences. This is where instructional technology can be an asset. Technology is particularly good at using multiple sensory channels. It allows us to combine text, graphics, audio clips, video, and "hands on" activities to help all students learn.
▶ We should help students understand how they learn best. This may involve helping them understand which sensory channel is most effective for them and helping them develop the other sensory channels.

	Characteristics	Technology Ideas
Visual Learners	• Learn best what they see • Are good at spatial relations • Will often use images or color to remember information	Present information in the form of graphs, pictures, animations, video clips, and other types of visuals
Auditory Learners	• Learn best what they hear • Have strong language skills • Will often sound things out or talk as a way of understanding something	Use audio to explain ideas or narrate
Kinesthetic Learners	• Learn best what they do • Are often well-coordinated • Will often physically explore his/her environment	Ask students to manipulate items

Check It Out

Learning Style and Instruction

Complete one or more of the learning style assessments available on the CD (**Chapter info and activities >>> Chapter 4 >>> live links >>> learning styles Inventories/Assessments**). Look over the description of your preferred learning style. Do you think it accurately describes you? What new information does it provide about the way you learn best?

Send the assessment to several friends and family members. Once they have been returned to you, tally the results.

Now, imagine that you had to teach the content of Chapter 2 (or a chapter from any other textbook) to a class made up of these friends and family members. Outline a plan for the instruction. Based on the results of the learning style assessment, what would you do to present the information? What would you do to actively engage the learners? How would you use technology during the lesson? What would you do to help these "students" understand how they learn best, and how would you incorporate this into the lesson?

Special Needs

Students are individuals, and differ from one another in a variety of ways. Sometimes students are different enough from their peers that they require special educational services to help them reach their potential. In recent years there have been increasing efforts to *mainstream* these students—to educate them as much as possible in regular classrooms with other students who do not have **special needs**—to ensure that all students have the same educational opportunities. At the same time, there have been increasing efforts to identify their special needs in order to provide them with school experiences that will enable them to reach their individual learning potentials.

Students may require special educational services for a variety of reasons, which can be classified into several categories:

▶ Learning disabilities, such as attention deficit/hyperactivity disorder (AD/HD), in which a student has difficulty concentrating on a single task for any length of time.
▶ Behavior disorders, which include both "acting out," marked by aggressive or disruptive behavior, and

"acting in," marked by anxiety and withdrawal (Eggen & Kauchak, 2001).
▶ Communication disorders, such as stuttering, in which a student repeats a sound while pronouncing words.
▶ Perception problems such as loss of vision or hearing.
▶ Motor problems such as cerebral palsy or epilepsy.
▶ Health problems such as asthma or diabetes.

For each of these types of special needs, we must reemphasize that students are individuals, as different from one another as they are similar. For example, visually impaired students are similar in that they all have a functional limitation. Like other students, however, they are likely to differ in terms of their cultural background, motivation, and learning styles. For a thorough discussion of special needs students and the issue of mainstreaming, see Salend (2005).

There is another category of special needs that is often not thought of as a "problem," but that requires special attention—giftedness. *Giftedness* refers to an exceptional talent or ability in one or more areas. Students may be gifted in any academic area—science, music, creative writing, and so on. Gifted students are often frustrated or bored in school and may become isolated from other students because of differences in their interests that may seem impossible to reconcile. Gifted students may benefit from planned instructional activities that challenge them and help them to develop their special talents.

Technology Literacy

Traditionally, literacy has meant the ability to read and write. However, with the growth of the information age, the definition of literacy has expanded to include visual literacy, information literacy, and technology literacy. **Technology literacy** refers to "computer skills and the ability to use computers and other technology to improve learning, productivity, and performance" (U.S. Department of Education, 1996, page 7). This includes

Accessibility issues need to be considered for students with special needs.

the variety of technology tools described in Chapter 3: word processors, graphics tools and desktop publishers, presentation software, computer databases and database management systems, electronic spreadsheets, and computer telecommunications and the Internet.

Knowing the technology literacy of your students has obvious benefits for instructional planning. If you're planning a lesson that asks the students to use a word processor, an electronic bulletin board, or a search engine, then it's a good idea to find out how familiar the students are with that technology.

Technology literacy is likely to vary in a particular class, depending on the students' ages, prior experience with computers, and access to computers outside of school. One way to assess technology literacy is to ask your students (or a sample of students) a series of questions about their computer skills, such as shown in Figure 4–4. This figure shows an excerpt from a survey used to assess the technology skills among a group of high school students. You can easily adapt the questions to fit the grade level of your students.

The figure shows a relatively formal assessment of technology skills. But it doesn't have to be done formally. It can be just as useful to ask students about their technology skills as part of short, informal "chats." In any case, the purpose is to find out how much your students know about technology so you can choose appropriate hardware and software, consider the value of creating familiarization activities for the students, and determine

how much technology support the students will require during the lesson.

Diversity as an Asset

Clearly, we've only scratched the surface of the dimensions that describe students. However, even these brief descriptions illustrate the important role student characteristics play in instructional planning. For example, Table 4–1 shows how the use of technology can be influenced by student characteristics. This is because virtually every group of students will be diverse in ways that are both apparent (gender, race) and hidden (learning style, motivation). For example, one in three students in elementary and secondary school belongs to a racial or ethnic minority; one in five lives in poverty; 11 percent are classified as disabled; and more than 50 percent will live in a single-parent home before they turn 18 (Sapon-Shevin, 2001). This diversity can be confirmed by looking into any classroom. Even in groups that are homogeneous on one dimension (e.g., single-sex classes), the students are likely to vary on other dimensions (e.g., SES, ethnicity, and learning style).

This diversity has benefits. For example, Terenzini and colleagues (2001) investigated the relationship between racial/ethnic diversity and student learning among college students. They found that students in diverse classes reported greater gains in both problem-solving ability and group skills. Similarly, in a review of

Can you edit, copy, cut, and paste a block of text within a document?	☐ I can do this ☐ I can probably do this ☐ I would have difficulty doing this ☐ I would not be able to do this
Can you create a table with 3 rows and 4 columns?	☐ I can do this ☐ I can probably do this ☐ I would have difficulty doing this ☐ I would not be able to do this
Can you insert a picture and wrap the text around it?	☐ I can do this ☐ I can probably do this ☐ I would have difficulty doing this ☐ I would not be able to do this
Can you change the size, color, font, and style of text?	☐ I can do this ☐ I can probably do this ☐ I would have difficulty doing this ☐ I would not be able to do this
Can you insert a formula that computes and reports sums, averages, and high and low scores?	☐ I can do this ☐ I can probably do this ☐ I would have difficulty doing this ☐ I would not be able to do this
Can you change the format of a number within a cell?	☐ I can do this ☐ I can probably do this ☐ I would have difficulty doing this ☐ I would not be able to do this
Can you select a range of rows and columns of data and create a chart?	☐ I can do this ☐ I can probably do this ☐ I would have difficulty doing this ☐ I would not be able to do this
Can you sort and filter data?	☐ I can do this ☐ I can probably do this ☐ I would have difficulty doing this ☐ I would not be able to do this

FIGURE 4–4   A sample set of technology literacy survey questions focusing on word processing and spreadsheet capabilities.

research, Milem (2003) reports that college students who interacted with diverse people and ideas showed greater intellectual engagement and academic motivation, along with greater gains in critical thinking.

So, classroom diversity is both inevitable and valuable. The question is how to deal with it. Traditionally, diversity has been viewed as a deficit—something that is lacking in students who don't fit the "norm." However, we propose a "difference" approach to diversity (Villegas & Lucas, 2002). A difference approach suggests that

a particular student's problems can often be attributed to a mismatch between the school experience and some characteristic of the student, rather than to something that is wrong with the student (a deficit). For example, using verbal descriptions to teach mathematics concepts may present a mismatch for students with more visual learning styles.

Putting this kind of difference approach into practice involves five basic principles that should be incorporated into your instruction.

TABLE 4–1 *Diversity and Technology*

Dimension	Characteristics	Possible Technology Implications
Gender	Boys may be more aggressive and dominate available equipment (Swain & Harvey, 2002).	Develop procedures to ensure equitable access
	Girls may focus more on the social functions of technology (Brunner & Bennett, 1997).	Choose software that emphasizes simulation and collaboration
	Girls may feel less confident in their ability to use and learn from technology.	Provide more guidance and feedback
SES	Low-SES children are likely to have less experience with technology than high-SES children (U.S. Department of Commerce, 1998).	Provide remediation or familiarization activities for low-SES students
Culture and ethnicity	African American and Hispanic children are likely to have less experience with technology than white children (U.S. Department of Commerce, 1998).	Provide remediation or familiarization activities for minority children
Learning preferences	Students with a visual preference learn best what they see.	Ask students to use drawing software to create concept maps for new information
	Students with an auditory preference learn best what they hear.	Use video conferencing and other types of communication tools to have students interact with experts
	Students with a kinesthetic preference learn best what they do.	Ask students to visit websites and scroll for information
Special needs	Students with impaired vision may not be able to read information on a monitor.	Provide a screen reader that will read aloud text and names of icons
	Students with motor problems may have difficulty with the fine motor coordination required to use a keyboard or mouse.	Provide switch-accessible software that allows them to control the keyboard or cursor with a head nod or puff of air

1. Recognize that, like your students, you are an individual. That is, you are a man or woman who has certain cultural and socioeconomic characteristics, learning styles, and motivational interests.
2. Get to know your students as individuals. Identify and support their specific cultural backgrounds, talents, accomplishments, and interests. These first two principles help us avoid the "ethnocentric" assumptions that our students are all alike and that they are all like us.
3. Teach each of your students as an individual, as much as possible. This means teaching each student to read, write, and solve mathematics problems. It also means teaching them to respect one another and to value the diversity among them.
4. Use teaching methods that incorporate their diversity. For example, Sapon-Shevin (2001) suggests three teaching strategies that make use of students' diversity:
    - Cooperative learning—This involves putting students into groups to work on a shared

learning task and making sure that the groups are diverse in one or more dimensions.
- Peer tutoring—This involves asking students to teach one another. An important consideration is making sure to allow all students to be the teacher at one time or

Selection of nontraditional professions has increased classroom and work place diversity.

another so that no one is permanently identified as less able.

- Multilevel teaching—This involves creating instruction that focuses on an essential idea and includes a variety of learning tasks to accommodate students with different cultural backgrounds, learning styles, and existing knowledge.

5. Represent diversity in the examples, stories, posters, and other classroom materials that you use. A key here is to make sure that each gender, race, and cultural group is represented in a positive light.

Following these guidelines will make it easier to understand any problems or concerns particular students are having and to plan instruction that will help overcome those problems. For example, you'll be able to:

- Encourage boys and girls in subject areas that do not fit traditional gender-related stereotypes
- Adjust instructional methods to allow for responses that are appropriate in students' home cultures
- Provide additional support (social and emotional as well as educational) for students (and their parents) from low-SES families
- Organize new information and plan instructional activities based on students' learning styles
- Develop strategies to increase students' intrinsic motivation
- Help identify students' special needs and obtain services to help meet those needs

OBJECTIVES

Imagine that you are taking a vacation trip. You will want to know where you're going so you can:

- Make reasonable decisions about what routes and means of transportation to take, what you might want to see along the way, what you'll need to take with you, and so on
- Manage your budget
- Monitor your progress and manage your time

- Tell concerned others (family and friends) where you're going and what your itinerary is so they will know where you are

A lesson is an instructional "trip," and, like a vacation trip, you'll want to know where you're going so you can

- Make reasonable decisions about what instructional methods and media to use, how long your students will take to reach the "destination," what else you might want them to learn along the way, what materials, facilities, and equipment you'll need, and so on
- Manage your budget
- Monitor students' progress and manage the time allotted for the lesson
- Tell concerned others (students, parents, principals, other teachers, etc.) where you're going and what your itinerary is so they will know where you are.

So, **objectives** are important because they define where you're going—the knowledge or skills the students should have at the end of the lesson. Refer again to Figure 4–1 and note that "Objectives" are critical to the planning process. Table 4–2 summarizes the practical benefits of specifying lesson objectives. As this table shows, objectives provide a useful communication tool as well as practical guidance for teachers, students, and others. However, researchers have raised questions about the value of specifying objectives in advance (Reiser & Dick 1996; Yelon, 1991). Following are several of the most common criticisms, together with our responses.

Criticism: Objectives dehumanize the instruction by focusing on the requirements rather than the students.
Response: Contrary to this common misperception, the purpose of objectives is to specify the knowledge and skills that are important for the students to acquire. This allows you to plan a way for *each* student to accomplish what you want him or her to. In addition, clearly stated objectives tell students where they will be

TABLE 4–2   *The Practical Benefits of Specifying Lesson Objectives*

	Guidance	Communication
Teacher	Guides selection and development of lesson content and activities. Guides selection and development of assessment instruments.	Reminds the teacher of what the expected outcomes are.
Students	Guides students' studying.	Tells students what will be expected of them.
Others	Guides the development of the overall curriculum into which the lesson or course fits. Guides the delivery of instruction by substitutes.	Tells interested others (e.g., principals, parents, substitutes) what the students are learning and what is expected of them.

going. This helps motivate them, guides their studying, and allows them to plan and monitor their own progress.

Criticism: Specifying objectives takes up valuable time.

Response: Time spent specifying objectives is an *investment* rather than an expenditure. As with any other investment, clearly stated objectives have a significant dividend: They help ensure that your instructional plan will match your students' needs.

Criticism: Objectives can't be specified for complex or intangible skills, such as problem solving or critical thinking. The result is a focus on low-level skills, such as memorization, which are easy to describe and measure but are not always the skills the students should be learning.

Response: It is easier to specify objectives for low-level skills such as memorization. However, objectives can be specified for all types of learning, including complex, high-level skills like problem solving or critical thinking. In fact, because of the greater complexity of high-level skills, specifying objectives for them may be more important than for low-level skills.

Criticism: Specifying objectives in advance "locks in" the curriculum and makes it difficult to change.

Response: Explicitly stating objectives doesn't necessarily mean they are written in stone. You can modify them as easily as you write them. Good teachers review their objectives periodically so they can modify those that are no longer relevant.

Criticism: Specifying objectives in advance leads to a rigid, mechanistic approach to teaching that reduces the teacher's ability to respond creatively and spontaneously to students and to the "teachable moments" that often occur in the classroom.

Response: When you're taking a vacation trip, having a destination doesn't necessarily mean that you can't or won't take side trips to explore other interesting places. Similarly, on an instructional "trip," having objectives doesn't mean that you can't or won't explore other interesting ideas.

Criticism: Specifying objectives in advance results in a tendency to "teach to the test."

Response: If your test accurately assesses your objectives, as it should, and you have designed your instruction to achieve your objectives, as you should, then your instruction will also help students succeed on the test.

Sources of Objectives

There are a number of sources to help you identify lesson objectives:

▶ *Curriculum guides.* General objectives are often provided in curriculum guides, competency lists, and content outlines that are set forth by state education departments, school districts, or professional organizations. You may then translate

these general course objectives into objectives for specific lessons.

▶ *Textbooks and instructional activities.* Textbooks and commercially produced instructional activities often include suggested objectives that identify what students should learn. These objectives may appear in an accompanying instructor's guide.

▶ *Tests.* Objectives can be derived from the tests used in a course. When the objectives, instruction, and tests are parallel, tests will indicate what the students should have learned. This is true for standardized tests as well as for tests you develop. The general principle is that if it is important enough to be on the test, it is probably important enough to specify as a lesson objective.

▶ *World Wide Web.* More and more lesson plans and instructional activities can be found on the World Wide Web. These often include objectives.

▶ *Your own ideas.* You will often have your own ideas about what students should learn from a lesson, especially if you have taught the lesson before or are familiar with the particular students.

Specifying Lesson Objectives

Objectives specify what the teacher wants the students to learn. Various methods for specifying objectives have been described (Jacobson, Eggen, & Kauchak, 1993). We suggest the method Mager (1997) describes, in which objectives include three components:

Performance: what students will do to indicate that they have learned

Conditions: the circumstance under which the students are expected to perform

Criteria: the standard that defines acceptable performance

Specifying the objectives for a lesson involves specifying each of these three components.

Specifying the Performance

What will students do or say that will indicate that they have learned? We suggest specifying the performance first because it is often the easiest component to identify. Teachers usually know what they want their students to learn in a lesson, even if they haven't thought out all the details. The key is to specify a performance that is an observable indicator of students' capabilities.

Observable Indicator. Assessing learning almost always involves inference. In some situations (e.g., learning to solve arithmetic problems) the inference is relatively straightforward, while in other situations (e.g., learning to think critically) the inference is more difficult. But in virtually every situation students must do something before you can infer their level of learning. To facilitate this inference, the objective should specify an observable performance. This will allow both you and the students to tell whether learning has occurred. One way to ensure the specification of an observable performance is to use verbs that describe observable actions—things you can see or hear students do. Table 4–3 lists some observable action verbs, along with verbs you should avoid because they aren't observable actions. These lists aren't exhaustive, but will give you an idea of the kinds of verbs to use when specifying lesson objectives.

Student Capability. Teachers are naturally focused on what is going to happen during the lesson (Sardo-Brown, 1990). One result of this is a tendency for the teacher's plans to focus on the activities (either the teacher's or the students') that will take place during the lesson. Developing these activities is an important aspect of planning. But the purpose of specifying objectives is to clearly identify the results, or destination, of the lesson rather than the route students will follow to reach that destination. What should students learn? One way to make sure you describe a student capability is to use the phrase "the students will be able to," before the action verb. Using this phrase will remind you that the objective of the lesson is a future capability of the student.

Specifying the Conditions

What are the circumstances under which students will be expected to perform? What will they be given to work with? The key is to specify conditions that will be in place *at the time of the expected performance*. One way to specify the conditions is to think about the questions students are likely to ask about the expected performance (Yelon, 1991). Their questions can be grouped into four categories:

Setting: Where will they be expected to perform?
People: Will they be working alone? With a team? Under supervision?
Equipment: What tools or facilities will they have to work with?

Information: What, if any, notes, books, checklists, or models will they have to work with?

For example, imagine that you want your students to describe the use of symbolism in *Macbeth*. The students might ask: Will we have to come up with the examples ourselves, or will we describe examples you give us (information)? Will this be an in-class assignment, or can we take it home (setting)? Can we use our books (information)? Can we work together (people)?

As shown in the following example, you can include your responses to these questions in the objective by using a word such as *given* or *using*:

▸ Given a scene from *Macbeth*, individual students will be able to describe the use of symbolism in the scene.

Specifying the conditions often helps you define what is important in the performance. For example, if you want your students to describe symbolism in *Macbeth*, you might consider the following questions: Is it important that they recall instances of symbolism, or is it enough that they can describe the identified symbolism? Is it important that they be able to perform under pressure, as in the classroom, or is it enough that they can perform in the more private and relaxed setting of home?

Specifying the Criteria

What is the standard that defines desired performance? How well must students perform? Some might argue that specifying criteria for students' performance is part of developing a test. However, criteria, like conditions, are an important component of an objective because they help you identify what is important in the performance. Consider wanting your students to describe symbolism in *Macbeth*. Will you accept just any description? Probably not. You want students' answers to be "correct" in some way. Thinking about what "correct" looks like will help you devise a lesson that will guide students to the objective. There are a number of possible ways of defining a "correct" performance. As Table 4–4 indicates, these can be classified into three broad categories: time, accuracy, and quality (Mager, 1997; Yelon, 1991). Of course, not all of these criteria will be relevant in every situation. The

TABLE 4–3 *Use Observable Action Verbs in Objectives*

Use Verbs Such As			Avoid Verbs Such As	
compare	construct	operate	understand	believe
translate	create	adjust	appreciate	become familiar with
describe	explain	replace	think	become aware of
measure	repair	compose	know	be comfortable with
identify	define	compute	recognize	
draw	administer	solve		

TABLE 4–4   *Categories of Criteria for Defining Acceptable Performance*

Category	Description	Example
Time		
Time limits	Specifies the time limits within which the performance must take place.	Given a "victim" with no pulse or respiration, the student will be able to begin one-person CPR *within 15 seconds.*
Duration	Specifies the length of the performance.	Given a "victim" with no pulse or respiration, the student will be able to maintain one-person CPR *for at least 15 minutes.*
Rate	Specifies the rate or speed at which the performance must take place.	Given a "victim" with no pulse or respiration, the student will be able to administer one-person CPR *at a steady rate of 12 compressions per minute.*
Accuracy		
Number of errors	Specifies the maximum acceptable number of errors.	Given a topic, the student will be able to compose a letter that contains *no more than two errors* in spelling, grammar, or syntax.
Tolerances	Specifies the maximum acceptable measurement range.	With the aid of a dial gauge, the student will be able to measure the lateral roll-out on a disc *to within 0.002 inch.*
Quality		
Essential characteristics	Specifies the characteristics that must be present for the performance to be considered acceptable. Often signaled by words such as "must include."	Without reference to books or notes, the student will be able to describe the causes of the American Revolution. The description *must include at least two of the significant events leading up to the war.*
Source	Specifies the documents or materials that will be used as a gauge of the performance. Often signaled by words such as "according to," or "consistent with."	Given a computer with a hard drive and a new software application, the student will be able to install the software onto the hard drive *according to the procedure described in the software manual.*
Consequences	Specifies the expected results of the performance. Often signaled by words such as "such that" or "so that."	Given a flat bicycle tire, a patch kit, and a pump, the student will be able to patch the tire *so that it holds the recommended air pressure for at least 24 hours.*

key is to identify those that are critical for successful student performance in your particular lesson.

Of course, an objective may use more than one type of criterion, as in the following example:

▶ Given a topic, the student will be able to compose a letter that contains no more than two errors in grammar or syntax (accuracy: number of errors). The letter must be at least one page long (time: duration) and contain a combination of simple and complex sentences (quality: essential characteristics).

Composing Objectives

Once you've considered each of the three components of an objective, you can put them together. You can simply list the components of the objective, as in the following example:

Performance: Solve simultaneous algebra equations
Conditions: Graphing calculators
Criteria: Accurate to two decimal places

Or, you can combine the components into a coherent sentence or two, as in the following example:

- With the use of graphing calculators, students will be able to solve simultaneous algebra equations. Solutions must be accurate to two decimal places.

LEARNING ENVIRONMENT

Simply stated, the **learning environment** is the setting or physical surroundings in which learning is expected to take place. At first glance this may seem obvious: Learning takes place in the classroom. It is more complicated than that, however, for two reasons. First, classrooms are different; they vary in size, layout, lighting, and seating, among other things. Second, learning takes place in a variety of settings besides the classroom: the laboratory (computer lab, science lab, or language lab), playground, beach, backstage at a theater, or at home. In fact, learning typically involves some combination of environments.

We said earlier that instruction should match the students for whom it is intended and the goals defined in the objectives. It is equally true that instruction should match the environment in which it will occur. If it doesn't, the instruction may be theoretically valid but practically impossible (Tessmer, 1990). Sometimes this is obvious, as in the following example:

- A biology lesson that includes a laboratory experiment in which the students use microscopes to identify the structures of the cell requires enough lab equipment and supplies for all students. When lab equipment is limited, it may be necessary to change the experiment to a group activity. When lab equipment is severely limited, it may be necessary to use a demonstration as the instructional method.

Sometimes this problem isn't as obvious, as in the following example:

- A mathematics lesson on solving algebra equations that includes a commercial computer-based tutorial requires a site license authorizing use of the tutorial at multiple workstations. Without a site license, the students may have to use the tutorial one at a time, requiring a reorganization of the lesson.

Instructional planning, therefore, involves asking several questions about the setting:

- Where will learning occur? A classroom? A laboratory? Some other area of the school? On a field trip? Or at home?
- What are the characteristics of those environments? In a classroom, how large is the space in relation to the number of students? How are the seats arranged? Can they be moved easily? How much noise do you anticipate in the setting? What other distractions are there? Is the lighting adequate? Can you adjust the lighting?
- How will these characteristics influence your instruction? Can the setting be modified to accommodate the instruction you're planning? If not, what constraints will the setting impose on the instruction?

Planning to incorporate instructional technology is becoming easier because computers are becoming more prevalent in schools. For example, describing the results

TECHNOLOGY COORDINATOR'S CORNER

Frank Bennett recently went to a national education conference where he listened to a seminar about celebrating the diversity in the classroom. He walked away wondering how he could integrate technology into his classroom in order to celebrate the diversity of the students in his, as well as other, classrooms. Frank approached Sara Gillespie, the technology coordinator for his school district, to see if she had any ideas. Sara suggested a couple of ways in which technology could support the diversity of the students. She recommended that Frank have his students create a database or spreadsheet of student information. This could be done through a survey of questions the students create themselves. It could comprise noninvasive information such as likes and dislikes of food, colors, hobbies, and so on, or could be more personal such as gender, hair color, eye color, heritage, and so on. The students could then graph the information and, using a chart, see the differences easily. To enhance this lesson, the students could converse with a school across the country in a different type of environment, such as rural versus an inner-city school, survey those students, and compare the results.

As Frank was considering these suggestions, he also began to ponder on how a similar student database could be used to impact how he designed his own lessons. Although it might get overwhelming to concentrate on all the differences among his students, Sara suggested that he might also look over the list and notice those things that were similar. Identifying the differences could help to show the variety needed in order to help all individuals accomplish the learning objectives; however, seeing the similarities would help identify the common ground that would allow him to build the confidence of the students by relating things to their common experiences, attributes, and so on. Frank quickly came to realize that understanding both differences and similarities of the students allows you to plan much more effective instructional lessons. In both cases, the technology facilitates how the information is gathered, stored, analyzed, and later accessed for use.

Check It Out

Kevin Spencer's Lesson Plan

Refer to Teacher Resource B on page 299. This Teacher Resource describes the instructional plan Mr. Spencer has developed for his sixth-grade social studies class. Read over the plan and answer the following questions.

STUDENTS

1. Do you think Mr. Spencer has done enough to accommodate the characteristics of his students? If not, what other accommodations would you suggest?
2. Is there anything more you would want to find out about these students? What, and how would this information help you in developing the instructional plan?

OBJECTIVES

3. Do the listed objectives include each of the three components described in the chapter? If so, label those components within each objective. If not, add the components that are missing.

LEARNING ENVIRONMENT

4. Do you think this plan is workable within the described learning environment? If not, in what ways is there a mismatch and what might you do to resolve this mismatch?

---

of an annual survey, Kleiner and Lewis (2003) report that the percentage of U.S. public schools with Internet access increased from 89 percent to 99 percent between 1998 and 2002. Similarly, the ratio of students to computers decreased from 12.1 to 4.8 during the same period. However, there are some differences among schools. The ratio is higher among larger schools, city schools, schools with a large proportion of minority students, and schools with a large proportion of low-SES students. But, in all schools, the ratio is decreasing.

SUMMARY

An instructional plan is like a jigsaw puzzle. It describes the pieces of the instruction and how they fit together to create a coherent lesson. This chapter began our description of the instructional planning process by describing the first three elements of a plan: students, objectives, and learning environment.

First are the students. Individual students invariably bring to any instructional situation a unique set of characteristics and a major part of the teacher's task is to fit the instruction to the students. This means gathering information about their background, what they already know about the content, their motivation for learning, and any special needs they may have. Second are the objectives. Objectives specify the intended results of the instruction: They define what the students should be able to do following the instruction. Objectives have three components: a performance, conditions under which that performance is expected, and criteria that define acceptable performance. Third is the

learning environment. It is as important to match the instruction to where learning will occur as it is to match the instruction to who will be learning (the students) and what is to be learned (the objectives).

SUGGESTED RESOURCES

CD Resources

To increase retention and transfer of this information, review the *Reflective Questions and Activities* located in the Chapter 4 section **(Chapter info and activities>>>Chapter 4>>> Reflective Questions and Activities)** of the text's accompanying CD.

In addition, you can access relevant Internet websites, NETS Connection exercises, and direct e-mail access to the text's authors.

Website Resources

Access the text's website **(www.prenhall.com/newby)**, navigate to Chapter 4, and review the Question and Answer section for relevant questions that have been generated by students and answered by the authors. You may also submit your own questions directly to the authors. In addition, you can access presentations by the authors about this chapter and gain insights directly from them about the topics that have been presented.

Print Resources

Achinstein, B., & Barrett, A. (2004). (Re)framing classroom contexts: How new teachers and mentors view diverse learners and challenges of practice. *Teachers College Record, 106*(4), 716–746.

Eggen, P., & Kauchak, D. (2001) *Educational psychology: Windows on classrooms.* Upper Saddle River, NJ: Prentice-Hall.

Gronlund, N. E. (2000). *How to write and use instructional objectives* (6th edition). Upper Saddle River, NJ: Merrill.

Powell, G. C. (1997). On being a culturally sensitive instructional designer and educator. *Educational Technology, 37*(2), 6–14.

Electronic Resources

http://www.educationworld.com/a_diversity
This website contains a variety of useful resources on diversity. For example, click on the <gender issues>link for an article titled "Educating girls in the tech age: A report on equity." Or, click on the <digital divide> link for an article titled "Caught in the digital divide."

5

Technology and Instructional Planning: Identifying the Plan's Key Activities

CHAPTER OBJECTIVES

After reading and studying this chapter, you will be able to:

▶ Specify the instructional activities for a lesson of your choice.
▶ Describe the practical benefits of an instructional plan.
▶ Develop an instructional plan for a lesson of your choice.

INTRODUCTION

In Chapter 4 we introduced the instructional planning puzzle and described the first three pieces of that puzzle—students, objectives, and learning environment. Those pieces provide the foundation for instructional planning by describing *who* we're teaching, *what* we want them to learn, and *where* the instruction will take place. In this chapter, we will begin describing *how* to present the instruction to the students by putting into place the next piece of the puzzle—instructional activities (see Figure 5–1).

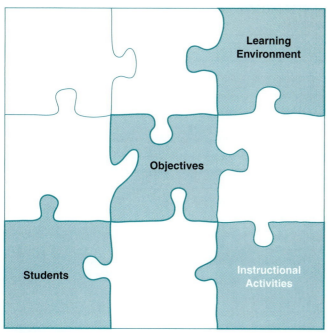

FIGURE 5–1   Instructional activities as the next piece of the puzzle.

DEVELOPING INSTRUCTIONAL ACTIVITIES

Simply put, an **instructional activity** refers to something that is done during a lesson to help students learn. Any lesson is made up of a collection of instructional activities intended to stimulate the students' curiosity, present new content, provide opportunities for practice, and so forth. Instructional activities can be thought of as the "script" for the instruction. In a play, the script directs the action, telling the actors what to do as the play progresses. Instructional activities serve much the same purpose for a teacher. Taken together, they tell the teacher what to do as the lesson progresses. Various

Using a script to direct the action of a play.

ways to organize this instructional script have been described (Gagne, Wager, Golas, & Keller, 2005; Hunter, 1982). We're going to use the five types of instructional activities proposed by Yelon (1996). Yelon suggests that every instructional plan should include:

- Motivation activities
- Orientation activities
- Information activities
- Application activities
- Evaluation activities

We will describe each of these types of instructional activity separately.

Motivation Activities

As described in Chapter 4, motivation refers to the internal interests that lead students to want to learn and to put in the effort required for learning. The purpose of a **motivation activity** is to gain the students' attention and maintain it throughout the lesson. The "and" is critical. It is, perhaps, obvious that generating interest in learning is important at the start of a lesson—to get the students' attention and help them focus on the lesson at hand. But it is just as important to hold their interest throughout the lesson—to maintain their focus and encourage their active participation.

One valuable approach to increasing student motivation is Keller's (1983) ARCS model. Keller describes four essential aspects of motivation, using the mnemonic ARCS (the mnemonic has given its name to the model):

Attention refers to whether students perceive the instruction as interesting and worthy of their consideration.
Relevance refers to whether students perceive the instruction as meeting some personal need or goal.
Confidence refers to whether students expect to succeed based on their own efforts.
Satisfaction refers to the intrinsic and extrinsic rewards students receive from the instruction.

One of the benefits of the ARCS model is that Keller and his colleagues (1987) have described a variety of techniques that can be used throughout a lesson to increase each aspect of motivation. Some of these techniques are shown in Table 5–1.

To develop the motivation activities for a lesson, consider the following questions:

- What will you do at the beginning of the lesson to gain the students' attention?
- At what points in the lesson will it be useful to build student motivation?
- What can you do throughout the lesson to increase each aspect of motivation: attention, relevance, confidence, and satisfaction?

TABLE 5–1 *Techniques to Increase Student Motivation*

To Increase:	Use One or More of These Motivational Techniques:
Attention	• Introduce an idea that seems to contradict the students' past experience • Vary the format of the instruction according to the attention span of the students • Build in problem-solving activities at regular intervals
Relevance	• Find out what the students' interests are and relate the instruction to those interests • Ask students to relate the instruction to their own future goals • Provide meaningful alternative methods for accomplishing a goal
Confidence	• Explain the criteria for evaluation of performance • Organize materials on an increasing level of difficulty • Teach students how to develop a plan of work that will result in accomplishing a goal
Satisfaction	• Allow a student to use a newly acquired skill in a realistic setting as soon as possible • Provide informative feedback when it is immediately useful • Provide frequent reinforcements when a student is learning a new task

Addressing the Standards

NETS Connection

Several of the key National Educational Technology Standards (NETS II, III, IV, and V) for teachers focus on *the effective use of technology to design, implement, and assess lessons that motivate, engage, and encourage student learning.* Motivation plays a significant role in the learning process. For a few moments think about the motivation you developed during a recent learning experience. Did the experience facilitate your learning by helping you attend to what was important? Did it help you come to see the relevance of the new materials? Did you develop the sense that it was possible for you to learn that task and that you had confidence in your learning abilities for that task? Were you satisfied with the results of your learning with the amount of effort you invested?

To take this one step further, think about the various types of technology that may have been used within your recent learning experience. To help guide your reflection, create a journal entry with a table similar to Table 5–2 and answer the questions posed in each of the cells.

Once you have addressed these questions, review your responses and think about the use of technology as a means to facilitate the design, implementation, and evaluation of a motivationally enhanced learning experience. In what ways could technology be used to ensure that key motivational elements of attention, relevance, confidence, and satisfaction are included within the lessons that one creates?

TABLE 5–2 *Elements of Motivation and Technology Integration*

Attention	How could technology have been used to help get and maintain your attention in the learning task?
Relevance	How could technology have been employed to help you see the relevance of the learning experience and why it is important for you?
Confidence	How could technology have been used to help you gain the confidence you needed in order to learn what was expected?
Satisfaction	How could technology have been used to help you achieve the level of satisfaction needed for investing effort into the learning task?

Orientation Activities

In general, orientation refers to knowing where you are in relation to your intended destination. In instruction, orientation refers to knowing where you are in terms of the intended objectives. Orientation activities go beyond the specific lesson. Any lesson fits into a sequence of lessons; it naturally follows some and leads to others. The purpose of an **orientation activity** is to help students see where they have been (what they have previously learned), where they are now (what they are currently learning), and where they are going (what they will subsequently learn). As a teacher, you will use orientation activities to introduce a lesson and link it to preceding lessons, to move from one part of a lesson to the next and help students monitor their progress, and to summarize a lesson and link it to subsequent lessons. To develop an orientation activity for an instructional plan, consider the following questions:

▶ What will you do to help students understand the objectives of the current lesson?
▶ What will you do to link the lesson to previous lessons?
▶ What will you do to provide smooth transitions within the lesson?
▶ What will you do to summarize the lesson and link it to future lessons?

Information Activities

Instruction generally includes some new ideas (facts, concepts, principles, procedures, etc.) and an opportunity for students to practice using those ideas. The purpose of an **information activity** is to help students understand and remember those new ideas. To be effective, information activities should focus on three different types of information—declarative, structural, and conditional. **Declarative information** refers to the new ideas themselves (e.g., Boyle's Law states that . . .). Declarative information is important but by itself is not enough. **Structural information** refers to the relationships that exist among those ideas (e.g., Boyle's Law is one of several laws meant to explain . . .). Structural information is important because it provides an organizing framework for the new ideas. This makes them easier to understand and remember because they are seen as part of a coherent whole rather than as isolated facts. Finally, **conditional information** refers to information about the potential usefulness of the new ideas (e.g., Boyle's Law can be used to explain . . .). Conditional information helps students internalize what they learn and transfer it to a variety of situations by showing them when the new ideas will be useful (the types of situations) and why they should use the new ideas (how they will help).

To develop the information activities for a lesson, consider the following questions:

▶ What major content ideas will you present? In what sequence? Using what examples?
▶ What will you do to help students understand and remember those ideas?
▶ What will you do to help students see the relationships among the ideas?
▶ What will you do to help students understand when and why the ideas will be useful?

Application Activities

Application activities involve practice, guidance, and feedback. First, the purpose of an application activity is to provide students with an opportunity to practice using what they are learning. Practice serves a diagnostic function. If students practice successfully, they can move on to evaluation. If, on the other hand, they have trouble, they might either repeat the practice, perhaps in a simpler form, or go back over the information, clarifying it as needed. To serve as an effective diagnostic tool, an application activity should ask students to demonstrate the performances called for in the objectives under the same conditions described in the objectives.

Second, an application activity may include varying amounts of guidance. In guided practice, students are given clues that suggest how they should proceed. In unguided practice, students must decide for themselves how to proceed. The amount of guidance that can be provided exists on a continuum and should be regulated to meet the needs of individual students. In general, practice that includes more guidance is less difficult than practice that includes less guidance. As a result, students who progress easily might benefit most from relatively unguided practice, while those who are having trouble might need more structured practice.

Finally, feedback is an essential component of an application activity. **Feedback** refers to giving students information about how well they are doing when they practice. Feedback comes in two forms: reinforcing feedback and corrective feedback. **Reinforcing feedback** is like a pat on the back (e.g., saying "Good job" or "I like the way you . . . "). You use it to acknowledge good performance and encourage continued effort. **Corrective feedback,** as its name implies, tells students specifically what they can do to correct or improve their performance (e.g., saying "What if you . . . " or "Next time try . . . "). These two forms of feedback are often used together, reinforcing what students have done well and correcting what they could do better. Practice and feedback are inseparable, or at least should be. Practice without feedback has limited value because it does not tell students whether they are progressing toward the objectives or what they can do to improve their

TOOLBOX TECHNIQUES

Using Questioning, Examples, and Feedback Effectively

You can use a variety of techniques to enhance the effectiveness of a learning experience. In particular, materials should incorporate questions, examples, and feedback. Listed below are several suggestions and guidelines for incorporating these techniques.

QUESTIONING

You can use questions to gain attention, maintain focus, pique interest, probe for depth of understanding, increase relevance for a topic of focus, or evaluate the quality of the instructional materials. Questions may be generated by the teacher or student, and answers can range from simple, to difficult, to unknown.

Several guidelines can help you incorporate productive questions into your instructional lessons (Dallmann-Jones, 1994; Wasserman, 1992).

When planning and developing questions:

▶ Determine why you will ask the question. Make sure each serves an important purpose.
▶ Use "who," "what," "when," and "where" questions to check information for review purposes. "Why" and "how" questions encourage higher levels of thought. Ask students to provide in-depth explanations or additional examples.
▶ Frame questions to invite, rather than intimidate. Help students feel safe to express their thoughts. Questions and responses should be respectful, nonthreatening, and productive.

When using questions:

▶ Sample class responses randomly; that is, ask questions of all students equally.
▶ Take time to pause after asking a question; provide students with time to think.
▶ Listen to students' responses before formulating your own so you can accurately reflect their ideas.
▶ Respond positively to appropriate responses, but never belittle incorrect answers.
▶ Allow students the chance to formulate questions in response to comments from you or from other students.
▶ When a student repeatedly provides incorrect answers, coach that individual during one-on-one sessions. Provide the student with opportunities to answer questions that you have previously discussed during your session.

EXAMPLES

Research has shown that examples are very effective in helping learners understand concepts and applications. Examples can highlight key characteristics and information about concepts, make ready comparisons, and illustrate how things are applied and generalized across different situations. Guidelines for using examples include the following:

▶ Begin with simple examples so students can readily identify their critical attributes. Simple examples can also increase your learners' confidence.
▶ Present examples in different formats, such as flowcharts, pictures, live demonstrations, and real objects.
▶ Use nonexamples (negative examples) to help highlight examples' critical attributes. Nonexamples may have some of the same attributes of the examples but vary on those features that make the critical difference. For example, to teach the concept "red" you may present learners with an example of a red ball. To make sure they understand the critical attribute of color, introduce nonexamples such as a blue ball and an orange ball. All of the attributes in the examples and nonexamples are the same, *except* for the critical attribute of color. The nonexample helps to identify the critical attribute.
▶ Gradually increase the difficulty level of the examples until you end with more difficult ones that approximate the real-world cases that students will encounter.

FEEDBACK

We are all familiar with the phrase "practice makes perfect," but is it true? With a short addition we can capture a more accurate picture—"Practice makes perfect, *as long as feedback is provided.*"

Feedback, according to Rothwell and Kazanas (1992, p. 13), is "a continuous process of providing information about an activity, sometimes during the activity itself." Feedback can serve two functions: (1) it can inform students about *how much* of the task they have completed, thus

TOOLBOX TECHNIQUES
(continued)

encouraging them to continue working, and (2) it can inform students *how well* they are performing and indicate what they can do to improve their performance.

As you design and implement instruction, it is important to make provisions for delivering feedback to students Without timely, reliable feedback, students may not know if their work is correct. Without some form of feedback, students could potentially continue practicing errors over and over. Use the following guidelines when designing practice and feedback exercises (adapted from Leshin, Pollock, & Reigeluth, 1992):

▶ Effective feedback should be delivered immediately (or as soon as reasonably feasible) after practice is completed.
▶ Well-designed feedback can motivate students to greater levels of performance.
▶ Informative feedback should function like a good example.
▶ Corrective feedback should require learners to think. Give hints but do not provide the correct answer immediately.

---

progress. To develop the application activities for a lesson, consider the following questions:

▶ What will you do to give students opportunities to practice using their new knowledge or skill?
▶ At what points will you build those opportunities into the lesson?
▶ How much guidance will you provide and what form will that guidance take?
▶ What will you do to give students both reinforcing and corrective feedback about their performance during the practices?

Evaluation Activities

In Chapter 12, we define evaluation as the process of gathering information about what students have learned and describe a variety of techniques that can be used before, during, and after instruction. This is the purpose of an **evaluation activity.** Like practice, evaluation serves a diagnostic function. Students who "pass" the evaluation are ready for the next lesson, while those who don't "pass" may need some additional instruction before they

proceed. We have purposely put quotation marks around the word "pass" to make a point. We often think of evaluation in terms of traditional paper-and-pencil tests. But there are a variety of ways to evaluate how well students have learned, and the meaning of "pass" will be different for these different evaluation methods.

To develop an evaluation for an instructional plan, consider the following questions:

▶ What will you do to determine whether students have achieved the learning objectives?
▶ How will you give students feedback about their performance during or after the evaluation?

INSTRUCTIONAL PLANS AS HEURISTIC GUIDES

We've suggested an instructional "script" that is flexible and adaptable to a variety of teaching and learning situations. Remember that an instructional plan, like a script, is a decision-making guide. It helps you decide what actions to take and how to combine those actions to help your students learn. The instructional plan we have presented is

---

Check It Out

Instructional Plans on the Internet

1. Choose a topic and grade level that is relevant and interesting to you.
2. Go to Kathy Schrock's Guide for Educators on the DiscoverySchool.com website (http://school.discovery.com/schrockguide/) or another site that allows access to various types of lesson plans.
3. Review and select two different plans.
4. Write out a brief description of the two plans.
   a. In what ways are they similar? Different?
   b. Which plan do you think does a better job of motivating the learners? Why?
   c. Which plan does a better job of helping the students understand and remember the new information? Are all three types of information (declarative, structural, and conditional) included?
   d. Which plan does a better job of providing opportunities for practice? How is feedback provided to the students?

TOOLBOX TECHNIQUES

Case Studies

The case study is a teaching approach that requires students to actively participate in real or hypothetical problem situations that reflect the types of experiences actually encountered in the discipline under study. After you read the following case study examples, reflect on the type of problem-solving lesson you could generate by using them.

▶ You are a botanist working to preserve the waters of Everglades National Park in Florida, the nation's third-largest national park, established in 1947. You have already documented the extent of the damage from surrounding farm chemicals that run off into the Everglades' vast swamps, saw grasses, and coastal mangrove forest. But recent attempts to reach agreement on the part of government and farmers' organizations have failed. How can you work to preserve these natural wonders of the country? (Barell, 1995, p. 126)

▶ Aurora is experiencing an increase in the crime rate. Currently, 30 percent of the cases admitted to hospital emergency rooms are victims of violent crimes, compared with a rate of 25 percent two years ago. What steps should the city take to find a solution to the problem? (from Gallaher, Stepien, & Rosenthal, 1992, as cited in Barell, 1995, p. 126)

The case "report" contains relevant (but not conclusive) data. You may present it to students, or they may develop it themselves. Individual or groupwork follows the case presentation, allowing students to analyze data, evaluate the nature of the problem(s), decide on applicable principles, and recommend a solution or course of action. A case discussion follows, which is useful in developing critical-thinking, problem-solving, and interpersonal skills. Although case methods may have strategies in common with other teaching techniques (particularly simulations and instructional games), the focus in all case methods is a specific set of circumstances and events. Whereas case methods are generally motivating to students due to the high level of involvement and can help bridge the gap between the "real" world and life in the classroom, they tend to be time consuming and require good management skills on the part of the discussion leader.

TOOLBOX TECHNIQUES

Role-Playing

Role-playing is a type of instructional simulation. It is like a drama in which each participant is assigned a character to depict, but must improvise their performance. Examples include learning how to interview for a job, managing a situation in which a hostile student threatens a teacher, discussing a questionable call with an umpire during a championship baseball game, and establishing a personal relationship.

Role-playing encourages creativity and allows students to express their feelings and attitudes. It is an effective means to develop and practice social skills, and it can help students learn to organize thoughts and responses instantly while reacting to a situation or question.

Consider the following guidelines when designing and implementing role-play in the classroom (see Dallmann-Jones, 1994; McKeachie, 1994):

▶ Design the situation in sufficient detail prior to class.
▶ Define participants' roles in terms of the situation.
▶ Ask for volunteers rather than choosing participants—volunteers are less likely to feel put on the spot.
▶ Allow participants a short time to get their thoughts together.
▶ Brief all students before role-play begins. Describe the situation and indicate what nonparticipants should look for.
▶ Don't let the role-play "run" too long. Three to six minutes is usually sufficient.
▶ Stop the role-play and reverse roles if a "hot" topic is encountered and emotions begin to get out of hand.
▶ Conduct follow-up discussion to analyze the performance. To avoid defensiveness, allow players to discuss their perceptions and emotional reactions first.

Using Analogies

At the beginning of Chapter 1 we referred to the way a master builder continually plans, implements, and evaluates his or her work. This is an example of the instructional technique of analogy. Its purpose is to help you learn by comparing a new concept with something familiar. An analogy consists of four parts:

1. the information to be learned (the subject)
2. the familiar thing to which the new information is compared (the analog)
3. the means by which the subject and analog are compared (the connector)
4. a description of the similarities and differences between the subject and analog (the ground)

In the builder analogy, we used the differences between how expert and novice builders would go about creating a structure (the analog) to describe the phases of learning (the subject). In both cases, experts plan their work, implement the plan, and evaluate the results (the ground).

Analogies have repeatedly been found to be effective in learning all types of subject matter (West, Farmer, & Wolff, 1991). To facilitate your own use of analogies, consider the following ABCDE method of constructing an analogy (adapted from Kearny, Newby, & Stepich, 1995).

A	Analyze the subject	What is it you most want the learners to understand about the subject?
B	Brainstorm potential analogs	What concrete items share the important feature(s) you have identified?
C	Choose the analog	Which candidate analog has the best combination of the following characteristics:
		▶ Familiarity—Will learners recognize the analog?
		▶ Accuracy—Does the analog accurately reflect the identified feature?
		▶ Memorability—Is the analog vivid; will learners remember it?
		▶ Concreteness—Is the analog something learners can directly perceive?
D	Describe the ground	How are the subject and analog alike? How are they different?
E	Evaluate the analogy	Does the analogy work with the intended audience?

designed to provide you with a set of **heuristic** guidelines; that is, it is a set of general rules that you can adapt to fit each situation, rather than a rigid procedure that you must follow in the same way every time. Our goal is to provide you with guidelines that are flexible enough to use with a variety of situations, yet structured enough to provide practical guidance. However, you must keep in mind that *there is no one "correct" instructional plan.* Instructional situations differ in terms of students' needs, interests, and experiences; the structure of the content; the available resources; and your preferences, interests, and experiences. Your task is to create a unique solution for the unique problem of helping your students learn; that is, you must develop a plan

that helps your particular students learn the particular content. There are several ways in which instructional plans may vary from one situation to the next.

Combining Instructional Activities

We think the five instructional activity categories (motivation, orientation, information, application, and evaluation) are basic ingredients that you should include in every lesson. However, that doesn't necessarily mean that each activity must be a separate entity in every lesson. For example, the purpose of an application activity is to allow students to try out their new knowledge or skill, and the purpose of an evaluation activity is to determine whether they have mastered the intended objectives. It is possible to present a sequence of application activities that will help determine whether students have mastered the objectives. In this case, you combine evaluation and application. The point to keep in mind is that each instructional activity has an important purpose in each lesson. Sometimes you can accomplish those purposes with greater efficiency by combining two or more instructional activities.

Emphasizing an Instructional Activity

Instructional activities are not all necessarily of equal importance in every lesson. For example, one lesson may present a lot of information and provide limited time for application, while another lesson on the same content may present a small amount of information and allow a lot of time for application.

The Manager of an Instructional Activity

The manager of an instructional activity is the person or thing that is primarily responsible for carrying out that activity, dictating the pace of the activity, controlling the flow of information, and determining what to do next. We say "primarily" because learning is always a collaboration among students, teacher, and instructional materials, and all are likely to influence each instructional activity. However, to what extent do students, teacher, and materials control the pacing, flow of information, and decision making? Note that the manager may vary from one activity to the next. For example, in a given lesson the teacher may manage the orientation while the material manages the information and the students control the application.

Encouraging students to manage their own learning is a powerful technique (refer to the discussion of constructivist learning theory in Chapter 2). Students often learn more from an instructional activity when they manage it themselves. However, this is an acquired skill, and students—especially younger or less-sophisticated ones—may require instruction and practice before they are able to do it well. Although teaching students to manage their own learning is beyond the scope of this book, we refer readers who are interested in learning more about this topic to Schunk and Zimmerman (1998).

The Amount of Detail or Structure in the Plan

You may describe an activity within an instructional plan with more or less detail or structure, depending in part on your experience with the technique being used. Teachers who are relatively inexperienced or who are using a new technique may want their plans to provide a lot of structure and will, therefore, describe activity content and materials in great detail. On the other hand, teachers using familiar techniques may need less structure and may, therefore, sketch out their activities rather than describe them in detail. Note that we're talking about individual activities rather than an entire plan. Different activities within a plan may be described at different levels of detail. For example, a teacher who has developed a new way to introduce a familiar topic may develop detailed motivation and orientation activities while briefly outlining the familiar information.

The Order and Number of Activities

We have listed instructional activities in an order that seems logical, but that isn't the only "correct" order. For example, you may decide to place an orientation activity at the beginning of the lesson as a natural introduction. Alternatively, you may decide to place an orientation activity after an information activity as a way of clearly connecting the new information to previously learned information. Or you may decide that an orientation activity would be useful in both places.

This last point highlights the idea that a lesson often contains more than one of each type of activity and that the activities may be clustered together or spread throughout the lesson. As shown in Figure 5–2, a lesson may include multiple motivation activities, information activities, and/or application activities in various configurations.

Making Plans Congruent

Instructional plans are flexible, designed to guide decision making rather than dictate the way to present a lesson to students. However, one thing should be true of every instructional plan: The components of the plan should be congruent with one another. That is, the objectives should match the instructional activities, and the instructional activities should match one another. For example, the objectives should accurately represent the knowledge and skills described in any information activities and measured in the evaluation activities. Similarly, the evaluation activities should measure the knowledge and skills described in the information activities and represented by the objectives. Students should be motivated to learn, and should be applying the knowledge and skills they will be evaluated on, and so on through all the combinations of instructional activities.

FIGURE 5–2   Varying sequences of instructional activities.

Motivation > Information > Information > Application > Application
Motivation > Information > Application > Information > Application
Motivation > Information > Application > Motivation > Application

Addressing the Standards

NETS Connection

In part, two National Educational Technology Standards (NETS II and III) for teachers focus on your being able to **connect curriculum and technology standards through creating and teaching technology-enhanced learning activities and experiences.** As a first step, go to your state's curriculum standards and review those that are relevant to your field of study (e.g., English, social studies, mathematics). In most cases, your state's education curriculum standards can be found quickly by going to the Web and searching your state government's website. Do a simple search using the following terms and then look for links to the curriculum standards: State name (e.g., New York) and then "Department of Education." You may have to explore the site a bit, but in most cases, the curriculum standards will be linked to your selected state's Department of Education home page. Once you have located and reviewed the relevant curriculum standards, do the following:

▶ Based on a specific curriculum standard, generate authentic problems that could be explored by students studying in that subject area.
▶ Outline a collaborative learning experience that would help students address the problem.
▶ Describe each of the five instructional activities (orientation, motivation, information, application, and evaluation) and how each would be addressed within your designed learning experience.
▶ Describe both the role of technology within each of the instructional activities AND its role in the design, implementation, and evaluation of your learning experience.

To illustrate the concept of parallel plans, consider the brief examples in Table 5–3. In Example A the objectives, information, application, and evaluation are all congruent. They all relate directly to learning how to solve algebra equations. In Example B, however, the objectives, information, application, and evaluation are all aimed at different aspects of algebra. Although they are all important, they are not parallel to one another.

How might you combine instructional activities to form a congruent instructional plan for a specific situation? The following two sample instructional plans will help answer that question. The situations are related, but begin with a different planning component. As a result, the plans are different. Look over each of the two sample plans. What differences do you notice? How might you explain those differences? What does this suggest about the flexibility of the instructional plan?

Scenario A

Ms. Heinrich teaches a beginning Spanish class for fourth-graders. A curriculum guide distributed by the school district specifies that students should be able to carry on simple conversations in Spanish and be able to use Spanish greetings (see Figure 5–3).

Scenario B

Mr. Delgado teaches a beginning Spanish class for fourth-graders in a different school. His objective is also to have students be able to use Spanish greetings. He has read about cooperative learning techniques, and he likes what he has read. He wants to try cooperative learning in his class (see Figure 5–4).

PRACTICAL BENEFITS OF PLANS

An instructional plan is a decision-making guide. It allows you to make sensible decisions about how to carry out instruction, respond to the changing needs of students and the situation, and make continual improvements in the instruction you provide. The practical benefits of having a plan can be described in terms of the functions the instructional plan serves before, during, and after the instruction (Borko & Livingston, 1992; Kauchak & Eggen, 1989; Reynolds, 1992).

Before Instruction

Bridge

The instructional plan serves two important linking functions. First, it is the *link between the curriculum goals and the students*. The plan is the vehicle you use to decide how to tailor the curriculum, which is often predetermined, to the needs of your particular students. Second, the plan is the *link among the objectives, instructional activities, and evaluation*. It is the means by which you can decide how to adapt the objectives, instructional activities, and/or evaluation to ensure that they match one another. The way these links are made depends on (1) the particular curriculum, (2) the students, and (3) your knowledge of the content, level of experience, beliefs about students and how they learn, and knowledge

TABLE 5–3 *Congruent Components in the Instructional Plan*

	Example A—Congruent	Example B—Not Congruent
Objective	Be able to solve algebra equations	Be able to solve algebra equations
Information Activity	Description of the notation used in algebra equations, followed by a demonstration of how to solve various types of algebra equations	Description of the historical development of algebra as a branch of mathematics
Application Activity	Problems asking the students to solve the types of algebra equations presented in the information activity	Problems asking the students to interpret various types of algebraic notation
Evaluation Activity	A set of algebra equations to solve	Questions about the importance of knowing how to solve algebra equations

Students: Fourth Grade Spanish I   Topic(s): Greetings

Objectives:

▶ Say the Spanish equivalent to a given English greeting.
▶ Say the appropriate Spanish greeting when meeting someone.
▶ Say an appropriate Spanish response when greeted in Spanish.

Learning environment: Classroom Activities

1. **Combined motivation–orientation activity**
   Present a series of situations, in English, calling for a greeting. Ask students what they would say. Show similar situations in Spanish on videotape. Present the objectives as steps toward being able to converse in Spanish. Emphasize the importance of practice.

   Method: presentation
   Medium: videotape

2. **Information activity**
   Demonstrate common Spanish greetings and responses (both formal and informal) for morning, afternoon, and evening. Write the words on the chalkboard, say them several times. Emphasize the greeting/response pairs. During the demonstration, clearly explain when each greeting and response would be used.

   Method: demonstration
   Medium: chalkboard

3. **Orientation activity**
   Before starting the practice activity, ask students when greetings are generally used and why. Then ask them when they would use the different types of greetings and why. Use this discussion to decide whether to review any of the previous information.

   Method: discussion
   Medium: audio (conversation)

4. **Combined application–evaluation activity**
   Pair the students up with an audiotape recorder. Instruct students to practice on the tape and to listen to the tape to see how they sound. Spend a few minutes with each pair after they have recorded a practice greeting and response. Listen to the taped practice with students (ask them to evaluate what they hear on the tape). Point out specific strong points in their pronunciation and give specific pointers for improving pronunciation.

   Method: drill and practice
   Medium: audiotape

FIGURE 5–3 Instructional plan for teaching Spanish greetings and responses.

Students: Fourth Grade Spanish I   Topic: Greetings

Objectives:
▶ Say the Spanish equivalent to a given English greeting.
▶ Say the appropriate Spanish greeting when meeting someone.
▶ Say an appropriate Spanish response when greeted in Spanish.

Learning environment: Classroom Activities

1. **Combined motivation–orientation activity**
   Greet students in English. Explain that all languages use similar greetings. Their task will be to learn greetings in Spanish. Each student will learn 1 greeting from audiotape and teach it to classmates. This is the beginning of being able to talk with people in Spanish. Once they've learned the greetings, they will be able to move on to other parts of conversation.

   Time: 5 minutes   *Add written materials showing*
   Method: presentation   *the words*
   Medium: audio (conversation)

2. **Information activity**
   Divide class into 3 equal groups for morning, afternoon, and evening greetings. Give each group an audiotape with the greeting and response for their time of day recorded on it. Review how to use the tape recorder.

   Directions—Each group is to practice their greeting and response so they can teach it to 2 classmates. Group members should listen to one another and help one another with pronunciation.   *Encourage them to practice as much as they can*

   In about 15 minutes the groups will switch around and each student will teach their greeting to the students in their new group. Ask if they need help. Circulate around the room. Keep students on track.

   Time: about 15 minutes
   Method: tutorial
   Medium: audiotaped Spanish greetings

3. **Orientation activity**
   Reorganize class into groups of three—one member from each of the previous 3 groups.

   Directions—Your task now is to teach as much as you can. Help one another out. Everyone in the group is to learn each greeting and response. After about 15 minutes I will start calling students to the front of the room in pairs to show me what you have learned.

   Time: about 15 minutes
   Method: cooperative learning
   Medium: audio (conversation)

4. **Evaluation activity**
   Call students to the front in pairs. Give first student an English greeting on a card. The student is to greet their partner with the corresponding Spanish greeting. Partner is to respond in Spanish.

   Time: 15 minutes   *Find an alternative. Students*
   Method: drill & practice   *need more time for practice*
   Medium: Spanish/English flash cards

5. **Information activity**
   Debrief the lesson:

   ▶ Recall when each greeting and response is used.
   ▶ Ask who else students might teach these greetings to (parents, friends, etc.)
   ▶ Suggest using the greetings with one another around school.

   Time: 15 minutes
   Method: discussion
   Medium: audio (conversation)

FIGURE 5–4   Instructional plan for teaching Spanish greetings and responses using cooperative learning.

about teaching methods that will help students learn. By making these links, you can ensure students meet the prescribed learning goals, thus making your instruction more accountable.

Checklist

The instructional plan encourages you to anticipate the specific materials, facilities, and equipment needed, as well as when you will need them. This helps you make sure that there will be enough materials on hand for all students.

Schedule

The instructional plan allows you to decide what activities you will use to help students learn, to put them in a logical sequence, and to allocate sufficient time to the different activities.

During Instruction

Road Map

The instructional plan describes the destination you want to reach and the routes you plan to follow to get there. This road map function helps you make adjustments in the plan. This is important for two reasons. First, interruptions in the classroom are inevitable (e.g., because of student absences or school assemblies). The instructional plan *helps you keep the instruction on track,* monitor students' progress toward the destination, and ensure the prescribed content is covered in the face of these inevitable interruptions. It does this by marking your place so you can return after the interruption. Second, students' needs and interests may change, and unanticipated learning opportunities may arise. *The instructional plan allows you to respond to these changing needs, interests, and opportunities* while continuing to

progress toward the destination. The plan is designed to be flexible, to allow you to improvise based on the students' responses.

Outline

The instructional plan provides a set of guidelines to follow in the classroom, allowing the teacher to concentrate on interacting with the students rather than trying to remember what comes next.

Compass

The instructional plan provides you with a clear sense of direction, and this helps to increase your confidence and reduce the uncertainty and anxiety that often accompany not knowing where you're going. This may be especially important if you are relatively inexperienced and need something to provide guidance.

After Instruction

Diary

The instructional plan provides you with a place to record what happened during the instruction (McCutcheon, 1980). It is also a place to record your observations and comments about what worked and what didn't. You can then use these notes to improve your instruction.

Briefing Book

It is often important that others know what is happening in the classroom. The instructional plan provides a convenient way to do this. For example, the plan will tell substitute teachers what parts of a lesson have been completed and what is yet to be done. Similarly, the plan will help principals keep track of what is happening in all classrooms in their building.

Check It Out

Kevin Spencer's Lesson Plan

1. Refer to Teacher Resource B on page 299. This appendix describes the instructional plan Mr. Spencer has developed for his sixth-grade social studies class. Read over the plan and label each of the five types of instructional activities within the plan. For example, what do you see within the plan that increases the students' interest in learning (motivation activities)? What do you see within the plan that gives the students opportunities to practice what they're learning (application activities)? The plan may not use these terms, so you'll have to read the plan carefully to see what is being done to carry out each type of instructional activity.
2. Write a brief description of at least one alternative for each of the five types of instructional activities.
3. Compare notes with one or two classmates. Use this as a brainstorming exercise. Briefly discuss each alternative you've come up with. What do you see as its strong points? What do you think might make it difficult to implement?

TECHNOLOGY COORDINATOR'S CORNER

The cross-curriculum theme at Lakeside Elementary this year has been "Cultures of the World." In keeping with this theme, two fifth-grade teachers, John Babcock and Rosie Avila, have recently finished the first draft of a new instructional website called "Traditional Japanese Holidays and Festivals." Before using it with their students, they asked several teachers including Michelle Asay, the school technology coordinator, to go through the website and offer suggestions. After a few days, they received the following e-mail message from Michelle.

March 23

John and Rosie,

Thanks for the opportunity to look over your website on Japan. I learned things that I had never known. Here are my brief comments about your work:

▸ Getting and maintaining the attention of students as they work through the website is critical. Your use of a variety of colored pictures and graphics should help in this regard. You may also want to think about helping the students understand how big the site is and how much they have to do. I have found that once they know this, they gain confidence that they can get it accomplished. Otherwise some might give up before getting to some critical parts of the site. In this regard, you may want to create a "site map" on the index/home page that should give students an overview of what they will experience plus it provides them direction as to where they need to go and what they have already covered.

▸ You have provided a lot of information about the holidays. Most of it is good information; but some students may see it as overwhelming and confusing. One suggestion would be to help them organize the information in some way. For example, you could group the holidays based on the season of the year. In this way the student begins to chunk them into groups that are more manageable. In addition (and perhaps more important), they may more readily make comparisons between the holidays/festivals of Japan and those with which they are more familiar. Adding "helps" for them to recognize the structure (e.g., simple but relevant pictures, graphics, and perhaps even music) is relatively simple within such web pages and it would provide the students with some interesting and memorable cues of your content.

▸ Finally, one element that I really think is lacking in your website is helping the students see how the information they are receiving can be applied and used. Knowing this, they should be able to retain it to a greater degree. One thought that I had is that since they will already be on the Web, why not have a page where they link to a school site in Japan where they

may be able to interact with students of their same age. Yes, the language may cause a problem, but I have found school sites where students are trying out their English writing skills and they would be thrilled to have students from our school interact with them in some fashion. You could have our students begin by sharing what we know about their traditional holidays and then ask questions such as which holiday they like the best, tell them about similar things we do here, and so on. Hopefully this interaction will develop into the students' learning about other similarities and differences in the cultures. After all, isn't that the goal of the school's theme this year?

I would be happy to brainstorm more with you about what could be done and how to get it accomplished. Thanks for allowing me to review your work.

Michelle

SUMMARY

An instructional plan is like a script. It describes the activities that will take place during the instruction, indicates how those activities are to be combined for a particular lesson, and is used as a flexible decision-making guide. Instruction is made up of varying combinations of five types of instructional activities: motivation, orientation, information, application, and evaluation. In instructional planning, the order in which components appear isn't as important as developing a plan whose parts are congruent. Such a plan offers a number of benefits before, during, and after instruction.

SUGGESTED RESOURCES

CD Resources

To increase retention and transfer of this information, review the *Reflective Questions and Activities* located in the Chapter 5 section (**Chapter info and activities>>> Chapter 5>>>Reflective Questions and Activities**) of the text's accompanying CD.

In addition, you can access relevant Internet web sites, NETS Connection exercises, and direct email access to the text's authors.

Website Resources

Access the text's website (**www.prenhall.com/newby**), navigate to Chapter 5, and review the Question and Answer section for relevant questions that have been generated by students and answered by the authors. You may also submit your own questions directly to the authors. In addition, you can access presentations by the authors about this chapter and gain insights directly from them about the topics that have been presented.

Print Resources

Gagne, R. M., Wager, W. W., Golas, K., & Keller, J. M. (2005). *Principles of instructional design* (5th ed.). Belmont, CA: Wadsworth.

Yelon, S. L. (1996). *Powerful principles of instruction*. White Plains, NY: Longman.

Electronic Resources

A quick search of the Internet, using the search term "lesson plans," will turn up a large number of websites with interesting and useful lesson plans. Most sites allow you to search for lesson plans for a specific grade level or within a certain subject area. As examples, look through the following websites:

Sponsor	Website Address
DiscoverySchool.com	http://school.discovery.com/lessonplans
NASA	http://imagine.gsfc.nasa.gov/docs/teachers/lesson_plans.html
The Peace Corps	http://www.peacecorps.gov/wws/educators/lessons.html
The National Geographic Society	http://www.nationalgeographic.com/education/lesson_plans
The Public Broadcasting System	http://www.pbs.org/teachersource
Mid-continent Research for Education and Learning	http://www.mcrel.org/topics/productDetail.asp?productID=80

6

Instructional Methods: Identifying Ways to Involve Learners

CHAPTER OBJECTIVES

After reading and studying this chapter, you will be able to:

▶ Define instructional methods and justify their importance in teaching and learning.
▶ Describe each method discussed in this chapter. Include with your description examples and guidelines for using each.
▶ Demonstrate the correct procedures for using each method discussed in this chapter.
▶ Discuss techniques for selecting and combining methods for instructional purposes.

INTRODUCTION

Assume you are planning a trip. There are many possible routes to reach the same destination. Some are quicker. Others are more scenic and fun. Airplane routes are the shortest and quickest, but you don't see the sights. Interstates are smooth, but they all look the same with little variety. The state highways are scenic, but may require a lot of stopping and starting. Back roads may take a winding and twisting path through the countryside. Traveling off-road may require a special vehicle like a Jeep or SUV.

After you decide where you want to go (objectives), there are many routes (methods) to get you there. Only after you learn the characteristics, advantages, and limitations of each are you prepared to select the route that best suits your travel plans.

Even though there are different roads to the same destination, traveling each one gives you a different experience. That experience for your students may be very important for their learning. Different types of learners and different types of desired outcomes will require different roads (methods) to be taken. The ability to select and use different methods is thus critical for every teacher. The different methods are all important—some may be used more frequently, but all are needed at one time or another to maximize learning.

As is shown in Figure 6–1, the instructional methods represent another piece of the planning puzzle. Chapter 5 began the discussion of how to present the instruction to the students through various instructional activities; in this chapter we expand that discussion to include the means and procedures that are used for the learner to experience those activities and the subsequent learning.

WHAT ARE INSTRUCTIONAL METHODS AND WHY ARE THEY IMPORTANT?

Traditionally, instructional methods have been described as "instructional formats" such as lecture and discussion.

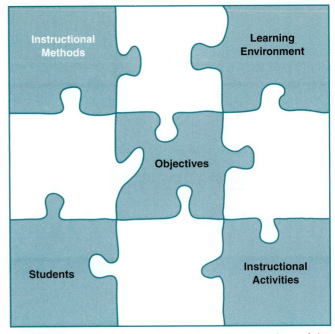

FIGURE 6–1   Instructional methods as the next piece of the planning puzzle.

Your methods are the procedures and actions used to help students achieve your stated lesson objectives. In Chapter 1 we introduced ten different types of methods (refer to Table 6–1). We discuss each of them in this chapter, beginning with the more teacher-centered approaches and proceeding to the more student-centered approaches.

Just like when you plan a road trip, the state highway may be the best way to see all the sights; a detailed discussion method in the U.S. Civil War lesson may be best for sixth-graders who are being introduced to the topic for the first time. (See the "Sample Lesson Plan" in Teacher Resource B, page 299.)

You should use a variety of methods in your teaching. However, some methods seem better suited for certain content or certain learners. You will learn which method or combination of methods is most effective only

Just as determining the optimal travel route helps to achieve the desired destination, determining the optimal instructional method helps to ensure the desired learning experience.

TABLE 6–1   *Instructional Methods*
Cooperative learning
Discovery
Problem solving
Games
Simulation
Discussion
Drill and practice
Tutorial
Demonstration
Presentation

by trying them with actual students. You will undoubtedly find yourself using a variety of methods to keep instruction interesting.

Methods of instruction vary in their interactivity and typical group size, just as the types of roads vary in their scenic views and number of lanes. Presentations and demonstrations tend to be less interactive, while drill and practice and tutorials are highly interactive. While most methods lend themselves to small-group instruction, presentations and demonstrations are more effective for larger groups. Tutorials and drill and practice tend to work best with individuals.

The purpose of this chapter is to help you identify the methods most appropriate for your planned instructional activities. Methods can be used to present information and to actively involve the learner. They are an integral part of learning and consequently of your learning plan.

Methods are different from the instructional activities. Methods are the heart of a lesson and contribute to learning. They, along with media (discussed in the next chapter), act like a road carrying the learners from where they are before the lesson (previous knowledge, skills, and attitudes) to where you want them to go (mastery of the objectives).

We now look briefly at each method, including examples and guidelines for using it. The methods are discussed in order of their increasing interactivity. Of course, the amount of interactivity can vary greatly for each method, depending upon the actual situation and how it is implemented.

Presentation

In a **presentation,** a source (often a teacher) relates, dramatizes, or otherwise provides information to learners. This method makes use of verbal information and/or visual symbols to convey material quickly. Presentations typically provide students with essential background information. A presentation can also introduce a new topic, provide an overview, and motivate students to learn. It is a one-way communication method controlled by the source, with no immediate response from, or interaction with, the audience. The source may be a textbook, an audiotape, a videotape, a computer, an instructor, a student, and so on.

In a presentation, the content can be presented verbally by the teacher or a student and the "audience" listens and takes notes. Video- and audio-taped presentations can also be used, either as the main way of presenting new material or as a supplemental approach for covering a specific topic in more detail.

Presentation Examples

1. In Jill Sanchez's sixth-grade class, a small group of students design and produce a mediated

Students share their knowledge through classroom presentations.

presentation on the origin and meaning of the Bill of Rights to summarize the content studied during a lesson. The presentation is given to the rest of the class.

2. The website from a major food company lists the nutritional information for all its products. Wanda Elliott's food and nutrition class learns the pros and cons of eating each of the products.

3. A videotape presents Ralph Watson's social studies class the television news coverage of the same story from four different cultures (United States, United Kingdom, Spain, and Israel). Students then compare and contrast the nature of coverage, length of coverage, content, and depth of coverage of the same news story from four different perspectives.

Principles for Using Presentations

▶ Inform students of the purpose of the presentation by providing them with an agenda or outline.

▶ Highlight the critical points of the presentation by showing a visual that illustrates a key point, by repeating the key points several times, by using voice inflection to emphasize important points, and by simply declaring a point as one of central importance.

▶ Make the presentation relevant. Learners need to be able to relate the information from the presentation to their own experiences. You can accomplish this by asking questions such as the following: How does this relate to you? Have you ever had a similiar kind of experience? How could you use this information now or in the future?

▶ Use variety to maintain attention. Add variety by introducing graphics or other forms of media, by asking questions, by incorporating relevant personal experiences, or even by making a simple change in your volume or rate of speech.

Demonstration

Demonstrations show students how to do a task as well as why, when, and where it is done. In this method, students view a real or lifelike example of a skill or procedure. Verbal explanations become more concrete by illustrating ideas, principles, and concepts. In addition, demonstrations can set performance standards for student work. By demonstrating how to properly perform a task, you establish the criteria you expect students to meet. You may use recorded demonstrations played back by means of a videotape or computer. Two-way interaction or student practice with feedback requires either a live instructor or a computer. The desired outcome may be for the student to imitate a physical performance, such as swinging a golf club or changing the oil in a car, or to adopt the attitudes or values exemplified by a respected person.

In a demonstration an individual performs a procedure in order to highlight an important principle or process. Demonstrations may be done live or recorded on a media format, such as videotape or CD-ROM.

You may use demonstration to illustrate how something works, to show how to perform a task, or to teach safety procedures. Demonstrations are essential when teaching a psychomotor procedure (such as jumping rope) or an interpersonal skill (such as participating in an interview).

Demonstration Examples

1. Molly Calhoun, a kindergarten teacher, demonstrates on the chalkboard how to form the capital and lowercase "letter of the week." The students then practice on their worksheets as Ms. Calhoun circulates throughout the classroom.
2. Jason LaJoy, the physical education teacher, demonstrates how to perform a forward flip on the trampoline as students watch. He describes each step and then demonstrates them in sequence. Next, each student is given an opportunity to practice the forward flip with feedback from Mr. LaJoy.
3. A CD-ROM program demonstrates how to deal with sexual harassment between students. The program dramatizes a variety of ways to deal with sexual harassment. Following the demonstration, students role-play how to deal with unwanted sexual advances.

Principles for Using Demonstrations

▸ While planning, preparation, and practice are important for all instructional methods, they are especially critical for demonstrations if you are going to be manipulating materials and equipment that you do not use regularly.
▸ Ensure that all can see and hear.

▸ Present the demonstration in small, sequential steps.
▸ Allow the audience to practice. It is often motivational for learners to watch a demonstration and then attempt to complete it themselves.

Discussion

Discussion is a dynamic method that encourages classroom interaction and actively involves students in learning. Discussion involves a group of individuals sharing information about a topic or problem. Students talk together, share information, and work toward a solution or consensus. They are given the opportunity to apply principles and information. This method introduces students to different beliefs and opinions, encouraging them to evaluate the logic of, and evidence for, their own and others' opinions. A major benefit of the discussion method is the amount of interaction that occurs and the learning that results from that interaction. It provides you with immediate feedback on students' understanding of course material.

Three important skills are associated with the discussion method: (1) asking questions, (2) managing the flow of responses to your questions, and (3) responding to students' questions. Discussions teach content as well as processes such as group dynamics, interpersonal skills, and oral communication. Discussion among students or between students and teachers can make significant contributions throughout students' learning. It is a useful way of assessing the knowledge and attitudes of a group of students. Discussion can foster collaborative and cooperative learning. In combination with written forms of student assessment, you also may use discussion to evaluate the effectiveness of your instruction.

Discussion Examples

1. A third-grade teacher may lead a discussion on the meaning of Thanksgiving Day when preparing his students to attend a Thanksgiving play presented

Students learn content and communication skills by participating in discussions.

Check It Out

Presentations, Demonstrations, and Discussions

Presentations, demonstrations, and discussions are instructional methods commonly used within classroom instruction. At this point in your learning career, you have probably experienced these methods literally hundreds of times. From those experiences, compile a list of evaluation criteria that you could use to determine the quality of these methods used within a classroom learning experience. With your list, assess three different classes that use one or more of these methods. Based on your criteria, what went well, what needed improvement, and what types of suggestions/recommendations could you offer? Did you find that you needed to adapt your evaluation criteria as you were using evaluating the quality of the methods? Are there ways in which to improve your set of selection criteria?

by high school students. A discussion after the play helps to answer students' questions and ensures that everyone understands the performance.

2. After reading different news articles, Jolene Moller's social studies students contemplate a current political issue or hot topic in the news through discussions and debates. Students then write up their own viewpoint on the topic based on the discussion.

3. Officer Richardson from the local police department shows a picture of a mangled car resulting from an auto accident involving a drunken driver to gain a student group's attention before discussing the problems of drug and alcohol abuse. She asks the students to discuss the consequences of drunk driving, particularly as it has affected their family and friends.

Principles for Using Discussions

▸ Provide inspiration/motivation before beginning a discussion by using a still picture, an audio recording, or a short video to secure the interest and attention of the participants.

▸ Encourage active participation from each group member. The exchange of ideas among group members is a critical factor in learning from discussion.

▸ Questions are needed to stimulate discussion, and should be prepared beforehand. Either you or your students may prepare questions.

▸ Summarize and/or synthesize the different viewpoints of various small groups discussing aspects of a specific topic.

Games

Instructional **games** provide an appealing environment in which learners follow prescribed rules as they strive to attain a challenging goal. It is a highly motivating approach, especially for repetitive content. Games often require learners to use problem-solving skills or demonstrate mastery of specific content such as math facts or vocabulary words.

Games have two key attributes—rules and competition or challenges. First, a clearly defined set of rules outlines how the game will be played, what actions are and are not allowed, what constitutes winning the game, and what the end result will be for a winning performance. Second, elements of competition or challenge provide players with an opportunity to compete against themselves, against other individuals, or against a standard of some type.

Spelling bees and speed math facts (e.g., students are given a number of problems to solve during a short time period; points are awarded for accuracy and speed) are common instructional games used in elementary classrooms to teach basic skills. You may easily adapt other games, such as *Trivial Pursuit* and *Jeopardy,* to contain relevant subject-matter content and at the same time retain the benefits of the game structure.

Game Examples

1. *Where in the World is Carmen Sandiego?* is a popular computer game that develops students'

Instructional games provide a challenging approach to experiencing a variety of activities.

understanding of geography and world culture. (See Figure 6–2.) Students assume the roles of detectives who must track down a thief who has stolen a national treasure from somewhere in the world. By gathering clues and conducting research, players are able to track the thief around the world, learning about geography as they go.

2. The religious education students in Reverend McCullan's class of middle school students enjoy playing *Jeopardy*. Rev. McCullan generates answers each week based on the reading assignment. The student teams actively participate to come up with the correct questions.

3. A group of high school chemistry students is given the assignment to memorize 15 element names and their associated numbers and symbols from the periodic table. The teacher has designed a board game in which four teams of two students each compete to complete the "experiment" by answering questions related to the 15 elements.

Principles for Using Games

▶ Students must have a clear concept of the instructional goal of the game. Ask yourself, "What do students need to learn, and how will a game help accomplish that?" Make sure to communicate the answer to these questions to your learners.

▶ Students must understand the procedures and rules for how the game will proceed and how all scoring

will occur. With a new game it always helps to have written rules.

▶ Make sure the game is structured so active involvement is maintained at the highest possible level for all participants. If groups are too large and long waits occur between "turns," the effectiveness of the game will wane. Allow enough time to play but not so much that students grow tired of the game.

▶ Include a debriefing or discussion following the game's conclusion. This should focus on the instructional content and value of the game and why it was played. Make sure the students understand that their participation in the game had an instructional purpose, and summarize what they should have learned from it.

Simulation

Using **simulation,** learners confront realistic approximations of real-life situations. Simulation allows realistic practice without the expense or risk involved in real situations, such as driving and flight simulators. The simulation may involve participant role-play, handling of materials and equipment, or interaction with a computer. This method promotes skills that emphasize accuracy and speed. Simulations also allow students to practice cooperation and teamwork, and can help foster leadership skills. Simulations can promote decision making and build positive values and attitudes by putting

FIGURE 6–2 A screen from *Where in the World is Carmen Sandiego?,* a popular educational computer game.
Source: Where in the World is Carmen Sandiego?®, © 1999. The Learning Company, Inc.

students in unfamiliar roles (see "Toolbox Techniques: Role-Playing" (see Chapter 5. page 92).

Laboratory experiments in the physical sciences are popular subjects for simulations because simulations avoid the risks and costs of real experiments. *Sim City* is a popular computer simulation. The program allows students to simulate the management of a city, including such elements as budget, construction of infrastructure, traffic, pollution, and crime. Students can build their own city from scratch or manage one of several well-known cities around the world.

Simulation Examples

1. The sixth-graders in Judy Krajcik's class learn about surviving in the inner city by playing a computer simulation about life downtown in a large city. She introduces the simulation to the entire class, then lets groups of four at a time participate on each class computer. She moves among the groups to answer questions, to monitor the progress of each group, and to discuss students' feelings about the conditions in the inner city.

2. Students in John Morales's middle school social studies class learn about the operations of government by participating in a role-playing simulation about creating and passing new legislation. John sits in the back of the room and lets the simulation progress at the students' pace. He takes extensive notes for a debriefing at the conclusion of the "legislative session."

3. High school students in Family Studies pretend that they are taking care of a baby. They are assigned a computerized doll that requires feeding, changing, and other baby functions. These simulated experiences give them insight into how they might respond in similar real-life situations.

Principles for Using Simulations

▶ Explain the purpose and procedures for the simulation. Make students aware of

oversimplifications implicit in the simulation. Explain the goal to be achieved and, where appropriate, the role of each student.

▶ Simulations can be confusing, and students may need guidance or direction in order to benefit from them. Questions, activities, and scenarios can fill this guidance role.

▶ Allow participants to play out their roles with minimum input from you.

▶ Conduct follow-up discussions or debriefing with students to maximize the benefit from the simulation. Provide feedback following the simulation (some commercial simulations provide feedback during their use).

Cooperative Learning

Many educators have criticized the competitive atmosphere that dominates some classrooms. They believe that pitting student against student in achieving teacher-assigned grades creates an adversarial relationship between students and teachers and is contrary to later on-the-job teamwork. Some teachers feel competition in the classroom can interfere with learning.

Cooperative learning involves small groups of students working together to learn collaborative and social skills while working toward a common academic goal or task. This method is specifically designed to encourage students to work together, drawing on their individual experiences, skills, and levels of motivation to help each other achieve the desired result. The central idea is that cooperation and interaction allow students to learn from several sources, not just the teacher, while also providing each student opportunities to share their own abilities and knowledge.

Each student in the group is accountable to the group for a different and specific aspect of the content. Individual students cannot complete the task on their own, but must rely on others in the group. In this method, students apply communication and critical-thinking skills to solve problems or to engage in meaningful work together. A growing body of research supports the claim

Check It Out

Simulations

Simulations of all varieties can be found on the Internet to download and explore. One example is a popular simulation known as *Roller Coaster Tycoon* (for a free trial, go to http://www.searchamateur.com/Tycoon-Games/Tycoon-Game-Download.htm). Additional simulations can be found by completing a search (e.g., using Google) with the search term *simulation game demo*. Locate a simulation such as *Roller Coaster Tycoon* and preview the software. From your experience with the software:

  a. Identify and describe the simulation aspects of the program,
  b. Identify and describe the game aspects of the program, and
  c. Describe how this program could be used within an educational setting.

Students learn interpersonal skills through cooperative learning.

that students learn from each other when they work on projects as a team (Sharan, 1990)

Cooperative groups have several uses including learning course content, promoting positive interactions and interdependence among groups of students, and teaching important social and communication skills. Another important reason for using such an approach is to teach individual accountability. When a group's success depends on the input of each individual in it, individuals learn to be accountable for their actions.

Cooperative Learning Examples

1. Recently the members of the fifth-grade Ecology Club and their advisor went on a field trip to view a creek near their school. Upon close observation of the creek, the students noticed patches of oil floating in the slow-moving water. After further investigation, the club advisor decided it would be a good project for the club to research what was occurring and to determine what could be done about it. He divided the students into four-person teams. Each team member was given a specific task. One student was to determine who should be contacted at the public health department. Another was to find out what the oily substance was and determine how it could have been introduced to the creek. Still another was in charge of identifying potential ways of publicizing what was occurring and determining the potential impact on the animals and community. The fourth was to review what the club could do to raise public awareness.

2. In the science lab, groups of middle school students work together as detectives to determine the nature of an unknown substance. In each group, one student is assigned to search the Internet, another goes to the public library for background research, others focus on designing and running experiments on the substance, while others work to locate someone who may be familiar with the substance. Together they pool their information to come to a combined, cooperative solution.

3. In a high school art appreciation class, groups of students were assembled to learn about the different forms of creative art. Each group was composed of three students: one who was accomplished at a musical instrument, another who had the ability to paint, and a third who had the ability to sculpt. The group's task was to learn about the different art forms and their relationships.

Principles for Using Cooperative Learning

▶ Build an atmosphere that encourages participation and cooperation. Help students realize the advantages of working together as a team. This can be facilitated by requiring that all members of the group have roles to fill that are necessary for the group's success.

▶ Teach group processes to the students. Effective group cooperative efforts do not happen by chance.

▶ Learn to facilitate, not dominate. It is important for you to take on the role of monitor, facilitator, and guide instead of director.

Discovery

The **discovery** method enables and encourages students to find "answers" for themselves. A principle of discovery learning is that students learn best by *doing,* rather than by just hearing and reading about a concept. With this method, your role is to arrange the learning environment so that "discovery" can occur.

Implementing a discovery method places students in a situation where they can learn through personal experience. Such experiences generally require learners to develop and use observation and comparison skills. Moreover, like detectives, students must learn to follow leads and clues and record findings in order to explain what they experience.

Discovery uses an inductive, or inquiry, approach to learning; it presents problems students must solve through trial and error. The aim is to develop a deeper understanding of the content through active involvement with it. For discovery learning in the physical sciences, students might view a video in which the narrator states a set of relationships and then go to the lab to discover the principles that explain those relationships. For example, after viewing someone saying, "Air has weight," they may then experimentally weigh a balloon before and after filling it with air, thus discovering that the statement is true.

Discovery Examples

1. Judy Lewis gives her first-graders a variety of watercolors and encourages them to mix any two colors together and see what color is produced. Judy uses the activity to teach color names. She has printed the color names on large cards along with a sample of the color. She also used cards with plus signs and equal signs to form equations such as "Blue + Yellow = Green." The activity allows students to "discover" the results of various combinations of colors. In addition, they learn to read the names of colors and are introduced to the basics of addition.

2. To help her middle school science students discover the relation between time and distance, Linda Harrison has them "experiment" with remote-control cars measuring the time it takes to go specific distances. Linda has the laboratory lesson carefully planned, but does not tell students what the result "should be." The students work in pairs and each lab pair manipulates the data with the aid of a computer, which constructs graphs of their data. Each pair shares its results with the entire class. Often, individual pairs' data do not show the function. However, when the class pools the data, the relationship among the variables becomes evident to everyone.

3. High school economics students "play" the stock market with $100,000 in pretend money. Students work in teams to gain the most from their "investments." Their success or failure is determined by the rise and fall of the real stock market during the time they are "investing."

Students discover how outside forces, such as the Federal Reserve, impact the value of stocks.

Principles for Using Discovery

▶ Be prepared for all types of "discoveries." Combining unique students with unique learning environments often leads to unique results. Be prepared for all types of standard and not-so-standard findings when students are allowed to make their own observations and draw their own conclusions.

▶ Encourage students to share their discoveries. Through the experience of discovery, students often gain both great insights into their subject and great enthusiasm for what they have learned. These important insights and feelings should be shared with other individuals.

▶ Make sure students understand that "one right answer" may not exist. They may need instruction and examples on how to observe, compare, and evaluate phenomena.

▶ Constantly encourage and reward students for being inquisitive, for asking questions, and for trying new approaches.

Problem Solving

The real world is filled with problems that need resolution. Some problems may be very well defined (e.g., determining if purchasing a new outfit is within one's current monetary means; finding the shortest route to travel to a nearby art museum). Other problems may be less well defined (e.g., determining how to increase neighborhood safety and finding the "best" postsecondary education). To fully participate in this world, students need to be able to analyze problems, form tentative hypotheses, collect and interpret data, and develop some type of logical approach to solving the problem.

In the problem-solving method, learners use previously learned content and skills to resolve a challenging problem. **Problem solving** is based on the scientific method of inquiry. The usual steps are (1) define the problem and all major components, (2) formulate hypotheses, (3) collect and analyze data, (4) formulate conclusions and/or solutions, and (5) verify conclusions and/or solutions. Learners must define the problem clearly (perhaps state a hypothesis), examine data (possibly with the aid of a computer), and generate a solution. Through this process, learners are expected to arrive at a higher level of understanding of the content under study.

One way to distinguish problem solving from discovery is that in problem solving students are *using* previously learned content and skills to solve problems while in discovery students are *learning* the content and skills.

Problem-Solving Examples

1. A computer program called *Thinkin' Things* makes use of various problem-solving strategies, such as working backwards, analyzing a process, determining a sequence, and thinking creatively. (See Figure 6–3.) The software provides the user with a factory that produces creative-looking feathered friends. The preschool-aged child selects from a set of options in order to create the next appropriate bird in the sequence.

2. Sister Anne is a sixth-grade science teacher at St. John's Catholic School. During a recent unit in science, she wanted her students to directly experience the impact of human population on the environment. She posed the following problem: "Does acid rain have an impact on the environment?" She quickly felt the need to clarify and redefine the question at her students' level, so she revised her question to, "In what ways does acid rain affect the growth patterns of common outdoor plants?" She asked her students to design an experiment that would provide an answer to that question.

3. Students in a business class are given information about a situation at a small manufacturing firm and asked to design a solution for a problem of low production. After gathering more data, they determine whether the solution should involve training or, perhaps, changing the environment or attitudes of the workers.

Principles for Using Problem Solving

▶ Clarify the problem when necessary. Especially with less mature students, one of the most difficult parts of problem solving is getting a true, accurate picture of the problem itself. In the initial stages of problem

FIGURE 6–3 *Thinkin' Things* allows the student to create a feathered friend based on a specific pattern and sequence. *Source: Thinkin' Things, Edmark Corporation. Reprinted with permission.*

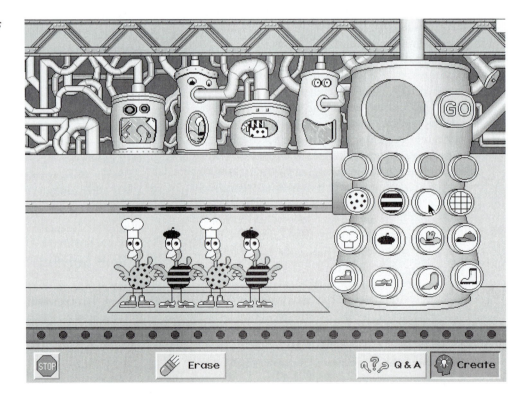

Addressing the Standards

NETS Connection

Several of the key National Educational Technology Standards (NETS I, III, V) address, in part, the need for teachers to *stimulate and facilitate the development of higher order and complex thinking skills (problem solving, critical thinking, creativity, etc.) through the use of technology resources.* Review these standards and their performance indicators in Teacher Resource A on page 297. Consider different ways in which technology resources could be used to develop better problem-solving abilities. Within the previous section, this text explained that problem solving is based on the scientific method. As a reflective journal activity, consider the following:

- List the steps involved to complete the scientific method.
- Note how technology could be used to help demonstrate and teach each of those steps.
- Take an alternative viewpoint and identify ways in which technology could be used by someone involved in the process of problem solving. How could technology tools assist in the process of discovering potential solutions to problems?

It is important to note that technology can often be used in multiple ways. In one case it may be used to teach individuals how to become more successful problem solvers. In another case it may be used as a tool of discovery and investigation in order to arrive at a solution to some problem.

---

solving, your role often involves helping students in identifying and outlining the specific problem. Be careful, however, to not overdo the clarification. If you explain the problem too thoroughly, the students won't have to work for the answer.

- Use additional resources and materials when necessary. It is important that students have access to additional resources, as well as instruction on how to use those resources most effectively.
- Keep groups small. Because of the uniqueness of the potential solution paths to the problems and the time required to complete the various steps, a smaller number of students is often essential.
- Help students understand the need for generalization. Students must recognize that problem solutions are generally unique and that no single answer works for all problems. This connotes an emphasis on learning general problem-solving strategies and procedures and adapting them as each new situation dictates.

Drill and Practice

Drill and practice is frequently beneficial when students need to memorize and recall information. During drill and practice, students are led through a series of practice exercises designed to increase proficiency in a newly learned skill or to refresh an existing one. To be effective, drill and practice exercises should include feedback to correct errors students might make along the way.

Drill and practice is a common classroom method for helping individual learners master basic skills or knowledge through repetitive work. Drill and practice is not designed to introduce new content. It is assumed that the skill or knowledge has already been introduced and, thus, its purpose is to give learners the opportunity to master the material at their own pace.

Drill and Practice Examples

1. To learn math facts to a level of automatic recall, students employ flash cards. On one side of the card is a simple arithmetic problem; on the other, the answer. Students attempt to answer the problem and then flip the card and compare their answer to the correct solution. This format can be used to learn states and their capitals, the names of animals and their young (e.g., goose and gosling, kangaroo and joey), foreign words and their translation, and other paired information sets.

2. Students in Wilber Groves's seventh-grade geography class work on their map-recognition skills using printed worksheets. He circulates throughout the classroom to monitor each student's work as they practice their skills in recognizing countries from their outline map. He also makes sure they all are getting the correct answers and gives them feedback as to the correctness of their answers.

3. Mary Owens uses a tutorial program on the computer to help her high school French students practice their vocabulary skills. Ms. Owens uses the quizzing ability of a voice recognition program that gives her students immediate feedback on their vocabulary pronunciation.

Principles for Using Drill and Practice

▶ Introduce content prior to the drill and practice session.

▶ Use many short drill and practice sessions instead of a few longer ones. Use both individual and group activities. Use competition (against self or others) to make drill more interesting.

▶ Make sure students are practicing the correct information or procedures. Only correct practice makes perfect!

▶ Provide opportunities for students to apply what they master through drill and practice.

Tutorial

Tutorials convey content from a tutor to a learner and may include instructor and student (interactive dialogue), student and student (tutoring or programmed tutoring), computer and student (computer-assisted tutorial software), and print and student (programmed instruction). The computer can play the role of tutor because of its ability to quickly deliver a variety of responses to different student inputs. Tutorials can be used for learning all types of content. Unlike drill and practice, which simply goes over previously presented information again and again, you can use tutorials to introduce new material to the student.

A *tutor*—in the form of a person, computer, or special print materials—presents content, poses a question or problem, requests student response, analyzes the response, supplies appropriate feedback, and provides practice until learners demonstrate a predetermined level of competency. Tutoring is most often done one to one and is frequently used to teach basic skills such as reading and arithmetic, although you may use it to teach higher-level skills as well.

Tutorial Examples

1. John Johnson uses a tutorial, in the form of an illustrated storybook on local history, as a makeup activity for his fourth-grade students who were absent when the topic was covered in class. He monitors their progress to check their understanding and learning.

2. A middle school math teacher uses a tutorial to teach her class how to calculate the area of a rectangle. First, she helps them recall relevant information from previous lessons (e.g., the concepts of rectangle, length, height, and multiplication). Then, she introduces and explains the concept of *area* as the product of the length of the rectangle multiplied by its height. She then demonstrates and shows a number of examples of determining the area of different sizes of rectangles. The students then attempt novel problems using the same format. The teacher gives them feedback on their performance, and they continue practicing until all students can successfully calculate a rectangle's area.

3. Jill Day, an industrial arts teacher, uses a video-based tutorial on shop safety as a prelude to having her students work with power equipment. The video shows each step of shop safety procedures and poses questions for students to answer.

Principles for Using Tutorials

▶ Present an overview of the material. Prompt students through content or skills, then release them to demonstrate content or skills on their own. Provide opportunities for students to apply what they have learned.

▶ Present content or skills one step at a time.

▶ Ask questions of the student, and encourage the student to ask questions.

▶ Plan for varying rates of completion. Monitor students' progress regularly to ensure that they are on task and learning.

CAN YOU COMBINE METHODS?

It's important to note that you may use multiple or mixed methods within a single lesson. In many instructional situations one method will not do the job. For example, you can combine a tutorial with drill and practice to strengthen the newly learned skills. The combination of methods may be more powerful and result in more learning than either method used alone. The key is to focus on what will work best to help *your* students learn *your* content. Try various methods with actual students

Check It Out

Kevin Spencer's Lesson Plan

1. Refer to Teacher Resource B on page 299. This teacher resource describes the instructional plan Mr. Spencer has developed for his sixth-grade social studies class. Read over the plan and identify several of the instructional methods that have been incorporated within the plan.

2. With a partner discuss the strengths and weaknesses of several of the selected methods. Convince your partner of an alternative method that should work effectively within Kevin Spencer's lesson plan. Justify your selection with information from Tables 6–2 and Figure 6–4.

3. With the selection of your alternative method, what alterations (if any) would have to be made for the selected instructional activities?

to help determine which method or combination of methods is most effective and consider using a variety of methods to keep the instruction interesting.

WHICH METHOD(S) TO USE?

Just as we described selecting a route when planning a trip in the introduction to this chapter, you must decide which instructional method(s) you will use in your lesson. For the methods we have just discussed, their advantages and limitations are listed in Table 6–2. These advantages and limitations provide a foundation for choosing methods for a particular lesson.

We have compiled the advantages of the various instructional methods into a checklist, shown in Figure 6–4. This table will help you select your method(s) for a particular lesson. The checklist will help you remember the factors to consider when selecting instructional methods. Without such a list, it is easy to make choices based only on what you like best or are most comfortable with. The list will remind you that there are other important considerations. It is not meant to replace your professional judgment, but to supplement or support it. We recommend that you use the checklist to narrow your choices and then rely on your experience and judgment to make a final decision. This will, of course, become easier as you gain teaching experience.

TABLE 6–2   *Advantages and Limitations of Instructional Methods*

Instructional Method	Advantages	Limitations
Presentation	Can be used with groups of all sizes Gives all students the opportunity to see and hear the same information Provides students with an organized perspective of lesson content (i.e., information is structured and relationships among concepts are illustrated) Can be used to efficiently present a large amount of content	Requires little student activity Makes assessment of student's mental involvement difficult Doesn't provide feedback to students; by definition, presentation is a one-way approach
Demonstration	Utilizes several senses; students can see, hear, and possibly experience an actual event Has dramatic appeal if the presenter uses good showmanship techniques, such as demonstrating an unexpected result or a discrepant event	May be difficult for all students to see the demonstration Is time-consuming if demonstrations are done live Demonstrations may not go as planned
Discussion	Allows students to actively practice problem-solving, critical-thinking, and higher-level thinking skills Is interesting and stimulating for teachers and students alike Can change attitudes and knowledge level Makes effective use of students' backgrounds and experiences	Students must have a common experience (reading a book, viewing a video, participating in an activity) in order to meaningfully participate and contribute Teacher must prepare and possess discussion-leading skills for the method to be effective
Games	Actively involves students and encourages social interaction through communication among players Provides the opportunity for practice of skills with immediate feedback Can be incorporated into many instructional situations to increase student motivation Helps students learn to deal with unpredictable circumstances	May involve students with competition more than content Can be impossible to play if pieces are lost or damaged Can be time-consuming to set up if games have many components

(Continued)

TABLE 6–2 *Continued*

Instructional Method	Advantages	Limitations
Simulation	Provides practice and experimentation with skills Provides immediate feedback on actions and decisions Simplifies real-world complexities and focuses on important attributes or characteristics Is appealing, motivates intense effort, and increases learning	Can cause deep emotional involvement (e.g., students in veterinary school get very attached to "sick" animals they diagnose and attempt to "save," even though the animals exist only within the simulation) Both setup and debriefing can be time-consuming
Cooperative Learning	Promotes positive interdependence, individual accountability, collaborative and social skills, and group processing Encourages trust building, communication, and leadership skills Facilitates student learning in academic as well as social areas Involves students in active learning	Requires a compatible group of students (this may be difficult to form) Takes more time to cover the same amount of content than other methods Is less appealing to individuals who prefer to work alone
Discovery	Encourages higher-level thinking; students are required to analyze and synthesize information rather than memorize low-level facts Provides **intrinsic motivation** (where merely participating in the task itself is rewarding) to discover the "answer" Usually results in increased retention of knowledge; students have processed the information and not simply memorized it Develops the skills and attitudes essential for self-directed learning	Allows for the discovery of "incorrect" or unintended information Can be time-consuming
Problem Solving	Increases comprehension and retention; students are required to work with everyday problems and to apply theory to practice Involves higher-level learning; students cannot solve problems by simple memorization and regurgitation Provides students with the opportunity to learn from their mistakes Develops responsibility as students learn to think independently	Limits the amount of content covered; can be time-consuming Selecting, modifying, and/or designing effective instructional problems can be time-consuming Requires teachers to have good management skills to coach students without giving them the "answer"
Drill and Practice	Provides repetitive practice in basic skills to enhance learning, build competency, and attain mastery Promotes psychomotor and low-level cognitive skills Helps build speed and accuracy	Students can perceive it as boring Does not teach when and how to apply the facts learned
Tutorial	Provides optimum individualized instruction; all students get the individual attention they need Provides the highest degree of student participation Expands the number of "teachers" in the classroom by using students or computers as tutors Frequently benefits student tutors as much as, or more than, the tutees Introduces new concepts in a sequenced, interactive way	May be impractical in some cases because appropriate tutor or tutorial material may not be available for individual students May encourage student dependency on human tutor; students may become reluctant to work on their own

Which Methods Should I Choose?

The Methods Selection Checklist will help you select the method or methods that will best fit your lesson. Each method has advantages, listed in the first column of the table. There are ten additional columns, one for each instructional method. To use the checklist, place a "√" in all the white spaces that best describe your instructional needs or situation. For example, if you think learning will be enhanced by allowing students to learn on their own, go to item 4 and place a "√" in the four columns that contain a white space. Continue this process for each of the items in the first column. When you have gone through the entire checklist, determine which column has the most "√s."

If most of the "√s" are in:	Select	If most of the "√s" are in:	Select
P	Presentation	CL	Cooperative Learning
DM	Demonstration	DY	Discovery
DN	Discussion	PS	Problem Solving
G	Games	DP	Drill and Practice
S	Simulation	T	Tutorial

It is possible that you will have more than one column with the same number of "√s." In that case you will need to choose which method is best or consider using multiple methods for your lesson.

Student learning will be enhanced by instructional methods that

	P	DM	DN	G	S	CL	DY	PS	DP	T
1. Are predominantly student centered										
2. Are predominantly teacher centered										
3. Provide a high level of interactivity										
4. Allow for students to learn on their own										
5. Allow several students (2–5) to be involved simultaneously										
6. Are appropriate for a small group (6–15)										
7. Are group oriented (16 plus)										
8. Provide information and content										
9. Provide practice with feedback										
10. Provide a discovery environment										
11. Present situations requiring strategy										
12. Can be completed in a short time (less than 20 minutes)										
13. Provide more content in a shorter time (are efficient)										
14. Enhance skills in the high-level intellectual skills domain										
15. Enhance skills in the low-level intellectual skills domain										
16. Enhance skills in the psychomotor skills domain										
17. Enhance skills in the attitude domain										
18. Are appropriate for a noncompetitive environment										
19. Promote decision making										
20. Provide a realistic context for learning										
21. Are highly motivating										
22. Enhance retention of information										
23. Use the inductive or inquiry approach to learning										

FIGURE 6–4 Method selection checklist.

Check It Out

Selecting Appropriate Instructional Methods

As practice, look over each of the following three scenarios. Decide what would be the best method for each situation. Then answer the following questions: What were the reasons you used to make your selections? Did you identify any potential problems with your selections? If so, what were those problems? What other methods could you also have selected? Under what conditions would you switch to those alternatives?

▶ *Scenario A:* The sixth-grade concert band instructor, Mr. Snyder, has decided that his students need to better discriminate between sharps, flats, and natural notes on the musical scale. He has 56 students currently in his band, and the instruction will take place in the band room, which is large enough to seat approximately 125 individuals.

▶ *Scenario B:* The instructor of an advanced survival training course needs to teach the six participants how to recognize edible versus nonedible desert plants found in the southwestern United States. Even though the course involves training for *desert* survival, it is being taught at a small college in Ohio.

▶ *Scenario C:* Mrs. Spence and her class of 25 tenth-grade students have been studying a unit on developing critical-thinking skills. One section of the content focuses on methods used to solve ill-defined problems and Mrs. Spence has decided that she wants to give the students practice using the different techniques they are studying.

To help you understand how factors such as the students, objectives, and learning environment might affect your choice of method in these scenarios, consider how your selections would change if the following aspects were different:

▶ *Scenario A:* Instead of being a band director, Mr. Snyder is a private flute teacher with 12 students of different ages who all come at different times during the day for individualized instruction. His goal is still to have the students increase their ability to discriminate between flats, sharps, and natural notes.

▶ *Scenario B:* The survival course takes place at the University of Nevada, Las Vegas, within minutes from large sections of desert.

▶ *Scenario C:* The focus of Mrs. Spence's class changes from being able to *apply* the problem-solving techniques to simply understanding them.

TECHNOLOGY COORDINATOR'S CORNER

Nancy Elder was a bit disconcerted. She had just come from a thought-provoking discussion in her evening educational psychology class. The dozen or so class members and the instructor had debated the benefits and challenges of a behavioral versus a constructivistic viewpoint of education. The debate was spirited, stimulating, and interesting. Nancy was convinced she had learned quite a bit about both sides of the argument. As they were wrapping up the discussion, the course instructor also noted to the class how highly effective he found their debate format to be. Then he jokingly said, "Hey, we did all this learning without touching a single piece of hardware. Sometimes I think technology just gets in the way."

Although Nancy was in her third year of teaching high school English and she had always been a strong proponent for integrating technology, now however, she wondered if more discernment should be used to determine when, or if, technology should be incorporated into her teaching methods. As she discussed this experience with the high school's tech coordinator, Nikki Sharp, Nikki reminded Nancy of a couple of things. First, learning is complex and thus a number of different methods and technologies may be needed in order to attain maximum effectiveness. There would always be times when one method of technology or another would be less appropriate. Second, the learners and the objective of the learning should dictate what types of methods are needed in order to accomplish the learning. It is important to understand different types of methods so that an optimal selection can be made. Finally, there will be times when technology is not needed as the primary means to attain learning; however, it may still play other important supporting roles to learning. For example, the actual debate in her evening class did not involve any technology; however, was technology used to facilitate gathering needed prerequisite information, to prepare the debaters to deliver their remarks effectively, and so on? Often technology has its greatest impact on learning as a support to other effective instructional methods.

SUMMARY

Just as we identified different forms of travel in taking a trip, there are different types of methods for learning. We presented the ten most widely used instructional methods, gave examples, and listed advantages and limitations of each method. You will need to select the appropriate method(s) for your students. Keep in mind that methods can be used in combination. There is no one best method for any instructional situation. For each lesson you will have to consider your objectives, your students, and your comfort level with each method.

Refer to Teacher Resource B on page 299 and review the sample lesson plan. Note the methods used for each of the sections. Would you consider using any different methods for any of the sections? Why or why not?

SUGGESTED RESOURCES

CD Resources

To increase retention and transfer of this information, review the *Reflective Questions and Activities* located in the Chapter 6 section (**Chapter info and activities>>> Chapter 6>>> Reflective Questions and Activities**) of the text's accompanying CD.

In addition, you can access relevant Internet web sites, NETS Connection exercises, and direct email access to the text's authors.

Website Resources

Access the text's website (**[www.prenhall.com/newby]**), navigate to Chapter 6, and review the Question and Answer section for relevant questions that have been generated by students and answered by the authors. You may also submit your own questions directly to the authors. In addition, you can access presentations by the authors about this chapter and gain insights directly from them about the topics that have been presented.

Print Resources

Barell, J. (1995). *Teaching for thoughtfulness: Classroom strategies to enhance intellectual development.* White Plains, NY: Longman.

Borich, G. D. (2004). *Effective teaching methods* (5th ed.). Upper Saddle River, NJ: Pearson.

Dallmann-Jones, A. S. (1994). *The expert educator: A reference manual of teaching strategies for quality education.* Fond du Lac, WI: Three Blue Herons.

Freiberg, H. J., & Driscoll, A. (2000). *Universal teaching strategies* (3rd ed.). Needham Heights, MA: Allyn & Bacon.

Jacobson, D. A., Eggen, P., & Kauchak, D. (2002). *Methods for teaching: Promoting student learning* (6th ed.). Upper Saddle River, NJ: Pearson.

McKeachie, W. J. (Ed.). (2001). *McKeachie's teaching tips: Strategies, research, and theory for college and university teachers.* Boston, MA: Houghton Mifflin.

Sharan, Shlomo. (Ed.) (1990). *Cooperative learning: Theory and research.* Westport, CT Praeger.

7

Instructional Media: Involving Multiple Senses of Learners

KEY WORDS AND CONCEPTS

Medium (plural, media)
Text
Visuals
Printed visuals
Projected visuals
Overhead transparencies
PowerPoint
Displayed visuals
Audiotape
Compact disc (CD)
Videotape
DVD
Real objects
Models
Multimedia
Computer software

CHAPTER OBJECTIVES

After reading and studying this chapter, you will be able to:

▶ Distinguish among the concepts of method, medium, and materials.
▶ Define instructional media and justify their importance in teaching and learning.
▶ Describe each medium discussed in this chapter. Include with your description, examples and guidelines for using each.
▶ Demonstrate the correct procedures for using each medium discussed in this chapter.
▶ Discuss techniques for selecting and combining media for instructional purposes.
▶ Select the most appropriate instructional media for a particular lesson.

INTRODUCTION

Let's assume you are buying your first vehicle. Which type of vehicle you buy will depend on how you define your needs. Do you have a family? If so, a two-seater sports car will probably not meet your needs. Do you go on frequent trips? If so, then you would probably look for a full-size car or van with a lot of passenger room and luggage space. If you have a trailer or camper, you will need one with a large towing capacity. Are you on a tight budget? If so, then you would probably look for a small, low-priced car that gets good gas mileage and is relatively inexpensive to maintain. Is safety a priority? If so, then you would probably look for a car with safety features such as antilock brakes, air bags, and side-impact protection.

After you define your needs, you should make yourself aware of the range of available vehicles. Only after you learn the characteristics, advantages, and limitations of each are you prepared to choose the one that meets your needs.

In the last chapter we showed how methods are like roads. Media, discussed in this chapter, are like vehicles. They help you and your students carry the content (information) along the road (methods) to learning. Just like most vehicles can travel on most roads, most media can be used by most methods. In this chapter you will learn how to select and use media to help your students learn.

To put these concepts into perspective, methods are procedures of instruction selected to help learners achieve objectives or understand content (e.g., presentation, simulation, drill and practice, cooperative learning).

Selecting an appropriate instructional medium is like selecting a vehicle; it depends on factors such as what is available, who will use it, under what conditions it will be used, and how it will be used.

Media are channels of communication that carry messages and means by which information can be delivered to the learner (e.g., text, visuals, video, multimedia). The specific items used in a lesson are called instructional materials (e.g., the *World History* textbook, *Where in the World is Carmen Sandiego?* computer software, the wall chart showing different types of insects).

As shown in Figure 7–1, a critical piece in the overall planning puzzle is that of the "instructional media." Just as there were a variety of instructional methods discussed within Chapter 6, the focus of Chapter 7 is to acquaint you with a variety of available media. The media help to determine how the instructional message is delivered and its overall impact on the learner. The strategic selection of media is based upon the needs of the learners, the desired outcome, and the constraints of the environment, as well as what methods and activities need to be supported.

INSTRUCTIONAL MEDIA

Media are essential to good teaching and, to get the most from them, they must be selected properly and used effectively. In this chapter we examine various types of media, including descriptions and examples of each, along with how to use them.

A **medium** (plural, **media**) is a channel of communication. Media are "carriers of information between a source and a receiver" (Smaldino, Russell, Heinich, & Molenda, 2005, p. 9). Examples of media include *PowerPoint* slides, videotapes, diagrams, printed materials, and computer software. These are considered

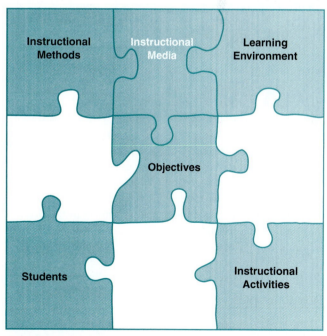

FIGURE 7–1 Instructional media as the next piece of the planning puzzle.

instructional media when they carry messages with an instructional purpose. The purpose of instructional media is to facilitate communication and to enhance learning.

Media serve a variety of roles in education. Their primary role is to *help students learn*. One way they do this is by providing an information-rich environment. Media can provide simulated experiences. Students don't have to go to a foreign country to "see" it. Visuals give added meaning to words. Students can see what a new invention looks like, not just hear or read a verbal description of it. Video or a series of pictures can demonstrate a process. It is better if learners see a skill demonstrated before being asked to practice it. The demonstration can be live, videotaped, or presented through a series of photographs. In addition, color, sound, and motion can increase student interest and motivation to learn.

Another role of media, often overlooked, is their use in assessment. You can ask students to identify an object or parts of an object in a photograph or to describe the movements in a musical composition recorded on audiotape. Videotapes can present the events leading up to a problem situation, and you may have students describe their responses to the problem.

Media commonly used in elementary and secondary schools include text, visuals, audio, video, real objects and models, and multimedia. We discuss each of these, along with examples of classroom applications.

Text

The term **text** refers to letters and numbers, usually presented in the form of printed materials or on a computer screen. Examples include study guides, manuals, worksheets, textbooks, and computer displays. Textbooks, such as this one, have long been used in the learning process. You can use many of the other media and computer formats discussed in this book along with textbooks.

The most common application of text is to present information. Students read text to learn the content. They are given reading assignments and are responsible for the material during class discussions and on tests. Text can also complement your presentation. Students may use study guides and worksheets to enhance information you present verbally or through other media. Worksheets allow students to practice what they have learned and to receive feedback. Additionally, students may use text references in the library media center or search computer databases to find information on a specific topic.

Text Examples

1. Jean Montgomery's fourth-graders are reading in their textbooks about the countries of Africa. Ms. Montgomery has taught them that reading is especially fun if you can share with others who are reading the same material. Students are working together in small groups, with each group studying a different country. The students take turns leading a discussion after reading a section of the text. Some students also refer to the encyclopedia on CD-ROM in the classroom to get additional information.

2. Students complete worksheets about the workings of an artificial heart after having viewed a videotape on the topic. The worksheet serves as viewing notes during the video. Each student practices applying the information presented and receives immediate feedback from the teacher.

3. Moderately handicapped industrial education students assemble a bicycle by following the directions in its accompanying pamphlet. The purpose of the activity is to promote reading and to encourage students to follow instructions. After assembling the bicycle, they disassemble it so other students can repeat the process.

Principles for Using Text

Textbooks and other text-based materials, such as those found on the Internet, should meet your students' needs rather than dictate what they do. As indicated in the PIE model (see Chapter 4), you should determine learning objectives and then select materials that will facilitate your students achieving them. Too often text is selected first, and then what the students learn and do is determined by what is in the text.

▶ Direct student reading with objectives and/or questions.
▶ Emphasize the use of visuals with text-based materials.
▶ Check the teacher's guide for additional materials and activities.
▶ Supplement text with other media.

Visuals

Visuals are two-dimensional materials designed to communicate a message to students. They usually include verbal (text or word) elements as well as graphic (picture or picture-like) elements. Figures and tables, such as the ones used in this book, are good examples of visuals.

We live in a very visual society. From pictures in the morning newspaper, to signs on the roadway, to graphics downloaded from the Internet, we constantly see visuals every day. Why are visuals used so frequently? Because they work! Visuals can increase instructional effectiveness by highlighting concepts through the use of graphs, illustrations, charts, and diagrams. They increase viewers' comprehension and understanding because they provide a summary or visual representation of the information presented in the text. For example, visuals can show real or abstract items, illustrate procedures, provide examples, identify parts and pieces, and draw attention to similarities and differences among various objects. Additionally, visuals can increase efficiency by representing, in a single form, what may take hundreds if not thousands of words to explain. Finally, visuals can increase appeal by attracting attention, as well as stimulating thought and inquiry.

Visuals have numerous applications. For example, you may use photographs or drawings to illustrate specific lesson topics, especially those explaining a process. Visuals are helpful when students are learning to identify people, places, or things. You may use them to stimulate creative expression such as writing stories or composing poetry. They can provide an excellent way to review or preview experiences of past or future field trips. Visuals also serve to pique interest and provide specific information for testing and evaluation purposes (see "Toolbox Techniques: Using Visuals in Instructional Materials").

Several types of visuals are used in teaching and learning. We look at three types here: printed visuals, projected visuals, and displayed visuals.

Printed Visuals

Printed visuals include drawings, charts, graphs, posters, and cartoons. Sources of visuals include textbooks, reference materials, newspapers, and periodicals, as well as those created by teachers or students. Several types of visuals are used in teaching and learning.

Printed Visuals Examples

1. Tom Keller selects one of his students' favorite books, *Alexander and the Terrible, Horrible, No Good, Very Bad Day,* to read to a small group of second-graders. Before beginning the story, he shows students pictures from the book to preview the story. This will help the students focus on the plot of the story. After reading the story, students will create their own drawings based on the important parts of the story.

2. Middle school science students are given a set of individual drawings showing the major steps involved in the production of oxygen by plants. As a group, they are to put the individual visuals into the proper sequence. Handling the visuals stimulates discussion and learning.

3. High school history students use geography maps to point out the difficulties an army would have if it attempted to invade Switzerland. Using topographic maps on a computer the students attempt to find possible routes before the teacher points out the routes actually used by invaders in the past.

Principles for Using Printed Visuals

A variety of pictures, drawings, charts, and other visuals are available or can be prepared for classroom use. Graphics are available in textbooks and other printed materials, in computer software and multimedia programs, and as separate paper-based visuals.

▶ Use simple materials that everyone can see.
▶ Provide written or verbal cues to highlight important aspects of visuals.
▶ Use one visual at a time except for comparison.
▶ Hold visuals steady.

Projected Visuals

Projected visuals include overhead transparencies and computer presentation software such as Microsoft's *PowerPoint.* **Overhead transparencies** are widely used in classrooms because of their many advantages. Basically, the overhead projector is a box with a large "stage" on the top. Light from a powerful lamp inside the box passes through a transparency (usually 8 inches by

TOOLBOX
TECHNIQUES

Using Visuals in Instructional Materials

Your selection and use of visuals are important when adapting or creating instructional materials. Just as the proper visual may lead to increased instructional effectiveness, efficiency, and appeal, one that is not appropriate may cause learner difficulties and frustration. Ask yourself the following questions when selecting visuals to use with your instructional materials:

▶ Is the visual relevant to the instructional outcomes?
▶ Is the information depicted accurately?
▶ Is the information current?
▶ Is the information presented clearly and simply?
▶ Will learners comprehend what is depicted?
▶ Will it be big/small enough for the given purpose and size of audience?
▶ Is it aesthetically pleasing?

10 inches) placed on the stage. A lens-and-mirror system mounted on a bracket above the box turns the light beam 90 degrees and projects the image onto a screen or blank wall. (See Figure 7–2 showing an overhead projector.)

Overhead transparencies may be created from clear plastic, photographic film, or any of a number of other transparent materials. You can write on clear plastic with colored markers and print on clear plastic using a computer. In addition, you can project a variety of materials, including cutout silhouettes, small opaque objects, and many types of transparent objects. Transparencies may be used individually or made into a series of images. You can explain complex topics step by step by adding a series of overlays one at a time to the base diagram (see Figure 7–3).

The overhead projector is one of the easiest devices to use. With a little practice, anyone—including your students—can make a professional presentation using overhead transparencies.

The overhead has many group-instruction applications. Commercial distributors of transparencies have made materials available for virtually all curricular areas, from kindergarten through adult education. These materials range from single, simple transparencies to elaborate sets with multiple overlays.

PowerPoint is an example of presentation software used on a computer connected to a data projector. It is possible for users without specialized training to create and project colorful and animated visuals. Students, as well as instructors, can use templates to produce very professional-looking presentations. *PowerPoint* allows the user to include text, draw pictures, produce diagrams, import digital photos, include music, and create animation.

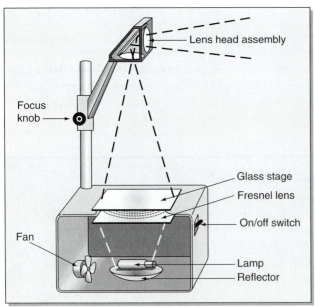

FIGURE 7–2   Key parts of the overhead projector.
Source: Smaldino, Sharon E.; Russell, James D.; Heinrich, Robert; Molenda, Michael. Instructional Technology and Media for Learning. *8e. © 2005. Reprinted by permission of Pearson Education, Inc., Upper Saddle River, NJ.*

Overhead Transparencies Examples

1. The chalkboard and overhead projector make a good team for teaching problem solving in Dianna Williams's physics class. After she demonstrates how to solve acceleration problems, Dianna projects similar problems with the overhead projector. Prior to class time she had prepared the problems on transparencies, using an 18-point font so all students would be able to see and read the problems. The screen is in the front corner of the room so it won't block the chalkboard. She randomly selects several students to do a problem on the chalkboard, telling them to print large enough so that everyone in the room can see their work. The other students work on the same problem at their desks. When all students are finished, Dianna leads a discussion on the various ways to approach the problem. Students indicate errors they find in the techniques and the calculations of each other's problems.
2. Students illustrate the flow of information between a computer's central processing unit and its random-access and read-only memories by drawing arrows on a transparency. All students will be expected to duplicate the flow on a paper-and-pencil test at the end of the unit.
3. Kindergarten students classify various items placed on the overhead projector stage as either circles, triangles, squares, or rectangles. The students are stimulated by the brightly colored clear plastic shapes and eagerly wait their turn to go to the overhead projector and manipulate the items.

Presentation Software Examples

1. In her sophomore-level history course, Brenda Horn uses *PowerPoint* to show an outline of her presentation about Lewis and Clark's expedition.

It is easy to use the overhead projector to show visuals to a group.

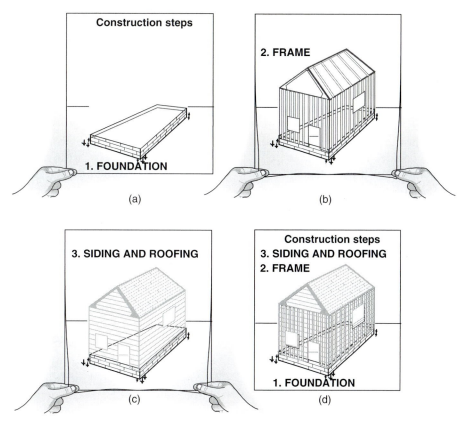

FIGURE 7–3 Transparency overlays can be used to build complex visuals step by step.
Source: Smaldino, Sharon E.; Russell, James D.; Heinrich, Robert; Molenda, Michael. **Instructional Technology and Media for Learning.** *8e. © 2005. Reprinted by permission of Pearson Education, Inc., Upper Saddle River, NJ.*

The phrases on the screen provide her students with the key words and they also serve as note cards for her. In addition she shows progressive maps of the westward progress of Lewis and Clark as she describes their important journey.

2. Charles Miller divides his eighth-grade general science class into groups of four. Each group draws from a jar a topic that they are responsible to present to the entire class. They are encouraged to use Apple *Keynote* on school Macintoshes for their presentations. Because science lends itself so well to visuals and diagrams, the students are encouraged to create their own drawings or to take photographs with the school's digital camera. However, in some instances Mr. Miller allows them to use material from the Internet, but they must properly cite their source.

3. Demetrius Brown uses a *PowerPoint* presentation that was developed by several local teachers to provide his fourth-graders with information and a "tour" of a local historical site. The old canal and locks could be visited as part of a field trip, but Demetrius would rather spend the available time and funds on another field trip, so he uses the multimedia presentation complete with sound (narration and music) as well as animation (video

shot by a local teacher) to introduce his students to the site. He also encourages his students to visit the site with their parents after the lesson.

Principles for Using Overhead Transparencies

- Focus the image so it fills the screen.
- Turn off lights over the screen if possible. The learners should be able to take notes and you should be able to see the class.
- Stand facing your class. Do not block the screen especially when using overhead transparencies.
- Use appropriate pacing. In most cases, do not show an overhead transparency for more than 20 to 30 seconds without adding to it or changing to the next transparency.
- Direct students' attention to the important parts of the overhead transparency.
- Summarize frequently. Every so often, assist your learners in their efforts to "see" the big picture.

Principles for Using Presentation Software

- Darken the room. Do not turn off all the lights. Turn off lights over the screen if possible. During the day natural light through windows may allow you to turn off room lights. The audience should be able to take notes and you should be able to see the audience.

▶ Introduce your presentation. Distribute handouts, if used. Provide an overview of the presentation. Indicate its purpose (objectives).

▶ Don't read from the slides. Your audience can read the text for themselves; just give them time to do so before you talk about the slide. You should elaborate upon and enhance what is on the slide. Provide additional information and clarify content.

▶ Minimize your need to look at the screen. Make notes or work from an outline with cues when to change the slide.

▶ Use appropriate pacing. In most cases do not show a slide for more than 20 to 30 seconds without adding to it or changing to the next slide.

▶ Summarize frequently. Every so often, assist your audience in their efforts to "see" the big picture. *PowerPoint*'s "Summary Slide" features may be helpful for this.

Displayed Visuals

There are many surfaces in the classroom on which to **display visual** materials, including chalkboards, multipurpose boards, and bulletin boards. The most common medium in the classroom is the chalkboard. Once called blackboards, chalkboards, like chalk, now come in a variety of colors. Although the chalkboard is most commonly used as a medium of verbal communication, you also may use it as a surface on which to attach or draw visuals. You can fasten pictures to the upper molding, tape them to the board with masking tape, or place them in the chalk tray to help illustrate instructional concepts and support verbal communication. You also may draw visuals, such as sketches, diagrams, charts, and graphs, on the chalkboard for display to the class.

Some classrooms are equipped with multipurpose boards (also called whiteboards or marker boards) instead of chalkboards. As their name implies, they have more than one purpose. Their smooth, white plastic surface requires a special erasable marker rather than chalk. The surface is also suitable as a screen on which you can project slides and overhead transparencies. Materials cut from thin plastic, such as figures and letters, will adhere to the surface when rubbed in place. Some of these boards have a steel backing as well and can be used as a magnetic board for displaying visuals.

A bulletin board's surface is made of a material that holds pins, thumbtacks, staples, and other sharp fasteners without damage to the board. In practice, bulletin board displays tend to serve three broad purposes: decorative, motivational, and instructional. The decorative bulletin board is probably the most common in schools.

Its function is to lend visual stimulation to the environment by using catch phrases or posters. Displaying student work illustrates the motivational use of bulletin boards. The public recognition offered by such displays can play an important role in classroom life. It promotes pride in achievement, encouraging students to do a good job.

The third purpose of bulletin boards is instructional, complementing the educational objectives of the formal curriculum. Rather than merely presenting static informational messages, you can design displays to invite participation. Such displays ask questions and give viewers some means of manipulating parts of the display to verify their answers (e.g., flaps, pockets, dials, or movable parts). Learners can also take part in the actual construction of the display. For example, to introduce a unit on animals, an elementary teacher might ask each student to bring in a picture of a favorite animal. Students would then make a bulletin board incorporating all the pictures.

Displayed Visuals Examples

1. Three of Carl Shedd's fifth-grade students print an outline on the chalkboard for their class presentation on the characteristics of gorillas. After describing each characteristic, one student puts a checkmark at the appropriate place on the outline so the students in the class can easily follow the presentation.

2. Bonnie Johnson uses a marker board and a variety of colored markers to diagram the relationships among the various components of several computer software applications. She leaves these diagrams on the marker board during class so students can refer to them. She also puts key commands on the board for her students' easy reference.

3. Students classify various types of igneous, metamorphic, and sedimentary rocks displayed on platforms secured to a bulletin board. Then they check their responses against the correct answer provided under a movable flap. Because the display is available in the classroom during the entire unit, they can check and recheck themselves until they are confident that they know all the types of rocks.

4. Students sing the simple notes of the treble clef displayed on a multipurpose board. As the teacher adds sharps and flats, different colors draw students' attention to these special notes. The notes can be easily moved around the board.

Principles for Using Displayed Visuals

In the classroom, the most widely used (and misused) tool is the chalkboard. Although chalkboards have been replaced by dustless multipurpose boards in some classrooms, the same simple techniques can increase the effectiveness of both.

- Check the visibility of the board from several positions around the room.
- Decide in advance how you plan to use the board.
- Print using upper- and lowercase, not all caps or in script.
- Face your audience; do not talk to the board with your back to the class.

Audio

In addition to the teacher's voice, there are numerous ways to bring sound (animal sounds, famous speeches, and foreign languages) into the classroom. The most common is the **audiotape.** Audiotape allows both students and teachers to make their own recordings to share with the class. Another medium is the **compact disc (CD).** Both are very durable.

For hands-on learning, you can record a tape from which students can receive step-by-step instructions. To be efficient and effective in their work, these students must have both hands free and their eyes on their work, not on a textbook or manual. Audiotapes allow students to move at their own pace and leave you free to circulate around the classroom and discuss each student's work individually.

Students with learning difficulties can revisit classroom presentations using audiotape. They can replay more difficult sections as often as necessary. The students practice their listening skills with tapes of recorded stories, poetry, and instructions. After the students have practiced their listening skills under your direction, you can evaluate them using a tape they have not heard before.

Audio Examples

1. The eighth-grade students at Fairfield Middle School are using cassette tape recorders to gather an oral history of their community. The project is a cooperative effort by all eighth-grade social studies teachers and their students. The teachers each chose to focus on an aspect of the community's history, such as transportation, government, business, industry, and recreation. Students spend many weeks deciding on important topics in the area assigned to their class, then work together to develop a set of questions to ask each individual they interview. Armed with tape recorders, students interview people from the community. Some of the citizens come to the school; the students visit others. Students edit the individual tapes into one tape that highlights important aspects of the community's history. The finalized copy is available for use by community groups and organizations.

2. High school students learn and practice Spanish conversation using audiotapes. The students enjoy recording and listening to the tapes. Using this technique, students learn conversational Spanish.

3. Students with visual impairments listen to recorded versions of novels being discussed in literature class. Other students also choose to listen to the tapes. All students, whether they read the novel or heard the tapes, then share their interpretations.

Students can share audio experiences.

Check It Out

Evaluating the Effectiveness of Visuals

Refer to the CD accompanying this text and access the media preview forms **(Chapter info and activities >>> Chapter 7 >>> Media Preview Forms)** for visuals and overhead transparencies.

1. Using the preview form for *visuals,* review a chapter in one of your textbooks and evaluate the visuals that are incorporated within the chapter. Rate the chapter's visuals for each of the criteria (it may be easiest to develop a 1 (low) to 5 (high) rating scale). Include comments about which photos should serve as examples and nonexamples for specific criteria rankings. What, if any, recommendations would you give the author for enhancing the visual quality of the chapter?

2. During the next lecture/oral presentation that you attend, use the preview form for overhead transparencies. During the presentation, evaluate the quality of the visual transparencies that are presented with the preview form criteria. What suggestions would you offer to the presenter in order for him/her to improve the presentation visuals?

Principles for Using Audio

In formal education, a lot of attention is given to reading and writing, a little to speaking, and essentially none to listening. Like all skills, listening and learning from audio can be improved with practice.

▶ Cue the audio material before you and your students use it.
▶ Make sure that all students involved can hear and that other students aren't distracted.
▶ Use a handout or worksheet to maximize learning from audio media.
▶ Use a follow-up activity after each audio lesson.

Video

Moving images can be recorded on videotape, DVD, and websites. All these formats offer ways to store and display moving images accompanied by sound. As we will see, the formats differ considerably in cost, convenience, and flexibility.

Video is the display of recorded pictures on a television-type screen. Any media format that uses a television screen or monitor to present a picture can be referred to as video: videotapes, DVD, and webcasts.

The VHS half-inch **videotape** is still used for commercial distribution of moving images. VHS can also be used for amateur video production in education. However, it is rapidly being replaced by a newer type of video medium—**DVD.** Some professionals refer to it as **digital video disc;** others use the term **digital versatile disc.** DVD is a compact disc format for displaying motion video. It offers truly digital, optical recording, storage, and playback of full-motion video and/or computer data (like a CD-ROM). The disc is the same physical size as an audio CD or a CD-ROM. Current DVDs can hold enough data for a full-length feature film—about two hours. Some DVD discs are able to hold about four times that amount. Like CDs and CD-ROMs, DVD has instant random access and is highly durable. Recordable DVDs are available. They have the potential to do for video what the CD did for music.

Both videotape and DVD have fast forward and reverse search capabilities. Video formats, particularly DVD, can be indexed, making it possible to locate specific sections of a program. Certain special effects, such as slow motion and still images, are available during the video presentation. Because the equipment is easy to operate, video lends itself to use by individual students.

Video Examples

1. Paige Ertmer's preservice teachers are viewing the acclaimed videotape *Good Morning, Miss Tolliver* in their mathematics methods course. Originally shown on public television, the video is a fascinating look at how Kay Tolliver, an East Harlem math teacher, combines math and communication arts skills to inspire and motivate her students. Dr. Ertmer is hoping this videotape will inspire and motivate her students, who will be doing their student teaching next semester. She has distributed a set of questions to direct students' viewing of the videotape, asking them to look over the questions prior to seeing the tape and to take notes during the viewing. These questions will form the basis of a class discussion following the video.

2. By watching a golfing video, physical education students use slow-motion and freeze-frame capabilities to practice imitating the grip and swing of a golf professional. Their coach is able to point out the critical parts of the pro's swing. Students can imitate the swing and also get feedback from their peers.

3. Students write a position paper after viewing videos presenting the opposing positions of the lumber industry and environmentalists on retaining the virgin forests of the northwestern United States. Viewing actual forests on videotape and hearing and seeing representatives of both sides of the issue stimulate the students to investigate the issue and to put their thoughts on paper.

Principles for Using Video

Video, regardless of its format, provides motion, color, and sound. Students are accustomed to viewing television passively at home. Therefore, you must prepare students for active viewing of video in the classroom.

Digital video discs (DVD) allow learners to view full-motion video on a computer.

- Check lighting, seating, and volume controls before the showing.
- Prepare students by reviewing previously learned content and by asking new questions.
- Stop the videotape at appropriate points for discussion.

- Highlight major points by writing them on the chalkboard or overhead.

Locate an instructional video (VHS, DVD, Internet). Check your school/university media center or on the Internet. How effective is the video in helping students

Check It Out

Microsoft's **PowerPoint** *and* **Producer**

Microsoft's *Office* suite of applications is one of the most popular collections of productivity software for both teachers and students. Within that suite, a popular application program is known as *PowerPoint*. To learn to use this application, complete the level 1 and level 2 activities in Chapter 5 of the book:

Newby, T. J. (2004). *Teaching and learning with Microsoft Office and FrontPage: Basic building blocks for computer integration.* Upper Saddle River, NJ: Merrill/Prentice-Hall.

Once you are familiar with creating *PowerPoint* presentations, go to the Microsoft website and examine and download their software known as *Producer. Producer* is a free video editor that was developed to work in conjunction with *PowerPoint*. With it, you can create a product that can incorporate audio, video, and *PowerPoint* slides simultaneously on the computer screen. See Figure 7–4 for an example of the *Producer* software editing screen and Figure 7–5 of a screen capture of the finished product.

To acquire information and to download the free *Producer* add-on to *PowerPoint,* visit Microsoft's website: http://www.microsoft.com/office/powerpoint/producer/prodinfo/default.mspx. For additional listings and updates on this and similar software, use your search engine with search terms such as *"Microsoft Producer."*

Note: These activities have also been placed on this text's accompanying CD-ROM. Launch the CD and click on the following links: **Chapter info and activities >>> Chapter 3 >>> Presentation software***. Read and study the materials and work through the various "Workout" exercises.*

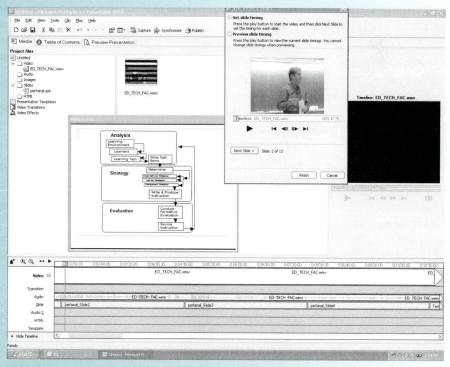

FIGURE 7–4 **Microsoft *Producer* video editing software.**
Reprinted with permission from Microsoft Corporation.

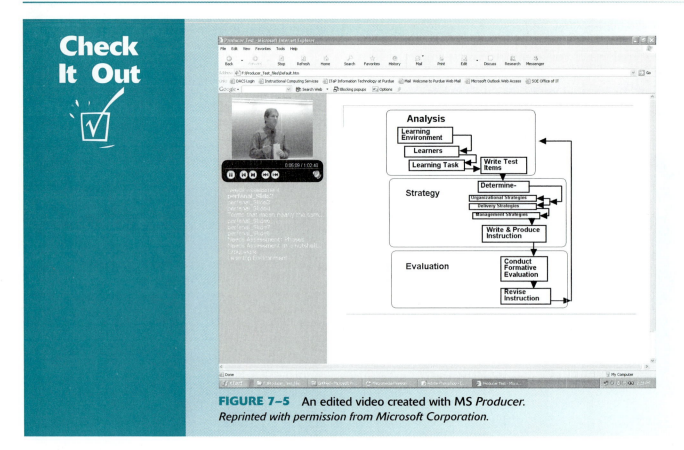

FIGURE 7–5 An edited video created with MS *Producer*.
Reprinted with permission from Microsoft Corporation.

learn? What does it do well? How could it be improved? How does the audio contribute to learning?

Real Objects and Models

Often not thought of as media, real objects and models can require learners to use all their senses—sight, hearing, smell, touch, and even taste! They bring the outside world into the classroom. **Real objects,** such as coins, tools, plants, and animals, are some of the most accessible resources available to promote student learning. **Models** are three-dimensional representations of real objects and may be complete in detail or simplified for instructional purposes. Models of almost everything are available from teacher supply companies and toy stores.

Often you can introduce a new topic with a real object or a model. Invite the students to see and handle it. Both elementary and secondary students can learn about objects in their own environment and those from foreign cultures and other times. Real objects and models add relevance for the students and can generate interest and enthusiasm for a topic. If you cannot bring real things into the classrooms, a field trip can take students to them. Another effective use of these materials occurs during assessment as students classify objects, describe their functions, and identify their components.

Real Objects and Models Examples

1. Nancy Foust, an instructor in the high school vocational-technical program, is demonstrating how automobile carburetors work so her students can adjust and repair them. She brings several different carburetors into the classroom to arouse interest at the beginning of the class. The students can handle and look at them before the class begins, then she puts the carburetors away. Nancy uses a larger-than-life model of a carburetor to show how the internal parts operate. Some of the parts are made of clear plastic, and many are color coded for easy identification. Having seen and manipulated the actual carburetors, Nancy's students know how big they are and what they look like. The enlarged model allows all of her students to see the various parts as she describes their functions.

2. Elementary students create a terrarium to observe the water cycle. All students are excited when they place the plants and animals in the terrarium. They work together in teams under the teacher's direction to complete the terrarium.

3. Students in a multicultural course discuss the impact of various artifacts (tools, dishes, etc.—real or replicas) on the lives of those from another culture. They then visit a museum. The artifacts hold the

Objects and models can bring the real world into the classroom.

interest and attention of all the students. The real objects and models make the cultures "come alive."

Principles for Using Real Objects and Models

There are countless things in the environment that you and your students can use to learn from—leaves, globes, dolls, manipulatives (objects designed for educational use, such as letter blocks and counting rods), tools, and so on. However, real objects and models will be effective only if they are used properly.

- Familiarize yourself with the object or model.
- Make sure objects are large enough to be seen.
- Indicate actual size, shape, and color of objects represented by models.
- Avoid passing a single object around class. It can be distracting and students may play with it while you are trying to move on in the lesson.

Multimedia

Multimedia is a conglomerate of a number of different media formats, including video, graphics, audio, text,

and real objects and models (Figure 7–6). These media can be used together as multimedia or can also be used individually. Multimedia are often under computer control. The computer—with its virtually instantaneous response to student input, its extensive capacity to store and manipulate information, and its unmatched ability to serve many individual students simultaneously—has wide application in instruction. The computer can also record, analyze, and react to student responses typed on a keyboard or input with a mouse. Some display screens react to the touch of a student's finger. **Computer software** refers to the program or instructions that tell the computer what to do. As noted, multimedia usually refers to the delivery of video, graphics, audio, and text by a computer using instructional software.

Multimedia Examples

1. Picture a student in a Spanish conversation class seated in front of a multimedia system. It looks pretty much like a typical computer system,

Students can learn from a variety of sources when using a multimedia kit.

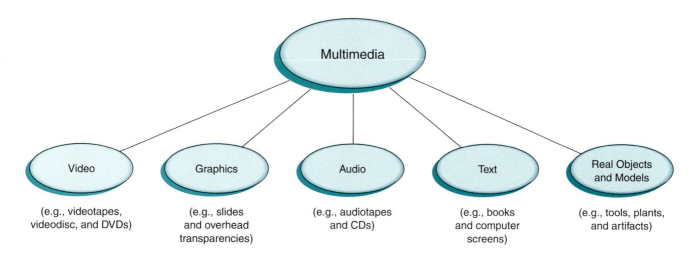

Video	Graphics	Audio	Text	Real Objects and Models
(e.g., videotapes, videodisc, and DVDs)	(e.g., slides and overhead transparencies)	(e.g., audiotapes and CDs)	(e.g., books and computer screens)	(e.g., tools, plants, and artifacts)

FIGURE 7–6   Multimedia is a combination of different media types.

perhaps with a few additional pieces of equipment installed. The student reads the directions on the computer screen and clicks the mouse to get started. The lesson begins with a video clip on a CD-ROM showing a conversation between two native speakers of Spanish. The video not only allows the student to see and hear two native speakers, but also provides a cultural backdrop, as it was shot on location in Spain. As the lesson progresses, the student makes use of a Spanish dictionary stored on the CD-ROM that provides definitions and translations, as well as the actual aural pronunciation of each word and phrase. The computer allows the student access to all of this information and provides periodic review questions and feedback about her progress. This is just one example of what interactive multimedia can be like.

2. Nancy Matson is presenting a unit on television violence, free speech, censorship, and the television industry in her eighth-grade social studies class. She has selected a multimedia program from Tom Snyder Productions titled *Rainforest Researchers* as the core of the unit (Figure 7–7). The program provides introductory material for both Nancy and her students. A teacher's guide and student booklets direct lesson activity. The students continue their learning adventure for several class periods. Students consider how ecosystems change and what caused the changes. Nancy accesses for students by their individual worksheets and teamwork.

3. Students in George Morgan's middle school mathematics class are using the computer simulation *Hot Dog Stand* to develop a variety of mathematical and practical skills. The simulation requires planning and recordkeeping, as well as judgments based on computational skills, to make as much money as possible while managing a hot dog stand during a season of various types of concerts. Random generation of variables ensures that the same students can use the program again and again. Participating students are gathered around a computer in the corner of the classroom while other students are engaged in different activities. Mr. Morgan has checked to be sure that all can see the screen and interact without disturbing other students. The students record data, enter the data into spreadsheets, and generate graphs. There is friendly competition to see which group of students can "earn" the most money from its hot dog stand.

Principles for Using Multimedia

When you use multimedia materials, you should test all of the components of the multimedia system well in advance of your lesson. Make sure you have all adjunct materials, such as printed materials, for all students.

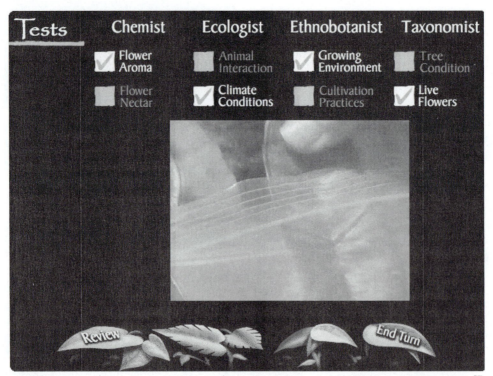

FIGURE 7–7 *Rainforest Researchers* is a multimedia instructional learning experience developed by Tom Snyder Productions. Students interact with various media to gain a greater understanding of the topic.
Source: Rainforest Researchers, *Tom Snyder Productions.*

Check It Out

Media Identification

In the blank before each description, write the name of the medium described. The media to choose from are text, visuals, audio, video, real objects and models, and multimedia. Our answers appear at the end of the chapter on page 138.

_____ **1.** Marketing students learn how to increase levels of consumer motivation for buying a specific product by combining dramatic music with emotional oral testimonies of the product's effectiveness and value.

_____ **2.** Learners study the *Titanic* by using an interactive program that provides diagrams of the ship's structure, biographies of individuals sailing on the ship, information about rescue operations, and video footage of the exploration and discovery of the wreckage.

_____ **3.** Students use photographs of local buildings to illustrate a unit on architectural styles.

_____ **4.** High school students research replicas of handwritten court records from the 1800s to discover information about their ancestors.

_____ **5.** Third-grade language arts students visit a museum's dinosaur exhibit to gain inspiration for creative story writing.

_____ **6.** Students view and compare short scenes of a typical school day for children from Taiwan, Germany, Ethiopia, Peru, and the United States.

Multimedia systems can be difficult to operate, and you want to make certain that everything will work when you are ready to use it.

▶ Use a display technology (computer monitors and/or projection systems) that is appropriate for the number of students. Be sure that all students can see projected computer images.

▶ Install and test all software in advance of the presentation.

▶ Run the software from the hard drive rather than from floppy disk, if possible. The computer program will respond more quickly.

▶ Encourage student participation through questioning and having students decide next steps.

Addressing the Standards

NETS Connection

A focus within several of the National Educational Technology Standards (NETS I, III, IV, and V) is for teachers to be able to ***promote creativity and facilitate academic learning through the use of technology.*** Taking that into consideration, imagine the following. You have asked two groups of middle school students to produce a short two-page paper on something they found of interest after they visit a local zoo or park. However, with one of the groups you provide each student with a digital camera and instructions and encouragement on how to incorporate the pictures within his/her report. Will there be a difference in what is reported and the quality of the reports? Does the technology allow the students to explore new avenues of being creative and perhaps find other ways to view the world? If it does, will this be academically beneficial or more of a distraction?

As you consider these questions, note your thoughts as a journal entry. Then expand that entry to other forms of media. For example, what about creativity and the use of a digital video camera, software to edit the video, and production and presentation software to incorporate the video within some type of presentation. This is a huge amount of work beyond reporting on basic facts of a field trip. Would it be worth the effort? In what cases would it be and in which cases would it not be worthwhile?

WHICH MEDIUM?

A decision you must make is which instructional medium or media to use. You are now familiar with six types of media: text, visuals, audio video, real objects and models, and multimedia. To make a good decision about the type of medium to use, you must know the advantages and limitations of each. Table 7–1 presents the main advantages and limitations of the media described in this chapter. These advantages and limitations provide your foundation for choosing which medium or media to use in a particular lesson.

As with instructional methods, we have compiled the advantages of the various media into a checklist, shown in Figure 7–8, that may facilitate your selection of the appropriate media for any particular lesson.

Selecting the appropriate materials for instruction is an important process.

TABLE 7–1   *Advantages and Limitations of Instructional Media*

Instructional Medium	Advantages	Limitations
Text	*Readily available.* Printed materials are readily available in a range of topics and formats. *Flexible.* Printed materials may be used in any lighted environment. They are portable. Properly designed text organizes the content and is very user friendly. *Economical.* Text can be used again and again by many students.	*Reading level of learners.* Many students are nonreaders or poor readers. *Memorization.* Some critics say textbooks promote memorization rather than higher-level thinking skills. *Passive.* Others contend that text promotes solitary learning rather than cooperative group processes. Textbooks may be used to dictate the curriculum rather than to support it.
Visuals **Printed Visuals**	*Realistic format.* Visuals provide a representation of verbal information. *Readily available.* Visuals are readily available in books, magazines, newspapers, catalogs, and calendars. *Easy to use.* Visuals are easy to use because they do not require any equipment. *Relatively inexpensive.* Most visuals can be obtained at little or no cost.	*Size.* Some visuals are simply too small to use with a large group and enlarging can be expensive. However, a document camera can project an enlarged image before a class. *Two-dimensional.* Visuals lack the three-dimensionality of the real object or scene. However, providing a series of visuals of the same object or scene from several different angles can address this limitation. *Lack of motion.* Visuals are static and cannot show motion. However, a series of sequential still pictures can suggest motion.
Projected Visuals	*Versatility.* The overhead can be used in normal room lighting. The projector is operated from the front of the room, with the presenter facing the audience and maintaining eye contact. All projectors are simple to operate. *Instructor control.* The presenter can manipulate projected materials, pointing to important items, highlighting them, and adding details with colored pens or covering part of the message and progressively revealing information. *Instructor preparation.* Teachers can easily prepare their own transparencies in advance for presentation at the proper time.	*Instructor dependent.* The overhead projector cannot be programmed to display information by itself. The overhead system does not lend itself to independent study. The projection system is designed for large-group presentation. *Preparation required.* Printed materials and other nontransparent items, such as magazine illustrations, cannot be projected immediately but must first be made into transparencies. This can be done using color copying machines.

TABLE 7–1 *Continued*

Instructional Medium	Advantages	Limitations
Displayed Visuals	*Versatile.* Both students and teachers can use display boards for a variety of purposes. *Colorful.* Display boards provide color and add interest to classrooms or hallways. *Involvement.* Students can benefit from designing and using display boards.	*Commonplace.* Instructors often neglect to give display boards the attention and respect they deserve as instructional devices. Displays can quickly lose their effectiveness if left in place too long. *Not portable.* Most display boards are not movable.
Audio **Audiotapes**	*Student and teacher preparation.* Students and teachers can record their own tapes easily and economically, erasing and reusing them when material becomes outdated or no longer useful. *Familiarity.* Most students and teachers have been using audiocassette recorders since they were very young. *Verbal message.* Students who cannot read can learn from audio media. Audio can provide basic language experiences for students whose native language is not English. *Stimulating.* Audio media can provide a stimulating alternative to reading and listening to the teacher. Audio can present verbal messages more dramatically than can text. *Portable.* Audiocassette recorders are very portable and can even be used "in the field" with battery power. Cassette recordings are ideal for home study since many students have their own cassette players.	*Fixed sequence.* Audiotapes fix the sequence of a presentation, even though it is possible to rewind or advance the tape to a desired portion. It is difficult to scan audio materials as you would printed text. *Lack of attention.* Students' attention may wander while they are listening to audiotapes. They may hear the message but not listen to or comprehend it. *Pacing.* Presenting information at the appropriate pace can be difficult for students with a range of skills and background experiences. *Accidental erasure.* Just as audiotapes can be quickly and easily erased when no longer needed, they can be accidentally erased when they should be saved.
CD	*Locating selections.* Students and teachers can quickly locate selections on CDs and can program machines to play any desired sequence. Information can be selectively retrieved by students or programmed by the teacher. *Resistance to damage.* There are no grooves to scratch or tape to tangle and break. Stains can be washed off and ordinary scratches do not affect playback.	*Cost.* The cost of CD players has limited their acceptance in the education market. *Limited recording capability.* Students and teachers cannot produce their own CDs as cheaply and easily as they can cassettes.
Video **Videotape**	*Motion.* Moving images can effectively portray procedures (such as tying knots or operating a potter's wheel) in which motion is essential. Operations, such as science experiments, in which sequential movement is critical can be shown more effectively by means of videotape. *Real-life experiences.* Video allows learners to observe phenomena that might be dangerous to view directly—an eclipse of the sun, a volcanic eruption, or warfare. *Repetition.* Research indicates that mastery of physical skills requires repeated observation and practice. Video allows repeated viewing of a performance for emulation.	*Fixed pace.* Videotape programs run at a fixed pace; some viewers are likely to fall behind, while others are waiting impatiently for the next point. *Scheduling.* Teachers normally must order videos well in advance of their intended use. Arrangements also have to be made for the proper equipment to be available. The complexity of the logistics discourages some teachers.

(continued)

TABLE 7–1 *Continued*

Instructional Medium	Advantages	Limitations
DVD	*Storage capacity.* Each disc holds two to eight hours of full-motion video. *High-quality audio.* The audio is high fidelity, comparable to that on a compact disc. *Digital format.* Because DVD is a digital medium, it is directly computer compatible.	*Limited materials.* At this time limited educational materials are available. *Few playback units available.* Many schools have few, if any, DVD players or player-equipped computers.
Real Objects and Models	*Less abstract and more concrete.* Real objects and models provide hands-on learning experiences and emphasize real-world applications. *Readily available.* Materials are readily available in the environment, around school, and in the home. *Attract students' attention.* Students respond positively to both real objects and their models.	*Storage.* Large objects can pose special problems. Caring for living materials such as plants and animals can take a lot of time. *Possible damage.* Materials are often complex and fragile. Parts may be lost or broken.
Multimedia	*Better learning and retention.* Interactive multimedia provides multiple learning modalities and actively involves learners. *Addresses different learning styles and preferences.* The incorporation of multiple modalities provides opportunities for teaching individual learners. For example, those with weak reading skills can use aural and visual skills to process verbal information. *Effectiveness across learning domains.* Interactive multimedia instruction has been shown to be effective in all learning domains. It can be used for psychomotor training, such as learning CPR techniques; to present simulations that provide opportunities for problem-solving and higher-order thinking skills; and even to address affective components of learning. *Realism.* Interactive multimedia provides a high degree of realism. Instead of merely reading about a speech by Dr. Martin Luther King, Jr., students can actually see and hear the speech as he originally gave it. *Motivation.* Learners show consistently positive attitudes toward interactive multimedia. For today's MTV-conscious youth, multimedia instruction represents a natural avenue for exploring the information revolution. *Interactivity.* The key element of computers is interaction with the user. The computer can present information, elicit the learner's response, and evaluate the response. *Individualization.* The computer's branching capabilities allow instruction to be tailored to the individual. The computer can provide immediate feedback and monitor the learner's performance. *Consistency.* Individualization results in different instructional paths for different learners. But it can be equally important to ensure that specific topics are dealt with in the same way for all learners. *Learner control.* Computers can give the user control of both the pace and the sequencing of instruction. Fast learners can speed through the program, while slower learners can take as much time as they need.	*Equipment requirements.* The equipment requirements for multimedia can be an impediment. While basic systems may involve only the computer and its built-in components, more complex systems may involve external DVD players, CD-ROM players, audio speakers, and so on. These can be difficult to hook up and maintain. *Startup costs.* Startup costs can be high. The computer itself can be expensive. Adding components and software may cost thousands of dollars. *Complexity and lack of standardization.* Interactive multimedia systems can be quite complex. Sometimes it is a challenge just to get the individual components to work together. Novices may become hopelessly lost. This is complicated by the fact that there is currently little standardization today in many facets of multimedia. *Compatibility.* The lack of compatibility among the various brands of personal computers limits multimedia transportability. Developers cannot always create a single package that will work across all types of computers. *Limited intelligence.* Most computer software is limited in its capacity for genuine interaction with the learner, and often relies on simple multiple-choice or true-false questions.

Check It Out

Media Selection

As practice, look over each of the following three scenarios. Decide what would be the best medium/media for each situation. Then answer the following questions: What were the reasons you used to make your selections? Did you identify any potential problems with your selections? If so, what would those problems be? What other media could you also have selected? Under what conditions would you switch to those alternatives?

▶ *Scenario A:* The sixth-grade concert band instructor, Mr. Snyder, has decided that his students need to better discriminate between sharps, flats, and natural notes on the musical scale. He has 56 students currently in his band, and the instruction will take place in the band room, which is large enough to seat approximately 125 individuals.

▶ *Scenario B:* The instructor of an advanced survival training course needs to teach the six participants how to recognize edible versus nonedible desert plants found in the southwestern United States. Even though the course involves training for *desert* survival, it is being taught at a small college in Ohio.

▶ *Scenario C:* Mrs. Spence and her class of 25 tenth-grade students have been studying a unit on developing critical-thinking skills. One section of the content focuses on methods used to solve ill-defined problems and Mrs. Spence has decided that she wants to give the students practice using the different techniques they are studying.

To help you understand how factors such as the students, objectives, and learning environment might affect your choice of medium/media in these scenarios, consider how your selections would change if the following aspects were different:

▶ *Scenario A:* Instead of being a band director, Mr. Snyder is a private flute teacher with 12 students of different ages who all come at different times during the day for individualized instruction. His goal is still to have the students increase their ability to discriminate between flats, sharps, and natural notes.

▶ *Scenario B:* The survival course takes place at the University of Nevada, Las Vegas, within minutes from large sections of desert.

▶ *Scenario C:* The focus of Mrs. Spence's class changes from being able to *apply* the problem-solving techniques to simply understanding them.

Check It Out

Kevin Spencer's Lesson Plan

1. Refer to Teacher Resource B on page 299. This teacher resource describes the instructional plan Mr. Spencer has developed for his sixth-grade social studies class.
2. Refer again to the Technology Coordinator's Corner for this chapter.
3. If Lizzy and Sally, the two ninth-grade multimedia developers, were asked by Mr. Spencer to review his lesson plan, do you think they might suggest some types of changes in the use of media within his plan? What parts do you think they would agree with? What types of suggestions do you think they would make regarding the use of media? How do you think they could justify their recommendations?

TECHNOLOGY COORDINATOR'S CORNER

There were a couple of students waiting for Jim Barrows as he approached his office. Sally and Lizzy were both ninth-graders and they explained to Mr. Barrows that they were working on a geography project together. Their assignment was to complete some research on a selected topic related to Africa and present it to their class. Almost all in their class were planning on making their presentation by verbally reading their reports. Sally explained that she found it really difficult to sit and listen to one oral presentation after another. They hoped to find a different way to present their project that might be more interesting and enjoyable for everyone.

Jim asked if they had ever thought about using some type of multimedia for their presentation. For example, using their topic of "Animals and Plants of the Serengeti" they could do all kinds of things. They could use either Windows *Movie Maker* or Apple *iMovie* and create short movies about their topic. They could integrate pictures from books, video from Internet sites, and even videos of themselves exploring the nearby zoo for the animals native to the Serengeti. With the software they could put the clips together, add titles, transitions between the segments, narration, and even add traditional African music in the background. Yes, it would be some additional work—but Mr. Barrows promised them that it would be worth it. They not only would have to do research on the content of the program, but would need to learn what it takes to design a successful instructional program, how to sequence the information, and how to write narration that actually makes sense. In addition, they would learn about shooting video and how to use editing software. He suggested a schedule of things that they needed to do and outlined a project plan of when he could meet with them to go over their progress and help to show them the software and technology they would be using. Although it was a bit overwhelming at first, Sally and Lizzy soon found that they could produce a successful project.

It wasn't long before other students were asking for help in deciding what types of multimedia projects they should be involved with. In many cases, Lizzy and Sally found themselves serving as consultants as they provided direction and help for other such projects.

Which Media Should I Choose?

As you begin planning your instruction, it is important to select a medium that will enhance your topic. The Media Selection Checklist will help you in the process.

Each type of media has a set of advantages (e.g., motion, realism) and a set of educational limitations (e.g., room size, group size). These specifications are listed in the first column of the table on the next page. There are seven columns next to the specifications. Place a √ in all the white spaces that best describe your instructional needs (or situations).

For Example

If it is important that you draw or write key words during your presentation, go to items #7 on the table (on next page) and put "√s" in the three columns to the right that are white. Continue the process for each requirement or item that best describes your instructional situation (needs). When you have gone through the entire table, determine which column has the most "√s" entered in the white spaces in the column. Select the media that has the most "√s".

If most of the "√s" are in:	Select the following media format:
T	Text (handouts, books, computer screen)
V-Print	Visuals-printed (graphics, photos, charts, diagrams)
V-Prj	Visuals-projected (overhead transparencies, *PowerPoint*-type slides)
A	Audio (tape, CD)
Vid	Video (DVD, tape, television)
RO	Real objects and models
MM/CS	Multimedia and other computer software

It is possible that you will have more than one column with most of the white spaces filled in. In that case you will need to choose which medium is best or consider using multiple media formats in your presentation.

FIGURE 7–8 Media selection checklist.

Media Selection Checklist

Student learning will be enhanced by media that:	T	V-Print	V-Prj	A	Vid	RO	MM/CS
1. Enable students to see and/or touch actual objects	▪	▪	▪	▪	▪		▪
2. Allow materials to be taken from the classroom	▪	▪	▪	▪	▪		▪
3. Can be used after the lesson as a reference, guide, or job aid		▪	▪	▪	▪	▪	▪
4. Allow several participants to respond simultaneously		▪	▪	▪	▪	▪	▪
5. Can be easily erased/modified		▪		▪	▪	▪	▪
6. Require minimal expense		▪	▪	▪	▪	▪	▪
7. Allow one to draw or write key words during the lesson		▪		▪	▪	▪	▪
8. Are appropriate for a small group (under 25)	▪		▪	▪	▪		▪
9. Use visuals that are easy to prepare		▪	▪	▪	▪	▪	▪
10. Allow advanced preparation of the visuals		▪	▪	▪		▪	▪
11. Present word cues or a lesson outline		▪	▪	▪	▪	▪	▪
12. Provide portability	▪	▪	▪	▪	▪	▪	▪
13. Offer commercially prepared visuals	▪	▪	▪	▪	▪		▪
14. Allow the order of the material to be easily changed	▪	▪	▪	▪	▪		▪
15. Allow the user to control pacing and/or to replay a portion of the presentation	▪	▪	▪	▪		▪	▪
16. Are appropriate for students who have difficulty reading or understanding English	▪		▪		▪	▪	▪
17. Reproduce an exact sound	▪	▪	▪	▪	▪	▪	▪
18. Are easily used by teachers or students	▪	▪	▪	▪	▪	▪	▪
19. Present high-quality, realistic images (color/graphics/illustrations/visuals)	▪		▪	▪	▪	▪	▪
20. Can be used independently of the instructor		▪	▪	▪	▪	▪	▪
21. Show motion, including sequential motion	▪	▪	▪	▪	▪	▪	▪
22. Allow observation of dangerous process; real-life reenactments	▪	▪	▪	▪	▪	▪	▪
23. Provide a discovery learning environment	▪	▪	▪	▪	▪	▪	▪
24. Present problem-solving situations that lead to group discussions	▪	▪	▪	▪	▪	▪	▪
25. Shape personal and social attitudes	▪	▪	▪	▪	▪	▪	▪

Adapted from © Claranne K. English, 1995 with permission.

FIGURE 7–8 *Continued*

SUMMARY

In this chapter you learned to complete an instructional plan by selecting instructional media that will match your students, objectives, learning environment, and instructional activities. We looked at the advantages and limitations of various media and introduced the media selection checklist.

SUGGESTED RESOURCES

 CD Resources

To increase retention and transfer of this information, review the *Reflective Questions and Activities* located in the Chapter 7 section (**Chapter info and activities>>>Chapter 7>>> Reflective Questions and Activities**) of the text's accompanying CD.

In addition, you can access media preview forms, tutorials on how to develop *PowerPoint* slides, relevant Internet websites, NETS Connection exercises, and direct e-mail access to the text's authors.

Website Resources

Access the text's website (**www.prenhall.com/Newby**), navigate to Chapter 7, and review the Question and Answer section for relevant questions that have been generated by students and answered by the authors. You may also submit your own questions directly to the authors. In addition, you can access presentations by the authors about this chapter and gain insights directly from them about the topics that have been presented.

Print Resources

Fleming, M., & Levie, W. H. (Eds.) (1993). *Instructional message design: Principles from the behavioral and cognitive sciences* (2nd ed.). Englewood Cliffs, NJ: Educational Technology.

Forcier, R. C., & Descy, D. E. (2005). *The computer as an educational tool: Productivity and problem solving* (4th ed.). Upper Saddle River, NJ: Merrill/Prentice Hall.

Kearny, L. (1996). *Graphics for presenters: Getting your ideas across.* Menlo Park, CA: Crisp.

Lever-Duffy, Judy, McDonald, Jean B., & Mizell, AI. P. (2005). *Teaching and learning with technology* (2nd ed.). Boston: Allyn & Bacon.

Moore, D. M., & Dwyer, F. M. (Eds.) (1994). *Visual literacy: A spectrum of visual learning.* Englewood Cliffs, NJ: Educational Technology.

Robyler, M. D., & Edwards, J. (2000). *Integrating educational technology into teaching* (2nd ed). Upper Saddle River, NJ: Prentice Hall.

Seamon, Mary Ploski, & Levitt, Eric J. (2003). *Digital cameras in the classroom.* Worthington, OH: Linworth.

Smaldino, S. E., Russell, J. D., Heinich, R., & Molenda, M. (2005). *Instructional technology and media for learning* (8th ed.). Upper Saddle River, NJ: Pearson.

Volker, R., & Simonson, M. (1995). *Technology for teachers.* Dubuque, IA: Kendall/Hunt.

Electronic Resources

http://online.fsu.edu/learningresources/ handbook/instructionatfsu/
Instructional media: Chalkboards to videos (chap. 9). (2004). Retrieved September 27, 2004, from Florida State University, Office for Distributed & Distance Learning website.

ANSWERS TO ✓ CHECK IT OUT: MEDIA IDENTIFICATION

1. Audio
2. Multimedia
3. Graphics
4. Text
5. Real objects and models
6. Video

8

Technology and Instructional Material Selection, Adaptation, and Creation

KEY WORDS AND CONCEPTS

Instructional materials
Formative evaluation
Copyright
Public domain
Fair use

CHAPTER OBJECTIVES

After reading and studying this chapter, you will be able to:

▶ Distinguish among the concepts of method, medium, and materials.
▶ Select the most appropriate instructional materials for a particular lesson.
▶ Identify sources of existing instructional materials.
▶ Select, modify, or design instructional materials for a particular lesson.
▶ Outline a procedure for acquiring computer software.
▶ Acquire instructional materials in a manner consistent with current copyright law.

INTRODUCTION

Imagine that you are the costume director for a high school's drama department. Each year the school puts on a winter play and a major spring musical. In each case, a unique set of costumes is required for those playing the various roles. Your job is to make sure that all costumes are suitable for the current production, that they fit appropriately, allow for the required movements and costume changes, and that their total cost is within the production's budget.

In order to accomplish your job, you need to ask two sets of key questions.

First set:

a. What types of costumes will match the needs of the production?
b. What special needs/requirements of each actor/actress should be considered (e.g., role of the character, size of each participant)?
c. What will the acts and scenes dictate that will impact the use of the costumes (e.g., movements that will require extra flexibility, rapid costume changes)?

Second set:

a. What costumes do we already have that will work for this production?
b. Do we currently have costumes that might be able to work if we can alter them appropriately?
c. What costumes will definitely need to be created?

The first group of questions focuses on the objectives of the production, as well as considerations for the actors and actresses and the stage/scene environment. The second set of questions focus on practical aspects of finding, adapting, and creating needed costumes given the budget constraints. All experienced costume directors know that answers to both sets of questions are critical for the success of the overall production.

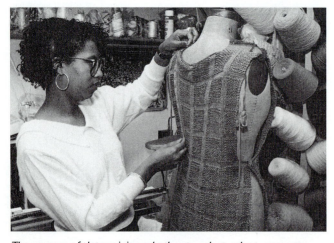

The process of determining whether to select, adapt, or create costumes for a drama production can be compared to the process teachers use to obtain needed instructional materials.

The design and development of instruction requires the teacher to seek answers to similar questions. In order to effectively select and use proper instructional materials, the goal and objectives of the lesson, as well as the needs of the learners and the demands of the learning environment, must be clearly understood. In addition, just as there are practical constraints (e.g., budgets for time and money) placed on the costume director, those same types of constraints are always found within education and the development of the learning experience. As the teacher goes about developing the learning experience, specific instructional materials will be needed to accomplish the desired learning. Those materials may already be available and can be used in their current format. However, in some cases, the available materials may only work by adapting them in some fashion. In still other situations, the materials may not exist in any available form and must then be created. As with the costume director, creating is much more expensive in time and cost than using what is already available.

Within this chapter we are going to finish the planning and development process. That will require us to look closely at the learning plan that was outlined in Chapter 5 and what was added in terms of methods and media in Chapters 6 and 7, respectively. We again add a piece to the puzzle as shown in Figure 8–1. This puzzle piece represents the need to add "meat" to the plan by identifying and including the proper instructional materials. To do so we must fully understand the objectives of the learning plan, the characteristics and needs of the learners, and the environment in which the learning will occur. Moreover, we must consider what is already available, how it can be identified and accessed, how it may need to be adapted,

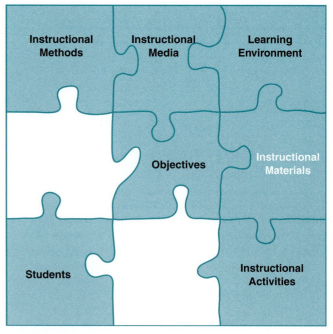

FIGURE 8–1 Instructional materials as another piece of the instructional planning puzzle.

and if additional materials will be required. In addition, we also need to evaluate the materials to make sure they accomplish what the plan has envisioned.

INSTRUCTIONAL MATERIALS

Instructional materials are the specific items experienced by students within a lesson that influence their learning. For example, a lesson for lower-elementary students may focus on learning simple addition problems. To accomplish this, a computer software program may be utilized that allows students to repeatedly experience the presentation of practice problems, generate a response to those problems, and receive feedback. The specific math problems and feedback experienced by the students on this software are the instructional materials. Another example would be the chapter that you are currently reading. These instructional materials consist of the written information and exercises found on these pages. The design and use of instructional materials is critical because it is the interaction of the student with those materials that generates and reinforces actual learning. If the materials are weak, improperly structured or sequenced in a poor manner, limited learning will occur. Powerful, well-designed instructional materials are experienced in such a way that they can be readily encoded, retained, recalled, and used in a variety of ways. These materials will be what the learners will remember and they must be created, integrated, and presented in a manner that allows them to have the needed impact.

INSTRUCTIONAL MATERIALS, METHODS, AND MEDIA: HOW THEY WORK TOGETHER TO ENSURE LEARNING

For an effective learning experience to occur, instructional materials, media, and methods work together in a coordinated manner. For example, instructional materials may be delivered and experienced by the student via a number of different media (see Chapter 7). In one case, part or all of a set of instructional materials may be experienced by viewing a video, whereas, in another case, part of the materials may be experienced by reading a text, viewing a graphic, or even listening to an audio CD. Combining several media formats together is often required in order for a set of instructional materials to be effectively experienced by the learners.

In addition to media, various instructional methods (e.g., cooperative groups, drill and practice, simulations, discussions; see Chapter 6) are incorporated within a lesson in order to adapt to levels of needed interactivity, size of the target group of learners, the learning environment, and so on. For example, in one instance, instructional materials may be needed as prerequisite information in order for a discussion to be successfully accomplished; whereas, in a different situation, the effectiveness of the instructional materials may be enhanced by providing the materials within a structured tutorial method.

Learners and learning situations can vary quite considerably. Consistent, meaningful learning requires well-designed instructional materials that are presented in a clear, motivating, and understandable manner. Integration and use of correctly selected and coordinated media and methods ensure that the materials impact students in the most effective, efficient, and appealing way.

Review the following classroom learning situation. Note how the methods, media, and materials are integrated to produce the final learning experience.

Mr. Hughes wants to teach sentence structure to his eighth-grade English class, which meets right before lunch. He decides to use a game to make the topic interesting and to give his students a chance to practice their skills and receive feedback. Not able to find any instructional materials in his school, he decides to design his own board game in which students roll dice, draw a card, and advance if they can correctly identify the part of a sentence highlighted on the card.

Within this situation, the instructional *materials* are the content and exercises found on the individual cards within the game. This is the focus of the overall learning task. In order to deliver this in an interesting and appealing way, a game *method* was employed with rules and directions on how to advance and compete. Real objects in the form of a tangible game board and dice were the *media* used to deliver the instructional experience to the learners.

WHEN AND WHERE ARE INSTRUCTIONAL MATERIALS INCLUDED WITHIN THE LEARNING PLAN?

As shown within the example learning plan in Teacher Resource B on page 299, the learning consists of a number of key activities—each of which plays a role in what the student experiences and what ultimately the student learns. Although not all lessons have each of these activities, a majority of the elements are found within most effective learning experiences. You can incorporate instructional materials throughout these lesson activities outlined in your plan, from the motivation component through the evaluation activities. For example, if you were designing a physics lesson on the characteristics of light, you may have several components of the lesson that require instructional materials. Note that each set of instructional materials may be presented via a number of different media and integrated within a variety of instructional methods:

▶ *Motivation lesson activity.* Gain attention for the topic with instructional materials that illustrate the behavior of light given different environmental situations.

Check It Out

Materials, Methods, and Media

Read the following situation and answer the questions that follow:

Ms. Roth, a fifth-grade teacher in the Midwest, wants to increase her students' awareness of the ways in which living things affect each other. She recently discovered software of a simulation titled *A Field Trip into the Sea* in the school library media center. After previewing it, she decided it matches the characteristics of her students and teaches the desired content. She is sure the software will motivate her students to develop an awareness of living things they have not seen.

▶ What constitutes the instructional materials that Ms. Roth's students will experience during this lesson?

▶ What principal instructional method is Ms. Roth going to use by implementing *A Field Trip into the Sea* software with her students?

▶ What is the primary medium that will deliver the instructional materials to the students?

▶ Could the students in Ms. Roth's class increase their understanding of the instructional materials if other instructional methods (e.g., discussions, cooperative groups, discovery learning) are included as additional parts to the overall lesson?

▶ What is the value of knowing a variety of methods and media and how they can be used with various types of instructional materials?

▶ *Orientation lesson activity.* Materials may be incorporated to focus on identifying and explaining the learning goals for the lesson.

▶ *Information lesson activity.* Instructional materials may provide key points on how light can be reflected, or refracted, as well as give students experience in achieving different results working with various types of light sources.

▶ *Application lesson activity.* Materials provide guidance and instruction on how to manipulate and use various forms of lenses, mirrors, prisms, and lasers to solve a variety of problems involving light.

▶ *Evaluation lesson activity.* Materials may help students question their abilities, ask self-reflective questions, and look for ways to improve how they approach problems and attempt solutions.

DETERMINING THE VALUE OF INSTRUCTIONAL MATERIALS

Selecting and/or creating proper instructional materials should be based on several criteria. These criteria allow us to determine if the materials will actually accomplish what they are intended to do, for the right group of students, under the restraints of the given time and cost elements. Table 8–1 highlights a set of key criteria to use when considering the selection and/or creation of instructional materials.

As an example of using these selection criteria, refer back to the example of Ms. Roth (in Check It Out above) and her instructional materials that involved the use of software simulation of ocean life. Before she selected that piece of software, she had to determine what she needed and if the selected software would deliver what she desired. To do so, she first needed to examine

the overall objectives of the lesson and determine if what was offered by the software would actually help her to accomplish those objectives. If there was little or no match between the software materials and her objectives, she should have dismissed the software outright and continued to search for more relevant materials. Second, once she found some materials that matched her objectives, she needed to make sure that those materials would work well with her particular students. A critical criterion in this case would be if the language level within the instructional materials matched with what her students could understand. Additionally, was the material something that wasn't a total repetition with something they already knew—but yet wasn't so far ahead of their level of understanding that they would not be able to grasp what it was explaining? Third, she needed to consider where the selected instructional materials would be used. Would the learning environment be conducive to students learning the material? In her case, if she didn't have access to a computer or computer lab, how effective would the software materials actually be? Finally, one should always consider time and cost of the materials. You can have a wonderful set of instructional materials, but if they take too long to use or they cost too much money to obtain, then they cannot be used.

There are three important things you should consider when thinking about such criteria. First, generally perfect matches between instructional materials and this set of criteria will not exist. Some will come closer than others, but there will always be some mismatches. In some cases, the instructional materials may be found to be acceptable with some slight modifications at certain points. Second, there will be times when you find powerful instructional materials that you know will positively impact your students; however, they may not match your

TABLE 8–1   *Criteria for Selecting and/or Creating Instructional Materials*

Criteria	Questions to Consider:
Objectives	• What are the learning objectives for this lesson?
	• What types of learning are required (e.g., problem solving, concept learning, rote memorization)?
	• What level of cognitive demand will be placed on the students?
	• In what sequence should the content be presented?
Students	• What are their general characteristics (e.g., age, grade level, socioeconomic status, previous experience, special needs)?
	• What specific knowledge or skills do they already possess?
	• What are their learning styles and preferences?
	• How many students will participate in the learning experience?
Learning environment	• How large is the space?
	• What distractions could there be?
	• What types of technology are available/accessible?
Available resources	• What resources do you have at your disposal (including materials, equipment, funds)?
	• What constraints are there on what you can do?
	• How much time is there to produce the materials?
	• How much time is there to prepare and utilize the materials?

current learning objectives. In such a case, you may find yourself adapting your objectives in order to effectively incorporate the instructional materials. Finally, watch out for slick packaging of instructional materials. Make sure you look closely at the content and not get lost in the glitz and shine of the color pages, the bells and whistles of the program, and so on. First and foremost, make sure it has sound content.

WHERE DO WE ACQUIRE INSTRUCTIONAL MATERIALS?

In the opening paragraphs of this chapter, the job of a costume director for a school musical was described. One major role of the costume director is to acquire the proper costumes for the actors and actresses. As explained at that point, the job is relatively easy and the cost is minimal if one can go to the school's storehouse of costumes and select the needed type and size of costume from an already existing inventory. However, for most high schools and local civic playhouses, the wardrobe inventory is very small. In such a case, the next alternative is either to borrow what is needed or to use what one has access to and adapt it to fit the style and/or needed size. This alternative is more time-consuming and generally more expensive than the first alternative. Finally, if all else fails, the costume director may be left with creating specific costumes. This is, by far, the most expensive in terms of both time and overall monetary cost.

These alternatives are similar to what is faced by individuals seeking proper instructional materials. In some cases, the materials are close at hand and are readily available; in other cases, materials can be used but there is a need to adapt the originals. Finally, there are times when the only thing that works is to actually create the materials. Although each alternative has its drawbacks, each also offers some interesting learning possibilities.

Selecting Existing Instructional Materials

As we noted at the beginning of the chapter, the simplest, most cost-effective way to incorporate instructional materials into a lesson is to use existing materials. Locating and selecting instructional materials involve the following steps:

1. *Determine needs.* What are you trying to accomplish? What needs might specific instructional materials address?

2. *Check a variety of sources.* There are a number of sources for instructional materials. Refer to the "Toolbox Techniques: Locating Relevant Instructional Materials" found in this chapter for several important ways to access relevant materials.

3. *Obtain and preview the materials.* Always preview all materials before using them to be certain they meet your needs and your students' needs. Go to the text's accompanying CD and access the preview forms **(Chapter info and activities >>> Chapter 7 >>> Media Preview Forms),** with which you can evaluate a single set of materials or compare two sets of materials.

Addressing the Standards

NETS Connection

Several National Educational Technology Standards (NETS I, IV, and V) emphasize, in part, that teachers should be able to *locate, collect, and evaluate information from a variety of sources using technology.* Read and review these standards and their performance indicators (see Teacher Resource A on page 297 for a full listing) and then complete the following:

▶ Create a simple Web search primer that will help you (and your students) use this technology more effectively in order to access needed instructional materials.
▶ Brainstorm potential things that should be listed within the primer (e.g., how to generate reliable search terms, the best advanced search techniques for your selected search engine, alternative search engine(s), tutorials to assist in Web searches and the evaluation of Web materials, etc.).
▶ Complete a search for two different sets of instructional materials. As you complete the searches, determine what additional information should be included within the primer and attempt to list those steps that you find helpful. Keep this primer close at hand and revise it as you attempt to locate, collect, and evaluate the materials that you need.

4. *Try out the materials with students.* How well do they like the materials? How effectively do the materials help them learn?
5. *Compare any competing materials.* If you have located more than one set of applicable materials, repeat the preview and tryout process to compare their effectiveness and appeal to students.
6. *Make your selection.* Use the information you have gathered to select the instructional materials that you think will work best in your situation.

7. *Keep accurate records.* After you have chosen materials, make sure you follow up on their effectiveness. By keeping records you also can determine how effective the materials could be in other lessons.

If the content of the instructional materials you find doesn't match the objectives of your instructional plan, you have two alternatives: (1) modify the materials so they do meet your objectives, or (2) create new instructional materials. We discuss these options in the next two sections.

TOOLBOX

TECHNIQUES

Locating Relevant Instructional Materials

Literally thousands of instructional materials are available to use in various learning situations—if one can locate them. In some cases, gaining ready access to these materials is not difficult if you actually have an idea of where they can be found. Some suggestions to help in your search are:

At school: Most schools maintain a computer database in the school library or media center. Some school districts also maintain a central collection of instructional materials. In addition, districts sometimes combine their resources to form a regional media center or service center housing a collection of instructional materials.

In the neighborhood: Many local libraries (including school libraries) supply not only books but other forms of instructional materials to those who visit. In many cases, those materials are accessible online.

On the Internet:

a. The World Wide Web can be a valuable source of instructional materials. In addition, Table 8–2 provides a number of popular teacher websites that contain downloadable instructional materials for various activities. Use of a general search engine should generate results when using the search terms "instructional materials" and your area of interest (e.g., "science").

b. Many museums and libraries have large collections of instructional materials. Searches of the websites for the Smithsonian museum, the Museum of Science and Industry, the Library of Congress, and so on will find significant portions of the sites devoted to education and provide ways for teachers to access and use their instructional materials when teaching a variety of different subject content and activities. For example, visiting the Smithsonian site (http://www.si.edu/) you will find a link to their teacher's site. In this location you can find all types of lesson plans linked to materials and activities associated with items within their museum.

c. Several comprehensive databases are available through which you can locate instructional materials. *A-V Online,* for example, is an automated index of commercially available materials. With it, you can locate the distribution sources for thousands of educational, informational, and documentary materials recorded in a variety of media formats. The database covers a range of subject areas at grade levels from preschool to graduate and professional school. *A-V Online* is continually being updated based on information from producer and distributor catalogs, the Library of Congress, media centers, and many other sources. In addition, *The Education Software Selector (TESS)* is a comprehensive database that includes information about educational software at every level, from preschool to college, in a variety of content areas. Each piece of software is described in terms of subject, learning approach, grade level, computer platform, pricing, and publisher contact. Entries include evaluation citations from educational journals, state evaluation agencies, and technology journals.

Through professional organizations: Professional meetings and trade shows held at local, state, and national levels provide opportunities to talk with vendors and other teachers to find out what is available.

Commercial vendors:

a. Most school textbook companies now include ancillary materials with their textbooks including software, workbooks, charts, lab manuals, and so forth, which can provide a wealth of additional materials to use within the classroom setting.

b. Commercial producers and distributors of instructional materials publish catalogs listing materials you can buy and, in some cases, rent. To obtain educational software, for example, use a search engine (e.g., Google) and search terms such as "Educational Software catalogs" to locate a number of websites that will list where and how to find commercial producers and distributors of materials. One such site, www.buyersindex.com, lists a huge number of commercial sites and catalogs—all online.

TABLE 8–2 *Education Websites with Instructional Materials*

Site Name	Web Address	Printable	Lesson Plan	Online Activities	Professional Development	Tools
Scholastic Teacher	http://teacher. scholastic.com/	Graphic organizers, worksheets, independent reading contracts, and many more printables to produce more effective and efficient learning.	Browse or search by subject, topic, and grade.	Interactive timelines, scholastic news, radio, and other resources for students to participate.	Tips and topics, newsletters and theories; this site has numerous links and information to assist in teacher development.	Lesson plan maker, test and quiz maker, presentation maker, website maker, and many more tools.

(continued)

TABLE 8–2 *Continued*

Site Name	Web Address	Printable	Lesson Plan	Online Activities	Professional Development	Tools
Teachers. Net	http://teachers. net/	Tons of printables ranging from calendars to check-lists, but no search function.	Browse or search by subject, topic, and grade.	Discussion board and chat functions for teachers.	Monthly news-letters concern-ing educa-tional practices.	No tools.
Houghton-Mifflin Education Place	http://www. eduplace.com/	Graphic organizers in PDF format and many other helpful activities that align to their textbooks, but can be used by any teacher.	There are excellent monthly aligned units with lesson plans and links. These are browsable.	Educational games are included in this section. Online activities are limited in topics, but provide quizzes, discussion boards, and more.	Difficult to find, although there are some.	No tools to use.
Web for Teachers	http://www. 4teachers.org/	There are no ready-made printables for teachers to use, but the tools provide teachers with their own customized printables.	Excellent lesson plans searchable by topic. They provide loads of good links to content information and innovative ideas.	The interaction for students is provided through the online and collaboration format.	There are num-erous links to websites and articles that will aid in profes-sional develop-ment questions the teacher may have.	Amazing tools rang-ing from RubiStar, Assign-A-Day, Quiz-Star, Web Worksheet Wizard, and many more!
Discovery Learning	http://school. discovery.com/	The tools allow you to create some custom printables.	This website does not provide many lesson plans, but they are searchable.	Short videos, quizzes, and brief educational games are provided.	There is more information on the Kathy Schrock section of this website. However, this is difficult to find and unless you know the link, there is no link from the home page.	Tools include puzzle maker, lesson planner, quiz cen-ter, and worksheet generator.
ABC Teach	http://abcteach. com/	This site is primarily made up of printables.				
Teachnology	http://www. teachnology.com/	There are a few common printables for teachers available.	Searchable lesson plans, although most lesson plans are links to outside websites.	There are some games for students, but many are not educational.	Tutorials, message boards, and different teaching ideas are provided by this website.	Make your own selected work-sheets, rubrics, and graphic organizers using these tools.
A to Z Teacher Stuff	http://www. atozteacherstuff. com/	Printables are organized by themes, although limited in scope for elementary.	The lesson plans are organized by theme. They can be sorted by grade level. The themes are specific and lack breadth.	Different discussion forums are the only source of interaction.	This site does a nice job of pre-senting different topics and ideas for teachers to develop within their profession.	There are no tools to use.

TOOLBOX

TECHNIQUES

Software Evaluation and Acquisition

We have examined issues related to selecting instructional materials in general and different media in particular. Here we discuss evaluating and selecting computer software.

In most school districts today, hardware decisions are centralized. An individual teacher cannot go out and select just any computer for his or her classroom. However, individual teachers often make software decisions. There is commonly an approval process that involves the technology coordinator, a technology committee, or an administrator, but software purchasing usually begins with the individual teacher. It is thus important for teachers to know how to evaluate and select software. Following are the steps involved:

1. *Determine needs.* As in any instructional activity, begin by assessing what you need. What needs might you address through the use of computer software?
2. *Specify desired software characteristics.* Your needs assessment should give you a general idea of the type of software you want. For example, if your students are having trouble adding mixed fractions, you may decide that you want a drill and practice program on this topic.
3. *Obtain or construct an evaluation form.* Many useful software evaluation forms are available from a variety of sources. We provide one in the accompanying CD **(Chapter info and activities >>>Chapter 7>>> media preview forms)**. Your school may have its own evaluation form. Alternatively, you could design one geared to your specific needs.
4. *Survey available sources of software.* Software is available from a variety of sources. Look through publishers' catalogs. Read software evaluations published in journals and magazines. Talk to your colleagues. Visit vendors' booths at professional meetings. Check collections of shareware.
5. *Obtain software for preview.* Many software companies now provide special demonstration disks for preview. Some are also providing demonstrations on CD-ROM. With these, if you like the software and buy it, the company provides you with a password that unlocks full access to the CD-ROM. Alternatively, you can often preview software via delayed-purchase-order billing. In this case, a purchase order for the product is submitted with the specification that it is for preview purposes. The vendor delays billing for a set period, usually 30 days. If you decide against purchase, simply return the software within the grace period, and the purchase order is canceled. Otherwise, keep the software, and the vendor processes the purchase order at the end of the grace period.
6. *Read the documentation.* While there is a temptation to simply jump into a software program, you should always read the documentation first. It should indicate the recommended audience for the program, and it will provide directions for how to properly use the software.
7. *Run through the software several times.* The first time you go through the software, simply concentrate on using the program correctly. How does it work? For a second pass, make certain that the software is "bombproof"; that is, make certain it doesn't fail when something unexpected happens. Purposely test for problems; if the program indicates, "Enter a number between 1 and 4," see what happens if you enter 5. Finally, run through the program with a pedagogical eye. Is the educational approach sound? Is it appealing? How does the software rate on the criteria given on the evaluation form you are using?
8. *Have students try out the program.* How do they like it? Do they learn from it?
9. *Complete the evaluation form.* Using the information gained from your review of the software, complete the evaluation form.
10. *Repeat the process for any competing products.* If you have more than one possible purchase, look at each competing product in the same way.
11. *Make your selection.* Select the desired software package. File your evaluation with the school, and be sure to enclose a copy of your evaluation with any product that is returned to the publisher.

Using a Software Evaluation Form

To really get a good idea of the value of using the preview forms, you should take the time to use several. On the accompanying CD in the folder for Chapter 8, there is a subfolder of "Software Evaluation Forms." Go to that link and launch Software Evaluation—Form A **(Chapter Info and Activities >>>Chapter 8>>>Software Evaluation Forms>>>—Form A)**. Locate a piece of educational software and evaluate it. For example, you can go to the River Deep website (www.riverdeep.com) and preview their educational software (note that you could also do a Web search using the term "educational software demo" and find other sites that will allow you to preview educational software). Using the form, check to see how easy/challenging it is to get a good idea of the value of that software. Once you have completed that, review the software again, only this time use the Software Evaluation—Form B **(Chapter Info and Activities >>>Chapter 8>>>Software Evaluation Forms>>>—Form B)** provided on the text's CD. Note the differences in the two forms. Determine what can be learned from using one and then compare that with what can be learned from using the other. Are there criteria that should be added to one or both of the forms that would make them more meaningful for your use? If the type of program changed, would a change in the criteria be needed? Although these forms were constructed for the preview and comparison of software, could they be adapted in certain ways to evaluate other forms/types of instructional materials?

Modifying Available Instructional Materials

If you cannot locate suitable materials, you may be able to modify what is available. In terms of time and cost, it is more efficient to modify available materials than to create new materials. It is also an opportunity for you to be creative. You can modify almost any type of instructional materials. For example, imagine that, for a piece of equipment being used in a middle school woodworking class, the only available visual is from a repair manual. The picture could be useful, but it contains too much detail and complex terminology for students. One possible solution would be to use the visual but modify the caption and simplify or omit some of the labels.

In another situation, the only videotape available shows a needed video sequence, but the audio is inappropriate because the vocabulary level is either too high or too low for your students. In such a case, you could show the videotape with the sound turned off and narrate it yourself. Videotapes can also be shown in segments. You can show a portion of a videotape, stop the VCR, discuss what has been presented, then continue with another short segment, followed by additional discussion.

Often, you can modify the audio portion of foreign-language materials (or English-language materials for a bilingual class). Narration can be changed from one language to another or from a more advanced rendition to a simpler one.

If you try out modified materials while they are still in more or less rough form, you can then make further modifications in response to student reactions until your materials meet their exact needs. A word of caution about modifying commercially produced materials: Be sure your handling and use of such materials does not violate copyright laws and restrictions. If you are in doubt, check with your school media specialist.

Creating New Instructional Materials

Teachers have long been known for their creative use of available tools and resources to produce instructional materials. Classrooms are usually filled with a variety of teaching materials, from concrete objects to posters, bulletin boards, and printed material of every kind. For several decades the tools for producing instructional materials changed relatively little, with typewriters and ditto machines doing the bulk of the work. But times have changed.

Photocopying machines, long commonplace in society at large, are now standard equipment in schools. Compared to a mimeograph or ditto machine, preparing copies with a photocopier is much simpler. In addition, the tools for creating the master copies of instructional materials have improved by leaps and bounds. The reason, of course, is the computer. Computer-based tools make it much easier to produce high-quality, professional-looking materials.

How Are Effective Materials Created?

For many teachers, creating ways to impact student learning is a key reason why they chose their profession. Creating materials allows you an opportunity to reflect on what is needed, use experiences from the past, synthesize new materials, and creatively bring together an effective learning experience. Is there a single recipe to creating effective instruction? Of course not. Just as there are different styles of learning, there are different ways to create learning experiences. Here is a general procedure that may help you in this process. It is a guideline

Check It Out

Adapting and Using Available Materials

Integrating New Technologies Into the Methods of Education (InTime) is a website that provides all kinds of online videos of teachers using technology within the classroom setting. An interesting part of that website is a tool that they have included that allows you to access and review the videos but more importantly to also create instructional materials/case studies that integrate the selected videos within your materials. For example, if you are creating some materials for a unit on brainstorming and problem solving, you could access via InTime relevant videos of teachers using brainstorming software within a classroom setting. With the use of their technology, clips of such relevant videos can be downloaded and adapted to be used within your lessons.

Go to the InTime website (http://www.intime.uni.edu/) and review the categories of the available videos. Access the section "Build Your Own Case Study" and walk through the process of selecting and identifying relevant information for a topic of your interest and how the materials can be selected and adapted for your use. Practice adapting one or more of your lesson plans with a video section provided by the website.

Think about the following questions:

▶ What additional materials will be needed to support the video in order to make it optimally effective?
▶ What issues of copyright will need to be resolved before such videos can be legally used within a classroom presentation?
▶ Are there other websites that may provide additional videos or additional materials from different content areas? How does one go about locating such sites?

---

only, and certainly not the *only* way to successfully construct instructional materials.

▶ Refer repeatedly to your instructional plan. The plan contains the direction and activities that you have determined your students need. Just as the general contractor of a large office building would not dream of beginning construction without the blueprints of the building, you should closely review your instructional plans.
▶ Within the plan, look closely at the overall learning objectives and the key activities that need to occur so that students meet them. Ask yourself, "What needs to be constructed so that the activities are successful?" For example, will the students need explanations, directions, examples, nonexamples, or guided practice? Will feedback be needed, and if so, how quickly should you deliver it? (See "Toolbox Techniques: Using Questioning, Examples, and Feedback Effectively" on pages 90 and 91 in Chapter 5.)
▶ Reflect on what you already know or have seen. If you determined that materials did not already exist, did you see pieces of different sets of materials that might give you insight into how to construct what you need? Can you talk with anyone who has taught these or similar concepts before?
▶ Put yourself in the "learner's shoes." What would you want to experience in order to effectively learn this material? Look for means to make materials relevant to students.
▶ Outline your materials. Have students review what you have thought through and determine what major changes need to occur.

▶ Construct a draft set of the materials. Incorporate the use of tools (e.g., copy machines, computers, clip art) to extend your creative development abilities.
▶ Review the materials to ensure that you make all needed changes. In most cases, you will not create perfect materials on the first attempt.

How One Teacher Created Instructional Materials

Nancy Piggot has taught fifth grade at Glen Acres Elementary School for a number of years. Increasingly, Nancy has felt the need to enhance her students' learning experiences as they study their science unit "Insects." She has located a number of great sources of visuals and textual materials, but in most cases they are above her students' level of understanding.

In reviewing and reflecting on her past "Insect" lesson plans, she noted that the different parts of the insect body consistently created problems for her students when it came to identification and descriptions. She determined that to facilitate learning she would assign her students live insects (large cockroaches from the local pet store) to care for. Students would observe their "pets" for a short time each day during the remainder of the insect unit. Students could name their pets and draw various pictures of them during the observation periods. In addition, her plan was to design and create a short multimedia program that would introduce students to their "pets" and show them things that they should observe. In particular, she planned for various pictures and drawings to explain how to identify the specific parts of the insect, highlight the body parts, and describe their functions.

During the development phase of the program, Nancy completed a number of interesting steps. First, she reviewed closely her overall lesson plan for the unit. She noted the weaknesses and the areas that she felt she could add to the instructional effectiveness. Through past experience, she knew that she would need to focus student attention via questioning, examples, practice, and feedback. Likewise, she knew it would be critical to use audio and visual stimulation techniques to effectively highlight key features. The multimedia software allowed her to include such features within a tutorial that students could review on their own. Nancy did one additional thing to ensure the success of the program: She began by drawing out all of the key concepts on 3 by 5 inch cards. She used rough sketches of what the actual program would look like. After developing several of these cards, she asked a few of her students to tell her what they liked and did not like about them. Her students actually helped her determine when more explanation was needed and when she was giving too much. By the time she actually sat at the computer, she had a good idea of the length of the program and that it would be effective. Figure 8–2 contains examples of some of the screens that students viewed as they worked through this program.

From start to finish, this project took Nancy a number of hours to complete. In fact, every year when she gets to the insect unit she finds herself adding new things based on her students' suggestions and new information she uncovers. She has found that this unit has really helped to increase her students' knowledge of insects and also has piqued their interest and motivation.

FORMATIVE EVALUATION OF INSTRUCTIONAL MATERIALS

Any time you modify or create instructional materials, you should assess how effective they are in helping students learn *before* you put the materials to use. This is done via the process of formative evaluation. **Formative evaluation** is evaluation done during the planning or production of instructional materials to determine what, if any, revisions should be made to make them more useful. Formative evaluation can help identify aspects of the materials that are unclear, confusing, inconsistent, obsolete, or otherwise not helpful to students. Chapter 12 provides guidelines for a number of techniques that you can use to carry out formative evaluation of instructional materials. The point we make here is that formative evaluation is a critical step in either modifying existing materials or creating new materials.

As an example, we noted earlier that one common way to modify existing materials is to show a videotape with the sound turned off, providing separate narration that better matches your students' vocabulary level. In this situation, formative evaluation would involve checking the narration to make sure it is, in fact, consistent with students' vocabularies and to identify any further revisions you might make to make it more useful.

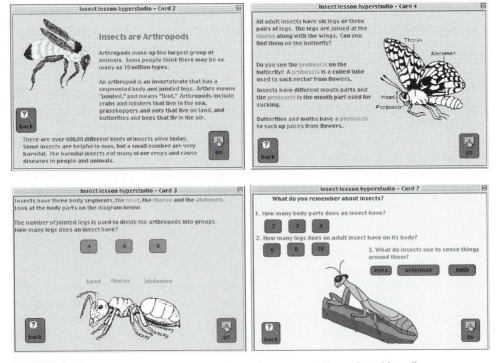

FIGURE 8–2   Instructional screens from a teacher-created "Insect" multimedia program.
Contributed by Nancy Piggott, Glen Acres Elementary, Lafayette, Indiana.

We also noted earlier that teachers commonly produce their own instructional materials. They may, for example, produce their own instructional game for a particular lesson. In this situation, formative evaluation would involve checking the game against students' needs and interests and against the lesson objectives. If the game matches both students and objectives, then it is ready for use. If, on the other hand, it doesn't match the students or objectives in some way, then it will be important to revise the game before using it.

LOCATING, ADAPTING, CREATING, AND EVALUATING INSTRUCTIONAL MATERIALS: HOW CAN TECHNOLOGY HELP?

Finding, selecting, adapting, and creating instructional materials all require time and effort. Can technology be used to help these processes in some way? Of course,

there are a number of ways that technology can be used. First, think of the ways in which technology can **access needed materials.** With the use of Internet search engines, for example, huge amounts of already prepared materials can be located and reviewed (see Chapter 10 for more information on this). Teachers are now able to use the Web to post materials they have found effective and others can then access, use, and adapt these materials for their own classroom situations. Moreover, once both websites and useable materials have been accessed, relevant information can be stored electronically in a way that can ensure rapid access in the future. Combining the use of large electronic storage devices (e.g., hard drives, CDs, and DVDs) with databases allows for the **storage of huge amounts of learning materials** and ways to immediately access them via keyword, subject, and grade level searches.

Second, think of how technology can be used to **create and/or adapt materials.** With the ability to electronically cut and paste within word processing and

---

Addressing the Standards

NETS Connection

As we have discussed the various aspects of the instructional planning process, we have shown repeatedly the potential role technology may play in that process. Standards I and II from the National Educational Technology Standards for teachers address (in part) this potential impact by indicating that teachers should be able to **analyze how technology may affect the instructional planning process.** For this NETS Connection, we want you to read and review these standards (see Teacher Resource A on page 297 for a full listing of the standards and their performance indicators) and then complete the following:

▸ As a journal entry, create a two-column table and put "With computer" and "Without computer" as the heading for each of the respective columns.

▸ Think about the design, creation, and production of a small set of instructional materials (e.g., a lesson on solar eclipses). In the "With" column, list what such design work would be like with the use of the computer and related technology. In the "Without" column, reflect on the same lesson but list what the main process would be without access to this technology.

▸ After listing a number of items within both columns, draw a horizontal line and below the line list the benefits and challenges of each design "With" and "Without" the computer. Although at first glance you might think that the list of benefits will be long with computer access, does it outweigh the list of the challenges that may also be listed?

▸ In your narrative, think about the following challenges that may be encountered when developing instructional materials with technology access:

   1. Electronic searches that turn up so much material that one is quickly overwhelmed with what is encountered. Sifting the materials becomes a major time commitment.
   2. Use of this technology "raises the bar" on production quality that now requires inordinate amounts of time to acquire the needed software skills.
   3. If you do develop the skill to effectively use the technology to produce quality materials, additional responsibilities for helping and mentoring students and other teachers may be "awarded."

▸ As you analyze when to use technology within the design and development process, make sure you realize that, just as there are times when the use of technology is critical, there will be other occasions where the use of technology is not warranted or necessary.

Check It Out

Instructional Materials and Technology

The use of the computer and various forms of software has become invaluable with instructional materials. Table 8–3 highlights a number of areas where the use of specific software may facilitate various steps in the process of finding and using instructional materials. After reviewing the ideas presented in the table, read the three different scenarios. Based on the materials within this chapter, determine which ways technology may be used to facilitate the access, storage, creation, publication, and evaluation of the needed instructional materials.

For each of the following situations, consider these questions:

▶ What should be your first considerations when determining how to obtain the proper instructional materials?
▶ In what ways could relevant materials be accessed, previewed, adapted, created, delivered, and evaluated?
▶ How could technology assist in the process of planning, adapting, producing, and delivering the instructional materials?

Situation A—A high school science teacher has the goal of having his students learn that common recycled materials (paper, plastic, glass) could be used in a number of different, productive ways. Currently, the students have a chapter in their science text that explains the need to recycle, but little is stated about adapting and using recycled materials. Could additional instructional materials be included into his lesson that would help his students attain the desired goal?

Situation B—Currently a teacher in the local middle school has a nice *PowerPoint* presentation that she gives to her science students that deals with the tides and phases of the moon. However, feedback from its previous use in other semesters indicates that some students are not able to fully grasp all of the concepts based on the presentation alone. The students seem to need more practice with the key concepts and they seem to falter when asked to explain how tides can be reliably predicted. In what way could additional instructional materials be included into this lesson?

Situation C—For an upper-elementary teacher, there was need for her Health students to develop healthy ways to properly interact within small groups and also to help them learn about various forms of communicable diseases. By working together in small groups on a project about a specific type of disease, the students may be able to gain insights into their content, develop their research skills, learn to work cooperatively, and also develop skills for writing, producing, and presenting an effective learning experience for others. What are some basic instructional materials that would help the learning within these small groups to occur?

---

desktop publishing programs, you can quickly add visuals, change text, and alter needed sequences. Even the creation and editing of video and audio instructional materials have become relatively easy. Along with the ease of using technology to create materials, the ***publication of the materials*** has also been simplified. Use of printers, copy machines, LCD projectors, and posting to the Web have all increased our ability to produce the materials and reach the students in a quicker, easier, and more cost-effective fashion.

Third, improvement of the learning experience should continually be sought through the ***evaluation of materials***. Technology can be used to transfer information between users of materials to gain insights into when, why, and how the materials are best implemented. Additionally, simple stored comments, ratings, and rankings on the effectiveness, efficiency, and appeal of the materials can be quickly completed and stored for quick review before the next use of the materials.

COPYRIGHT ISSUES

One of the most important issues related to the acquisition or creation of instructional materials, especially in this age of computers and digital reproduction, is copyright. **Copyright** refers to the legal rights to an original work. Schools have an obligation, both under the law and from an ethical standpoint, to adhere to the law and to instruct students in proper behavior. The penalties for violation of copyright law can be severe, and, as a number of schools and businesses have found, publishers' groups are willing to take action against organizations that are in violation. To avoid problems, schools should establish clear copyright policies and make those policies known to both teachers and students.

The origin of copyright can be found in the U.S. Constitution. Article I, section 8 specifies: "[Congress shall have power] to promote the progress of science and useful arts, by securing for limited times to authors and inventors the exclusive right to their respective writings

TABLE 8–3   *Instructional Materials and the Use of Technology*

Planning for the Instructional Materials

What Is Needed	Potential Useful Software
Questionnaire development to get information from students	Word processing (e.g., MS *Word*)
Means to assemble, sort, store, and analyze the collected information	Database (e.g., MS *Access*), spreadsheet (e.g., MS *Excel*), word processing
Determine potential types of materials needed by the students for the lesson	Brainstorming software (e.g., *Inspiration*)
Development of preliminary outlines, flowcharts, and/or planning cards of the needed materials	Flowcharting software (e.g., *Inspiration*, MS *PowerPoint*, MS *Word*)

Identifying and Accessing Potential Instructional Materials

What Is Needed	Potential Useful Software
Finding and reviewing potential materials	Internet browsers (e.g., MS *Internet Explorer*) Website search engines (e.g., *Google, Yahoo*) Library search software
Reviewing critiques provided by others who have used the materials in the past	Internet browsers and search engines

Creating and Adapting Potential Instructional Materials

What Is Needed	Potential Useful Software
Adding text, questions, written examples, exercises, and directions for use	Word processing
Creating and integrating needed audio, visuals, graphics, and video	Word processing, graphics, video and audio editing software Scanning software Clip art software
Adding graphs	Spreadsheet
Creating actual presentations and/or publications	Presentation software (e.g., MS *PowerPoint*); desktop publishing (e.g., MS *Publisher*, Adobe *PageMaker*)

Delivering the Instructional Materials

What Is Needed	Potential Useful Software
Delivery of written materials	Word processing; desktop publishing
Delivery of Web-based materials	Web editing software (e.g., Macromedia *Dreamweaver*)
Delivery of presentations	Presentation software

Evaluating the Instructional Materials

What Is Needed	Potential Useful Software
Complete reviews of the materials	Word processing
Comparison with results from other similar materials	Web search software
Storage of results for future access and use on revisions	Word processing, database

and discoveries." Current law governing copyright can be found in Title 17 of the U.S. Code (available online at: **http://www.law.cornell.edu/uscode/17/**). Although a complete discussion of copyright law is beyond the scope of this book, in this section we provide some basic guidelines. For more information, contact your school's library or media specialist or consult references on the subject.

In the following questions and answers, we cover some of the most important points of copyright law.

◗ What are copyrighted materials?

Copyrighted materials are original works of authorship that are fixed in any tangible medium of expression. This includes such things as written works, works of art and music, photographs, and computer software. Basically, any tangible authored work qualifies. A work does not have to be registered to be protected under copyright law; such protection is automatically granted to the creator of the work when it is produced. Ideas, concepts, and procedures cannot be copyrighted. This means the little copyright symbol © is a symbol of convenience and it is not required to signify copyrighted materials.

◗ How long does copyright last?

Under current law, copyrighted works are protected for the life of the author plus 70 years. Works for hire are protected for 95 years from the date of publication or 120 years from the date of creation, whichever comes first. Similar rules apply to works created before 1978.

◗ What rights does the law give copyright owners?

The copyright owner is the person or entity that holds the copyright to a work. Usually, this is the creator of the work, except in the case of work for hire or when copyright is transferred (e.g., to a publisher). The owner of the copyright to a work has *exclusive* rights to:

◗ reproduce (copy) the work,
◗ create derivative works,
◗ sell or distribute the work, and
◗ perform or display the work in public.

◗ Are there any limitations or exceptions to copyright owners' rights?

The law spells out several specific exceptions to the exclusive rights of copyright owners. For example, libraries are allowed to make copies under certain circumstances, which allow us to enjoy things like interlibrary loans of materials. Also, works produced by the U.S. government cannot be copyrighted; they are in the **public domain**. This means that students or teachers can use things like NASA photographs (those deemed public domain) in their multimedia projects without special permission. There are also important exceptions related to software backup, teaching, and fair use of materials. Because these are so relevant to teachers and schools, we discuss them here in more depth.

Software Backup

Under copyright law, computer software may be duplicated when such duplication is essential to the use of the software on a particular computer or to create an archival backup copy of the software to be used if the original fails. Other copying of computer software, except as may be allowed by the license for a particular software product, is illegal. This applies to networks as well as to stand-alone computers. While a network file server actually holds only one copy of a particular program, multiple copies can be operated on the network. This is illegal if only a single copy of that software was purchased. Schools must purchase network licenses or multiple copies of the software to run multiple copies on a network, and the network must monitor use to prevent violations if the license is restricted to a specific number of copies.

Teaching

For some time, educators have been given some latitude under copyright law to publicly display copyrighted works for the purpose of face-to-face teaching. For example, a teacher may show a videotape in the classroom, even one labeled FOR HOME USE ONLY, as long as the tape was legally purchased, is materially relevant to the subject being taught, and is used in face-to-face teaching at a nonprofit educational institution.

This particular exception in copyright law was, to some degree, recently extended to distance education through the Technology, Education and Copyright Harmonization Act (TEACH Act) of 2001. This means that an instructor within a distance education course now is allowed to transmit materials to students within the distance course. There are limitations; for example, "the TEACH Act covers works an instructor would show or play during class such as movie or music clips, images of artworks in an art history class, or a poetry reading. It does **not** cover materials an instructor may want students to study, read, listen to or watch on their own time outside of class" (Harper, 2001). These excluded works include items typically purchased by students (such as textbooks and coursepacks) for a normal class. Additional restrictions on how the works are transmitted, which types of institutions and courses are eligible, and the length of retention for the materials are also specified within the Act. Crews (2003) offers a full discussion about the meaning and importance of the TEACH Act and its implications for teachers.

Fair Use

Fair use applies to situations involving criticism, comment, news reporting, educational use, and research associated with copyrighted material. Researchers, for example, can make single copies of articles from library journals as part of their research. A critic can excerpt dialogue from a book as part of a published review of the work. Fair use can also apply to education, and it is one of the most important exceptions for teachers and students. There are no absolute guidelines for determining what constitutes fair use in an education setting. Instead, four factors must be weighed:

◗ The purpose and character of the use (e.g., using a copyrighted work for an educational objective is

A teacher contemplates making copies of a textbook illustration for her students.

more likely to be considered fair use than using it for commerical gain)

▶ The nature of the copyrighted work (e.g., if the work itself is educational in character, this would tend to support a judgment of fair use)

▶ The amount of the work used in relation to the whole (e.g., using a smaller amount of a total work is more likely to be fair use than using a larger amount)

▶ The effect of the use on the potential market for the work (e.g., if the use negatively impacts potential sales of the original work, this weighs against fair use)

Fair use guidelines must be applied case by case. However, guidelines on the subject suggest that educational use of a copyrighted work can meet fair use guidelines if (1) only a brief excerpt is used (e.g., an excerpt of less than 1000 words or less than 10 percent of the whole written work), (2) it is a spontaneous use (e.g., a teacher could copy an article for a class if the decision to use it was on the spur of the moment, occurring too late to reasonably seek permission), and (3) there is no cumulative effect (e.g., the use doesn't occur in more than one course, it isn't repeated, and it doesn't serve as a substitute for purchase). Other rules govern the use of specific media, such as taped television broadcasts. Consult with your media specialist for specific guidelines.

Digital Media.   With the advent of digital media and the Internet, copyright issues have become even more important and more difficult to sort out. While it is possible to scan images or digitize audio and video and incorporate the digital representations into multimedia presentations or World Wide Web pages, is it legal? In most cases, the answer to that question is "Probably not," although matters are not altogether clear today. A number of groups around the country are working on revisions to copyright law, or interpretation guidelines for specific situations, that would clarify issues related to digital media and other new technologies. But, as of this writing, nothing has been settled.

The best advice is for teachers and students to treat digital media according to established fair use guidelines. That is, use of copyrighted material in digital format (text, graphics, audio, or video) is likely to be considered fair use when (1) the use is of an educational nature (e.g., part of classroom instruction, including student-created projects), (2) the material itself is educational in nature, (3) relatively little of the original material is used (and credit is given to the source of the materials), and (4) it is unlikely to detrimentally affect the market for the original materials. However, use or distribution beyond the classroom is a problem. So, for example, putting copyrighted materials on the Web without permission is almost certainly contrary to copyright law.

Avoiding Problems.   There are several ways teachers and students can avoid problems with copyrighted material. One solution is to request permission to use the material. Publishers are often willing to permit copyrighted material to be used free of charge for nonprofit educational purposes in the classroom. Another solution is to obtain "royalty-free" collections of media. Many vendors now sell CD-ROMs that contain collections of images and sounds that can be used in presentations or other products without payment of royalties. Be sure to read the fine print, however. What is meant by "royalty-free" varies from one collection to the next. In some cases, there are almost no restrictions on the use of materials; in others, you may not be allowed to use the materials in any kind of electronic product.

Many collections of images and other materials are on the World Wide Web. While images available on the Web are often described as "public domain," they may not be. Use caution when acquiring materials this way. Some websites permit you to use materials from the site as long as you give proper attribution and create a link to the site on your web page. This can be a small price to pay for good material. Another way to "get" images or other materials on the Web is to create a link on your site to the original source. In this way your site provides access to the information without actually copying it. If you adopt this approach, it is considered polite to request permission from the source site to create a link, and you need to be alert to the possibility that your link may be broken if something changes on the source site.

For more information about copyright, or to track the latest developments in the debate about copyright law and new technologies, visit the websites shown in Table 8–4.

TABLE 8–4   *Websites Related to Copyright and Fair Use*

Website	URL
Title 17 of the U.S. Code—copyright law. This is the law and how it is stated.	http://www.law.cornell.edu/uscode/17/
U.S. Copyright Office. U.S. government's official website dealing with copyright.	http://www.copyright.gov/
Stanford University Copyright and Fair Use site. One of the most comprehensive sites on copyright and education. Highly recommended.	http://fairuse.stanford.edu/
Copyright Management Center at Indiana University–Purdue University at Indianapolis. Excellent site that offers all aspects of copyright for educators and librarians.	http://www.copyright.iupui.edu/
Copyright Quick Guide. Quick reference to the key questions about copyright and the issues involved with it. This is part of the Copyright Management Center.	http://www.copyright.iupui.edu/quickguide.htm
Copyright Crash Course. University of Texas tutorial and quizzes dealing with all aspects of copyright and fair use.	http://www.utsystem.edu/OGC/IntellectualProperty/cprtindx.htm

Addressing the Standards

NETS Connection

The National Educational Technology Standard VI (Social, Ethical, Legal, and Human Issues) for teachers emphasizes the need to *identify and understand copyright and the ethical and legal issues that it involves.* At times, faithfully adhering to this law can be confusing and difficult. One way to explore some of these difficulties is for you to go to one of several Internet sites and take a short "Copyright quiz." Consider completing the following:

1. Review one or more of the sites below:

   http://www.esu7.org/~sgsweb/copyquiz.html
   http://www.mediafestival.org/quiz1.pdf
   http://www.techlearning.com/db_area/archives/TL/2002/10/copyright quiz.html

   Additional copyright quizzes may be located by completing an Internet search (e.g., Google) using the keywords: copyright quiz.

2. Compare the answers you gave with those presented within the quiz and note any differences.

3. Investigate several Internet information and tutorial sites about copyright and fair use to resolve misunderstandings about the law. Example sites may include:

   http://fairuse.stanford.edu/
   Stanford University's comprehensive site about copyright and fair use.

   http://www.utsystem.edu/OGC/IntellectualProperty/cprtindx.htm#top
   University of Texas crash course on copyright.

   http://copyright.iupui.edu/
   Indiana University Purdue University in Indianapolis's Copyright Management Center.

4. Describe in a journal entry the need for copyright and why a teacher should model correct behavior in this regard.

TECHNOLOGY COORDINATOR'S CORNER

Recently, Marion Parker received a call from one of her second-grade teachers. Two weeks earlier this same teacher had created a class website that explained the activities occurring in her class, the important assignments for the kids, her teaching philosophy, and reports on several field trip activities in which her students participated. She had published her course site and had asked Marion to create a link on the school's website to her course site. Everything seemed to run fine—until last Friday. On that day, she had received a call from one child's grandparent. The child had called his grandmother and told her to visit his class's website to see what he and his class were doing in school. However, when Grandma visited the site, she was worried by what she saw. She first expressed concern about why a teacher would spend so much time creating the site. She thought it was pretty, but she didn't see the educational value of the site and she worried about the investment of time on the site and if that took away from classroom time she spent with her students. Second, and more importantly, she found several pictures of class members working on projects and her grandson and his name were prominently displayed below one of those pictures. Although she found it interesting to read about the activity, she was worried that the publications of the name of her grandson, an address of the school, and a picture broadcast to the entire world, via the Internet, would place him in danger in some way. She called the teacher to ask if she had permission to use her grandson's picture and if she was concerned about safety issues.

The second-grade teacher was not overly concerned about the value of the course website. In discussions with Marion, she had planned out what was to go within the site and what value it had. She had already witnessed in her own class how it had helped students to remember assignments and how it helped parents stay connected to their children's school activities and work. In addition, she had other things planned to be added to the site in the near future that would allow additional interactive activities, examples, and more practice exercises for her students. Each of these additions would extend the learning that was currently occurring in her classroom. The technology coordinator also suggested that to ensure those visiting the site fully understood its value, additional explanation of what the site contained and why it contained that material should be added to the opening (index) page. The other issue of safety, however, was something that the tech coordinator wanted to see cleared up. In today's world, one can't be too careful. It is important that before publishing anyone's picture permission is granted and, in the case of minors, they remain anonymous or identifying pictures, identities, and locations are not revealed. Marion suggests that she and the teacher review the site and remove or adapt any and all identifying pictures and names of her students.

SUMMARY

In this chapter you learned to complete an instructional plan by selecting instructional materials that match your students' objectives, learning environment, and instructional activities. In acquiring instructional materials, select existing materials whenever possible. If appropriate materials are not available, try to modify existing materials to meet your students' needs. Only as a last resort should you attempt to create new materials. In all cases, whether selecting, modifying, or creating, you should follow established copyright guidelines.

SUGGESTED RESOURCES

CD Resources

To increase retention and transfer of this information, review the *Reflective Questions and Activities* located in the Chapter 8 section **(Chapter info and activities >>>Chapter 8>>> Reflective Questions and Activities)** of the text's accompanying CD.

In addition, you can access software evaluation forms, relevant Internet websites focusing on sites that have large quantities of instructional materials, additional sites with a focus on copyright issues, NETS Connection exercises, and direct e-mail access to the text's authors. Also refer to the completed students' projects to see what types of instructional materials can be created.

Website Resources

Access the text's website (**www.prenhall.com/Newby**), navigate to Chapter 8, and review the Question and Answer section for relevant questions that have been generated by students and answered by the authors. You may also submit your own questions directly to the authors. In addition, link to some of the finished example instructional materials. Review these for ideas on what can be accomplished through use of technology and the principles of designing instructional materials. Finally, also access the presentations by the authors about this chapter and gain insights directly from them about the topics that have been presented.

Print Resources

Clark, R. C., & Lyons, C. (2004). *Graphics for learning: Proven guidelines for planning, designing, and evaluating visuals in training materials.* San Francisco: Jossey-Bass/Pfeiffer.

Crews, K. D. (2000). *Copyright essentials for librarians and educators.* Chicago: American Library Association.

Fleming, M., & Levie, W. H. (Eds.). (1993). *Instructional message design: Principles from the behavioral and cognitive sciences* (2nd ed.). Englewood Cliffs, NJ: Educational Technology Publications.

Kearny, L. (1996). *Graphics for presenters: Getting your ideas across.* Menlo Park, CA: Crisp.

Layng, J. M., & Rosner, R. (2004). *Media design: The practice of communication technologies.* Upper Saddle River, NJ: Pearson/Prentice Hall.

Moore, D. M., & Dwyer, F. M. (Eds.) (1994). *Visual literacy: A spectrum of visual learning.* Englewood Cliffs, NJ: Educational Technology Publications.

Smaldino, S. E., Russell, J. D., Heinich, R., & Molenda, M. (2005). *Instructional technology and media for learning.* Upper Saddle River, NJ: Merrill/Prentice Hall.

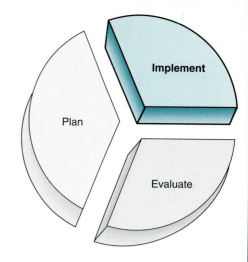

MEANINGFUL INTEGRATION OF TECHNOLOGY

Although we have covered a lot of ground to this point, our question now is, "If your students interact with your instructional materials, will they learn?" The answer is, "It depends." Moving to the "I" in the PIE model, in the next section of this textbook we concentrate on how instructional materials are best *implemented*. We will illustrate how you *must* couple an excellent plan and set of instructional materials with good integration and implementation strategies for your students to achieve the highest-level learning. Consider the last few times you experienced *poor* results from instruction. Was your learning inhibited by poorly planned materials, by the manner in which the materials were integrated and/or implemented, or by some combination? Were there, for example, distractions because of poor-quality video, inaccessible websites, uninterpretable audio, or visuals that weren't relevant to the information being presented? What about class discussions that were not available to students who were absent, lab experiences that didn't work because of limited software access, or network problems that created slowed or halted Internet access?

The point is, you may have the best instructional plan ever developed and a wonderful set of instructional materials, but if you do not properly implement them, your students will not learn as they should.

In this section we emphasize that learning is a function of both instructional content and the manner in which students interact with the content. There are principles of utilization that can help to ensure that learning occurs. It is not enough to know the different types of technology tools that are available and when they could be used; you must also know *how* to use them effectively.

To begin this section, Chapter 9 examines the computer specifically as a means to support student learning. This chapter is followed by Chapter 10, which deals with the Internet and how it is integrated within the classroom setting to effectively impact both teaching and learning. This section on integration and implementation concludes with a focus on distance education (Chapter 11) and how it can be used to deliver instructional materials in a unique manner and impact students in a unique way.

9

Integration of Computers to Support Learning

KEY WORDS AND CONCEPTS

Integrated learning
   systems
One-computer classroom
Programming language
Hypermedia

CHAPTER OBJECTIVES

After reading and studying this chapter, you will be able to:

▶ Describe the characteristics and give at least one example of each common category of computer-assisted instruction.
▶ Discuss a rationale for having students learn through developing their own multimedia/hypermedia projects.
▶ Discuss ways that students can learn by using the computer as a teacher, as an assistant, and as a "learner."
▶ Identify and discuss issues related to the use of the computer in the classroom.

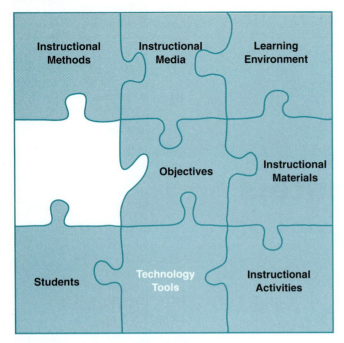

FIGURE 9–1   Technology tools as a piece in the development of the learning experience puzzle.

In this chapter, we begin to explore how to integrate technologies to enhance the learning experience. As shown in Figure 9–1, the integration of such technology tools can be viewed as being a vital puzzle piece in the design, development, and implementation of the learning experience. This chapter focuses specifically on the computer and how you can use it in the classroom to promote student learning. Recall that in introducing the computer and its uses in education in Chapter 3, we briefly explained three ways of using it: as a teacher, as an assistant, and as a learner. We revisit and expand that classification scheme in this chapter with a special focus on using the computer to promote student learning. In Chapter 10, we look specifically at the Internet and ways that you can use it in the classroom; and in Chapter 11, we will examine ways to integrate distance education technologies to enhance learning.

INTRODUCTION

Have you ever played chess? If you have (and probably even if you have not), you know that it is a game of strategy in which players maneuver their playing pieces against those of an opponent. The goal of the game is to checkmate the opposing player's king. This goal can be accomplished in millions of different ways.

Each of the playing pieces in chess has its own characteristic ways of moving and hence strengths in different situations. Bishops, for example, move along diagonals and can exert an influence far across the board.

Rooks can also exert influence from far away, but move straight along rows or columns only. Knights move in an L-shaped pattern that allows them to slip into spots that other pieces cannot. Good players understand the different strengths of each piece, from the lowly pawn to the powerful queen, and as a result they are able to successfully use these pieces to achieve the goal of the game.

What does the game of chess have to do with using computers in education? Education, of course, is about learning, not about beating an opponent. But when using computers in the classroom, as when playing chess, there is more than one way to achieve your learning goal. In chess, players must understand each piece's strength to find ways to checkmate their opponent's king. In the classroom, as we pointed out in Chapter 3, there are multiple ways to use computers and related technologies. To teach with them effectively, you must understand the strengths of different computer applications so you can use them to achieve your ultimate goal in the classroom—enhancing student learning.

In Chapter 3, we introduced you to Taylor's (1980) simple but useful categorization scheme for educational applications of computers: computer as teacher, computer as assistant, and computer as learner. In the first category, the computer presents instruction to the learner much as a teacher or tutor might. In the second category, the computer assists the learner in performing routine tasks such as writing, calculating, or presenting information. In the final category, the student takes on the role of a teacher by trying to "teach" the computer (the "learner") to perform a task or to instruct others. Like chess pieces, each way of using computers in education has strengths that make it suitable for different classroom learning situations. In this chapter, we revisit this organizational scheme to help you better understand how to use computers to promote student learning.

Instructional technology tools, similar to chess pieces, have different strengths.

TECHNOLOGY INTEGRATION PROCESS: PREPARING TO INTEGRATE THE COMPUTER IN THE LEARNING EXPERIENCE

This chapter explores options for integrating the computer in the classroom to enhance the learning experience for your students. As you plan to integrate the computer in learning activities—whether as teacher, assistant, or learner—what should you consider?

First, consider the knowledge, skills, and dispositions of your students. What capabilities do your students possess as they come to the learning activity? At a minimum, to use today's computers students need to be able to use a mouse, select options from menus, and otherwise navigate the computer's interface. Just as one does not need to know all of the intricacies of chess to begin playing, detailed knowledge of specific applications is usually *not* necessary to get started using the computer. However, students do need to know the basics of whatever software you plan to utilize, just as one would need to know the basics of how chess pieces move to begin playing that game. If students do not have the necessary knowledge and skills, you should plan on introducing them as part of your lesson.

Consider your objectives. What is it that you want your students to learn and how can the computer be of benefit? As you will see in this chapter, the computer can help to address many learning objectives. However, it is certainly not appropriate for all. A computer would be of limited value in helping a student to learn to distinguish different fruits by their smells or to estimate the length of a parking lot.

Of course, in order to use the computer, the learning environment must include at least one. In schools, available computer technology can range from a single computer in the classroom (see "Toolbox Tips: One-Computer Classroom" on page 170) to a cluster of classroom or library computers to a computer laboratory where each learner has access to his or her own machine (see "Toolbox Tips: Using Computer Laboratories" on page 176). Each configuration has its own challenges, and you must plan appropriately to use what is available.

When using the computer with students, as with any instructional activity, be sure to prepare the instructional materials, prepare the learning environment, and prepare the learners. While preparing your learning environment, check that the computer or computers are working properly. Make sure that you are familiar with the software that you intend to use, whether that is a computer-assisted instruction package, an office application, or a multimedia authoring tool. Prepare your students for the activity. If necessary, introduce the basic operations of the software that they will need to complete the activity. Discuss the purpose (objectives) of the lesson, develop written instructions and supplemental instructional materials for the activity, and remind students of the rules for proper care and use of the computers.

During implementation of a computer-enhanced lesson, monitor individual students to check for understanding and to head off any problems they may encounter in using the software. Encourage students to use each other as resources if they have questions or problems. Be sure to integrate the use of the computer with other classroom methods and media so that the use of the computer builds upon and adds to the existing curriculum.

Of course, following a lesson, you and your students need to take time to evaluate how well it worked. Was the use of the computer helpful? How could it be improved in the future?

COMPUTER AS TEACHER

The oldest use of the computer in education, dating back to the early 1960s, is as a tool that presents instruction directly to students. Such use is usually termed *computer-assisted instruction (CAI), computer-based instruction (CBI),* or *computer-assisted learning (CAL).* In this mode, the computer can present instruction, use various media (text, graphics, audio, video), provide instructional activities or situations, quiz or otherwise require interaction from learners, evaluate learner responses, provide feedback, and determine appropriate follow-up activities.

The chief advantage of the computer is its interactivity. Whereas a printed worksheet may leave space for a student's answer or an instructional video may pose a question for the viewer, there is no guarantee that the student will in fact respond. The computer can require a response; it can demand the learner's active involvement. When used as a teaching machine, the computer can be highly interactive, individualized, engaging, and infinitely patient. Research analyses of studies comparing computer-assisted instruction with traditional methods suggest that it produces slightly superior achievement, often in less time, and may produce improved attitudes toward computers and sometimes toward the subject matter itself (Kulik & Kulik, 1991; Niemiec & Walberg, 1987). The positive effects are somewhat greater in the lower grades. More recent analyses (Kulik, 2003) suggest that the results of integrating instructional technology in instruction are mixed, but do indicate that integration of instructional technology during the past decade has been more successful than earlier attempts.

CAI has a long history of use, and it remains a popular option in classrooms today, especially at the elementary level. Consider the scenario that follows. As you read, identify how Ms. Stanley uses the computer as a teacher.

Scenario: States and Capitals

Sue Stanley is a fifth-grade teacher at Riverside Elementary School. The school district's social studies curriculum guide calls for all students in the fifth grade to be able to name and correctly spell all of the fifty U.S. states and capitals from memory. To help her students meet this requirement, Ms. Stanley set up a series of activities stretching over several weeks.

At the beginning of the unit on U.S. geography, Ms. Stanley handed out a labeled U.S. map and a printed list of all fifty states and capitals to her students, and explained that each student would be responsible for learning the names and correct spellings of all fifty states and capitals. Realizing that this task can be daunting to fifth-graders, she looked for ways to make it easier and to give her students plenty of opportunities for practice.

First, she broke up the task into more manageable pieces. She divided her class of twenty-four students into four groups of six students each. Students in each group were assigned the task of becoming class "experts" on the states and capitals from one of four geographical regions of the United States: the Northeast, the South, the Midwest, and the West. Each student was responsible for learning information about the states and capitals in his region. Ms. Stanley set up the two computers in her classroom as learning stations. One station had a CD-ROM almanac that students could use to research each state, its major points of interest, population, and so forth. The other had a drill and practice program that allowed individuals to quiz themselves over the states and capitals. As students worked, Ms. Stanley circulated throughout the classroom, helping those students who needed assistance.

After giving the students time to develop their expertise, Ms. Stanley set up a rotating system where a student from one group was paired with a student from another group. The students took turns peer tutoring and drilling each other over the states and capitals in their respective regions, and, through the rotation schedule, they were able to practice all fifty states and capitals by the end of the week. Each week, Ms. Stanley gave each student a worksheet on a subset of states and capitals to complete, and gave a quiz over the subset each Friday.

To help students with particular learning difficulties, Ms. Stanley worked closely with Ms. Epstein, the school's special education teacher. Some special practice activities were arranged and assignments were adjusted for students with special needs. She also talked to Ms. McHenry, the music teacher, who was able to help by using music time to teach the class a song that helped everyone learn the names of the fifty states.

Ms. Stanley also scheduled the computer lab several times during the unit. On computer lab days, students played the educational game, *Where in the USA is Carmen Sandiego?* In this game, students must use geographic clues about the United States to track a criminal who has stolen a national treasure. The first few lab days, Ms. Stanley had students work in pairs on the game. She found that students working in pairs more

quickly grasped how the game worked and were able to get through any problems that arose. In later sessions, she had students work alone, so that she could get a sense of how well individual students were progressing.

After several weeks, most of the students became fairly proficient at writing the names of U.S. states and capitals from memory. Ms. Stanley was pleased with their progress, and gratified that her unit had been successful in meeting the district objective. As a culminating activity, the class put on a "United States Day." Each student took one of the states and prepared a short oral presentation about it. Ms. Hopper, the art teacher, helped them create illustrations for their presentations. Many drew maps of their state, but some did other projects; one student even made a papier mâché model of Mount Rushmore for her presentation about South Dakota. Parents were invited, and everyone made their presentations, then sang the song they had learned to end the program. The day was a big hit with the kids and their parents, and it was a great way to wrap up the unit.

What can this scenario tell us about using the computer as a teacher? We can note the following:

▸ *CAI is usually used in a supporting or adjunct role.* In this example, educational software was only one part of a broader strategy of classroom activities. Since the earliest uses of CAI, there has been an enduring myth that computers will become perfect teaching machines and one day will replace human teachers. This has not happened, and does not seem likely anytime in the near future. Few computer programs approach the capabilities of a human tutor. We see little evidence to suggest that computers will ever replace teachers. CAI is merely one more tool at your disposal for helping students learn.

▸ *Certain types of CAI are appropriate for certain learning goals.* In this example, the specific learning goal of the school district was to have every student learn the fifty U.S. states and capitals. Sue Stanley wanted to make certain that each child had the opportunity to master this rote task. The CAI she used, a drill and practice program and an educational game, was appropriate to this learning goal. These programs were able to engage students' interest while providing opportunities for practice and repetition. Other forms of CAI may be appropriate to higher-level learning goals. (See the next subsection, "Categories of Computer-Assisted Instruction.")

▸ *CAI can help students and free time for the teacher.* Not only were students able to benefit from the software, but it gave the teacher the opportunity to address individual learners' needs. When the learning stations were operating, Ms. Stanley could help those students who needed the most help. Later, when all of the students were playing the game, she could take time to assess the progress of individual students.

In Chapter 6, we introduced you to various instructional methods including the two employed here: drill and practice and instructional game. Other common methods that are embodied in instructional software include tutorial, simulation, and problem solving. Keep in mind, you can use the computer as a teacher in many other ways that do not neatly fit these categories, such as with demonstrations, content review or testing programs, dialogues, context-sensitive help systems, and others. It is important to recognize that categories are a useful place to begin discussions, but they should never be allowed to restrict your thinking about computer applications in education. There are many forms of CAI and many ways to view the role of the computer in education. As software and our knowledge of human learning evolve, we may invent new categories or change old ones to better reflect the reality in the classroom. Next we look at the most common current categories of CAI, the characteristics of these computer-based methods, and examples.

Categories of Computer-Assisted Instruction

Drill and Practice

As you learned in Chapter 6, a drill and practice application is designed to help learners master already introduced basic skills or knowledge through repetitive work. Compared with noncomputer drill and practice, the computer offers significant advantages:

▶ *Interactivity.* The computer can present many problems and require student responses.
▶ *Immediate feedback.* The computer can immediately inform the learner if an answer is right or wrong and, in a well-designed program, tell the learner why. Many drill and practice programs automatically recycle missed items until they are mastered.
▶ *Infinite patience.* A computer drill and practice program can go all day without getting tired or irritable.
▶ *Variable level of difficulty.* The computer can adjust the level of difficulty. This might be set by the teacher or the learner, or the program may adjust automatically based on the student's performance.
▶ *Motivation.* Through the use of challenge and gaming elements, or just because it is on the computer, a computer drill and practice program may be more motivating to students than similar paper-and-pencil exercises.

These characteristics make the computer an excellent tool for drill and practice applications and explain why they are among the most popular of all computer applications in education, especially in the elementary grades. In the previous scenario, Ms. Stanley used a drill and practice program on the states and capitals as a learning station in the classroom. Drill and practice programs tend to be used for basic information and skills in a variety of subject areas. They are most effective for rote learning or where automatic student responses are desired. The *Stickybear Typing* and the *Reader Rabbit* series are examples of computer drill and practice programs (in the content areas of arithmetic computation and beginning reading skills, respectively) that are popular in the elementary school. *Reader Rabbit* helps students practice beginning word-recognition and word-construction skills. In *Stickybear Typing,* students are drilled on basic typing skills and facts in a game format. As the student answers each question, the program provides reinforcement. Figure 9–2 shows a sample screen from *Stickybear Typing.*

Students can usually gain some benefit from drill and practice programs even with relatively little exposure per session. As a result, such programs are a popular option when computer hardware is scarce. A common strategy is to rotate individual students through the program so that each student is able to get 10 or 20 minutes of practice at a time. Over time, many short practice sessions can build skills. Refer to the utilization guidelines in Chapter 6 for more tips about using drill and practice and the other methods discussed in this chapter.

Tutorial

In a tutorial application, the computer assumes the primary instructional role of teacher or tutor. It presents new content and assesses learning. A tutorial typically contains an organized body of knowledge, one or more pathways through that knowledge, specific learning objectives, and built-in tests of student learning. Computer-based tutorials offer a number of advantages:

▶ *Embedded questions.* Like computer drills, tutorials on the computer have the advantage of being interactive. Students must take an active role by answering embedded questions. As with drills, immediate feedback is provided.
▶ *Branching.* Computer tutorials can automatically branch, that is, adjust content presentation order according to the learner's responses to embedded questions. Remediation or advancement can be built in to meet the needs of individual learners.
▶ *Dynamic presentation.* The computer can present information dynamically, such as by highlighting important text on the screen to capture the learner's attention or by depicting processes using animated graphics. A multimedia computer system may also employ audio and video.
▶ *Recordkeeping.* Computer tutorials can automatically maintain student records, which inform students of their progress. In addition, you can check the records to ensure students are progressing satisfactorily.

While a poorly designed tutorial may be little more than an electronic page-turner, a well-designed one can

FIGURE 9–2 A screen from *Stickybear Typing*, a popular drill and practice computer program.
Source: Stickybear Typing, Optimum Resources, Inc. Used with permission.

be a highly interactive and effective form of instruction that responds to the needs or wants of individual learners. They are often used to address verbal and conceptual learning. Tutorials are available for a range of subject matter and at all grade levels. Use of tutorials in the social and natural sciences has been found to be consistently effective (Kulik, 2003). *Science Smart* is an example of a tutorial program designed to teach key anatomy concepts (Figure 9–3). *Rosetta Stone* from Fairfield Language Technologies is a popular tutorial series for foreign language learning. *World History* from ABC-CLIO provides a comprehensive treatment of historical developments from about 1500 to the present. Also, many popular computer office applications come with associated tutorials that provide instruction on how to use the package.

In many cases, computer tutorials are used in schools to supplement regular instruction rather than to replace it. Because tutorials often require a significant time commitment (a student may require hours to complete an extensive one), it is difficult to use tutorials effectively with large numbers of students without access to a computer laboratory. Where computer hardware is limited, you may use computer tutorials with selected students for remediation, enrichment, or makeup work.

Simulation

A *simulation* is a representation or model of a real (or sometimes imaginary) system, situation, or phenomenon.

In most cases, this representation is simplified to make learning easier. Simulations make excellent use of the computer's capabilities:

▶ *Control of multiple variables.* Computers can manage multiple variables simultaneously. As a result, they can realistically depict complex phenomena, such as the growth and change of a city or the physics of bodies in motion. Learners can manipulate these variables to observe their effects on the system being modeled.

▶ *Dynamic presentation.* As with tutorials, the computer's ability to dynamically present information is important in simulation. Simulated instrumentation can change like the real thing, and processes such as plant growth can be graphically depicted.

▶ *Time control.* The computer can contract or expand time to allow study of phenomena that are too slow (e.g., population growth) or too fast (e.g., chemical reaction) for normal classroom observation. The computer can also depict historical situations (e.g., a nineteenth-century wagon train).

▶ *Effects of chance.* Many simulations include an element of chance or randomness that makes them even more realistic, allowing students to interact with them differently on different occasions.

Simulations have found their greatest use in the natural and social sciences. While evaluations of simulations'

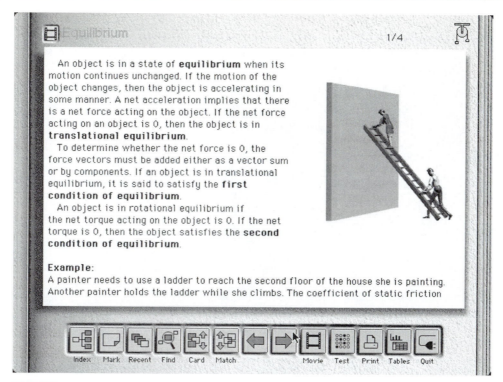

FIGURE 9–3 A screen from *Science Smart,* a popular tutorial program.
Source: The Princeton Review "Science Smart". Used with permission.

effectiveness have been mixed (Kulik, 2003; Lee, 1999), there are many good examples of educational simulations, including *SimCity* (management of a growing city), *CatLab* (simulated cat breeding), *Decisions, Decisions* (social studies role-playing simulation series), and *The Oregon Trail* (travel by covered wagon). Most simulations are designed to promote application of information, thinking, and problem-solving skills. Most tend not to teach basic concepts. As a result, it is usually important for students to be well grounded in the underlying concepts of the simulation before use, and guidance is often needed during use. For example, *The Oregon Trail* simulates pioneers crossing the United States by covered wagon in the nineteenth century. Students must make decisions about the amount of food and ammunition to take at the start, and they must decide what to do when they encounter various problems and opportunities along the trail. But to make the experience meaningful as a historical exercise, students may need background about the westward expansion, the factors that promoted it, and nineteenth-century life in general. Figure 9–4 shows a sample screen from *The Oregon Trail.*

Simulations vary in the degree to which they accurately depict what they are modeling. Educational simulations are simplified, and students should be made aware of this. Simulations also vary in the time required for use. Simple simulations of some processes may require

only a few minutes of student time; others may demand hours. So, you must plan accordingly. You may effectively use computer simulations with both individuals and small groups of students.

Instructional Game

Instructional games add an element of fun to CAI. In most cases, games are simply modified versions of other types of CAI, such as drill and practice or simulation, but are distinguished by having the following characteristics:

▶ *Motivation.* The chief advantage of computer games is the variety of motivational elements they may employ, including competition, cooperation, challenge, fantasy, recognition, and reward.
▶ *Game structure.* The game structure means that there are rules of play and an end goal.
▶ *Sensory appeal.* Games on the computer often appeal through the use of graphics, animation, sound, and other sensory enhancements.

Computer games, as noted, are usually modified forms of other types of CAI. A game may have begun as a drill and practice, problem-solving, or simulation program to which gaming elements were added. *Physicus* is a computer game that involves the application of principles of physics on a mysterious island. A popular

FIGURE 9–4   A screen from *The Oregon Trail*, a popular educational simulation.
*Source: The Oregon Trail, © 1999. The Learning Company, Inc. Used with permission.
All rights reserved.*

geography computer game is *Where in the World is Carmen Sandiego?* In this simulation game, a student assumes the role of a detective who must use geography clues to track a thief around the world. In this role, the student experiences an element of fantasy. There is challenge in that the player must locate the thief within a set amount of time by using clues embedded in the game. Students may compete against one another for the best times or cooperate with one another to help catch the villain. All of these elements make the program a terrific game. It has proven so popular that it has spawned a series of other similar games (including *Where in the USA is Carmen Sandiego?* mentioned in the previous scenario), a line of merchandise, and a television series. Figure 6-2 (page 106) shows a sample screen from *Where in the World is Carmen Sandiego?*

Addressing the Standards

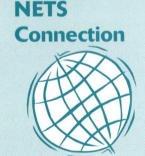

NETS
Connection

Several National Educational Technology Standards (NETS II, III, IV, and V) emphasize the need for teachers to create lessons that involve the use of technology to *engage, motivate, and encourage self-directed student learning.* Imagine being asked to help mentor a student teacher who is attempting to create such a lesson. Review these standards and their performance indicators (see Teacher Resource A on page 297 for a full listing) and then complete the following:

▶ Create an e-mail message to your mentee that defines and explains "self-directed student learning." Also, make suggestions about the potential role of technology in developing such learning. Make sure to explain the benefits (and challenges) associated with learner-controlled learning environments.

▶ Your mentee will greatly benefit from seeing some high-quality examples of computer-assisted software and how it could be integrated within instructional activities to increase self-directed student learning. Offer some of the best examples you know of and give a rationale for your selection.

Computer games vary in their time requirements. Some may require only a few minutes. More complex games may extend over hours or even days. Probably the biggest concern about educational computer games is that the education should not take a backseat to the game. You must take care to carefully integrate these games into your curriculum.

Problem Solving

Some CAI applications are designed to foster students' problem-solving skills but don't fit into any of the previous categories. Computer problem-solving applications have certain advantages:

▶ *Focus on specific problem types.* Specific problem-solving programs often focus on specific skills (e.g., spatial ability, logic).

▶ *Quantity.* The computer can provide students with practice over a large number of problems in a short period of time, requiring interaction and providing feedback as in other forms of CAI.

▶ *Variety.* The computer is capable of presenting a variety of problems. This helps students to generalize their problem-solving skills.

Problem-solving applications are designed to promote students' higher-order thinking skills, such as logic, reasoning, pattern recognition, and strategies. Problem-solving software often helps students by providing concrete representations of abstractions. Examples of problem-solving programs include *Zoombinis Island Odyssey* (reasoning and logic in science) and *Geometric Supposer* (geometry). Some teachers use this software to enhance students' problem-solving skills for their own sake. Others link it to relevant curricular areas such as mathematics.

Most problem-solving programs, like drill and practice, require relatively short stretches of time for use. As a result, programs can often be used by individuals or small groups of students in rotation when computer hardware is limited.

Integrated Learning Systems

Integrated learning systems (ILSs) are the most complex and sophisticated computer systems that function as a teacher. They combine comprehensive computer-assisted instruction (CAI), any or all of the categories mentioned previously, and computer management features into a single networked computer delivery system. They are designed to provide a cycle of instruction, assessment, and prescription for a particular subject matter—all on the computer.

ILSs are usually supplied by a single vendor that provides all of the hardware and software. Leading ILS producers today include CompassLearning and Pearson Digital Learning. While ILSs are expensive, they provide a lot for the money. The hardware consists of a local area network (LAN) of computers linked to a large file server that contains all of the software. The software includes a fully articulated curriculum in a particular subject area, such as mathematics or language arts, as well as software that tracks students and manages their progress.

Students in schools that have ILSs typically use the system regularly, from daily to once or twice per week. The computer delivers instruction, most often tutorials and drill and practice exercises, and tests students. Instruction, testing, and test scoring are all managed by the system. Because the curriculum is well integrated and spans a number of grade levels, students may work on the ILS over a period of years and progress at their own rate. Teachers like the fact that the instruction is individualized. In addition, because the computer handles both the instruction and the assessment, the teacher is freed to provide individualized assistance, plan ancillary learning activities, and guide the learning process. Administrators like ILSs because they provide detailed information about the levels of mastery of the student body. A recent summary of the effects of using instructional technology in elementary and secondary schools by Kulik (2003) reported that the use of ILSs had an effect too small to be educationally meaningful on students' achievement in reading. However, the use of ILSs did have a positive effect on students' achievement in mathematics.

Problems and Pitfalls

We have emphasized the many advantages of using the computer as teacher, and rightly so. CAI has much to offer. However, there are concerns that we must consider, as well. Critics charge that CAI is a low-level use of the computer that simply puts a new face on old busywork and that is not consistent with a view of learning as knowledge construction. In some cases this charge is surely justified. Some drill and practice programs are little more than electronic worksheets. Some tutorials are mere electronic page-turners. There is a tendency for the first uses of a new technology to be simply re-creations of older forms. For example, many early films and television programs were just stage plays performed in front of a camera; it took a while for these media to develop their own unique forms. In similar fashion, many early CAI programs were simply adaptations of older instructional forms such as paper-and-pencil worksheets. But that is changing. Newer software releases tend to make better use of the computer. However, it remains your responsibility to see that CAI is used productively in the classroom to help students learn and not simply as busywork.

Classroom management is also an important consideration in the use of CAI. Effective use often requires special classroom management strategies. If you have only one or perhaps two computers in the classroom, you must devise mechanisms to ensure that each student gets access (see "Toolbox Tips: One-Computer Classroom"). If a computer laboratory is available, you must plan computer activities well in advance in consultation with the school's technology or media coordinator. Laboratory settings, too, have their own challenges (see "Toolbox Tips: Using Computer Laboratories"). You often will need careful planning and structured activities to provide the direction required to keep students productively on task.

COMPUTER AS ASSISTANT

In the role of assistant, the computer aids the learner in performing routine work tasks. In Chapter 3, we introduced important computer applications that fall into this category including word processors, graphics tools, presentation software, computer databases, electronic spreadsheets, and telecommunication/Internet tools. Both teachers and students can use these programs in a variety of ways.

In this chapter, we focus on the use of computer productivity tools that can assist the learner. This use of computers in the classroom is one of the most important, and it is one of the most common as well. In many

TOOLBOX TIPS

One-Computer Classroom

Classrooms with a single computer are common in many schools across the country. Despite the fact that millions of computers are now installed in U.S. schools, the **one-computer classroom** remains a fixture of the educational landscape. What can be done with a single computer in the classroom? The answer is, a lot!

All of the methods of using computers in the classroom discussed in this chapter can apply to the one-computer classroom. Students can work on computer-assisted instruction, either individually or in small groups. The computer can be used as a productivity tool, for example, to graph data from a science experiment or make an in-class multimedia presentation. One computer can even be used, with appropriate management, for "computer-as-learner" activities.

One simple but useful approach to utilizing limited hardware is to provide individual students access in rotation. This model is especially popular at the elementary level, where the computer is often established as one of a number of learning centers through which students rotate. For example, primary-age learners working on basic arithmetic skills might rotate through several related learning stations featuring concrete manipulatives, traditional flash cards, and a computer drill and practice game. While time on the computer is necessarily limited in this approach, it does give an entire class at least some access. You, the teacher, must effectively manage students' access to the computer to avoid conflicts and to keep those students who are not working on the computer productively engaged in other activities. Sign-up sheets, schedules, fixed time intervals, and other similar techniques can help with the management challenge.

Students can also use the computer in small groups. Research suggests that for many types of computer-assisted instruction there are benefits to having small groups, as opposed to individuals, work on CAI programs (Johnson, Johnson, & Stanne, 1985; Lou, Abrami, & d'Apollonia, 2001). Cooperating students can learn from and help one another, where a single student might become confused or stuck. Small groups can also use the computer to do such things as create presentations or develop hypermedia projects. Even whole-class use of a single computer is possible. Using an appropriate large-group display (see "Toolbox Tools: Presentation Hardware," later in this chapter), you might lead a whole class through a session with a program such as *The Oregon Trail*, calling on different students to make decisions along the trail. Some CAI programs are even designed to support whole-class use with a single computer. A notable example is Tom Snyder Productions' *Decisions Decisions* software line. The whole-class activities in these role-playing simulations are orchestrated by a single computer.

Finally, although the emphasis in this chapter is on students' learning, one should not overlook the single classroom computer as a tool for you, the teacher. Word processing is a great tool for producing printed material. With a single computer equipped with word processing software and attached to a printer, you can produce printed instructional materials you can then copy for the whole class to use. Many textbooks today come with computerized question banks; you can make copies of selected questions to help guide review activities. You may use a database to keep student records, a spreadsheet to maintain student grades, and so on. As some experts have argued, if you have only one computer in a classroom, the most useful place for it is on your own desk!

ways, this is only natural. When computers are used in the workplace, they are most often used as a tool to assist the worker. Secretaries prepare documents using word processors, businesspeople store customer records in databases, accountants use spreadsheets to calculate, graphic artists use drawing programs, and so on. So, it makes sense that students should learn to use computers in schools in the same ways that they are used in the workplace.

In this section, we will revisit the popular computer applications that we introduced in Chapter 3. To begin, read the following scenario, looking for examples where students use the computer as an assistant.

Scenario: Stock Market Game

Bob Goins is an economics and social studies teacher at George Washington Carver High School. For the past several years, he has used a popular unit as part of his economics class. In this unit, students "play" the stock market by creating and tracking a portfolio of investments. Bob uses the unit as a synthesizing activity in which students learn and apply information about investing, the market, and financial tracking. Here's how it went last year.

To ensure that his students were adequately prepared, Mr. Goins waited until the start of the second semester of his economics class to begin the game. Once started, however, the activity spanned the entire semester. At the beginning of the unit, the class was divided into teams of three or four students each. Each team was given an initial investment of $100,000 of play money. Teams were allowed to invest in the stock market in any way that they wanted, and they could change their investments during the game by buying or selling stocks (taking sales commissions into account). Each team's goal was to have its initial investment grow as much as possible by the end of the game. The teams competed against one another to achieve the best overall performance, and Mr. Goins added an extra incentive by offering to treat the winning team to pizza at the end of the semester.

Before the teams actually made their first investments, Mr. Goins set aside two weeks for research. During this period, each team investigated stocks that it might want to purchase. Using computers available in the Business Department's lab, students used the Internet to do online research of various companies and mutual funds. Mr. Goins provided the class with the URLs of online brokerage houses and other sources of investment information on the Web. When teams identified promising investments, they requested more information online or used the lab's word processor to compose a letter requesting more information. Mr. Goins also invited a local stockbroker to talk to the students about investing and to provide some tips about

possible investment selections. At the end of the two-week research period, each team made its mock purchases, and the game was under way!

To keep track of their investments, Mr. Goins had each team maintain an investment spreadsheet. To help the students learn to use the software, Mr. Goins briefly demonstrated it during class, and provided a handout that covered the basics. However, he let the students figure out the details, and they seemed to do just fine. Mr. Goins required the students to design the team spreadsheet so that it listed each individual investment and calculated the total value of the portfolio. He required that each team update its spreadsheet weekly, though most teams were so engaged in the game that they checked their stocks daily. Each team created a graph from the spreadsheet to show the overall performance from the beginning of the game to the current week. These graphs were posted on the classroom bulletin board every Friday, so all of the teams knew where they stood. A few of the teams went further and used their spreadsheets to do projections—calculating what would happen if market conditions changed in certain ways. They used their projections to decide whether to buy or sell certain stocks.

As a final activity at the end of the semester, each team prepared a presentation to summarize their investments, the strategies they used during the game, and their results. The students developed their presentations in the computer lab using *PowerPoint* software. With the presentation software, the students were able to import graphs and data from their spreadsheet. Finally, each team presented its report using the classroom computer and a portable LCD projector that Mr. Goins checked out from Ms. Habib, the technology coordinator. The unit went well, it was a favorite of the students, and Mr. Goins expects that it will be a part of the curriculum in his economics class for many years to come.

A team of students uses spreadsheet software on the computer to prepare a graph showing their investments as part of a stock market game lesson.

What can we learn about the use of the computer as an assistant from this scenario? Consider the following points:

▶ *Content comes first.* When the computer is used as an assistant, the computer and its software play a secondary role to the subject matter itself. In this example, the goal of the activity was for students to learn economics. The computer simply helped them achieve this goal.

▶ *The computer as assistant offers benefits over traditional tools.* The students in this example were able to easily create a graph of their investment history each week because they had the data in a spreadsheet. They could have done this by hand, but the computer made the job much quicker and easier, and the computer-generated graph was neater and more accurate than one created by hand. However, it is important to point out that initial time and effort is needed, often *more* than is required with conventional tools. The students had to create the spreadsheet before they could realize the advantages it provided.

▶ *The computer as assistant can help students achieve various learning goals.* While some applications are relatively basic (e.g., totaling the value of the stock portfolio), others can foster more high-level learning (e.g., using a spreadsheet to do projections based on market changes, communicating information to an audience). See the discussion in the next subsection for ways to use the various computer tools.

▶ *Extensive software instruction is not necessarily required.* Some teachers are reluctant to have students use the computer as an assistant unless the students (and the teacher too) have extensive knowledge of the software. But, as with Mr. Goins in the scenario, many teachers find that students are able to function adequately when they have just the basics, whether from prior exposure (e.g., a computer application class) or, as in this example, from instruction such as a handout or in-class demonstration. Students tend to learn computer applications rapidly and can often learn what they need to know while using them.

In Chapter 3, we introduced you to a number of the most popular computer productivity tools. Refer to the information there for their features and advantages. Here, we examine these tools—word processors, graphics tools, presentation software, databases, and spreadsheets—to see how students can use them as assistants. We consider the Internet and how to integrate it into the learning experience in Chapter 10.

Common Computer Assistant Tools

Word Processors

As we indicated in Chapter 3, word processors take much of the drudgery out of creating and editing written work. As a result, they are useful for a variety of student learning activities that involve literacy. Students can use word processors to do the following:

▶ *Write papers, stories, poems, and other in-class work.* The major emphasis today is on the process of writing. With almost any written work, students can use the word processor to practice creating a draft, editing the work, and producing a new draft. The ease with which they can do this encourages students to write more and do more revising.

▶ *Write letters.* In the stock market game, students wrote letters to obtain information during their initial research. This is one way to encourage students to reach out beyond the classroom. Many teachers have students write to other students through pen-pal projects. Writing to another student seems to provide an extra motivation for students to do their best.

▶ *Do writing-related activities.* The word processor can be useful for any type of writing-related activity. Students can use it singly or in groups to take notes, to record an experiment's or project's progress, or to collect ideas from a brainstorming session.

▶ *Do individual language arts exercises.* Students can use the word processor, for example, to type spelling words, science vocabulary words, or other language exercises as a way of practicing these skills.

▶ *Type handwritten notes as a way to study.* By typing their own handwritten notes on a word processor, students can reinforce learning or study for an exam.

Research on the effectiveness of word processors in writing instruction, while not unequivocal, suggests that they can be beneficial if used appropriately. In a statistical review of 32 studies, Bangert-Drowns (1993) concluded that using word processors in writing instruction results on average in both longer documents and better-quality writing. However, much of the research is mixed, and you should not assume that any use of word processors in a classroom automatically results in better student performance. The effects of word processors in instruction derive from the teacher's methods and the classroom organization (Cochran-Smith, 1991). As a result, it is important to integrate word processors into a well-conceived process approach to writing, provide students with adequate opportunity to learn to use the software, and take into account the particular classroom environment where the word processors are used.

Graphics Tools

Graphics tools provide students with the capability to work with images of all types (e.g., photographs, clip art, charts, graphs). See Chapter 3 for basic information about these tools. Students can learn by using these tools for the following:

▸ *Creative drawing.* Students can use drawing or painting programs to produce original artwork.
▸ *Illustration of work.* Students can use drawing or painting programs and clip art to illustrate written stories, reports, or hypermedia projects.
▸ *Charting or graphing.* As in the stock market game scenario, students can chart or graph data. This is especially applicable in data-rich subjects such as mathematics, science, and economics.

While graphics tools reduce the effort it takes for students to produce visual materials, they still rely on users' abilities to effectively communicate ideas. You need to help your students find the best ways to visually present information.

Presentation Software

As we pointed out in Chapter 3, presentation software is designed for the production and display of computer text and images, usually for presentation to a group. Appropriate presentation hardware is needed for group display; see "Toolbox Tools: Presentation Hardware" for more information. While presentation applications are often seen as tools for the teacher to enhance lectures and other presentations, students can use them as well. In general, these packages are quite similar to hypermedia authoring tools, discussed later in this chapter. Students can use presentation software to do the following:

▸ *Make in-class presentations or reports.* Presentation packages make it easy for students to create professional-looking electronic reports complete with multimedia elements.
▸ *Store and display electronic portfolios.* Because presentation packages are capable of handling multimedia elements, students can use them to assemble a portfolio of work including text, graphics, and even digital audio and video.
▸ *Transfer work to other media.* Many presentation packages provide a simple mechanism for converting electronic slides to print, photographic slides, or web pages. As a result, they can be used as authoring tools.

Presentation software, because of its multimedia capability, shares usage characteristics with graphics software as well as hypermedia authoring software. For all of these programs, it is important that students avoid becoming caught in the trap of form over substance. You must emphasize to your students that *what* they are presenting is as, or more, important than *how* they are presenting it. You and your students also need to be aware of copyright regulations to avoid making improper use of copyrighted material in presentations or other multimedia products. See the discussion on copyright in Chapter 8 for more information.

Databases

As you have already learned, computer database software provides the capability for creating, editing, and manipulating organized collections of information. Students can use databases and database management software to do the following:

▸ *Locate information in prepared databases.* Given the widespread use of computer databases today, at a minimum, students should be able to use database software to find information (e.g., locate a book in the school library's electronic card catalog or find the name of the nineteenth president in a database of U.S. presidents). As students progress, they should learn to apply the Boolean (logical) operators AND and OR to narrow or expand searches, respectively.
▸ *Develop problem-solving and higher-order thinking skills.* Databases make excellent tools for the development of problem-solving and higher-order thinking skills. Using a database of U.S. presidents, for example, students might explore questions such as: "How does war impact presidential elections?" or "Is there a relationship between the rate of increase in federal spending and the political party of the president?"
▸ *Develop original databases.* Students can learn a great deal about research, information organization, and a particular content area by developing their own databases. For example, as a social studies class project, students might develop a database of historical sites within their community.

Research into the use of databases in the classroom suggests that students can acquire information from databases and can learn from them but that they often need assistance to do so effectively (Collis, 1990; Ehrman, Glenn, Johnson, & White, 1992; Maor & Taylor, 1995). Just because students have access to databases does not ensure that they will learn. Students often exhibit poor inquiry skills. They may have difficulty formulating appropriate questions and corresponding searches, and they have difficulty interpreting results. You should help students understand the structure and organization of the database, and guide them through the process of using it.

TOOLBOX

TOOLS

Presentation Hardware

To make the computer's display visible to a group, you must choose one of several hardware options. The most common choices include a large television or video monitor usually with special computer-to-video conversion hardware and video projectors. We look at each of these options.

LARGE TELEVISIONS OR VIDEO MONITORS

Most schools possess large televisions or video monitors, often mounted in classrooms or available on carts, for use with VCRs or other video programming. For classroom use, sizes ranging from 21 inches to 35 inches are common. Large-screen televisions, although less common, can also be used for group presentations.

Today most personal computers are incapable of working with standard video monitors or televisions without special hardware. However, a number of vendors supply the special hardware needed to convert the computer's output to standard video. These devices, called scan converters, convert the computer's display output into standard video (often referred to as NTSC, the U.S. video standard). Most of these products, which typically cost a few hundred dollars, provide composite video output (the standard used by most VCRs), and some also support S-video output (super VHS video, a better quality). This output can be directed to a large video monitor or video projector for group presentations.

Computer-to-video conversion devices provide one convenient option for displaying computer images in the classroom. However, they have a disadvantage. Standard video cannot reproduce the high resolutions found on most personal computers today. As a result, when the computer image is converted to video, there is some degradation of the image. The output may become somewhat fuzzy, and small text fonts are likely to be completely unreadable. To compensate for this loss of resolution, some scan converters support magnification of the image. If this is not an option, select larger text fonts (at least 18 point) when using a computer with a video scan converter.

VIDEO PROJECTORS

Video projectors provide the capability to project a video or computer image onto a screen, much like a motion picture projector projects an image onto a screen. Most projectors today use liquid crystal display (LCD) technology, the same technology as is found in laptop and now desktop computer displays. However, some newer technologies are also beginning to be used in projectors. Because video projectors are capable of producing very large images—in some cases, 20 feet or more across—these devices provide an option for very large groups. Indeed, they are popular in classrooms, lecture halls, auditoriums, and other facilities that seat large numbers of people.

Different video projectors are distinguished by such features as the maximum screen resolution supported, the number of colors simultaneously displayed, and how rapidly the display is "refreshed" or renewed, an important consideration when tracking rapid motion such as the movement of a mouse cursor on the computer screen. Most projectors today can display video (e.g., from a VCR) as well as computer output from either *Windows*-based or *Mac OS*–based computers, usually with only an appropriate cable connection. Costs vary, but typically run a thousand dollars or more.

Some LCD projectors are so bright that they can function effectively in fully lighted rooms; no other common presentation device can accomplish this feat. LCD projectors are portable; most weigh under 20 pounds and are usually equipped with a carrying handle or come in a transportable case (see Figure A). In a classroom, they can be mounted on the ceiling for a permanent installation or wheeled into the classroom on a cart. Many projectors come with their own speakers to support audio as well as video. They are an especially attractive option for classroom display of computer images.

FIGURE A   An LCD projector.
Photo courtesy of ViewSonic Corporation.

Spreadsheets

Spreadsheets, as we noted in Chapter 3, are tools for calculating. In many cases, they include enhancements such as database elements and the capability to graphically depict data. Students can use these versatile tools to do the following:

▶ *Track financial information.* Spreadsheets first became popular tools for helping businesses track finances. Students, likewise, can use them for tracking financial information ranging from personal budgets to the finances of student clubs and organizations to class projects such as the stock market game in the previous scenario.

▶ *Keep records.* Although primarily calculating tools, spreadsheets can be used for simple recordkeeping, such as maintaining lists of information you may need to quickly sort or otherwise manipulate.

▶ *Create charts and graphs.* In addition to the previously mentioned graphing software, spreadsheets are excellent tools for quickly producing a chart or graph from data. In the stock market game scenario, students graphed their investment data using a spreadsheet.

▶ *Perform complex calculations.* Spreadsheets can quickly produce results involving complex calculations. For example, students in an economics or business class might generate loan amortization tables, while students in a trigonometry class could calculate trigonometric functions of various triangles.

▶ *Perform "what-if?" simulation or hypothesis-testing activities.* Because of their rapid recalculation, spreadsheets are well suited to having students investigate how changes in one factor impact other factors—"What will happen if I change . . . " Using a spreadsheet, students in a high school business

Addressing the Standards

NETS Connection

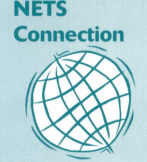

As we have discussed the various aspects of the instructional planning process, we have shown repeatedly the potential role technology may play in that process. National Educational Technology Standards I, III, IV, and V (see Teacher Resource A on page 297 for a full review of these standards and their performance indicators) for teachers emphasize one's need to *use technology tools to process data, report results, prepare publications, solve real-world problems, produce creative works, and facilitate higher-order thinking skills.* Often a stumbling block in using such tools is generating ideas of when and how it could be used. Below we have listed a variety of ways a database might be used. Note that some of the tasks are quite mundane things that perhaps would save some time and energy; whereas some others may help you see how real-world problems might be addressed.

Database tool	• Organize a personal DVD collection that would filter for story line, age appropriateness, actors, etc.
	• Create biographical information on your students that would allow you to identify students, parents, addresses, who to contact in emergencies, favorite pets, birthdays, etc.
	• Create a storage and retrieval database that would include all of your lesson plans and accompanying ancillary materials (printables, weblinks, etc.) and would filter based on content, learners, instructional method, and/or media.
	• Create a database of information that would allow students to compare the best theme parks of the world and then create vacation plans based on location, types of rides desired, cleanliness of the park, type of park visitor, etc. Moreover, they could use the data from the database to make recommendations about where new amusement parks could be built, the types of entertainment that should be developed, etc.
	• Create a database that a pharmacist might use to compare drug interactions. Given various types of drugs, taken in close contiguity for specific types of patients, could specific interactions be predicted?

Ponder ways in which other software applications (e.g., word processing, spreadsheets, presentation software, Web editing, desk top publishing) might be used along a similar continuum from simple uses to more complex, real-world problem-type tasks. For each of these, create a journal entry and record some of your ideas.

class, for example, might examine the effects of changing insurance rates on the cost of owning and operating a car. Students in a biology class could explore the effects of changing birth and death rates on the growth of populations. Students in a geometry class could examine the relationship between perimeter and area in various geometric shapes.

Spreadsheets allow students to concentrate on real-world problems without becoming bogged down in the calculations. However, you need to make certain your students understand that the results from spreadsheets are only as good as the data and formulas entered in them. An incorrect formula or bad data can lead to erroneous results. The relevant old expression in the computer world is "garbage in, garbage out." If what you start with is not correct, the computer cannot magically fix it. Spreadsheets are great tools, but like any other computer tool, they must be used properly.

Problems and Pitfalls

Problems and pitfalls are associated with each of the computer-as-assistant productivity tools discussed here. Refer to the discussion in this chapter for specific concerns associated with each type of software. As with any instructional tool, the important thing to remember is that computer use should be appropriate to the specific instructional goals, the educational context, and the students. Keep in mind that you may need special hardware and/or software to meet students' special needs. See the section on assistive technology in Chapter 3 for more information.

TOOLBOX

TIPS

Using Computer Laboratories

Computer laboratories are commonplace in most schools, and they offer the advantage that each student, or perhaps pair of students, is able to work on an individual machine. This makes it possible for an entire class to simultaneously use computer-assisted instruction software, work with an office application such as a word processor or spreadsheet, or do multimedia authoring. However, just as there are challenges in using a single computer in the classroom, working with an entire class of students in a computer laboratory brings its own set of challenges. How can you effectively make use of a computer laboratory?

For starters, consider the configuration of the laboratory. Many different configurations for computer laboratories are common in schools, and these configurations are suited to different instructional purposes. Four of these are shown in Figure B. As shown in the figure, the peripheral layout works well for monitoring laboratory activities. The classroom layout is effective for teaching computer applications. The back-to-back rows layout maximizes utilization of space in individualized student work situations. The cluster layout supports small-group activities well. Plan to make the best use of whatever configuration is available to you.

It is important to recognize that computer laboratories are shared resources within schools. Typically, a number of classes, perhaps even the entire school, may use a computer laboratory. As a result, you must plan in advance for the use of a laboratory and expect that your time will be limited. In some schools, computer laboratories can be reserved for a specific period of time by making a request to the technology coordinator or media specialist. In other schools, a fixed rotation schedule may be utilized to allow each eligible class to have some time in the lab. Regardless of the particular method, it is likely that you will have only a limited amount of time, such as an hour a day for several consecutive days or perhaps only an hour once per week in the lab. You must be prepared to effectively utilize the laboratory by planning your lessons around the available times.

Sessions in computer laboratories have the potential to become chaotic because of the fact that many students are working on computers simultaneously and may need assistance at once. How can the teacher manage the laboratory environment so that time is productively spent? Try the following tips to make best use of laboratory time.

▶ Obtain assistance, if possible. It never hurts to have more hands and eyes in the computer lab. The school's technology coordinator may be able to assist during laboratory activities. Teacher's aides, parents, or others may be able to help.

▶ Prepare students for the laboratory experience. Complete preparatory work in the classroom before going to the lab. Make sure students know the rules for how to work in the lab (e.g., proper lab behavior, how to save work, how to print) and what they are to do when they go to the lab. Create instructions, worksheets, checklists, and other materials to guide students' activities. Discuss with students the amount of time their activities will entail, and schedule the lab accordingly.

TOOLBOX TIPS
(continued)

▶ Monitor students during the laboratory activity to make certain that they are on task. Break down the laboratory activity into steps and require students to check in or complete work at each step to ensure that they make adequate progress throughout the assigned laboratory time.

▶ If you need to address all of the students in the lab, have the students turn off their monitors/displays so that they will focus their attention on you.

▶ Encourage students to help one another. "Ask three before me" is a laboratory rule used by many teachers that means students should ask three other students before asking the teacher if they have a question or problem. Develop student "experts" who are knowledgeable about particular computer applications and can assist others.

▶ Have students use visual signals to indicate when they need help. For example, if students have noncritical questions or problems, instruct them to put a yellow card or cup on the computer or monitor. If students have critical questions or problems, such that they cannot continue without help, instruct them to put a red card or cup on the computer or monitor. These visual signals make it easier for the teacher and aides to determine who is in need of immediate assistance.

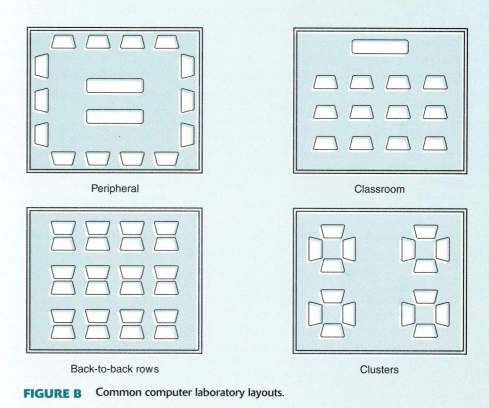

Peripheral

Classroom

Back-to-back rows

Clusters

FIGURE B Common computer laboratory layouts.

COMPUTER AS LEARNER (STUDENT AS TEACHER)

When the computer functions as learner, the roles of computer and student that we see in traditional computer-assisted instruction are reversed. The computer becomes the "learner," and the student becomes the "teacher." The objective is for the student to teach the computer to perform some task (e.g., draw a geometric figure) or to use the computer to teach others relevant content (e.g., concepts about the solar system). To achieve this objective, the student must come to understand a problem or body of content and be able to communicate this to or through the computer. This requires organization, logical thinking, and problem-solving skills; as a result, many experts believe that this is one of the most valuable ways to use a computer in education.

Using the computer as learner is an open-ended approach that relies on students' abilities to construct their understanding about some body of content and how to use the computer. In the classroom, this approach can be implemented by having students program the computer using a traditional computer **programming language** such as Logo, BASIC, or C. Programming, while once a popular way to use computers for problem solving in the classroom, today is little used outside of computer science classes. However, another way to implement this approach is to have students develop interactive multimedia/hypermedia products using authoring tools such as *HyperStudio, eZedia,* or *Flash*. Using multimedia authoring tools, students must gather content, organize it, put it into the program's multimedia format, and create mechanisms within the software for others to interact with the content. This approach remains popular in many classrooms today.

We look here at the ways that students can learn by creating products on the computer. Begin by reading the scenario that follows. Identify how the students use the computer to present content to others in this example.

Scenario: Multimedia Reports

Peggy Gambrel teaches sixth grade in a self-contained classroom in William McKinley Middle School. Last year, in response to a call from the school for more emphasis on mathematics, science, and technology, she developed a number of new activities for her students. One of these activities was a modification of a history/language arts assignment that she had used in previous years. In the past, Ms. Gambrel had assigned her students the task of writing a report about a famous American "pioneer" (i.e., explorer or scientist such as Meriwether Lewis, Thomas Edison, or George Washington Carver). To fit last year's new theme, she changed the assignment to one in which pairs of students were to do research and create an interactive multimedia program about a famous mathematician or scientist.

At the beginning of the two-and-one-half week activity, Ms. Gambrel made the assignment to her class and paired off the students. Each pair's initial task was to decide on the subject of their report. To help them choose, Ms. Gambrel decorated her room by hanging pictures of famous mathematicians and scientists on the walls. With the help of the school librarian, Ms. Keck, she also gathered a number of print materials about famous scientists and mathematicians. After surveying the available materials, each team wrote the names of their top four preferred choices on a card and turned it in to Ms. Gambrel. By looking through all of the requests, she was able to assign a subject to each team so that there were no duplicates in the class, and every team was able to get its first, second, or third choice.

During the remainder of the first week, students researched their choices. Ms. Gambrel set aside time each day for students to go to the library. All of the students were able to access relevant print materials, and they were also able to go online to find information on the Web. To ensure that everyone had a chance to do online research, Ms. Keck set up a sign-up system where each team was assigned two 30-minute blocks during the week. She helped the students during their searches so that they were able to make productive use of the limited time.

During the second week, students created their multimedia programs using *HyperStudio,* a popular hypermedia authoring tool, using the school's minilab as well as the two computers in their classroom to work on their projects. Ms. Gambrel didn't feel that she was an expert in *HyperStudio* herself, but she could handle the basics. The students had used *HyperStudio* on a couple of occasions earlier in the year, so Ms. Gambrel did not spend time teaching them how to use the software for this activity. The kids just dove right in! Ms. Gambrel gave them some time each day to work on their reports.

All of the teams built *HyperStudio* projects, called *stacks,* consisting of several cards. Ms. Gambrel provided some general guidelines for the multimedia report, but each team had to determine exactly what content to include and how to present it. Ms. Gambrel was amazed at how hard the students worked—much harder, she thought, than when they did their usual written reports—and how creative they were. Each team included textual information about its subject, navigational buttons to allow others to go through the stack, interactive questions about the subject, and multimedia elements. Lauren and Katie, for example, like many of the other students, scanned a picture from a book for their report on Jane Goodall. They also added a sound effect that played each time someone went to a new card in their stack because they thought it sounded "cool." Tim and Jim used a picture of Marie Curie that they found on the Internet for their project. Chris and Sean used *HyperStudio*'s ability to record speech to add their own narration to their project. David and Nancy found a digital video clip of Albert Einstein for their report. No two projects were alike.

At the end of the project, the class had a show-and-tell session. Ms. Gambrel hooked one of the computers in her classroom to an LCD projector that she checked out from the media center so that everyone could see. Each team then presented its multimedia report. The students really enjoyed the assignment, and they loved sharing their projects. During the school's science night, the students set up their projects in the school's computer lab so that their parents could stop by to see them. Ms. Gambrel received notes of thanks from several of the parents. She was pleased with the new class activity and glad that she had tried it.

What does this scenario tell us about using the computer as learner? There are several things to note:

▶ *Students must learn both the content and how to present it.* When the computer functions as "learner," students become the "teacher" and have a two-part task. They must learn the content at hand, and they must learn how to present it via the computer. This requires organization, logical thinking, and problem solving.

▶ *Students are actively involved.* Although it is certainly not the only way to accomplish this aim, having students create computer-based projects gets

Student working on hypermedia project.

them actively involved in learning. It is motivating. It is consistent with a view of learning as construction of understanding.

- *There is more than one way to achieve success.* A characteristic of most situations where students assume the role of teachers using a computer is that there are many ways they can succeed. In the previous scenario, no two students' projects were the same, yet all met the goal. Just as in much of "real-world" problem solving, different approaches can and do work.
- *Extensive prior knowledge is not necessarily required.* As with the use of the computer as assistant, teachers are sometimes reluctant to try using the computer as learner without a lot of prior knowledge. However, as with computer productivity tools, a little knowledge can go a long way in the classroom when it comes to using the computer as learner. In this example, Ms. Gambrel didn't feel she was expert with the software, but her students were able to dive in and get the job done.

While students can "teach" the computer using programming languages such as Logo, BASIC, or C, programming is usually taught only in computer science or technology courses today. However, students can assume the role of teacher by using multimedia authoring tools to create interactive multimedia software to teach others. We look next at multimedia and hypermedia authoring, specifically *HyperStudio,* an authoring package widely used in schools. Web page authoring tools can be used in a similar way; this option is discussed in more detail in Chapter 10.

Multimedia and Hypermedia Authoring

Multimedia refers to the use of a variety of media formats (e.g., text, graphics, audio, video) in a single presentation or program. **Hypermedia** refers to a system of multimedia information representation in which the information is stored digitally in interlinked chunks called *nodes.* The process of creating multimedia or hypermedia products is called *authoring.* Because of the growth and popularity of multimedia and hypermedia, many schools are now teaching students how to author multimedia and hypermedia works.

The rationale for teaching students to author multimedia/hypermedia is that engaging in this process causes students to be actively involved and often highly motivated. Further, multimedia development is consistent with the view of learning as knowledge construction. To develop a multimedia project, the learner must research, evaluate, organize, and present information in a variety of formats. Because hypermedia is rapidly becoming the norm of the computer world, teaching students to author hypermedia can prepare them for future study and work. Further, hypermedia project development serves double duty in the classroom. Not only is the creation of a hypermedia project a learning activity, but the process and the end product can serve as a form of assessment.

Hypermedia Authoring Fundamentals

In popular stand-alone hypermedia programs, nodes are usually referred to as *cards* in a *stack* (like a stack of index cards) or *pages* in a *book* (like a traditional print book). On the Web, we talk about *web pages* in a *website.* The concept is the same. You can think of a hypermedia node as a card or page on which you can put information of various sorts, and the card/page can be linked to one or more other cards/pages of related information. Unlike a print book, however, nodes in hypermedia are often linked to other nodes in a nonlinear fashion.

On any given node, one can place different things, such as text, graphics, and links to other nodes (sometimes depicted as buttons). Each thing that one can put on a node is an "object." There can be text fields (objects containing text), graphics (picture objects), buttons or links (linking or action objects), and perhaps other objects such as sounds, videos, and so on. Because they treat things as objects, hypermedia systems have the characteristics of what are known as *object-oriented programming systems* **(OOPS).** In addition, hypermedia systems are **event driven,** which means that they respond to events in the computer environment. For example, when the user clicks on a button or a *hot link* (an active link to another node often appearing as highlighted text), this triggers a *mouse click event.* The hypermedia system can respond to this event with some action, such as navigating to another card or page.

With hypermedia authoring tools, students can create hypermedia products with relative ease. By placing objects (text, pictures) on cards/pages and creating links, it is a simple matter to create functional and effective hypermedia projects. Little if any programming knowledge is needed. However, many hypermedia authoring tools have programming available if the student wants to do something more complex. Macromedia's *Director* uses a scripting language known as *Lingo*. *HyperStudio* uses a scripting language called *HyperLogo*, a version of the Logo programming language. In the next subsection, we focus on *HyperStudio* as an example of a hypermedia authoring tool. *HyperStudio* has become a popular hypermedia tool in schools because of its ease of use, its many features, and its availability for different types of computers. In Chapter 10, we will look at tools and techniques for authoring Web-based hypermedia materials.

HyperStudio

HyperStudio is a popular hypermedia authoring tool produced by Roger Wagner Publishing. The program is available for both *MacOS* and *Windows*-based computers. Using it, students can create hypermedia projects that operate on stand-alone computers or can be shared over the Internet. While the complete *HyperStudio* package is needed for authoring, a freely distributable player program can be used to present or play back finished projects on computers that do not have the complete program.

In *HyperStudio,* nodes are referred to as *cards* and complete projects are called *stacks*. The task of creating

content on a card is relatively straightforward. When first starting a new stack, the program automatically creates the first card just as word-processing software begins with a blank page. Additional cards can be added as needed. Through a combination of menu options and tools, hypermedia authors can add objects to a card and subsequently edit them. Authors can add text objects (known as *fields*), graphic objects (pictures or clip art), and *buttons* (objects used for navigation or to invoke actions). Figure 9–5 shows an example of a *HyperStudio* card with a variety of hypermedia objects.

Several options are available in the program to permit authors to create cards with visual interest. The objects on a card rest in layers on top of a background. Authors can paint the background with a color or a pattern or place a graphic in the background to give the card an interesting look. In text objects, the author can control the color of the text and the color of the background field in which the text sits. Buttons can also be colored, and the author can select from a number of available icons to represent buttons. In addition to the ability to import pictures and clip art, *HyperStudio* also provides basic drawing tools so that student authors can create their own illustrations.

HyperStudio also provides a high level of multimedia support. Special multimedia options are made

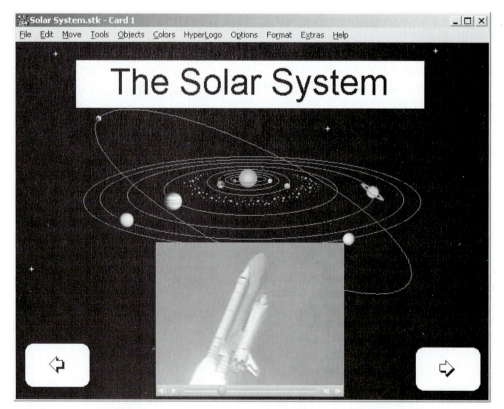

FIGURE 9–5   A screen from a *HyperStudio* stack showing multimedia elements including text, a graphic, a digital video clip, and navigational buttons.
Source: HyperStudio, Roger Wagner Publishing. Used with permission.

available as actions associated with buttons. Available actions include playing a digital sound, playing a digital movie (e.g., a QuickTime movie), playing an animation, using a built-in timer function, and using one of several special actions (such as a function that causes credits to roll up the screen like a movie). *HyperStudio* even has some rudimentary test tracking features that can be used for embedded quizzes. Finally, for students who may not be satisfied with the range of available options in the program, buttons can be programmed using *HyperStudio*'s built-in scripting language, HyperLogo.

Hypermedia Authoring in the Classroom

Student development of hypermedia offers many opportunities for classroom activities.

▶ *Hypermedia projects.* Perhaps the most common application of hypermedia authoring in the classroom is student development of hypermedia projects or reports. Hypermedia projects allow students, either individually or in groups, to create reports that summarize a major effort such as a science experiment or interdisciplinary project. Rather than simply writing about it, students can include written work, pictures, sound clips, video, and links to describe what they did and/or to present background information. This application is similar to the use of presentation software, but students can create interactive projects with built-in questions and extensive hyperlinking that other students can use to learn about the content.

▶ *Multimedia presentations.* Students (and teachers) can use hypermedia authoring tools to create multimedia presentations or slide shows. While perhaps not as easy to use for linear presentations as presentation software (e.g., *PowerPoint*), tools such as *HyperStudio* are well suited to branched or linking presentations.

▶ *Nonlinear fiction.* Some teachers have begun to have their students experiment with the possibilities of hypermedia for authoring nonlinear fiction. The branching capabilities of hypermedia offer students the option to create stories that may have more than one ending.

▶ *Portfolios of student work.* Hypermedia authoring tools are excellent for building portfolios of student work in many subjects.

Problems and Pitfalls

Programming is, and probably will remain, a controversial aspect of computers in education for some. Detractors point out that few students will ever become programmers, and early claims of the problem-solving benefits of learning programming tended not to be borne out by research. Having students develop hypermedia projects seems to be less controversial, although its aims are similar. There is evidence that students are motivated by and can benefit educationally from developing hypermedia projects (Ayersman, 1996; Chen & McGrath, 2003). However, you must plan and prepare in order for hypermedia development to pay dividends in the classroom.

When students develop hypermedia projects, structure and advance planning are important. Two forms of advance planning, often used by programmers and instructional designers, are also helpful in getting students to think about their projects *before* getting on the computer. These two techniques are storyboarding and flowcharting. Software designers often use storyboarding, originally borrowed from animators and filmmakers. **Storyboarding** is a technique for illustrating, on paper, what the computer screen displays will look like in a program. Students can design a *HyperStudio* project, for example, on index cards before making the real thing.

Multimedia Projects

How can multimedia/hypermedia authoring tools be used by students and teachers? To find out more, visit the following websites that include examples of multimedia projects.

Website	URL
HyperStudio Showcase	http://www.hyperstudio.com/showcase/index.html
eZediaMX Showcase	http://www.ezedia.com/support/resources/showcase/

Look at an example of a multimedia lesson from one of these sites. Imagine that you are a teacher of a relevant subject and grade. Using the Preview Form: Multimedia focus on the accompanying CD **(Chapter INFO and Activities >>> Chapter 7 >>> Media Preview Forms)**, review the lesson. How effective do you think it was? How would you integrate it in your own teaching? What ideas do you have for multimedia development projects in the classroom?

Addressing the Standards

NETS Connection

Several National Educational Technology Standards (NETS II, III) focus on teachers being able to help their students *use technology to address and solve authentic problems through collaborative learning activities.* Review the related standards and performance indicators in Teacher Resource A on page 297 and focus on the concepts of technology, authentic problems, and student collaborative learning.

Consider ways that you might use different technologies to facilitate collaborative efforts in learning. Reflect on the possibilities of having your students do the following:

▶ Outline ways for groups of students to work collaboratively using *HyperStudio, PowerPoint,* or similar software, to produce a set of student-centered individualized instructional materials on a topic of interest.

▶ Students today often use IM (instant messaging) software to communicate with one another. Have students create a short, concise lesson on what IM is and how it is typically used to be presented to parents at the upcoming parent/teacher conferences. Create ways for the students to use IM to actually develop the project and report on their procedures, as well as what worked and what didn't.

▶ Have students develop another project using IM or e-mail as a tool to help them communicate and accomplish the goals of the project.

In a journal entry, describe the potential value and challenges of such an activity. How could you emphasize the need to transfer what is learned so that students see the utility of the tool and what can be learned through the group collaboration?

They can redesign and rearrange the cards before making the effort to create the project on the computer. Most programmers describe the logic of a program using **flowcharting,** a graphical means of representing the flow of a program. The flowchart illustrates where the links go in a hypermedia stack or a web page. This can be especially important in a highly linked hypermedia project. Figure 9–6 shows samples of a storyboard card and flowchart for a card in a *HyperStudio* project.

ISSUES INVOLVED IN INTEGRATING THE USE OF COMPUTERS

We hope that this chapter provided you with many good ideas about how your students can learn using computers. Just as there is no one right way to win a game of chess, there is no one right way to help your students learn. Different approaches, like the different chess pieces, have their own strengths and weaknesses. It is the situation, the audience, and the goal that determines which approach to choose. In chess, the pawn is a relatively weak piece that usually moves forward only a single square. But, in some situations, it is possible to mount a winning attack by making a succession of small pawn moves. In the classroom, a single drill and practice session, like a single pawn on the chessboard, may not accomplish very much. But, many drill and practice sessions, like a sequence of pawn moves, can have a big impact on student learning. The important thing is to match the learning demands of the instructional situation to the particular method of computer use.

When using computer-assisted instruction, select the category of CAI that best meets your needs. Drill and practice programs can help learners to master basic skills. Tutorials can help students to learn concepts. Simulations and problem-solving software offer the opportunity for learners to apply what they have learned to solve problems. However, always keep in mind that any use of CAI must be part of an overall learning strategy in the classroom. Appropriate preparatory and follow-up activities are essential to success.

Computer productivity applications can be used in the computer as assistant mode by students as they learn in almost any content area. As we have suggested in this chapter, students do not necessarily need to have extensive knowledge of particular productivity applications in order to effectively use the computer in this way. A little knowledge is enough to get started. When using the computer in this way, it is important to bear in mind that the focus should be on the learning task rather than on the software, which is just a tool to help achieve the learning goal.

By developing multimedia or hypermedia projects, students can take on the role of teachers. From a learning perspective, this requires the students to develop their own understanding of a body of content and effectively communicate it to others. When using the computer in this way, students need to be made aware of

Storyboard Card

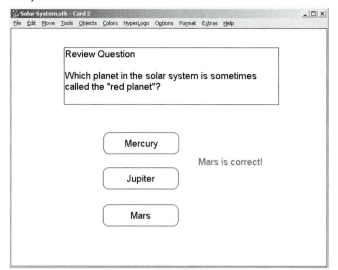

Flowchart of Card

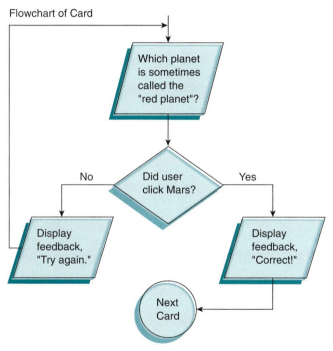

FIGURE 9–6   Sample flowchart and the resulting screen shot for an interaction question in a *HyperStudio* project. *Reprinted with permission from James D. Lehman.*

copyright laws. (See the discussion in Chapter 8.) While students' classroom uses of copyrighted material in developing multimedia projects may be protected under the fair use provisions of copyright law, it is important for students to understand that they do not have carte blanche to use copyrighted materials in any way that they wish. When using the computer in this way, teachers also need to make sure that the content remains the focus of students' efforts. Students sometimes are guilty of emphasizing form over substance when developing multimedia projects.

TECHNOLOGY COORDINATOR'S CORNER

Recently, technology coordinator Phyllis Parker consulted with one of her fourth-grade teachers, Bonnie Anderson. They talked about the evolution of Ms. Anderson's uses of the computer in her classroom. Ms. Anderson noted that when she first started teaching, she only thought about using the computer as a teaching machine. She described how she found a few computer-assisted instruction software packages that she was comfortable using with her students. In those days, she had the kids work on math exercises and an occasional science simulation perhaps once a week. It was okay, and some use of CAI was still a part of what she did in the classroom. But Ms. Anderson shared with Ms. Parker her desire to do more.

At Ms. Parker's urging, beginning a couple of years ago, Ms. Anderson began asking her students to word process some writing assignments. She also introduced an assignment to have her students do an oral report using *PowerPoint*. Both she and her students became increasingly comfortable doing work using the computers in her classroom and the school's lab. That successful experience had given Ms. Anderson the courage to take another step and try hypermedia this year. She decided she wanted her students to develop hypermedia stacks about state historical sites as part of their history curriculum. However, she was nervous about it and sought advice from Ms. Parker.

Ms. Parker was encouraging, and she made some suggestions for how Ms. Anderson might approach having her students use the hypermedia authoring package available in the school. First, she recommended that Ms. Anderson go through the tutorial for the software or attend a district workshop so that she could become familiar with the basics of how the software worked herself. Next, she advised Ms. Anderson to introduce her students to the software through a warm-up activity such as creating a small hypermedia project about their hobbies or pets. She assured Ms. Anderson that the students would be quick to learn. During the history unit, Ms. Parker suggested that Ms. Anderson have her students design their projects on note cards before ever going to the computer. This would allow the students to do their preparatory work in the classroom so that the lab time could be used productively for the task of putting the content into the hypermedia authoring program. When they did begin work on the computers, Ms. Parker urged Ms. Anderson to designate student helpers in the laboratory, those students who knew their way around the software, to help manage the questions that would come up. In this way, Ms. Anderson would be able to spend her time circulating throughout the laboratory and helping those students who needed it the most. Ms. Anderson agreed to try these suggestions as she tried a new way to use the computer to help her students learn.

SUMMARY

In this chapter we explored ways that students can use computers for learning, examining three basic categories of computer use: computer as teacher, computer as assistant, and computer as learner. Computer as teacher is often labeled computer-assisted instruction (CAI), where the computer delivers instruction to the student. Common forms of CAI include drill and practice, tutorial, simulation, instructional game, and problem solving. Computer as assistant refers to the use of the computer as a productivity tool for common tasks. Typical computer applications in this category include word processor, graphics package, presentation software, database, and spreadsheet. When the computer plays the role of the learner, the student assumes the role of the "teacher" through the use of a hypermedia authoring tool such as *HyperStudio*. This requires developing content expertise and communicating it to others in an organized fashion.

SUGGESTED RESOURCES

CD Resources

To increase retention and transfer of this information, review the *Reflective Questions and Activities* located in the Chapter 9 section **(Chapter info and activities >>> Chapter 9 >>> Reflective Questions and Activities)** of the text's accompanying CD.

In addition, you can access relevant Internet websites, NETS Connection exercises, and direct e-mail access to the text's authors.

Website Resources

Access the text's website **(www.prenhall.com/newby)**, navigate to Chapter 9, and review the Question and Answer section for relevant questions that have been generated by students and answered by the authors. You may also submit your own questions directly to the authors. In addition, you can access presentations by the authors about this chapter and gain insights directly from them about the topics that have been presented.

Print Resources

Chen, P., & McGrath, D. (2003). Moments of joy: Student engagement and conceptual learning in the design of hypermedia documents. *Journal of Research on Technology in Education, 35*(3), 402–422.

Johnson, R. T., Johnson, D. W., & Stanne, M. B. (1985). Effects of cooperative, competitive, and individualistic goal structures on computer-assisted instruction. *Journal of Educational Psychology, 77*(6), 668–677.

Jonassen, D. H. (1999). *Computers as mindtools for schools: Engaging critical thinking* (2nd ed). Upper Saddle River, NJ: Prentice Hall.

Kulik, C. C., & Kulik, J. A. (1991). Effectiveness of computer-based instruction: An updated analysis. *Computers in Human Behavior, 7*, 75–94.

Kulik, J. A. (2003). *Effects of using instructional technology in elementary and secondary schools: What controlled evaluation studies say*. Arlington, VA: SRI International. Available: http://www.sri.com/policy/csted/reports/sandt/it.

Lee, J. (1999). Effectiveness of computer-based instructional simulation: A meta-analysis. *International Journal of Instructional Media, 26*, 71–85.

Lockard, J., & Abrams, P. D. (2004). *Computers for twenty-first century educators* (6th ed.). New York: Allyn & Bacon.

Lou, Y., Abrami, P. C., & d'Apollonia, S. (2001). Small group and individual learning with technology: A meta-analysis. *Review of Educational Research, 71*(3), 449–521.

Roblyer, M. D. (2004). 2004 Update: *Integrating educational technology into teaching* (3rd ed.). Upper Saddle River, NJ: Prentice Hall.

Taylor, R. (1980). *The computer in the school: Tutor, tool, and tutee*. New York: Teachers College Press.

Electronic Resources

http://www.ezedia.com
eZedia

http://www.hyperstudio.com
HyperStudio

http://www.macromedia.com
Macromedia

http://www.yahoo.com/Computers/
Yahoo Computers and Internet

http://www.yahoo.com/Education/
Yahoo Education

10

Integration of the Internet to Support Learning

CHAPTER OBJECTIVES

After reading and studying this chapter, you will be able to:

▶ Discuss applications of the Internet in education that fall into the categories: (1) communication, (2) information retrieval, and (3) information publishing.

▶ Distinguish between synchronous and asynchronous forms of Internet communication.

▶ Identify three or four websites that could be used by students to locate age-appropriate information related to an educational topic of your choosing.

▶ Define WebQuest, and describe the common components of a WebQuest.

▶ Describe how teachers and students can use the Internet for information publishing.

▶ Identify and discuss issues related to the use of the Internet in the classroom.

This chapter focuses on using the Internet and World Wide Web as tools to enhance the learning process. Chapter 9 examined the use of the computer as a tool that can be used as a teacher, as a learner, and as an assistant. Here, we extend that notion to include the use of the Internet. In Chapter 11, we will continue our look at technology integration by considering distance education technologies.

INTRODUCTION

Think about the library in your school or community. On the shelves of the library you will find a large collection of information resources of various types. There are books, magazines, and newspapers. There are reference materials such as dictionaries and encyclopedias. In most libraries today you will also find collections of nonprint media such as music CDs and videos. A library contains a substantial collection of accumulated knowledge that has been brought to one location where you can browse through it, search for items of interest, and explore topics of interest to you.

In some ways, the Internet is like a vast library. The Internet brings information resources including text, pictures, sounds, and video from all over the world into your classroom or home. As in a library, you can browse through available information resources to pick and choose what you need to learn about a topic of interest or to create lessons and learning experiences for your students. Many Internet information resources are updated daily, or even minute by minute, making them very up-to-date. Unlike a library, however, there is no

card catalog for the Internet, no librarian to help you find materials, and no assurance of the quality of what you might find. Indeed, there are many things on the Internet that we would prefer our students did *not* find. Yet, it is an unparalled information resource.

The Internet is more than just a repository of information, however. It is also a communications tool that gives you and your students the capability to interact with others around the world. It is also a tool for information publishing, where you can make your own materials available to others as if you could simply slide your own book onto the shelves of your local library. This power and versatility make the Internet a truly revolutionary tool for teachers and learners.

TECHNOLOGY INTEGRATION PROCESS: PREPARING TO INTEGRATE THE INTERNET IN THE LEARNING EXPERIENCE

As when planning any instructional activity (see Chapters 4 and 5), you need to develop a plan for using the Internet in the classroom. First, consider the characteristics of your students. When using the Internet, you must give special attention to their abilities to access the Internet for communication, information retrieval, and information publishing. If your students don't have these skills, you will need to teach them.

In specifying objectives for your students, determine if using the Internet will enhance their ability to meet the objectives. In many cases, the Internet can provide up-to-date information on the content they are studying. In other cases, your students might need to communicate with others outside the classroom to meet their objectives. These are reasons to use the Internet in the classroom, but you should not have students use the Internet just for its own sake. Students should not use the Internet to find information readily available in the classroom. Use the Internet when it adds real value to your lesson.

Of course, in order to use the Internet, the learning environment will need to include access to a computer with an Internet connection. It may be one computer in the classroom or a computer lab where all students can access the Internet simultaneously. Be aware that the type of connection you have available may limit your options. A dial-up connection to the Internet can be slow, limiting what can be done in a class period. Even a fast connection may slow to a crawl if a whole class of students attempts to access the same website at the same time.

When selecting methods and media as well as specific instructional activities, you will need to preview the material on the Internet related to content and objectives.

In some ways, the Internet is like a vast library where resources of many kinds are available.

This is no different than previewing a videotape before you decide to use it with students. Selecting websites for a lesson is no different than selecting any instructional materials (textbooks, videotapes, audio recordings, etc.) as described in Chapter 8. See the "Web Page Evaluation Form" in this text's accompanying CD **(Chapter Intro and Activities >>>Chapter 7>>> Media Preview Forms)** for criteria for evaluating websites. There are countless websites for students and teachers, and we have included a few of our favorite examples in this chapter.

When using the Internet with students, follow the same general process as you would for any lesson implementation: prepare the instructional materials, prepare the learning environment, prepare the learners, and proceed with the lesson. Preparation is the key to success! While preparing your learning environment, check that the computer or computers are working properly and that they have Internet access. Schedule the computer laboratory if you plan to have many students access the Internet simultaneously. If you are going to demonstrate the Internet to a class, be sure that the computer projection equipment is working properly and that all students will be able to see the image. Preparing materials requires that you determine that the websites you plan to use are still available. Check the sites you plan to use a week or so before the planned use date at the same time of day that you plan to have students access them, if possible. Prepare your students for the lesson activity whether it is to be done individually, in small groups, or as a class. Discuss the purpose (objectives) of the lesson, provide written guidelines for the activity, and remind them of the copyright guidelines and acceptable use policies for your school.

When the lesson begins, monitor individual students to keep them on task and to be sure that they are following the Internet use guidelines for your school (see "Toolbox Tips: Acceptable Use Policies"). For group use of the Internet, you will be able to monitor what students are doing. Make certain they do not wander off into cyberspace or to an inappropriate site. Just as a student who is directed to find information in a standard encyclopedia may be sidetracked by unrelated pictures and content, students are often distracted on the Internet.

Of course, following a lesson, you and your students need to take time to evaluate how the Internet worked (or didn't work) within the lesson. You need to determine if the students learned from the experience. If the lesson was less successful than expected, think of ways in which you could improve on your use of the Internet in the future.

You and your students must have realistic expectations of the Internet. It will not answer all questions and solve all learning problems. The Internet is a learning tool (admittedly a powerful one), and like all tools, you must use it properly. You cannot just turn students loose and hope for the best.

WHAT IS THE INTERNET AND HOW DO I CONNECT?

As you learned in Chapter 3, the **Internet** consists of thousands of connected computer networks around the world that connect millions of computers and tens of millions of people. The Internet is also referred to as the "Net," the "Information Superhighway," and "cyberspace." The many different kinds of computers on the Internet communicate with one another by means of a common communications *protocol* (a set of common rules) known as **TCP/IP** (Transmission Control Protocol/Internet Protocol). Every computer on the Internet has a unique address, expressed in numeric form, called its *IP address*. A computer communicates with another computer on the Internet by sending information to its IP address.

How is information communicated through the Internet? Information is sent through the Internet in **packets** (see Figure 10–1), little bundles of information. The packets of an individual message are sent along any available path through cyberspace. Packets are reassembled when they arrive at their destination. A network device called a **router** regulates traffic on the Internet and determines the most efficient route for each packet. So, when you send an e-mail message, for example, the message is broken into packets, sent across your local area network (LAN) to a router, which then shunts the packets to their destination. Packets may travel through many computer networks on their journey, but because they travel at the speed of electricity the journey usually takes only seconds. Today, almost all schools, most classrooms, and most homes in the United States are connected to the Internet.

USES OF THE INTERNET

You and your students can use the Internet in a wide variety of ways. As we noted in Chapter 3, the most common applications can be grouped into three categories: communication, information retrieval, and information publishing. We introduce them here, and discuss them at length over the course of this chapter.

Communication

Electronic mail (e-mail) is the most widely used service on the Internet. Anyone with a computer connected to the Internet can communicate with anyone else in the world who is also connected. It is fast, inexpensive, and saves paper. You and your students can also join discussion groups where you can ask questions, discuss problems, and share experiences.

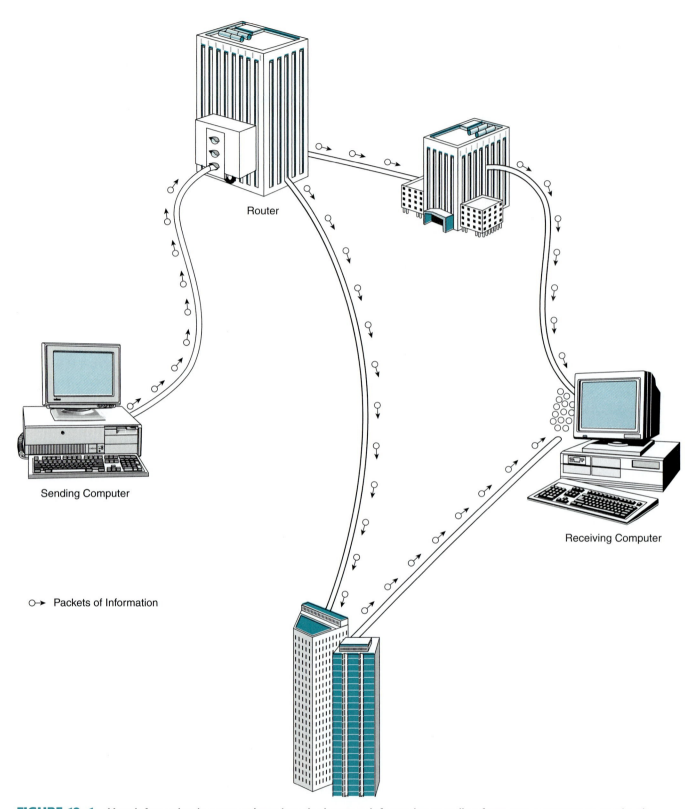

Sending Computer

Router

Receiving Computer

○→ Packets of Information

FIGURE 10–1 How Information is communicated on the Internet. Information traveling from one computer to another is divided into packets. Each packet travels independently, sometimes taking different paths. The packets are reassembled at their destination.

TOOLBOX

TIPS

Computer Communication over Telephone Lines

For most users, the Internet is accessible from a personal computer over telephone lines on a dial-up basis, although an increasing number of people have always-on connections through a cable TV network or a telephone digital subscriber line (DSL). What is required to make a dial-up connection to the Internet? In addition to the computer itself, one must have a modem, communication software, and a clear telephone line. When two computers communicate, each one must be so equipped (Figure A).

Telephone lines were designed to carry human speech (i.e., sound) between two points. Computers using telephone lines for communication must adapt their information to this format. A modem (short for modulator/demodulator) converts a computer's outgoing digital information into analog format (sound) so it can be transmitted over telephone lines, and performs the reverse action on incoming signals. Modems come in both internal (built in the computer) and external (connect to the computer's serial port via a cable) varieties. Modems are distinguished, among other things, by their maximum speed of transmission, which is measured by the baud rate, the approximate number of bits transmitted or received each second. Today, nearly all modems are capable of 56 kilobytes per second (kbps), although this theoretical maximum is rarely possible over standard telephone lines.

Communication software controls the modem and computer-to-computer communication. If you subscribe to a commercial service provider such as America Online (AOL) or MSN, the service provides communication software specifically designed for its system. AOL, for example, is well known for sending disks with their software in the mail to entice people to subscribe to its service. If you go through another Internet service provider (ISP), you can establish a connection using the TCP/IP software built into the operating system of your Windows or Mac OS–based computer. You must configure the software with some key pieces of information, including the IP address for your computer (if it is not assigned automatically); the location of a domain name server (DNS), a computer that translates Internet names into numeric IP addresses (usually your ISP); the location of your e-mail post office; and possibly other specific identifying information. Your Internet service provider will supply the information you need to establish a proper connection, and wizards, or helper applications, will help walk you through the process.

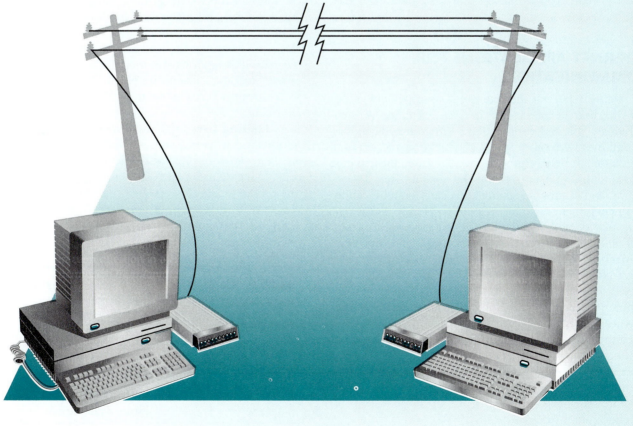

FIGURE A   Computer-to-computer communication via modems.

Information Retrieval

There is a lot of interesting and varied information available on the Internet for students and teachers. Most of this information is up-to-date, available free of charge, and can be accessed in seconds. Computer programs, like word processors, databases, and spreadsheets, as well as lesson plans, are also available.

Information Publishing

You and your students can publish material on the Internet. Publishing on the Internet is quicker than traditional channels. It is also cheaper than "publishing" with a copying machine and sending the documents through the mail. Students' short stories and poems can, with parental approval, be posted on the Internet for the world to read. You can also share your teaching ideas with others in your discipline.

INTERNET APPLICATIONS FOR COMMUNICATION

A valuable aspect of the Internet is its capability of facilitating human interaction and the exchange of data and ideas. You and your students can communicate via the Internet with other students, teachers, and experts in a particular field around the world. Three basic types of communication are e-mail and mailing lists, newsgroups, and instant messaging and chat. Communication by e-mail (electronic mail) is analogous to writing a letter to one person. Mailing lists, also called listservs, are like bulk mailings. You and your students can subscribe to receive topic-specific information (like magazines) delivered to your electronic doorstep. A newsgroup is a discussion group that allows teachers and students with common interests to communicate with each other. The sites are typically dedicated to a single subject and allow you and your students to read comments and questions, and to post comments, questions, and answers of your own. While newsgroups are asynchronous, instant messaging and chat support instant (synchronous) communication. We look here at each of these types of communication in more detail.

E-mail and Mailing Lists

Any communication sent from one individual or group to another over a computer network is called **electronic mail (e-mail)**. It may be sent to or received from another teacher or student in your school or a scientist in Antarctica. Every individual or corporate Internet account holder has at least one unique e-mail address (see Table 10–1 and Figure 10–2). Because e-mail is transmitted over phone or network lines, it is transmitted in seconds rather than in the days required for postal mail. E-mail is usually a person-to-person communication, and you can provide "enclosures" (called **attachments**) as you would in a letter. In addition, you can send the same letter to multiple individuals as you would copies of a letter sent by the postal service. Using e-mail, you and your students can exchange information with people all over the world. Popular programs for composing, sending, and receiving e-mail include Qualcomm *Eudora*, Microsoft *Outlook* and *Outlook Express*, and Netscape *Messenger* as well as the e-mail software built into services such as America Online and MSN. Free e-mail accounts are available to individuals on the Web through services such as Yahoo! Mail and MSN Hotmail.

Mailing lists use e-mail to deliver topic-specific information to your computer on a regular basis. They are like electronic magazines. When a mailing list receives a message, a copy of the message is sent to everyone on the mailing list. To subscribe to a mailing list, all you have to do is send a message to the **listserv** (the computer that controls, sorts, and distributes incoming

TABLE 10–1 *The E-mail Addresses of the Authors of This Text*

Author	E-mail Address
Tim Newby	newby@purdue.edu
Don Stepich	dstepich@boisestate.edu
Jim Lehman	lehman@purdue.edu
Jim Russell	jrussell@purdue.edu

E-Mail Addresses

Internet Addresses (URLs)

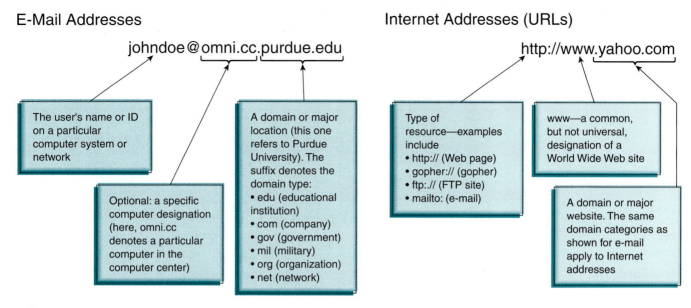

FIGURE 10–2   Finding your way in cyberspace—the anatomy of e-mail addresses and URLs.

information on a particular topic). See Table 10–2 for a small sample of mailing lists available for teachers and students. To subscribe to a listserv, contact the computer that administers the list you are interested in. In most cases, you just send an e-mail message with the following in the body of the e-mail message: the word "subscribe," the name of the list to which you wish to subscribe, and your name (not your e-mail address). Leave the subject line of the e-mail blank. After you send the message, you will receive a confirmation that you are subscribed. You should keep the welcome message that you receive, because it will contain information about the list and how to unsubscribe if you decide you do not want to stay subscribed to the list. Just as you can publish in a journal, you can "post" to a listserv. Likewise, just as you don't have to renew your subscription to a journal, you can stop your subscription to the listserv by sending an "unsubscribe" message to the host computer.

TABLE 10–2   *Sample Mailing Lists for Teachers and Students*

List Resource	Internet Address	Description
Community Learning Network	http://www.cln.org/lists/home.html	Good source for locating educational mailing lists
The Teacher's Guide	http://www.theteachersguide.com/listservs.html	Reference for dozens of educationally oriented mailing lists
ACSOFT-L	listserv@wuvmd.wustl.edu	Educational software discussion
AERA-A	listserv@asu.edu	AERA division A: Educational Administration Forum
ECENET-L	listserv@listserv.uiuc.edu	Early childhood education discussion
EDINFO	listproc@inet.ed.gov	Updates from the U.S. Department of Education
EDNET	listproc@lists.umass.edu	Discussions about a variety of educational topics
EDTECH	listserv@h-net.msu.edu	Educational technology discussion
TEACHNET	listserv@byu.edu	Exchanging ideas, articles, research, experiences, and questions about teaching
WWWEDU	wwwedu-subscribe@yahoogroups.com	The World Wide Web in Education

TABLE 10–3 *Sample Newsgroups for Teachers and Students*

Newsgroup	Description
http://groups.google.com	Web access to UseNet discussion forums through the popular Google site
K12.chat.teacher	Casual conversation for teachers in grades K through 12
K12.ed.math	Mathematics curriculum in grades K through 12
K12.ed.music	Music education and performing arts curriculum in grades K through 12
Alt.parents-teens	Discussions about raising teenagers
Alt.education.distance	Distance education via the Internet
Alt.prose	Original writings, fiction and nonfiction
Soc.culture.german	German culture and history

Newsgroups

Newsgroups are like bulletin boards devoted to specific topics. Just as there are bulletin boards in many classrooms, there are bulletin boards on the Internet through a service called UseNet. You can access UseNet newsgroups through your e-mail client, if your ISP is set up to support it, or there are various websites that now provide access to UseNet. Newsgroups and bulletin board systems allow you and your students to post information/messages and to read others' messages (Table 10–3). You can "go look at" electronic bulletin boards, just as you might look at a real bulletin board that you pass in the hall each day. For example, you can put a message on the electronic bulletin board for art education and ask for ideas for teaching the color wheel to elementary students. Later that same day or several days later when you log onto that newsgroup, you may find one or several suggestions. With a newsgroup you can read all *postings* (questions or information), post your own question or information, and receive answers to your questions. Unlike an e-mail list, you do not have to subscribe to a newsgroup. You can read and post to any newsgroup you wish to at any time, just as you would a bulletin board in your school. Use caution in selecting newsgroups for student use; many newsgroups have content that is inappropriate for school-age children.

Instant Messaging and Chat

Whereas e-mail and newsgroups support asynchronous communication, **instant messaging (IM)** allows two users on the Internet to synchronously communicate by typing messages back and forth to one another in real time. IM resembles a telephone conversation, except that the conversation in most cases is written rather than spoken. However, recent developments in IM software permit audio and video communication as well as textual communication. Whereas it is possible to communicate with any other user who is online at the same time

and using the same instant messaging software, most IM users maintain a list of particular users, or buddies, with whom they regularly communicate. Common instant messaging programs include *AOL Instant Messenger* (AIM), *MSN Messenger, Yahoo! Messenger,* and *ICQ.*

Chat, like instant messaging, is a form of synchronous communication in which users communicate mainly by typing messages to one another. However, in a chat room, you and your students can "chat" with one person or many people at the same time. Various software programs for Internet chat are available including the software built into popular course management systems such as Blackboard and WebCT. Some chat software uses *avatars,* pictures that represent the individuals chatting. Like e-mail lists, chat rooms tend to be topic specific (Table 10–4). While chat can be a time-consuming and confusing way to communicate, most kids love it. It does allow people from all over the world to communicate with each other in real time. However, chat rooms can become addictive and some conversations may not be appropriate for young people, or even for older folks! Just as parents say to their children, "Never talk to strangers," be sure to admonish your students, "Never give out personal information!"

Because e-mail, instant messaging, and chat lack the cues of face-to-face conversation, conventions have been developed for conveying emotion via text. **Emoticons** are "e-mail body language" and are usually combinations of characteristics that resemble human faces when turned sideways (Table 10–5). Emoticons are used to indicate the writer's feelings because we can't see the writer or hear voice inflection in chat rooms or over e-mail. Acronyms are also commonly used in e-mail and instant messaging messages to convey emotion or simply as brief shortcuts for common expressions.

Others

Many think of the Internet as just a transmitter of text material. But graphics, sound, and video can be sent

TABLE 10–4   *Examples and Sources of Chat Rooms for Teachers and Students*

Name	Web Address	Description
About.com	http://kidswriting.about.com/mpchat.htm	Creative writing chat room for teens
Big Pond	http://bigpond.com/chat/rooms/default.asp?k=Education	Chat rooms for gifted students, parents, and teachers
ESL Chat Central	http://www.eslcafe.com/chat/chatpro.cgi	English as a second language provides a forum to chat with ESL/EFL students and teachers from around the world
Tapped In	http://ti2.sri.com/tappedin/	An international community of education professionals
Teachers Net Chatboard	http://www.teachers.net/chatboard/	Dedicated to open discourse among teachers of the world

TABLE 10–5   *Emoticons and Message Acronyms*

:-)	happy	:-D	laughing
:-(	sad	;-)	a wink
:'-(	crying	:-I	indifferent
:-X	writer's lips are sealed	:-O	surprised
:-/	skeptical or confused	:-&	tongue tied
BBFN	bye bye for now	BTW	by the way
FYI	for your information	<G>	grinning
IMHO	in my humble opinion	JK	just kidding
LOL	laughing out loud	ROF	rolling on the floor
TTYL	talk to you later	TY	thank you

A "video phone" can transmit sound and pictures across the Internet.

over the Internet. With a microphone and speaker connected to your computer you can communicate with someone whose computer is similarly equipped as you would during a telephone conversation and not have to pay long distance toll charges. Internet telephony, also called voice over IP (VoIP), is becoming an increasingly popular option for businesses and consumers, and a number of companies now offer services. Add an inexpensive camera to each of your systems, and you have a "video phone." With a high-speed Internet connection and good quality equipment from companies such as Polycom and Sony, it is possible to conduct high-quality video-conferencing sessions over the Internet.

Another form of communication on the Internet is peer-to-peer (P2P) networking. In peer-to-peer networking, individual computers on the Internet connect directly with one another, without the need for a server, to exchange information. While P2P has gotten a lot of negative press because of its association with the illegal sharing of music files, the technology has great potential for enhancing Internet communication. Programs such as *Groove Virtual Office* from Groove Networks use P2P technology to allow individuals or groups to share data and work collaboratively on projects without the need for a central server to store documents and manage the communication.

Classroom Applications

Learning experiences can be enhanced in a number of ways through the communication application of the Internet. Communicating with other individuals and groups allows for the exchange of ideas, insights, and cultures. The following are typical applications of the Internet for communication.

▶ Use e-mail "e-pals" or electronic pen pals to exchange ideas, cultures, and to learn about and from each other. This might occur between two 8-year-olds, or it might be effectively used between students of different countries, or even different age

Addressing the Standards

NETS Connection

The ability to *use telecommunications to interact and collaborate with students, peers, experts, and other audiences* is an emphasis within the National Educational Technology Standards I and IV for teachers. Listed below are a number of forms of telecommunications. Think about each and then generate one or more ways in which each could be used to increase interaction between teacher and students, between students and students, and between teachers and other teachers.

Internet website

Teacher-to-student collaboration:
Student-to-student collaboration:
Teacher-to-teacher collaboration:

Electronic mail

Teacher-to-student collaboration:
Student-to-student collaboration:
Teacher-to-teacher collaboration:

Discussion boards found in most course management systems (e.g., WebCT, Blackboard, Angel)

Teacher-to-student collaboration:
Student-to-student collaboration:
Teacher-to-teacher collaboration:

Live "Net" meetings

Teacher-to-student collaboration:
Student-to-student collaboration:
Teacher-to-teacher collaboration:

groups (e.g., a college preservice teacher and a group of fifth-grade students).

▶ Use newsgroups involving science experiments in which students from many locations share data. For example, middle school students in New York City could measure air quality data from their city and compare it with similar data received from students in Mexico City, Mexico, and Sydney, Australia.

▶ Use live chat discussions in which student teachers discuss problems they are encountering within their current classroom settings with other student teachers or individuals who have been through that experience.

▶ Create an e-mail list for individuals within a common group like a Spanish club or an afterschool service organization to disseminate information rapidly to all members. For example, the next meeting time, topic of discussion, advance reading, and some reflective questions could be posted on the Spanish club's listserv to allow all members to quickly receive the

relevant information and make comments back to the listserv as they deem necessary.

▶ Conduct an Internet-based "video phone" session to link a scientist in a local research laboratory with a science class or science club in your school. Have the students prepare questions ahead of time to pose to the scientist during the video conference.

INTERNET APPLICATIONS FOR INFORMATION RETRIEVAL

Both students and teachers can access valuable resources and a wealth of up-to-date information on the Internet. You are no longer limited to textbooks and resources in the library. Today you and your students have access to the latest, most up-to-date information located far beyond the walls of the schools building (see Figure 10–3 on page 196). Like the library we discussed at the beginning of the chapter, the Internet makes available information resources from around the world. The information

TOOLBOX

TIPS

Netiquette

The informal rules for appropriate etiquette on the Internet are often referred to as **netiquette.** The following guidelines apply anytime you or your students are using the Internet to send e-mail or other text messages (Figure B):

◗ Keep your message short and simple. Try to limit your message to *one* screen. Make it brief, descriptive, and to the point.

◗ Identify yourself as sender. Include your name, school's postal address, and school Internet address. Do not use your or your students' home addresses and telephone numbers.

◗ When replying to a message, include the pertinent portions of the original message.

◗ Don't write anything you would not want someone other than the receiver to read. E-mail can be intercepted and/or forwarded.

◗ When joining a newsgroup or listserv, take some time to get acquainted with the topics and typical pattern of postings before contributing your own message. If **FAQ** (frequently asked questions) files are available, read them.

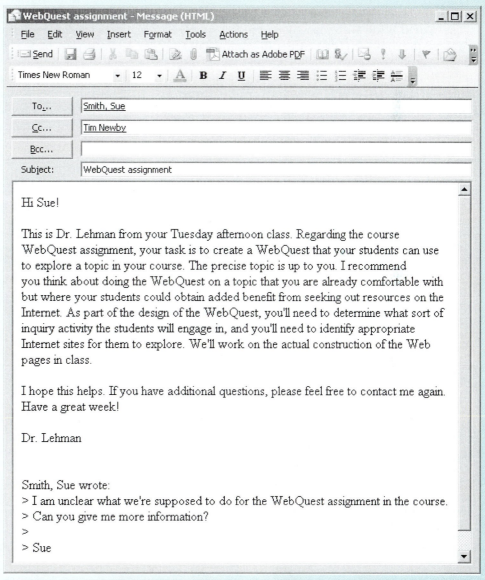

FIGURE B An e-mail message showing proper netiquette.

is available on the Web in the form of databases, documents, government information, online bibliographies, publications, and computer software.

The **World Wide Web** (usually referred to simply as WWW or the Web) is a part of the Internet. Countless information resources (including text, graphics, sound, video, and even virtual reality) are stored on computers around the world in documents called **web pages.** A **website** is a collection of web pages maintained by a school, university, government agency, company, or individual. A **home page** is the first or main page in a website. A **Web server** is a computer connected to the Internet that makes web pages and websites available to other computers.

Each web page, and individually accessible component of a web page, has a unique Internet address called a **Uniform Resource Locator (URL)**. See Figure 10–2 for the components of a URL. Web pages are hypertext documents, which means they contain highlighted text that connects to other pages on the Web,

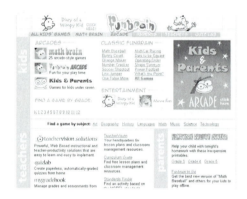

Funbrain
http://www.funbrain.com

NASA
http://www.nasa.gov

Online Frog Dissection
http://curry.edschool.virginia.edu/go/frog

Discovery School
http://school.discovery.com/

FIGURE 10–3 Websites of interest to teachers and students for information retrieval from the Internet. *Note: Type all URLs as a single unit, with no internal spaces. Follow all punctuation and capitalization exactly as written, using slashes, hyphens, and underscoring as shown.*

often at other diverse locations. Hypertext allows you to quickly move from one web page to another.

A software program that allows you to move around the Web and locate specific information is a *Web browser*. A **browser** allows you and your students to navigate through information on the Web by choosing nonsequential pathways. Popular browsers include Microsoft *Internet Explorer,* Netscape *Navigator,* Apple *Safari,* Mozilla *Foxfire,* and *Opera.* Most browsers are available free of charge or at low cost on the Web, and one or more is probably already installed on your home or school computer.

While exploring the Web, you may find sites of interest and wish to return to them in the future without having to remember where you were or to retrace your path. A **bookmark** allows you to return to interesting sites without having to remember and retype the URL. Browsers include easy ways to create, store, and retrieve bookmarks. The computer stores the website address and allows you to easily recall it using a pull-down menu. Bookmarks may also be filed and divided into many different file folders for easier access if you have a lot of them. For a class, each student may want their own file folder.

Another browser feature is image capture, which allows you and your students to "copy" images from others' web pages and add them to your own. A reminder about copyright is in order here. *Assume that all images on the Internet are copyrighted!* You must have permission to use any image from the Internet (see the discussion on copyright and the Internet later in this chapter). You can purchase collections of ready-made images, called *clip art,* which come with permission to use them for certain purposes. Some websites make clip art available for certain purposes free of charge. In other cases you and your students must ask for permission from the copyright holder *before* including the image on your own web page or with any other materials—even for educational purposes.

Plug-ins allow you and your students to display or play certain types of files on the Internet. A plug-in performs tasks the Web browser cannot perform on its own. You must install the appropriate plug-in before you can work with that particular file. For example, Adobe System's *Acrobat Reader* lets you view and print Portable Document Format (PDF) files. PDF files are an Internet standard for cross-platform distribution of formatted documents. *Acrobat Reader* is available free of charge at **http://www.adobe.com.** *Shockwave* and *Flash* plug-ins (available at **http://www.macromedia.com)** let you view certain kinds of animations and interactive applications via your Web browser. In order to see some multimedia presentations on the Web, you will need the *Quick Time* plug-in **(http://www.apple.com/quicktime)** or *RealPlayer* plug-in **(http://www.real.com)** to view video files in those formats. There are literally hundreds of plug-ins available, many at your browser's home website.

Because the information resources available on the Internet are vast and often ill-structured, students often need guidance and structure to make effective use of them. Students need to be able to use search engines to locate relevant information. (See "Toolbox Tips: Using Search Engines.") In addition, teachers can shape and guide students' use of online resources by creating activities such as online scavenger hunts and WebQuests.

TOOLBOX TIPS

Using Search Engines

Search engines are websites designed to help people locate information of interest on the Internet. Search engines do not search the Internet in real time. Instead, each search engine maintains a database of information accumulated from the Internet. When you use a search engine and submit a query, the database is searched to yield web pages, and sometimes other sources of information (e.g., newsgroups, images), that fit the search criteria. These are returned as a list of "hits," rank-ordered according to criteria applied by the search engine. Different search engines maintain different databases of information, and they apply different criteria to rank-order the list of potential sites. So, it is a good idea to use those search engines that best fit your needs, or use a variety of search engines when you are looking for information.

Although the specifics of searching for information vary from engine to engine, basic techniques apply across most. Search engines allow you to search for topics using key words. Pick relevant nouns or proper names as key words. Avoid common words (e.g., education, computer) that will return too many hits. Use several key words together to narrow your search (e.g., lesson, biology, plant, elementary). When you want to search for a specific term or phrase, enclose it in quotes (e.g., "lesson plan," "American history"). Many search engines allow you to include key terms with + and exclude other terms with a − (e.g., the key terms "recipe, cookie, +oatmeal, −raisin" would yield a search for cookie recipes containing oatmeal but not raisins). Many search engines permit you to use an asterisk (*) as a wild card at the end of a term to broaden the search (e.g., the key term "planet*" would yield hits for planet, planets, planetary, etc.). Some search

TOOLBOX TIPS
(continued)

engines also allow the Boolean (logical) operators OR and AND to be used with key words to expand or narrow searches, respectively. Popular search engines appear in the following table.

Search Engine	URL
Altavista	http://www.altavista.com
Dogpile	http://www.dogpile.com
Excite	http://www.excite.com
Google	http://www.google.com
Hotbot	http://www.hotbot.com
Infospace	http://www.infospace.com
Lycos	http://www.lycos.com
Metacrawler	http://www.metacrawler.com
Netscape	http://www.netscape.com
Vivisimo	http://www.vivisimo.com
Yahoo	http://www.yahoo.com

Note: Type all URLs as a single unit, with no internal spaces. Follow all punctuation exactly as written.

There are also search engines, or subsets of existing search engines, that are specifically designed for use by children. These include Ask Jeeves for Kids (http://www.ajkids.com), KidsClick! (http://www. kidsclick.com), and Yahooligans (http://www.yahooligans.com). These sites filter out websites that might have content inappropriate for children.

For more information about how to search the Internet, visit the listed search engines and view the guidelines associated with each. You can also visit any of a number of sites that provide information about how to use search engines and locate information on the Web, including Search Engine Watch (http://www.searchenginewatch.com/), Search Engine Showdown (http://www.searchengineshowdown.com/), and the UC Berkeley Library guide to the best search engines (http://www.lib.berkeley.edu/TeachingLib/Guides/Internet/SearchEngines.html).

Scavenger Hunts

Scavenger hunts or treasure hunts are one popular way for teaching students how to find and use information resources available on the Internet. Like their real-life counterparts, online scavenger hunts involve searching for specific items. But rather than searching in the real world, students search for items of information on the Web. Elementary students might search for facts about specific animals in the rain forest, middle school social studies students might search for information about American presidents, or high school students might investigate issues facing Native Americans.

Scavenger hunts are structured around a series of questions or searching tasks for students. To help the students locate information, the URLs for specific, relevant websites are provided by the teacher or scavenger hunt designer, although the students must search through those sites to find the information needed to answer the questions or complete the tasks. Scavenger hunts can be fun and informative while helping students to practice their Web searching skills. They can be adapted to almost any grade level or curriculum

area. See Table 10–6 for some sites about scavenger hunts.

WebQuests

WebQuests are inquiry-oriented activities in which some or all of the information used by learners is drawn from resources on the Web (see Figure 10–4). This approach was developed by Bernie Dodge and Tom March at San Diego State University, and it has become one of the most popular ways of using the Web in education. Web Quests ordinarily contain several specific components as described below.

▶ Introduction—introduces the activity, sets the stage, and provides basic background information to engage the learner
▶ Task—describes what the learner is to do and identifies the culminating performance or end product of the activity
▶ Process—outlines the steps the learner is to follow, identifies the resources to be used, and provides guidance or scaffolding to assist the learner

TABLE 10–6   *Scavenger Hunt Websites*

Site	Web Address	Description
Education World	http://www.education-world.com/a_curr/curr113.shtml	Curriculum resources related to Internet scavenger hunts
LT Technologies Internet Hunts	http://www.lttechno.com/links/hunts.html	Information about scavenger hunts and examples in various curriculum areas
Internet Hunts by Cindy O'Hora	http://homepage.mac.com/cohora/ext/internethunts.html	A collection of Internet scavenger hunts arranged by curriculum areas
Vicki Blackwell's Internet Guide for Educators	http://www.vickiblackwell.com/hunts.html	A collection of Internet scavenger hunts on various topics
Yahooligans Scavenger Hunt	http://yahooligans.yahoo.com/tg/basil.html	A scavenger hunt related to the book *From the Mixed-Up Files of Mrs. Basil E. Frankweiler*

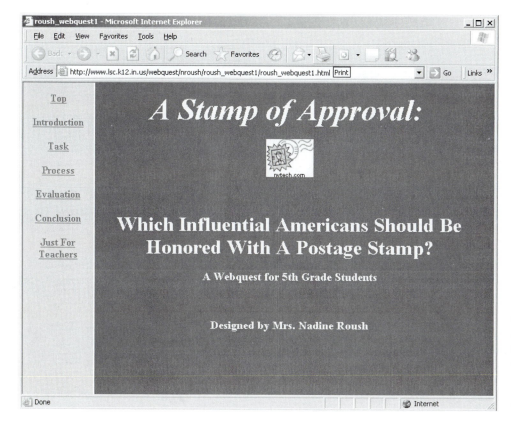

FIGURE 10–4   A screen from a WebQuest, a popular way for learners to use the Internet for inquiry-based learning in the classroom.
Reprinted with permission from Nadine Roush.

▸ Evaluation—describes the evaluation criteria to be applied to the activity; this is often in the form of a rubric

▸ Conclusion—provides closure for the WebQuest and encourages the learner to reflect on the activity

▸ Teacher Page—provides key information about the WebQuest for other teachers (e.g., target learners, standards addressed, suggestions for implementation)

WebQuests are often designed as group activities with different students assuming different roles in the activity. This approach not only encourages cooperative learning but motivates the learners by giving them realistic scenarios as a context for the activity. The best WebQuests focus on developing students' higher-order thinking skills using Internet resources. Like scavenger hunts, WebQuests are available for and can be developed for almost any grade level or curriculum

Designing a WebQuest

Suppose that you will have the opportunity to help students learn about a particular topic in a subject area and grade level of your choice. After studying the information provided about WebQuests, design a WebQuest that the students could use to learn about the topic. Determine the introduction, task, process, evaluation, conclusion, and teacher information. Identify at least three to five online resources that students could use during the WebQuest to obtain information about your topic.

Once you have designed your WebQuest, consider actually developing it by using Web authoring software. See the section that follows (Table 10–7) for more information about Web authoring.

TABLE 10–7 *WebQuest Resources*

Site	Web Address	Description
The WebQuest portal	http://webquest.org	Up-to-date news and information about WebQuests and a matrix of examples by grade level and curriculum area
San Diego State University WebQuest site	http://webquest.sdsu.edu	The original WebQuest site with articles and resources about WebQuests
BestWebQuests.com	http://bestwebquests.com/	A collection of the best WebQuests maintained by Tom March, one of the developers of the approach
WebQuest Direct	http://www.webquestdirect.com.au/	A searchable directory of thousands of teacher-reviewed and -rated WebQuests
Saskatoon East School Division Teacher Resources	http://sesd.sk.ca/teacherresource/webquest/webquest.htm	A collection of over 1000 WebQuests

area. See Table 10–7 for some sites that have example WebQuests.

Classroom Applications

The information retrieval aspect of the Internet offers exciting application possibilities within all classrooms. With access to so much information, you and your students will need to develop skills to be able to effectively wade through all of the possibilities, find that which is most relevant, and determine its quality. Here are just a few ideas of how you can use access to this unlimited information to enhance students' learning experiences:

▶ Conduct online research using databases and other online resources. Here you and your students can access information on almost any topic, from a variety of sources, very quickly. Finding huge amounts of information on topics such as whales, tax laws, soccer rules, trigonometry equations, and kindergarten safety is no longer difficult.

Additionally, this information frequently includes visuals, audio, and other media formats beyond text.

▶ Monitor current events through online newspapers and magazines. Access to the Internet allows you and your students to get up-to-the-minute information on critical news stories and read it from a variety of sources. Now students can access and read what their local newspapers have to say about some current event and immediately compare that with what is being written by the national news organizations and even those from countries around the world.

▶ Use scavenger hunts or WebQuests to direct students' online explorations of particular aspects of the curriculum. A wide variety of existing activities are already available, and it is easy to develop your own.

▶ Access Web-based archives of teaching methods, instructional strategies, and lesson plans. Finding information on what to teach and how to teach is now easy. From hands-on science experiments to drama techniques, lesson plans are available to give ideas to both new and experienced teachers.

◗ Retrieve information on possible job opportunities. Information on potential employment, contact personnel, and how to prepare (e.g., résumé development) for job interviews is readily available.

INTERNET APPLICATIONS FOR INFORMATION PUBLISHING

Everyone likes to see his/her writings in "print." You and your students can publish material on the Internet. The Internet is a quick and inexpensive method for sharing ideas. Students' short stories and poems can, with parental approval, be posted on the Internet for the world to read. You can also share your teaching ideas with others in your discipline.

The procedures for publishing on the Internet are becoming steadily easier. Publishing on the Internet is almost as easy as generating an e-mail communication. Many schools, teachers, and even students have their own home pages. People often create personal home pages that show their hobbies, pictures, and family. It is best *not* to put pictures and personal information of students on web pages created at school.

The explosive growth of the World Wide Web has led to a surge of interest in web page authoring in K–12 schools. Most schools now have their own home pages, and an increasing number are using the Web as a vehicle for students to make their work public. As a result, a student's hypermedia project that once may have been seen only by her teacher and classmates may now be available for viewing by anyone in the world. Realistically, of course, the world will probably not beat an electronic path to every school web page in cyberspace. However, the mere idea that the world can see their work is highly motivating to students, and posting students' hypermedia projects to the Web for all to see does give parents, grandparents, and members of the community an opportunity to keep tabs on what is happening in the school.

Web Authoring

When the World Wide Web first burst onto the scene in the 1990s, tools for creating web pages were few and far between. As a consequence, many people jumped into learning Hypertext Markup Language (HTML), the underlying language of web pages. While there may still be merit in understanding a bit about HTML (see "Toolbox Tips: HTML, the Language of the Web"), today it is no longer necessary to know HTML in order to create functional and attractive web pages. Web page authoring tools allow you to create pages using a simple interface similar to a word processor or presentation package.

Among the simplest to use of all the tools for creating HTML documents is a basic word processor. The latest versions of most popular word processors (e.g., Microsoft *Word,* Corel *WordPerfect*) now provide an option to save documents as web pages. Simply create your document onscreen as you would if you were writing any document, and select the Save as Web Page or Save as HTML option. It is simple and easy. However, word processors were not designed specifically for web page creation, and they may not be as easy to work with or provide results as good as products designed for that purpose.

A number of programs specifically designed for web page creation are on the market today. Among the most popular Web authoring programs are Macromedia *Dreamweaver,* Microsoft *FrontPage,* and Netscape *Composer.* These programs allow one to visually design and save individual web pages (see Figure 10–5). More advanced features available in some packages include page design from templates, website management tools, sitewide spell checking, link testing, and search and replace. Today, better Web authoring products are also providing support for the latest developments in Web creation including Java and JavaScript language support, cascading style sheets, and dynamic HTML.

When creating web pages, students experience benefits and encounter difficulties similar to those associated with authoring other forms of hypermedia (see Chapter 9). When students author web pages, they must gather, evaluate, organize, and ultimately present information on a topic. This requires students to develop logical thinking and planning skills, and the process is active and often motivating to learners. For teachers, it is important to help guard against students' tendency to want to jump right in and begin authoring web pages without planning. As in other types of development efforts, a little planning at the beginning pays great dividends later on. In addition, as with other forms of visual expression, there is a need for students to adhere to good design guidelines (see Table 10–8).

It also very important for you and your students to remember that the Web is a public medium of expression. When a student makes a mistake on a paper written in the classroom, probably only the teacher and the student see that error. An error on a web page has the potential to be seen by many people, which can be very embarrassing. There is also significant potential for students to get into trouble with copyright infringement on the Web (see the discussion on copyright later in this chapter and in Chapter 8). A student who scans a picture from an encyclopedia for a report in class is probably protected under fair use guidelines. But displaying that scanned picture on the Web without permission would be a clear violation of copyright law. As a general rule, you should assume that material gathered from other sources, including the Web itself, is copyrighted and cannot be displayed on the Web without permission. When in doubt, err on the side of caution.

FIGURE 10–5 A screen from Macromedia *Dreamweaver*, a popular Web authoring software tool.
Reprinted with permission from Macromedia, Inc.

TABLE 10–8 *Guidelines for Designing Web Pages/Sites*

Start with users.	Know who your users will be and what they are interested in learning.
Identify your purpose.	Describe in writing what you want your users to gain from the web page/site to keep you on target as you design it.
KISS Principle—Keep It Simple for Students.	Present information clearly and simply. Also, do not assume that users will have the latest and fastest technology to access your web page/site.
Write clearly and succinctly.	Write in a clear, simple style that is easy for users to scan. Use headings to help organize content and make it easy for users to find what they want.
Limit information on each page.	A guideline is that pages should be no larger than about 50K to download reasonably quickly, usually in no more than about 10 seconds, using a 56K modem.
Use simple graphics that load quickly.	To keep pages small enough to load quickly, limit the number and type of graphics. Convert graphics designed for print to the lower resolution needed for viewing on the Web to reduce file size.
Follow guidelines for text development and designing visuals.	See Chapter 8, Table 8–3, "Guidelines for Designing Instructional Materials."
Limit number of links to other information.	Too many links without structure and guidelines can cause users to get lost in cyberspace.
Provide navigational support.	Use clear and consistent navigational elements. Don't assume users know as much about the site as you do. Use linking text that describes the destination; never use "click here" without explanation.
Avoid useless and annoying animation (blinking and movement).	Put your emphasis on the content, not the glitz.
Limit use of cutting-edge technology.	Minimize the use of technologies (e.g., video streaming) that require plug-ins and use a lot of bandwidth. Many of your users may not be able to access these technologies.
Make sure your pages are accessible.	Follow accessibility guidelines (see http://www.w3.org/WAI/) to ensure that your web pages can be accessed by everyone.

Classroom Applications

Student development of web pages offers many opportunities for classroom activities that parallel those that we cited for hypermedia authoring packages in the last chapter. Typical applications of the Web for information publishing include the following:

▶ Students can create hypermedia projects or reports on the Web in much the same fashion as they might use a hypermedia authoring tool such as *HyperStudio*. Such projects can contain textual information, pictures, and other multimedia elements. Significantly, on the Web, they can also contain links to further information at that site or on other websites.

▶ The Web is a great tool for displaying examples of students' work. Parents and members of the community can get a sense of what goes on in the school by seeing posted work. Remember, always get permission from *both* students and their parents/guardians before displaying students' work on the Web.

▶ Learning how to develop web pages may be an educational goal in and of itself. Students, for example, might learn web page development skills by helping to construct or maintain a portion of the school's website. This "win-win" situation gives

students experience and helps schools to maintain a Web presence by using an inexpensive pool of student labor.

PROBLEMS AND PITFALLS

The Internet is a rich source of information for students and teachers (see Table 10–9). It can also provide quick communication and a place to display ("publish") materials. However, these benefits can have a downside as well. For one thing, there is a financial cost to access the Internet. Costs can vary greatly from school to school depending on arrangements with local Internet Service Providers (ISPs). Once the connection is there and paid for, there still may be a problem gaining access. Websites may be busy or not available when you or your students want to access them. This is especially true for popular educational sites during the school day. Other times the school's connection to the Internet may be down. It is important to have backup plans when planning to use the Internet in the classroom.

The ease with which students can access information on the Internet can sometimes be a detriment. Students doing research for a class paper may search the Internet only and assume that they have found all that there is to find. While the Internet is often a great research tool, students still need to be able to use traditional library

---

TOOLBOX

TIPS

HTML, the Language of the Web

HTML, Hypertext Markup Language, is the underlying "language" of all web pages. Each web page is derived from an HTML document; you can see the document that gives rise to any web page by choosing the option to view the page source in your Web browser. (This is a great way to learn HTML.) HTML is not a language in the same sense as a computer language such as Logo or BASIC. Rather, it is a set of conventions for embedding tags or markup labels within a text file. Because HTML documents are plain text files, you can create them with any text editor, including simple ones such as *Windows WordPad* (or the older *Notepad*) or Apple's *SimpleText*. Alternatively, students can use any word processor to create the HTML document as long as the document is saved in plain text (or ASCII) format. While it is not necessary to know HTML to create web pages today, a little knowledge of HTML can be useful. Popular course management systems, such as Blackboard and WebCT, as well as other Web-based programs often allow individuals to use HTML tags to format text entered by the user.

HTML **tags** tell Web browsers how to interpret the text that is marked up. In most cases, the tags tell the browser how to display information on the computer's screen and how to do things like link to other web pages. Most tags come in pairs, a beginning tag and an ending tag. For example, the tags <b> and </b> are used to bracket text that is to be boldfaced (e.g., <b>some text</b> would be displayed by a Web browser as **some text**). All tags are set off by angle brackets (< >). Capitalization of tags is ignored. Tags can be nested within other tags to create compound effects (e.g., <b><i>boldface and italics</i></b> would yield ***boldface and italics***). In addition to text formatting, tags also control text layout. For example, one can center or otherwise align page elements. In addition to formatting, tags are used to embed pictures and links to other web pages. The <IMG> tag is used to insert a graphic image. Links are accomplished using the anchor (<A>) tag. An example of a web page and its corresponding HTML are shown in Figure C.

For more information about the latest developments in HTML, visit the World Wide Web Consortium's website (http://www.w3.org/).

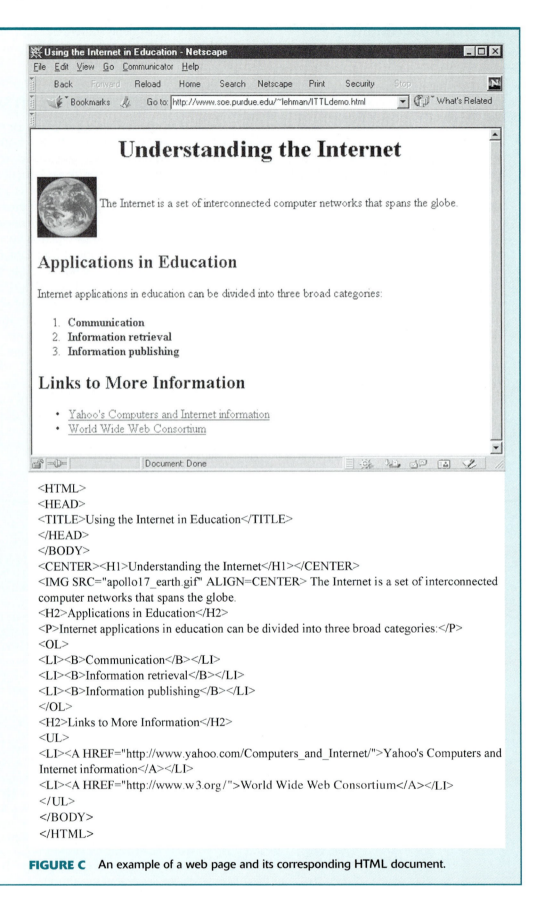

```
<HTML>
<HEAD>
<TITLE>Using the Internet in Education</TITLE>
</HEAD>
</BODY>
<CENTER><H1>Understanding the Internet</H1></CENTER>
<IMG SRC="apollo17_earth.gif" ALIGN=CENTER> The Internet is a set of interconnected
computer networks that spans the globe.
<H2>Applications in Education</H2>
<P>Internet applications in education can be divided into three broad categories:</P>
<OL>
<LI><B>Communication</B></LI>
<LI><B>Information retrieval</B></LI>
<LI><B>Information publishing</B></LI>
</OL>
<H2>Links to More Information</H2>
<UL>
<LI><A HREF="http://www.yahoo.com/Computers_and_Internet/">Yahoo's Computers and
Internet information</A></LI>
<LI><A HREF="http://www.w3.org/">World Wide Web Consortium</A></LI>
</UL>
</BODY>
</HTML>
```

FIGURE C   An example of a web page and its corresponding HTML document.

TABLE 10–9   *Popular Educational Websites*

Name	Web Address	Description
The CIA World Factbook	http://www.cia.gov/cia/publications/factbook/	A well-organized, easy-to-use website containing maps and data on population, geography, economics, and governments of countries throughout the world.
CNN.com	http://www.cnn.com	An up-to-the-minute source of news, weather, sports, and other information from the TV network.
The Crayola Site	http://www.crayola.com/	A colorful site with activities, stories, and games for young people.
Department of Education	http://www.ed.gov/	The U.S. Department of Education's website, with information on its programs and services.
Discovery Channel School	http://school.discovery.com/	Resources from the Discovery Channel for teachers and students.
Educator's Reference Desk	http://www.eduref.org/	A collection of resource guides, lesson plans, and access to the ERIC education database.
Kathy Schrock's Guide	http://school.discovery.com/schrockguide	A well-organized guide to Internet sites of all types for educators.
Library of Congress	http://www.loc.gov/	The Library of Congress website that contains online exhibits, information about American history and culture, and Thomas legislative information.
LION (Librarians Information Online Network)	http://www.libraries.phila.k12.pa.us/lion/	An information resource for K–12 school librarians.
National Education Association	http:/www.nea.org/cet/	The NEA's Technology in Schools department.
TeachNet's Teacher Activities	http://www.teachnet.org/	A collection of lesson plans, online courses, and other information resources of interest to teachers.

Note: Type all URLs as a single unit, with no internal spaces. Follow all punctuation and capitalization exactly as written, using slashes, hyphens, and underscoring as shown.

resources to find information. Further, Internet resources, more so than traditional print resources, can be inaccurate, biased, or misleading. Students need to understand how to evaluate the quality of the Internet resources that they do find. See the discussion below about evaluating the quality of websites.

Educators also need to be vigilant when students use the Internet. Many educators believe that the biggest problem with the Internet is students deliberately or accidentally gaining access to inappropriate material. To discourage this—it can never be totally prevented—requires close monitoring. Students also may choose to "play" on the Internet. They may gain access to materials that are not relevant to lesson content, such as the "Hot Wheels" website or a sports website during a social studies lesson on World War II. It is also important to

monitor students when they use the Internet for communication. Students may send inappropriate e-mails to others, or they may receive inappropriate messages from individuals in chat rooms or on discussion boards. Always caution students to *not* give out personal information over the Internet; you can never be certain who might be on the other end of the connection.

Any use of the Internet also introduces vulnerability to problems such as viruses, spam (unwanted e-mail advertisements), and computer attacks. Caution students against downloading files, which might contain viruses. Advise them to avoid clicking on advertisements or responding to e-mail advertisements that they might receive. Also, make sure that they understand the importance of maintaining computer security. See the discussion below for more about security and information privacy.

ISSUES INVOLVED IN THE USE OF THE INTERNET IN THE CLASSROOM

In addition to the problems and pitfalls noted above, the use of the Internet in the classroom brings with it some special issues and concerns. Several of these key issues are identified and briefly discussed below.

Copyright and Fair Use of Materials on the Web

Teachers have an obligation to make students aware of copyright laws and how they apply to the Internet. *All* materials on the Internet are copyrighted! It is no different from materials published in a textbook. Just because something can be copied electronically doesn't mean it can be distributed legally without the copyright holder's permission. You and your students may use Internet materials personally, but you may not make copies, modify them, or incorporate them into commercial materials without the permission of the copyright holder.

Likewise, you should *not* post on a website any materials (stories, artwork, photographs, poems, etc.) created by your students or photographs of your students *without* the written permission of their parents or guardians. You should spend some class time discussing copyright rules and guidelines with your students. Check with your school administration about the local policies. Refer again to the information on copyright in Chapter 8.

Security and Information Privacy

Always monitor your students when they are using the Web. Discourage students from exploring inappropriate websites either accidentally or deliberately. While many schools now use filtering software to prevent students from accessing inappropriate sites, students may still encounter unsuitable content. The amount and level of your monitoring will be determined by the maturity of your students and local school policies. (See "Toolbox Tips: Acceptable Use Policies.")

Make certain that students understand that computer security is important and personally meaningful. Instruct students to *not* give out personal information such as phone numbers and addresses on the Internet. If students are using the Internet for gathering information for a school project, instruct them to receive the information at school using the school's electronic address or postal address.

Spam, unwanted e-mail advertising, is becoming an increasing problem for all users of e-mail, including teachers and students. While spam cannot be completely eliminated, it can be limited. Use e-mail filters to catch spam before it gets to your inbox. Avoid giving out your e-mail address online; it may end up on a spam list.

Avoid posting your and your students' e-mail addresses on a web page; some spammers obtain e-mail addresses by scanning web pages for them. Never respond to spam; just delete it. Responding to spam verifies that your e-mail address is valid and just invites more spam.

To avoid problems with viruses, never allow students to download programs from the Internet. Even apparently innocuous programs, such as screen savers, may harbor viruses or **spyware,** programs that covertly gather information and transmit it to someone else over the Internet. Likewise, instruct students to never open e-mail attachments from unfamiliar sources or that contain executable files (in the Windows world, files with extensions such as exe, com, bat, pif, ocx, and vbs, among others). Of course, anti-virus software should always be installed and kept up-to-date.

To minimize problems with outsiders gaining access to school and home computers, Internet firewalls should be installed. Most schools now maintain **firewalls,** combinations of hardware and software that prevent outsiders from gaining access to private networks connected to the Internet. In addition to network-level firewalls, personal firewalls can be installed on individual computers to limit the danger from viruses and hackers. It is also important to make students aware that their passwords must be kept private in order to keep school computers secure. Students and teachers should create hard-to-guess passwords (e.g., consisting of nonsensical mixtures of upper and lowercase letters and numerals) and change passwords often. Passwords should never be shared with others or written down where someone else might get them.

Evaluating the Quality of Websites

We conclude our discussion of using the Internet in education by exploring *evaluation*—the E in our PIE model. As we noted at the beginning of the chapter, unlike a library the Internet has no librarian and no assurances of quality. Therefore, you must evaluate the resources that are brought to you via the Internet. How can you and your students determine if information on the Internet is credible and of quality? For most printed materials, especially textbooks, there are editors who review the materials and make sure what is presented is accurate. However, this is not the case for most sites on the Internet. You and your students need to understand that what you read on the Internet may not be correct. To assist you, we have included a "Preview Form: Web Pages/Sites," in this text's Accompanying CD **(Chapter Info and Activities >>> Chapter 7 >>> Media Preview Forms).** However, even if the web page meets these criteria, it is still no guarantee that the information on it is up-to-date, unbiased, and accurate.

One of the most important rules is to evaluate the content and to separate it from the glitz. It goes back to

TOOLBOX

TIPS

Acceptable Use Policies

Some information on the Web is inappropriate for students. What you might consider appropriate might be considered inappropriate by parents or your school administration. It is the responsibility of your school board to establish acceptable use policies for your district. **Acceptable use policies** are signed agreements among students, parents/guardians, and the school administration outlining what is considered to be proper use of the Internet and Web by all persons involved (Figure D). Locate and read your local policies very carefully *before* you use the Internet or Web with your students. Protocol will vary from one community to another.

Internet Use Agreement

The intent of this contract is to ensure that students will comply with all Network and Internet acceptable use policies approved by the District. In exchange for the use of the Network resources either at school or away from school, I understand and agree to the following:

A. The use of the network is a privilege which may be revoked by the District at any time and for any reason. Appropriate reasons for revoking privileges include, but are not limited to, the altering of system software, the placing of unauthorized information, computer viruses or harmful programs on or through the computer system in either public or private files or messages. The District reserves the right to remove files, limit or deny access, and refer the student for other disciplinary actions.

B. The District reserves all rights to any material stored in files which are generally accessible to others and will remove any material which the District, at its sole discretion, believes may be unlawful, obscene, pornographic, abusive, or otherwise objectionable. Students will not use their District-approved computer account/access to obtain, view, download, or otherwise gain access to, distribute, or transmit such materials.

C. All information services and features contained on District or Network resources are intended for the private use of its registered users. Any use of these resources for commercial-for-profit or other unauthorized purposes (i.e., advertisements, political lobbying), in any form, is expressly forbidden.

D. The District and/or Network resources are intended for the exclusive use by their registered users. The student is responsible for the use of his/her account/password and/or access privilege. Any problems which arise from the use of a student's account are the responsibility of the account holder. Use of materials, information, files, or an account by someone other than the registered account holder or accessing another person's account without permission is forbidden and may be grounds for loss of access privileges.

E. Any misuse of the account will result in suspension of the account privileges and/or other disciplinary action determined by the District. Misuse shall include, but not be limited to:
   1) Intentionally seeking information on, obtaining copies of, or modifying files, other data, or passwords belonging to other users.
   2) Misrepresenting other users on the Network.
   3) Disrupting the operation of the Network through abuse of or vandalizing, damaging, or disabling the hardware or software.
   4) Malicious use of the Network through hate mail, harassment, profanity, vulgar statements, or discriminatory remarks.
   5) Interfering with others' use of the Network.
   6) Extensive use for non-curriculum-related communication.
   7) Illegal installation of copyrighted software.
   8) Unauthorized downsizing, copying, or use of licensed or copyrighted software or plagiarizing materials.
   9) Allowing anyone to use an account other than the account holder.
   10) Using the Internet without a teacher's permission.
   11) Violating any local, state, or federal statutes.

FIGURE D Sample statement of Acceptable Use Policy from Crawfordsville (IN) School Corp.
Source: Crawfordsville Community School Corporation, Crawfordsville, IN 47933.

Addressing the Standards

NETS Connection

In part, the National Educational Technology Standards V and VI for teachers emphasize that one should **model safe and responsible use of technology.** Read those standards, study their performance indicators (see Teacher Resource A on page 297 for a full listing), and then complete the following:

▶ Obtain and review your school's Acceptable Use Policy (AUP). This generally can be found on the school or school district's website. Identify the main safety issues that it outlines.
▶ Based on the AUP, develop a list of "Things to Do" and "Things Not to Do" when working with the Internet.
▶ Create a journal entry that includes your lists and how you would model those behaviors if you were teaching in one of that school district's elementary schools. Would what and how you model differ if you were teaching at a secondary school level? Why or why not?

Check It Out

Evaluating the Quality of Websites

Because of the lack of controls on the Internet, anyone can put anything on a website. Therefore, it is important for users to learn to judge the quality of information on the Web. Website evaluation is an important skill for teachers and students alike.

Some sites that provide information about website evaluation include:

▶ http://school.discovery.com/schrockguide/eval.html (Kathy Schrock's Guide for Educators)
▶ http://www.lib.berkeley.edu/TeachingLib/Guides/Internet/Evaluate.html (Guidelines from the University of California at Berkeley Library)
▶ http://lib.nmsu.edu/instruction/evalcrit.html (Web evaluation criteria from the New Mexico State University Library)
▶ http://www.library.cornell.edu/olinuris/ref/research/webeval.html (Web criteria and tools from the Cornell University Library)

Use the "Preview Form: Web Pages/Sites" to evaluate the following websites:

Site	URL
Boilerplate: Mechanical Marvel	http://www.bigredhair.com/boilerplate/
Dihydrogen Monoxide	http://www.dhmo.org/
Faked Moon Landings	http://batesmotel.8m.com/
Gettysburg Address	http://www.loc.gov/exhibits/gadd/
Harriet Tubman and the Underground Railroad	http://www2.lhric.org/pocantico/tubman/tubman.html
Institute for Historical Review	http://www.ihr.org/
Martin Luther King	http://www.martinlutherking.org
Tobacco Control Archives	http://www.library.ucsf.edu/tobacco/index.html
U.S. Holocaust Memorial Museum	http://www.ushmm.org/

Which of these websites do you think are or are not credible sources of information? Why?

the old proverb, "Never judge a book by its cover." Many websites are pretty, but also pretty shallow in terms of content. Inaccurate and inappropriate content beautifully presented is still inaccurate and inappropriate! Examine the content of websites closely. Pay attention to indicators

of quality and the qualifications of the author. Typical criteria that can be used to judge Web resources include:

▶ Authority—Who is the author of the site? What information can you glean from the website itself about the person or organization that created the site? Do other reputable sites link to the site?

◗ Accuracy—Is the content of the site correct? How can you judge the accuracy of the content? Does the author document information sources? Do other reputable sites support the information?

◗ Currency—Is the site up-to-date? Were the pages last modified recently or long ago?

◗ Objectivity—Does the site present a biased or slanted point of view? How can you tell?

◗ Coverage—What is the scope of topic coverage on the site? For whom was the site written?

To practice judging the quality of websites, complete the "Check It Out: Evaluating the Quality of Websites" activity on page 208.

TECHNOLOGY COORDINATOR'S CORNER

Don Bauer, a district computer coordinator, was in his office recently when two teachers separately stopped in for some advice about how to make use of the Internet in their classrooms. They came to Don with different needs and levels of experience but a common desire to integrate the Internet.

Linda Owens, a fifth-grade teacher, had relatively little experience using technology in the classroom. She wanted to find a way to begin to integrate the Internet to support her curriculum. She had a unit coming up on tropical rain forests and asked Bob for advice on how to get started using the Internet in her class.

Don discussed with Linda the different ways that the Internet can be used from communicating across distances to gathering information on all sorts of topics. He suggested to Linda that having her students use the Web to retrieve up-to-date information would be a relatively easy way to meaningfully integrate use of the Internet into her rain forest unit. Linda agreed that this would be a good way to get started with the Internet.

Don gave Linda some advice to get ready for the activity. He suggested she prepare by locating websites where her students could find relevant information about tropical rain forests. He suggested that she record the addresses of those websites, put them on a worksheet for her students, or, better yet, save them as bookmarks that could be put on the computers in the school's lab. With a bookmark file, students would be quickly directed to relevant sites, and this would help to keep them from wandering aimlessly or getting off task. Don also suggested that Linda consider locating an existing WebQuest that would work with her rain forest unit. A WebQuest would make sites available for student research within the context of some sort of inquiry activity. Don suggested that Linda might want to learn to make her own WebQuest for the future. Linda agreed to try Don's suggestions. She thanked him and left the office.

A few minutes later, Phil Nelson, a high school social studies teacher, stopped in Don's office. Unlike Linda, Phil had used the Internet for information retrieval in his class for a number of years. However, he was interested in doing something more than he had done in the past as part of an upcoming unit on the history of the civil rights movement.

Don suggested that Phil think about having his students focus on primary source materials. The Web is a great repository of many original materials that would be relevant to the social studies objectives of the planned unit. For example, the American Memory collection at the Library of Congress (**http://memory.loc.gov**) is a site that has many excellent primary source materials. With students who are already fairly capable users of the Web, the task of finding primary source materials to do reports would be challenging but doable. The students could also use e-mail to communicate with experts or people who were involved in the civil rights movement to get some first-hand accounts. Don also suggested that another way for Phil to take his use of the Internet up a notch would be to have the students put the results of their research on the Web for others to see. Rather than just doing reports in class, the students could design Web reports using the Web editing software (e.g., *FrontPage* or *Dreamweaver*) available on the computers in the school's lab. Don indicated he could provide space on the school's server to host the students' Web reports.

Phil agreed that these were interesting suggestions. He commented that he knew of another teacher at a nearby school who also planned a unit on the civil rights movement, and he imagined that they might work together to have their students share evaluations of each other's projects via e-mail. Don agreed that this sounded like a good possibility.

Don reminded Phil to make certain the students obtained permission to post anything copyrighted on their websites. He also reminded Phil that the students could create links to the original sites, if they found relevant materials on existing websites, rather than copying the work to their own sites to avoid the copyright issues. Phil agreed to remind his students about copyright issues, thanked Don for his assistance, and left to plan his civil rights unit.

SUMMARY

In this chapter, we examined uses of the Internet to enhance learning. Applications of the Internet in education can be put into one of three broad categories; communication, information retrieval, and information publishing. Asynchronous forms of communication include e-mail, mailing lists, and newsgroups, while synchronous forms of communication include instant messaging and chat. These technologies allow for rapid communication between individuals or groups. Students and teachers can retrieve text, graphics, audio, and video information from the World Wide Web. Structured approaches for integrating information retrieval in educational lessons include scavenger hunts and WebQuests. The Internet can also be used for information publishing. Using Web authoring software, students and teachers can create materials that can be accessed by others on the Internet.

Teachers and students need to be aware of issues related to the use of the Internet in the classroom. Copyright laws apply to materials on the Internet just as they do to materials in other media. Security and information privacy are of concern when using the Internet, and precautions should be taken to minimize problems. Finally, because information sources on the Internet can be inaccurate or biased, students need to understand how to judge the quality of websites.

SUGGESTED RESOURCES

CD Resources

To increase retention and transfer of this information, review the *Reflective Questions and Activities* located in the Chapter 10 section (**Chapter info and activities>>>Chapter 10>>> Reflective Questions and Activities**) of the text's accompanying CD.

In addition, you can access relevant Internet websites, NETS Connection exercises, and direct e-mail access to the text's authors.

Website Resources

Access the text's website (**www.prenhall.com/newby**), navigate to Chapter 10, and review the Question and Answer section for relevant questions that have been generated by students and answered by the authors. You may also submit your own questions directly to the authors. In addition, you can access presentations by the authors about this chapter and gain insights directly from them about the topics that have been presented.

Print Resources

Ackerman, E., & Hartman, K. (2002). *Learning to use the Internet and World Wide Web*. Wilsonville, OR: Franklin, Beedle, & Associates.

Bissell, J. S., Manning, A., & Rowland, V. A. (2001). *CyberEducator: The Internet and World Wide Web for K–12 and teacher education with free student CD-ROM and PowerWeb*. New York: McGraw-Hill.

Ertmer, P. A., Hruskocy, C., & Woods, D. M. (2002). *Education on the Internet, 2002–2003 update*. Upper Saddle River, NJ: Prentice Hall.

Heide, A., & Stilborne, L. (2004). *The teacher's Internet companion*. Markham, Ontario: Trifolium Books.

Herring, J. E. (2004). *The Internet and information skills: A guide for teachers and school librarians*. New York: Neal Schuman.

Lamb, A., Smith, N., & Johnson, L. (1998). *Surfin' the Internet: Practical ideas from A to Z* (2nd ed.). Emporia, KS: Vision to Action.

Miller, E. B. (1997). *The Internet resource directory for K–12 teachers and librarians, 2000–01*. Englewood, CO: Libraries Unlimited.

Nielsen, J. (2000). *Designing Web usability*. Indianapolis, IN: New Riders Publishing.

Provenzo, E. F. (2004). *The Internet and online research for teachers*. Boston: Allyn & Bacon.

Rivard, J. D. (1997). *Quick guide to the Internet for educators*. Needham Heights, MA: Allyn & Bacon.

Roblyer, M. D. (2002). *Integrating educational technology into teaching* (3rd ed). Upper Saddle River, NJ: Prentice Hall.

Roblyer, M. D. (2002). *Starting out on the Internet: A learning journey for teachers* (2nd ed.). Upper Saddle River, NJ: Prentice Hall.

Ryder, R. J., & Hughes, T. (2000). *Internet for educators* (2nd ed.). Upper Saddle River, NJ: Prentice Hall.

11

Integration of Distance Education to Support Learning

CHAPTER OBJECTIVES

After reading and studying this chapter, you will be able to:

◗ Define distance education, and identify the needs it addresses.
◗ Compare and contrast distance education technologies on the basis of capabilities, advantages, and limitations.
◗ Describe examples of the use of audio-based, video-based, and computer-based distance education technologies.
◗ Identify basic utilization guidelines for the use of distance education technologies in teaching and learning.
◗ Discuss issues related to the use of distance education.

In the two preceding chapters, we have explored how to integrate computers and the Internet into the classroom. In this chapter, we continue to examine the classroom integration of technologies. This chapter focuses on distance education technologies. Distance education is growing rapidly today, and a variety of distance education technologies are available for use in the classroom. This chapter summarizes common audio, video, and Internet-based distance education technologies and their applications.

INTRODUCTION

When you go shopping at a grocery store, have you ever thought about the convenience provided? Goods are brought to the store to save you from traveling to many locations around town, as your grandparents and great grandparents did, or even around the world to get the items you want to buy. On the shelves of the store you can get coffee from Colombia, cheese from Wisconsin, meat from a butcher shop, pineapples from Hawaii, rice from Japan, bread from a bakery, and fresh produce from California. Fresh goods from throughout the world are brought to one location where you can pick and choose from what is available.

Just as a grocery store brings items from around the world to one location, distance education brings teaching and learning resources into your classroom or home. Without having to travel, learners can receive a variety of learning resources including printed matter, pictures, audio, and video that may come from another city, another state, or another country. Distance educa-

tion can deliver a complete set of instructional materials and experiences to the learner, substituting for what might ordinarily take place in a classroom, or it can supplement and enrich what learners experience in a traditional educational setting. Like a grocery store for learning, distance education makes it convenient for learners to get the education that they want without having to travel to get it.

TECHNOLOGY INTEGRATION PROCESS: PREPARING TO INTEGRATE DISTANCE EDUCATION IN THE LEARNING EXPERIENCE

As we have emphasized throughout this text, planning is an important precursor to any instructional activity. However, it is doubly important in distance education. Just as you should plan a trip to the grocery store to ensure that you get all of the items needed for a particular recipe, you should carefully plan distance education experiences to avoid leaving out a critical component. Because of the separation of teacher and learners in distance education, instructional activities must be thoroughly planned in advance. Whereas a teacher who is present in the classroom with his or her students may be able to adjust planned activities, such adjustments can be difficult or even impossible at a distance. If students participating in a biology course at a distance are to compare plant specimens during a particular class session, they will be unable to do the needed work if the instructor forgets to make the plant specimens available at the remote class location. So, a key to successful distance education is careful advanced planning.

As with any learning experience, in distance education you must prepare your learners, the learning environment, and the learning materials. Because distance education may be unfamiliar, learners should be informed of what to expect during a distance education experience. They may need to know how to operate whatever technology is being used (e.g., switching on a microphone to make a comment or ask a question, controlling a video conferencing camera, using an asynchronous discussion board in an online course). The learners also need to know expectations and norms for participation (e.g., how to ask a question from a remote site, etiquette for participating in an online chat), and they need to prepare themselves to participate (e.g., jotting down questions to ask during an audio teleconference). Of course, the learning environment must be set up to facilitate the distance education experience. Technical support staff may be needed to set up the distance education technology to be used (e.g., a satellite video linkage with remote sites). For an online course, learners may need to adjust their browser settings so that the course management software works properly. Finally,

Just as a grocery store makes items from around the world available in one location, distance education makes teaching and learning resources conveniently available to the learner.

learning materials must be prepared in advance so that the learners at the remote sites will have them in time for the distance education experience.

When implementing a distance education lesson, the teacher often must manage both the implementation of the lesson and the distance education technology being used. This adds a layer of complexity to the teaching experience. It is particularly important for the teacher to use available communication channels to check for learners' comprehension and engagement. In a classroom, it is relatively easy for the teacher to monitor learners' understanding by observing facial expressions and body language. These cues are often absent in a distance education environment, so it is important for the teacher to ask questions and actively check for understanding.

Of course, following a distance education learning experience, you and your students need to take time to evaluate the success of the experience. Because of the separation of teacher and learners, this can be more challenging than in the traditional classroom. Therefore, it is important for the teacher to plan in advance to gather evaluative information in a distance education environment.

WHAT IS DISTANCE EDUCATION?

Distance education refers to an organized instructional program in which teacher and learners are physically separated. Distance education addresses problems of educational access. Obviously, distance itself can be a major barrier to educational access. Just as people in rural or remote locations often have more limited selections at the grocery store than those in urban areas, educational access may also be limited in rural or remote locations. Resources may be scarce, and, in the worst cases, there may not be enough teachers to reach the students. For example, a small, rural school may not be able to justify the cost of a teacher to teach advanced physics or Japanese to the handful of students who might be interested in the subject. Problems of access may be manifested in other ways as well. For example, learners who are home-bound due to illness or physical disability may not be located far from an educational institution, but they are effectively isolated. Adults who wish to pursue education may lack the time needed to travel to a local school or college to pursue traditional coursework. For them, home study may be the only option. Distance education can overcome many of these problems of access and provide educational opportunities.

Figure 11–1 shows a matrix of educational settings formed by crossing the factors of both place and time. Traditional classroom instruction involves teacher and learners meeting at the same time and in the same place. Time-shifted classroom instruction occurs when teacher and students meet in the same place but at different

	Same Place	Different Place
Same Time	Traditional Classroom	Synchronous Distance Education
Different Time	Time-Shifted Classroom	Asynchronous Distance Education

FIGURE 11–1 Matrix of educational settings based on time and place.

times, such as when a teacher records video cassettes for student viewing at another time. Distance education, of course, occurs when teacher and learners are in different places. **Synchronous** distance education refers to situations where teacher and students meet at the same time but in different places, as in a live video broadcast or an audio teleconference. **Asynchronous** distance education refers to circumstances where both time and place are different, as is the case with most Web-based distance education.

Traditionally, distance education has referred to educational experiences that are apart from conventional in-class learning experiences. When most people think of distance education, they think of an instructor at one site teaching learners at another site or sites via television, the Internet, or another communication channel. However, distance education technologies are increasingly being used to augment conventional instruction. So-called **hybrid courses** are courses that combine elements of face-to-face teaching and learning with elements of distance education. They are becoming increasingly common on college campuses and even beginning to appear in K–12 education. The term *distributed education,* while sometimes used interchangeably with distance education, is better thought of as a broader term that encompasses this use of distributed learning resources to support learners who may be situated locally or at a distance. In this chapter, we examine technologies and approaches that support education at a distance but that in most cases can also be used to enhance traditional face-to-face educational experiences.

DISTANCE EDUCATION TECHNOLOGIES

The earliest efforts at distance education involved correspondence study in which individuals used self-study printed materials. While useful and still in existence today, print-based correspondence study is limited, especially because of the limited interaction between instructor and learners. Over the years, various technologies have been employed to enhance distance education, including radio, television, and the telephone. Today, a variety of telecommunication technologies are available for support of distance education. Often, a key element of

Check It Out

Defining Distance Education

Conceptions of distance education vary even among experts in the field. Review the following websites that provide information about definitions of distance education.

Website	URL
Distance-Educator.com Knowledge Netbook (follow the definitions link)	http://www.distance-educator.com/knb/
Instructional Technology Council Definition of Distance Education	http://144.162.197.250/definition.htm
University of Idaho Engineering Outreach Distance Education at a Glance	http://www.uidaho.edu/eo/distglan.html
University of Wisconsin Distance Education Clearinghouse Definitions	http://www.uwex.edu/disted/definition.html

Why do you think there are differences of opinion in how distance education should be defined? What are the common elements in most of the definitions of distance education? How do you personally think distance education should be defined?

these technologies is their ability to enhance communication between teacher and learners and among learners who may be at different locations. We look at three broad categories of distance education technologies: audio-based, video-based, and computer-based.

Audio-Based Technologies

Audio technologies have been used in distance education for many years. Options include audio cassettes and CDs, radio, and audio teleconferencing. See Table 11–1. Audio technologies are familiar and readily available. While not as widely used as computer and video technologies, they offer a cost-effective alternative that can effectively meet many distance education needs.

Video-Based Technologies

Video overcomes the lack of visual elements in audio-based distance education. Video may be delivered over distances using a variety of means including video cassettes, broadcast television, satellite and microwave transmission, closed-circuit and cable systems, and, today, the Internet. A key distinction between various video distance education options is the degree of interactivity. See Table 11–2. Video technologies are familiar, widely available, and one of the most popular options for distance education.

Video technologies are widespread in K–12 schools. Even the most advanced of these technologies, two-way video, is now becoming more common in pre-college education, and considerable enthusiasm surrounds the potential of this medium. However, it is

Using a speakerphone, students can engage in an audio teleconference with individuals at a distance.

A two-way, interactive video classroom.

important to recognize that this technology is still relatively young. Video compression, which is needed to support two-way video transmission over telephone lines or the Internet, requires specialized equipment and

TABLE 11–1   *Audio-Based Distance Education Technologies*

Technology	Description	Examples
Audio cassettes and CDs	Audio cassettes and CDs, often supplementing print material, provide a convenient, easy-to-use, and inexpensive way to deliver audio-based instruction. They are often used for self-study or correspondence courses.	• Foreign language self-study programs • "How-to" instructional modules
Radio	Radio has the capability to reach a relatively broad geographical region at relatively low cost when compared to a delivery technology such as television. Radio broadcasts adhere to a fixed schedule. Also, radio is a one-way medium; it sends a message from the instructor to the learners, but it doesn't allow learners to send messages back to the instructor.	• Educational programming on National Public Radio • Instructional lectures to remote regions, such as some parts of the developing world
Audio teleconferencing	*Audio teleconferencing* extends a basic telephone call to permit instruction and interaction between individuals or groups at two or more locations. By using a speakerphone or more sophisticated audio equipment (e.g., microphones, amplifiers, high-quality speakers), members of the audience can both hear and be heard. This allows for live, two-way interaction between two or more physically separated sites. It can be supplemented by print-based or graphical materials distributed to the remote sites in advance or by transmission of visuals. Audiographics refers to the use of audio teleconferencing along with the transmission of still pictures or graphics via fax or computer.	• Chat session between elementary students and the author of a children's book recently read in class • Dialogue between foreign language students and native speakers of the language • Project collaboration between students at two different schools

can be subject to problems with sound and picture quality. While some two-way interactive video equipment can be quite complex and expensive to set up and operate, the development of relatively easy-to-use Internet-based video conferencing equipment from companies such as Polycom (**http://www.polycom.com**) promises to make video conferencing more accessible. A room-to-room video conferencing unit includes a camera, microphone, and built-in codec (compressor/ decompressor)

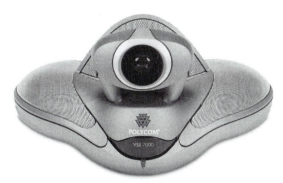

This unit from Polycom supports video conferencing over digital telephone lines or the Internet.

for transmitting video over digital telephone lines or the Internet. Schools interested in exploring this technology should consult experts in the field for advice about equipment and requirements.

Computer-Based Technologies

Computers represent one of the newest tools for distance education. In addition to the use of packaged software as part of correspondence courses, the computer can be used as a communication tool and as a tool for gathering information and resources. **Computer-mediated communication (CMC)** is the term given to any use of the computer as a device for mediating communication between teacher and learners and among learners, often over distances. Common CMC applications include e-mail, computer conferencing, chat, and the Web (see Table 11–3).

The computer is now the most widely used platform for distance education delivery. In the past decade, the emergence of the World Wide Web has led to a proliferation of online learning courses and virtual schools. Institutions specializing in distance education, such as

TABLE 11–2   *Video-Based Distance Education Technologies*

Technology	Description	Examples
Video cassettes, CDs, and DVDs	Video cassettes, like their audio counterparts, are a convenient and easy-to-use technology. VCRs are widespread in U.S. homes, and therefore video cassettes provide a familiar way to deliver instruction into people's homes. As DVDs supplant VCRs, more educational materials are likely to be released on this newer medium.	• Basic skills and literacy self-study courses • Musical instrument (e.g., guitar, piano) home study courses • Career development training courses
One-way video	Broadcast video, like radio, is a synchronous technology that involves transmission of both audio and video information to a mass audience. It is a relatively cost-effective way to reach a broad geographical area. Its chief limitations are time dependence (i.e., programs are broadcast only at certain times) and the lack of interaction between instructor and learners.	• Educational programming on public television stations • School-based offerings such as Whittle Communication's *Channel One* and CNN's *CNN Newsroom* • Instructional courses offered via local cable companies
One-way video with two-way audio	This technology combines one-way video with audio "talkback" capability, usually added by means of a simple telephone connection between the originating video location and the receiving sites. Students can call the instructor with questions or comments, allowing the students to be active participants rather than passive receivers of a video-based message. Limitations include the added cost of talkback capability, the instructor's lack of visual contact with callers, and problems of access that can arise when many receiving sites attempt to call a single originating site.	• Satellite teleconferences in which a small group of experts at one site presents information to and accepts input from various receiving sites • College and university courses broadcast live to multiple receiving sites
Two-way video	In two-way interactive video, also called *video conferencing*, both sending and receiving sites are equipped with cameras, microphones, and video monitors. Some means of transmission—satellite, microwave, cable, digital-grade telephone line, or the Internet—links the two (or sometimes more) sites together permitting a high level of interaction. This is the closest approximation to face-to-face instruction via technological means.	• Advanced physics course taught at one site by a teacher who teaches and interacts with both local students and students at another school • Students at two different schools working on the same science project make live presentations to each other about their research findings

the University of Phoenix and Western Governors University, have grown by leaps and bounds. Many states now have virtual high schools. It is not hard to understand the attraction. Computer technologies have grown to encompass many of the other technologies that have traditionally been used in distance education. Computers and the World Wide Web can deliver textual information, graphics, audio, and even video to learners in remote classroom locations or in their own homes. They make education more accessible and more convenient than ever before.

PLANNING FOR DISTANCE EDUCATION

Distance education allows students to obtain learning experiences, from enrichments of traditional lessons to complete courses and degree programs, at places and often at times that are convenient for them. Distance education technologies can be used to meet any of the educational goals one would have in a typical classroom, but sometimes modifications of traditional approaches are required for the distance education environment.

TABLE 11–3 *Computer-Based Distance Education Technologies*

Technology	Description	Examples
Diskettes, CD-ROMs, and DVD-ROMs	Just as audio cassettes and video cassettes can be used to supplement print-based correspondence study, computer diskettes, CD-ROMs, or DVD-ROMs can be mailed to learners for correspondence study on home computers. While Web-based instruction can often replace packaged software today, some bandwidth intensive applications, such as digital video, work better when delivered on computer-readable media.	• Technical skills courses, such as "how to" courses for using various computer applications • Self-study courses in disciplines such as foreign language and business education.
E-mail	E-mail supports asynchronous personal communication between teacher and learners, between teacher and parents, or among individual learners. It is rapidly becoming an essential communication channel not only for distance education courses but in traditional educational settings as well.	• Electronic communication between an instructor and students or instructor and parents • Class "discussions" via an e-mail list
Computer conferencing	Computer conferencing systems, also known as discussion forums or bulletin boards, permit two or more individuals to engage in an asynchronous text-based dialogue. Individuals type messages and post them to the conference at any time, and the computer maintains and organizes the messages. A computer conference discussion resembles conversation, in printed form, where participants can drop in and out at any time. Some conferencing systems operate on dedicated computers that users access through a dial-up or network connection. Popular electronic course support systems such as Blackboard and WebCT have built-in computer conferencing capabilities.	• Online class discussions, forums, or debates • Sharing student works, such as papers or projects, to permit peer review and critique
Chat or instant messaging	Synchronous or real-time interaction in which individuals interact by typing messages back and forth to one another. Chat room interactions resemble group conversations, except in printed form, and chat rooms have become popular places for electronic socializing. Instant messaging is similar to chat but normally involves only one-to-one communication. In addition to asynchronous discussions, course support systems such as *Blackboard* and *WebCT* have chat capability.	• Live student interaction with an expert such as a scientist • Collaboration between students from different schools about a mutual project • Online "office hours" when distant students can contact their instructor
Web-based instruction	Web instruction, also known as **online learning,** can present content, provide links to information at other locations, and serve as a focal point for a distance education experience. Web courses and programs are proliferating rapidly at all educational levels. Online course management systems, such as *Blackboard* and *WebCT*, consolidate a number of functions (content presentation, discussion forums, live chat, quizzes, and grading) that an instructor might desire. (See "Toolbox Tools: Course	• Complete courses on almost any topic • Online supplements to traditional face-to-face courses

TABLE 11–3   *Continued*

	Management Systems.") Newer technologies, such as *Tegrity* and *Breeze,* allow presentations to be captured and put on the Web. Software tools originally designed for collaborative work, such as Lotus *Notes* and *Groove,* can also support online learning.	
Internet-based audio and video conferencing	Computers connected to the Internet can be used for audio and video conferencing, replacing other types of audiovisual equipment. Internet-based telephony makes it possible to conduct telephone calls that are routed across the Internet. Computers can also be used for what is known as **desktop video conferencing,** the computer equivalent of video conferencing or what is sometimes called *video phone* technology. Software for Internet or IP-based video conferencing includes White Pine's *CUSeeMe,* Microsoft's *NetMeeting,* and Polycom's proprietary *ViaVideo* package.	• See examples under audio-based and video-based technologies above

Addressing the Standards

NETS Connection

One of the National Educational Technology Standards (V) for teachers focuses on one's ability to *engage in lifelong learning that includes technology-based opportunities, which would include distance education.* Reflect on that standard (see Teacher Resource A on page 297 for a full listing) and then complete the following:

▶ Imagine obtaining a teaching job that is located far from the nearest community college or university. But at the same time, you find the need to take classes to keep current with changes in your field, as well as the need to keep your license up to date.

▶ From this perspective, explore the possibility for taking some online, graduate-level, distance education courses. How would you go about finding and selecting the class? How do you determine the quality of such programs?

▶ Investigate two or three online distance education programs and their list of relevant classes. If one or more of the programs offer example courses to investigate, review those samples. Record in your journal the following:

  ▶ How difficult would you perceive it to be to take such a course? What would be some barriers that you would have to overcome? What would be some of the advantages?

  ▶ Do you really think it is possible to learn when you don't physically attend the class? In what ways would you have to adapt your "normal" way of learning in order to learn in this distance-type environment?

  ▶ Could you see the possibility of your actually teaching a distance course some day? What challenges does the distance bring to the instructor of such courses?

Benefits of Distance Education

Consider the benefits of distance education identified below. When planning for distance education activities, look to take advantage of these benefits.

▶ Distance education allows individuals isolated by distance, geography, or other barriers, as well as

nontraditional populations of learners (e.g., adult learners, homebound individuals), to gain educational access.

▶ Distance education can deliver remediation or enrichment to students (e.g., instruction in a specialized subject area, such as advanced

Course Management Systems

Course management systems are software programs that integrate a variety of functions in support of teaching and learning activities in an online environment. Popular course management systems include *Blackboard, WebCT,* and *Angel* among others. (See Figure A.) Most course management systems integrate multiple course support functions including content organization and presentation, student record/grade management, communication tools (e.g., e-mail, chat, and asynchronous discussions), online quizzing/testing, and other tools for managing course content and activities. In recent years, these systems have become very popular in higher education for offering online courses and for supporting traditional face-to-face courses, and they are beginning to appear in K–12 education as well.

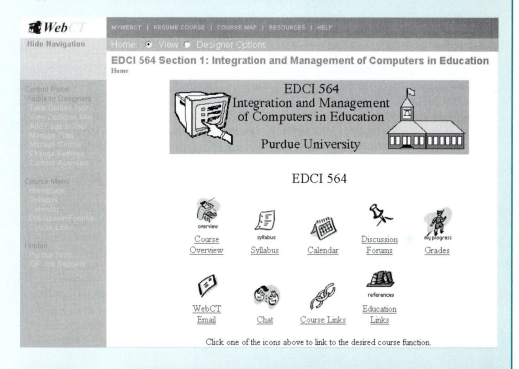

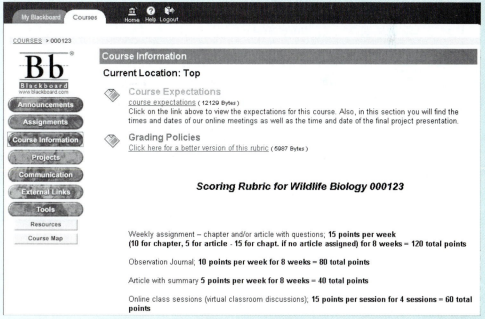

FIGURE A Screens from *WebCt* and *Blackboard,* two popular course management systems. *WebCT is a copyright of WebCT, Inc. Reprinted with permission of WebCT, Inc. and Blackboard, Inc. All rights reserved.*

TOOLBOX TOOLS
(continued)

Course management systems provide students with a central point of access for information about a course, and they give faculty the tools to make course content and information available to students through a secure Web interface. Unlike typical web pages, where anyone on the Internet has access to the information contained therein, a course management system can restrict access to only those students who are actually enrolled in the course, because students must log in with an ID and password. In addition, features such as online testing and discussion boards provide new ways of performing typical classroom instructional activities. As these systems continue to evolve, we are likely to see an even greater range of functionality.

Addressing the Standards

NETS Connection

Several of the National Educational Technology Standards (e.g., I [Technology Operations and Concepts], III [Teaching, Learning, and the Curriculum], IV [Assessment and Evaluation], and V [Productivity and Professional Practice]) for teachers emphasize the need *to use technology tools to increase the level of academic learning by students, as well as to augment personal productivity.* Reflect on those standards (see Teacher Resource A on page 297 for a full listing) and then complete the following:

▶ Create a grid similar to the one provided below. In one column list the current courses you are taking as a student. If you don't have any, think back to the last semester when you had a full slate of courses (even back into high school) and list those.

▶ In the other column list ways in which the course could have been improved if additional experts had been able to visit the course and impart their wisdom and experiences in some way. For example, if you are in a children's literature class, you might think of one or more authors who could have added a great deal by visiting and explaining their literary work, their current projects, their aspirations, their challenges, and so on.

▶ Below the grid, record how technologies today may be used to bring some of those individuals into your future classrooms. How can technology eliminate some of the problems imposed by distance and time when it comes to adding knowledge experts to your future classrooms? What advantage would this be to your learning and to the learning of your future students?

Your list of classes	The learning in the class could have been improved by having subject matter experts visit. Example visitors could have included . . .

mathematics or a foreign language), which may not be available locally.

▶ The technology offers a way to bring experts, outside consultants, or other individuals into the classroom from a distance (e.g., having the author of a children's book interact with a class of elementary students who have just finished reading the book).

▶ Distance education technologies can link together two or more classrooms at disparate locations so that students can interact with one another to learn, solve problems, and communicate (e.g., cross-cultural interactions between students from two different countries or two regions of the same country).

▶ Using distance education technologies, teachers can consult with experts or peers at remote locations regarding teaching practices, curriculum, research, and so on.

Understanding the Distance Education Learner

Distance education technologies may be used across a variety of grade levels and subject matter. Because of this, there is no single profile that describes distance education learners. However, many learners who take courses taught completely at a distance are working adults, and the characteristics of this population of learners often are different from those of learners in traditional educational settings. Even in K–12 schools, distance education learners may have characteristics that set them apart from the general student population. When planning for distance education, it is important to take into account the special characteristics of these learners.

◗ Adult distance education learners are often older, work full-time during the day, and have family obligations. As a result, they seek learning opportunities that are flexible in terms of time and place. They often pursue distance education for career or personal advancement and can bring workplace experience to their coursework.

◗ Many distance education learners, whether K–12 students pursuing advanced coursework or working adults, are highly motivated and self-directed because they seek out learning experiences to fulfill personal or professional needs.

◗ Some distance education learners, such as adults who have been away from traditional schooling for a while or K–12 students who have been unsuccessful in traditional classroom settings and are completing remedial coursework at a distance, have anxiety about their ability to perform at least when first starting a distance education course or program.

◗ K–12 students who enroll in remedial distance education courses may have difficulty academically, and, as a result, they may need higher levels of support and assistance than the average student. On the other hand, those who pursue advanced coursework at a distance (e.g., AP physics course) may be strong students who require higher levels of challenge than the average student.

◗ Distance education learners across all settings may be more prone than traditional learners to drop out or fail to complete a course/program because of competing obligations, the need to maintain self-direction when learning at a distance, and the difficulty of receiving adequate support at a distance.

Preparing for Distance Education

As we have noted above, planning and preparation are key to successful learning experiences at a distance. Below are tips for preparing the learning materials, the learning environment, and the learners for distance education.

Preparing the Learning Materials

◗ Provide thorough information for learners including explicit directions, a clear time line, guidelines for how to participate, grading information, what to do in the event of technical problems, and where to seek assistance. An extensive course syllabus, distance learning handbook, or website can provide the necessary information. When teaching online, create a FAQ file for learners to access.

◗ Take advantage of the medium when preparing distance education materials. Video, for example, can be used to show action or zoom in on something of interest; avoid "talking heads" as they will become boring in a short time. When teaching on the Web, take advantage of the Web's ability to link to information resources and facilitate communication among learners; avoid static pages of Web content that offer no improvement over the pages of a book.

◗ Make certain that learners at a distance have all learning materials in advance of when they will be needed. This may require sending materials to a remote site or making them available on the Web.

◗ Make back-up plans in the event of technical problems, and be sure to inform the learners what to do in the event of unforeseen problems.

Preparing the Learning Environment

◗ Arrange for the use of the distance education technology well in advance of when you will need it. Some technologies, such as broadcast and two-way video, may require significant lead time to reserve a studio, obtain network time, and so on.

◗ Prior to beginning a distance education lesson, test the equipment to make certain that it is working. If you are using Web resources, check links to make sure they still work. Make sure that browser settings are properly configured to use the resources you will access.

◗ If using video or audio technologies, adjust the audio and video levels so that all of the learners will be able to see and hear.

Preparing the Learners

◗ Inform learners of what to expect during a distance education experience. Whether using an audio teleconference, two-way video conference, or online discussion forum, learners may be unfamiliar with distance education and could benefit from an orientation.

◗ Have students practice using the technology in advance so that they become familiar with how it works. If using video conferencing equipment, for example, arrange for a local connection that can be

Students should practice with video conferencing equipment in advance of actual use to become familiar with its operation.

used for practice in advance of the real thing, or spend time during the first class having students practice. In an online course, have students do a nongraded activity, such as posting a personal biographical sketch to an online discussion forum, as a warm-up.

▶ Set expectations and establish norms for participation (e.g., inform users in an online discussion forum of when, how often, and in what ways they should contribute to the online discussion).

▶ Make certain that learners at a distance have access to the resources that they need, know how to contact you or other sources of help, and know what to do in the event of problems.

Problems and Pitfalls

▶ *Monetary cost.* All distance education technologies entail some real monetary cost. In the case of simpler technologies, such as audio teleconferencing, this may be as little as the cost of a long-distance telephone call. That alone, however, may be a barrier to implementation in some schools. More advanced distance education technologies, such as two-way interactive video that uses satellite or digital phone line transmission, can be very costly. The required equipment is often expensive, and the recurring costs associated with actually connecting two sites can be quite high as well. Schools should weigh the costs of using particular technologies against the benefits.

▶ *Technical difficulty.* Distance education technologies can be technically complex. While an audio teleconference may not be too difficult to set up, video conferencing may require expert assistance and may involve the coordinated efforts of local personnel, vendors, telecommunication company technicians, and others. This complexity

also increases the chance that something may go wrong.

▶ *Need for planning.* As we have emphasized, distance education requires careful planning. This is true even for simpler forms of distance education. Advance scheduling of equipment and facilities may be required. Materials must be prepared in advance and may need to be sent to participants at remote sites. In many cases, teachers need to redesign curriculum and learning activities to accommodate or take advantage of the distance education medium.

▶ *Need for training and support.* Teachers may need training to effectively use distance education technologies. Learners may need assistance in learning via these unfamiliar means, and provisions for assisting participants need to be made. These may involve onsite coordinators, telephone help, e-mail, and so on. In short, there is a lot to distance education, and teachers and schools shouldn't expect to engage in it without significant effort. As with any other educational enterprise, distance education requires time, effort, commitment, and resources. The technology is only a tool that helps schools meet existing needs.

▶ *Not all content works well.* Some content cannot effectively be taught at a distance. For example, you would not want to fly in a plane that has been serviced by a mechanic who has only learned about aircraft engines on the Internet. Hands-on experience would be essential.

IMPLEMENTING DISTANCE EDUCATION

Following are some examples of ways that distance education technologies can be implemented for teaching and learning at a distance. Following these examples, we discuss strategies for teaching at a distance and utilization guidelines for distance education.

Distance Education Examples

▶ A high school teacher offers a specialized class (e.g., AP physics, Latin, Russian) to interested students in his own school as well as several other schools using a one-way video with two-way audio connection.

▶ A teacher invites an expert (e.g., book author, scientist, public figure) at a distance to interact with her students via an audio teleconference using an available speakerphone.

▶ A high school student with a talent for mathematics would like to take advanced calculus, but it isn't offered at her school. She enrolls in a Web-based course from a nearby university and takes the class online using a computer at home.

▶ A zoo in a major metropolitan center offers virtual field trips to classes in schools through a statewide two-way video network.

Students can take classes online in specialized content areas that may not be available locally.

- Using desktop video conferencing and electronic mail, preservice teachers at a college tutor elementary school students to help them improve their reading and mathematics skills.
- Searching for lesson ideas, an English teacher posts a question to an Internet discussion group and receives several helpful suggestions from other teachers around the country.
- Students in classes at two different high schools work on a common project (e.g., investigating local water quality) and prepare presentations that they share with each other using desktop video conferencing over the Internet.
- After getting parental permission to display work, students create websites that showcase their work (e.g., poetry, local history project, artwork) and post them to the school's Web server. The work is reviewed by parents, community members, and students at other schools.
- To get practice doing research and making presentations, middle school students prepare informational presentations on animals for elementary age learners. They make the presentations from a television studio in their school to several elementary classrooms simultaneously using a cable television network within the school district.

Strategies for Teaching at a Distance

In many ways, teaching at a distance is no different than teaching face-to-face. The same instructional methods that are commonly used in the traditional classroom—presentation, demonstration, discussion, cooperative learning, drill and practice, simulation, etc.—can also be used in distance education, although some modifications may be necessary. A class discussion, for example, can be conducted at a distance using audio teleconferencing or two-way video. However, it may be necessary for the instructor to call on students at distant locations to make certain they stay actively engaged in the discussion. In an online class, a discussion could take place via chat or in an asynchronous discussion forum although individuals will type their contributions rather than speaking. A presentation or demonstration can be done at a distance, via one-way or two-way video, by sending a videotape to the learner or by posting a *Tegrity* or *Breeze* presentation (which combines *PowerPoint* with the accompanying video or audio) to a website (Figure 11–2). Cooperative learning can take place using two-way video or Internet-based collaboration tools.

In other ways, strategies for teaching at a distance depend on the particular technology being used. For example, when using video for distance education, it is important to be aware of the characteristics of the medium. Video is a visual medium, so it is important to use visuals (e.g., pictures, graphical organizers) to convey information. When creating visuals for video (e.g., *PowerPoint* slides), use a large font size and avoid the edges of the screen to adapt to the characteristics of video monitors. When teaching for video, make eye contact with the camera, and speak loudly and clearly. Avoid clothing that can cause visual effects on television (e.g., checks, all white). Camera shots and pacing should be varied and activities should be changed frequently to maintain the interest of the distant learners.

When teaching online, make resources available online; this may entail designing web pages or creating materials for a course management system such as *Blackboard* or *WebCT*. Establish regular office hours so that distant learners can make contact by e-mail, chat, or telephone. When conducting online discussions, establish guidelines and norms for participation (e.g., set the

Check It Out

Observing Distance Education

What does distance education look like in practice? Sit in on a distance education class or session at a nearby school. If you are unable to observe distance education at a K–12 school, try observing a distance education class at your college or university.

What technologies are used for information delivery and communication? How would you characterize the learners? How did the instructor prepare learning materials, the learning environment, and the learners for the distance education class? Were there any problems or difficulties that had to be overcome during the class?

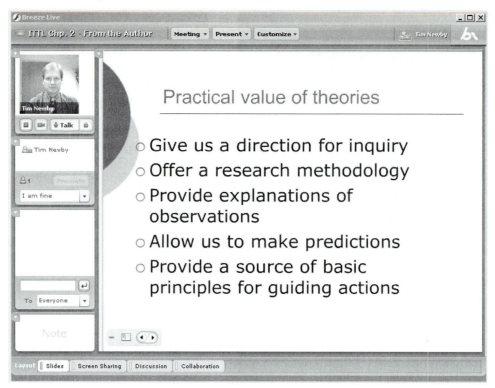

FIGURE 11–2   A screen from a Macromedia *Breeze* presentation showing audio- and video-enhanced *PowerPoint* slides for online delivery.
Reprinted with permission from Macromedia, Inc.

Addressing the Standards

NETS Connection

Two of the National Educational Technology Standards (III [Teaching, Learning, and the Curriculum] and VI [Social, Ethical, Legal, and Human Issues]) for teachers deal specifically with the ability to *address specific learner needs and affirm diversity while using technology resources that increase student learning.* Reflect on those standards (see Teacher Resource A on page 297 for a full listing of the standards and their respective performance indicators) and then complete the following:

▸ Imagine teaching a class that had a student(s) who was not physically able to be present in the classroom (perhaps due to physical disability, illness, or distance to the school).
In what way could distance education technology be used to help this student become a "normal" part of the class and experience and learn what was required?

▸ What would you perceive to be the specific challenges that this would add to your normal teaching load? For example, what types of additional training would need to be provided to use the distance technology? What types of compensation would have to be made for your normal instructional materials, for group activities, and for classroom interactions and discussions?

▸ Record your thoughts and ideas within your journal.

time line for the discussion, set parameters for number and length of postings, establish guidelines for online etiquette). See the "Toolbox Tips: Managing Asynchronous Discussions Online" for more information.

Regardless of the particular delivery system, instructors teaching at a distance must create ways for learners to interact with the content, with the instructor, and with one another. The teacher must set up and moderate class discussions, oversee individual and group assignments, and answer questions about the course and the technology being used. It is the teacher's job to foster interaction, motivate students, and help

Managing Asynchronous Discussions Online

A common feature of many online distance education courses is asynchronous discussions. Because students taking online classes generally are separated from the instructor and from one another, online discussions provide one of the only mechanisms for interaction and exchange. They not only replace traditional live discussions in a classroom, but often provide a vehicle for communicating information about the course and assignments, fostering collaborative learning, and sharing student work. While asynchronous discussions naturally will vary depending on the specific topics discussed and the purposes of the discussion, some general tips for conducting online discussions are given here.

▶ Establish a clear time line for each online discussion, and be specific about the expectations for when and how often students should contribute. Set parameters for length and quantity of messages.

▶ Build discussions around specific topics from the course. This will help to provide focus and establish a clear schedule.

▶ Assess students on both the quantity and quality of their participation. If you value the discussion, students are more likely to value it as well.

▶ Establish basic ground rules for participation and etiquette in the online discussion, and model appropriate behavior. This can help to head off problems and misunderstandings.

▶ Create an open and welcoming atmosphere for the discussion. Refer to students by name and share relevant personal experiences to build a sense of community.

▶ Use techniques to structure the online discussion (e.g., case studies, debates, assigning roles to students).

▶ Encourage students to quote from the original message when making replies. This makes it easier for readers to follow the discussion thread.

▶ Allow students to take leadership at times by starting a discussion topic, developing a discussion question, or synthesizing comments from classmates.

▶ Do monitor the discussion to make certain that students stay on the topic and do not get off on tangents. However, avoid intervening in a discussion too quickly; the pronouncement of the teacher can sometimes squelch further discussion.

▶ Ask good questions to stimulate thought and discussion. Occasionally summarize points from the ongoing discussion to help synthesize the topic. At the end of the discussion, bring closure by wrapping up the key points.

▶ Provide feedback to the learners. You need not acknowledge every message a student posts, but regular feedback is essential to let the students know how they are doing and that you are involved.

▶ Be available to students who might want to contact you outside of the discussion. Monitor e-mail and establish regular hours when you will be in your office or available online.

them to engage. The teacher must establish the mechanism by which student assignments are submitted for grading, and, of course, the teacher grades the assignments and returns them to the students. Giving regular feedback is essential because distant learners often feel out of touch. Although the teacher is at a distance, the teacher's role remains crucial to effective learning in distance education.

ASSESSING STUDENT PERFORMANCE IN DISTANCE EDUCATION

Approaches to assessing student performance at a distance, like approaches to teaching at a distance, are often no different from those used in face-to-face educational settings. However, just as teaching approaches must sometimes be modified for teaching at a distance, assessment techniques must sometimes be modified for effective use at a distance.

Traditional tests—whether multiple choice, true-false, short answer, or essay—are one of the mainstays of assessment in education. In the typical classroom setting, tests are administered by the instructor who monitors the students during the exam and enforces a specific time limit. Can tests be used when learning occurs at a distance? The answer is yes, although issues of identity authentication and test security must be addressed. The traditional solution to the testing problem in distance education has been the use of proctors at remote sites. Tests are mailed to a proctor, and students then take the test from the proctor in the usual way. This solution works well for distance learning situations in which a group of students are located at a single remote site, such as a video-based course that is transmitted to a remote school or workplace site.

The use of exam proctors is less suitable for online courses where individual students may be scattered across the country or even around the world. However, online testing is becoming an increasingly viable option. Course management systems such as *Blackboard* and *WebCT,* as well as stand-alone testing software, can generate and administer quizzes and tests online (see Figure 11–3). Various options are available within most testing software packages to generate a pool of items, draw test questions from the available pool, randomize the order of multiple-choice responses, and so forth. In addition, online test taking can be limited to particular time frames and even particular Internet domains or addresses to limit access. The issue of authentication of student identification online can be addressed through system logins and the use of personal identification information (e.g., asking for mother's maiden name), but one can never know for certain if an online learner working from home has someone else in the room helping with the test.

Many distance education instructors simply avoid the issue of online testing by using other means of assessment. For example, rather than giving timed exams, one can give students in a distance education course a take-home exam that stresses application, analysis, synthesis, and evaluation of course material rather than recall of content. Traditional in-class forms of assessment such as papers and projects can also be used in distance education. Alternative forms of assessment such as portfolios can also be done at a distance just as well as in the traditional classroom. Thus, instructors have a full range of options available for assessing student performance in distance education.

UTILIZATION GUIDELINES FOR DISTANCE EDUCATION

▶ *Plan thoroughly in advance.* As we noted at the beginning of this chapter, good instruction always requires planning, but it is doubly important in distance education. It is difficult, if not impossible, to teach at a distance "on the fly." You need to set schedules in advance, prepare materials, ensure that distant students have access to necessary resources, establish office hours for distant students, arrange for synchronous connections, practice with the equipment, and so on. Careful advance planning is the single most important thing that you can do to ensure a successful distance education experience for yourself and your students.

▶ *Make contingency plans.* The technologies involved in distance education can and do fail. The speakerphone for an audio teleconference may not work, your video connection to a remote site may fail, or your connection to the Internet may go "down." Always have backup plans that you and your students can follow in the event things do not work as expected.

▶ *Use the medium.* Make effective use of your particular medium of communication. When using

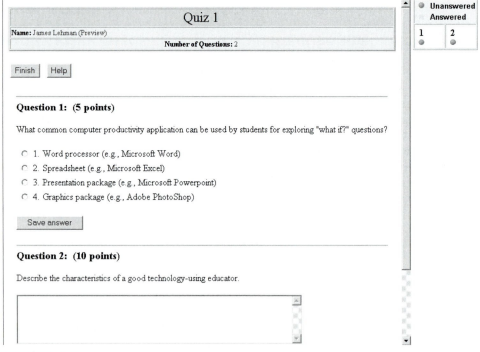

FIGURE 11–3 A screen of an interactive quiz in *WebCT.*
Reprinted with permission from WebCT, Inc.

video-based distance education, prepare effective visuals, do demonstrations, and otherwise make use of what video offers. When teaching an online class, link to Web-based resources that your students can use and take advantage of the computer's ability to store materials and make them accessible at any hour of the day.

▶ *Encourage active participation.* Regardless of the particular medium of communication, encourage active student participation. During a synchronous audio or video conference, call on distant students by name. If a local class is listening to a speaker at a remote location, have each student prepare a question to ask the speaker. During asynchronous online discussions, respond directly to students' comments; use private e-mail if you need to prod a reluctant student to participate more fully.

▶ *Vary activities and approaches.* Almost nothing is as boring as a "talking head" lecture on video. Change your activities and instructional approaches to add variety and maintain students' interest. During audio or video conferencing, change activities every 15 to 30 minutes. Mix online and off-line activities. In Web-based instruction, use a variety of approaches such as self-study content modules, Web information retrieval, asynchronous discussion forums, synchronous chat sessions, and so on to keep things interesting for your learners.

▶ *Guide your students.* Students at a distance often feel isolated and out of touch. You can help them by providing explicit guidance. Provide a clear schedule of when things will be happening and when any assignments are due. Prompt students about proper forms and level of participation (e.g., asking questions during a video conference, posting comments to an online discussion board). Summarize audio/video conferencing sessions or online discussions to help students understand the main points.

▶ *Use appropriate assessment methods.* As with all instruction, match your assessments to your learning objectives. If traditional testing is called for, consider using proctors or testing online. Use other forms of assessment (e.g., take-home exams, papers, projects, portfolios) as appropriate to your content and the needs of your students.

ISSUES RELATED TO DISTANCE EDUCATION

Copyright

As you have learned, copyright refers to the legal rights applied to original works authored in a tangible medium of expression. (Refer again to the information on copyright in Chapter 8.) Copyright law grants copyright owners certain exclusive rights including the rights to copy or make derivatives of a work, sell or distribute the work, and perform or display the work in public. These rights are tempered by certain limitations including fair use and the face-to-face teaching exemption. Teachers can benefit from fair use and the face-to-face teaching exemption because they permit certain uses of copyrighted works without permission from the copyright owner.

Distance educators, however, need to be aware that the face-to-face teaching exemption is limited in the distance education setting. Prior to 2002, copyright law did not permit the use of audiovisual materials, allowed under the face-to-face teaching exemption, in situations involving transmission from one location to another (i.e., distance education). Further, only nondramatic literacy or musical works (i.e., no dramatic plays) could be transmitted and then only into classrooms or other instructional locations (except where disabilities or special circumstances prevented individuals from being in the classroom). Needless to say, this was a significant hindrance in the rapidly growing field of online education where learners often access distance education materials in their homes.

In 2002, the Technology, Education, and Harmonization (TEACH) Act was passed by Congress and enacted into law. It amended copyright law to extend many of the protections afforded by the face-to-face teaching exemption to distance education settings. Under the provisions of the TEACH Act, it is not a copyright violation when teaching at a distance (i.e., via transmission or digital networks) to perform or display reasonable and limited portions of legally acquired works, comparable to what would typically be displayed in the course of a live classroom session, as long as this occurs as a material part of instruction under the supervision of an instructor in a class at a nonprofit educational institution. The law further stipulates that policies regarding copyright must be implemented by the institution, and students must be informed that materials used within the course may be subject to copyright protection. Further, to the extent technically feasible, any performance of works in conjunction with distance education should be restricted to the students officially enrolled in the course, and technological measures should be employed to prevent retention or further dissemination of any copyrighted work beyond the class session.

Thus, distance educators now have many of the same affordances as classroom instructors, but limitations are designed to protect the interests of copyright owners. For example, one cannot simply put a copyrighted work on an unprotected web page as part of an online course, because individuals other than the students in the class could easily access and copy the work. Measures such as password protection must be employed to limit access to only the students in the class

Check It Out

Copyright and Distance Education

Copyright law can be confusing, especially to those unfamiliar with it. To learn more about copyright law and how it applies in distance education, check out the websites below.

Website	URL
Copyright Management Center at Indiana University Purdue University at Indianapolis	http://www.copyright.iupui.edu/
North Carolina State University Libraries TEACH Act Toolkit	http://www.lib.ncsu.edu/scc/legislative/teachkit/
University of Idaho Engineering Outreach Distance Education at a Glance Guide #12	http://www.uidaho.edu/eo/dist12.html
University of Wisconsin Distance Education Clearinghouse Intellectual Property and Copyright	http://www.uwex.edu/disted/intprop.html

Suppose a teacher that you know tells you that she is planning to teach an online course at a nearby school and asks you how copyright applies. What would you tell her are the key things to know about copyright and distance education? What cautions would you give?

and prevent unauthorized use. To learn more, see "Check It Out: Copyright and Distance Education."

Support

Support tends to be a critical component of successful distance education. Technical support is often necessary to get the delivery technology (e.g., video, Web) up and running. In addition, technical support staff may be needed to assist learners if problems arise during a distance education course or lesson. Because learners are often located far from the campus or school where a distance education course originates, support is needed to help students get enrolled and acquire books and other course materials. As we have noted, it may also be necessary to have support staff at remote sites to distribute materials, assist learners, or proctor examinations. Most institutions that do significant amounts of distance education have an entire support structure dedicated to the distance education enterprise. Schools that are considering launching new distance education initiatives should carefully examine support needs before proceeding. As with other aspects of distance education, planning for support is important for a successful experience.

Policy Issues

Several policy issues can arise with respect to distance education. One fundamental issue is the certification or accreditation of distance education courses and programs.

Although research has tended to demonstrate that learners at a distance perform as well as or even better than those in traditionally delivered courses (Bernard et al., 2004; Machtmes & Asher, 2000; Neumann & Shachar, 2003; Russell, 1999), there has traditionally been skepticism about the quality of distance education experiences in comparison with those delivered by traditional means. As a result, distance educators often must establish for institutions and accrediting bodies that courses taught at a distance are equivalent to those taught face-to-face. As distance education has expanded in recent

Teaching load and intellectual property rights are issues related to faculty who teach at a distance.

years, many of these accrediting hurdles have diminished as it has become apparent that distance education courses can be just as rigorous and just as effective as traditional instruction.

Faculty issues can also arise in distance learning situations. How is a distance education course factored into a faculty member's load? Is it equivalent to a traditional course? Many faculty members who teach at a distance report that distance education requires more time and effort than traditional instruction. Intellectual property rights are also an issue for faculty teaching at a distance. Who owns the distance education course, the faculty member or the institution? These are important issues that must be addressed by institutional policies.

Basic administrative issues also need to be addressed by policy. How are costs determined and revenue shared in programs involving distance education? Because of the costs of the delivery technology and support structures, distance education programs may be more expensive than traditional programs. Further, all of the costs may not be borne by the originating site. When distance education programs are delivered at remote sites, there may be costs associated with the remote sites (e.g., support staff, proctors). This may necessitate models of revenue sharing that differ from those in traditional education.

TECHNOLOGY COORDINATOR'S CORNER

Miranda Allen, a high school Spanish teacher, wanted to use distance education technologies to provide the students in her advanced Spanish course with a new educational experience. Her class was studying the culture of Mexico by reading articles about various regions of Mexico, and browsing the Web to look at various sites including Mexican newspapers online. Miranda decided to cap off the unit by providing her students with the opportunity to interact directly with people living in Mexico. She e-mailed a colleague in Mexico City, Señora Diego, a high school English teacher, to ask if it might be possible to do a "real-time" conversation between the students in Señora Diego's English class and her own advanced Spanish class. Señora Diego was enthusiastic about the idea and promised to cooperate if Miranda could make the arrangements.

Miranda checked with the principal, Mr. Taylor, to make sure it would be all right. He told Miranda that as long as there was no extra cost, he would support it. Miranda then went to her school's technology coordinator, Dorothy Simpson, to see what could be done. She explained to Ms. Simpson that her goal was to have her students get experience speaking to native speakers of Spanish, and she hoped they could arrange a live video connection between their schools in the United States and Mexico. Ms. Simpson agreed to investigate options,

confer with the support staff in Señora Diego's school, and report back to Miranda.

A few days later, Ms. Simpson explained the options to Miranda. She said, "You have a few options. I looked into the possibility of a video teleconference. While we have satellite uplink capability, Señora Diego's school does not have a satellite receiver. The class would have to go to a university receiving site, which might be a problem. The other catch is that it would be very expensive. Then, I looked into the possibility of an Internet-based video conference. Unfortunately, Señora Diego's school has a relatively slow Internet connection. We could use a small PC-based video camera, but the quality would not be very good, especially for a whole class of students. Your other option would be to do an audio teleconference. That really just involves the use of a speakerphone to make a long distance phone call. You'd have the cost of the international phone call, but it would give your students the chance to speak to native Spanish speakers."

After weighing her options, Miranda decided to try an audio teleconference. Mr. Taylor okayed the idea when the Spanish Club agreed to pay for the call. Dorothy advised Miranda to consider several things in planning the activity. She pointed out the time difference, and she advised Miranda to have her students prepare for the audio teleconference by preparing questions in advance. She also advised Miranda to have a backup lesson plan in case things didn't work.

About a week later, using a speakerphone borrowed from the media center, Miranda called Señora Diego at the arranged time. Her students took turns asking their prepared questions and answering questions from the students in Mexico. Miranda's kids spoke Spanish, and Señora Diego's kids spoke English. It was pretty crazy, but somehow they all managed to understand each other. As a follow-up activity, Miranda's students and Señora Diego's students became e-pals (e-mail pen pals). So, the students got to practice their writing skills as well as their speaking skills. They were motivated to do well because they knew someone real was on the other end. It turned out to be a great way to harness the power of distance education technologies to make the classroom learning experience more real, more engaging, and just plain fun.

SUMMARY

In this chapter we examined distance education, any organized instructional program in which the teacher and learners are physically separated. Distance education addresses problems of educational access caused by distance, disability, or work and family obligations, among others. Technology is often used in distance education to facilitate communication between teacher and learners. We examined the characteristics of three categories of distance education technologies: audio-based, video-based, and computer-based.

Planning is especially important for successful distance education. When planning for a distance education lesson, you should take advantage of the benefits of the technology, understand the characteristics of distance education learners, prepare for the experience, and avoid problems and pitfalls. Examples of distance education were presented, and strategies for implementing distance education were described. Assessment of student performance at a distance was considered, and utilization guidelines for distance education were presented.

Issues associated with distance education were also presented. These issues include copyright, the need for support, and issues related to policy.

SUGGESTED RESOURCES

CD Resources

To increase retention and transfer of this information, review the *Reflective Questions and Activities* located in the Chapter 11 section (**Chapter info and activities>>>Chapter 11>>> Reflective Questions and Activities**) of the text's accompanying CD.

In addition, you can access relevant Internet websites, NETS Connection exercises, and direct e-mail access to the text's authors.

Website Resources

Access the text's website (**www.prenhall.com/newby**), navigate to Chapter 11, and review the Question and Answer section for relevant questions that have been generated by students and answered by the authors. You may also submit your own questions directly to the authors. In addition, you can access presentations by the authors about this chapter and gain insights directly from them about the topics that have been presented.

Print Resources

Berge, Z. L., & Collins, M. P. (Eds.). (1994). *Computer-mediated communication and the online classroom* (Vol. 1). Cresskill, NJ: Hampton Press.

Bernard, R. M., Abrami, P. C., Lou, Y., Borokhovski, E., Wade, A., Wozney, L., Wallet, P. A., Fiset, M., & Huang, B. (2004). How does distance education compare with classroom instruction? A meta-analysis of the empirical literature. *Review of Educational Research, 74*(3), 379–439.

Bonk, C. J., & King, K. S. (Eds.). (1998). *Electronic collaborators: Learner-centered technologies for literacy, apprenticeship, and discourse*. Mahwah, NJ: Erlbaum.

Cyrs, T. E. (1997). *Teaching at a distance with the merging technologies: An instructional systems approach*. New Mexico State University: Center for Educational Development.

Harasim, L., Hiltz, S. R., Teles, L., & Turoff, M. (1995). *Learning networks: A field guide to teaching and learning online*. Cambridge, MA: MIT Press.

Kearsley, G. (2000). *Online education: Learning and teaching in cyberspace*. Belmont, CA: Wadsworth.

Keegan, D. (1996). *Foundations of distance education*. London: Routledge.

Machtmes, K., & Asher, J. W. (2000). A meta-analysis of the effectiveness of telecourses in distance education. *The American Journal of Distance Education, 14*(1), 27–46.

Moore, M., & Kearsley, G. (2005). *Distance education: A systems view* (2nd ed). Belmont, CA: Thomson Wadsworth.

Neumann, Y., & Shachar, M. (2003, October). Differences between traditional and distance education academic performances: A meta-analytic approach. *International Review of Research in Open and Distance Learning, 4*(2). Available at **http://www.irrodl.org/content/v4.2/shachar-neumann.html.**

Russell, T. L. (1999). *The no significant difference phenomenon*. Available at **http://www.nosignificantdifference.org/.**

Simonson, M., Smaldino, S., Albright, M., & Zvacek, S. (2003). *Teaching and learning at a distance: Foundations of distance education* (2nd ed.). Upper Saddle River, NJ: Merrill/Prentice-Hall.

Electronic Resources

http://www.ed.psu.edu/acsde/
(American Center for the Study of Distance Education, Penn State University)

http://www.adec.edu/
(American Distance Education Consortium)

http://www.uidaho.edu/evo/distglan.html
(Distance Education at a Glance, University of Idaho Engineering Outreach)

http://www.uwex.edu/disted/home.html
(Distance Education Clearinghouse, University of Wisconsin-Extension)

http://www.distance-educator.com/
(Distance-Educator.com)

IV

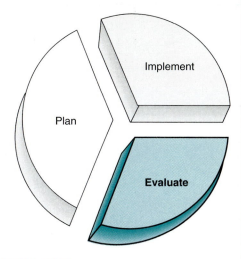

ENSURING SUCCESSFUL TECHNOLOGY-ENHANCED LEARNING EXPERIENCES

Evaluation is, and probably always will be, anxiety provoking. That is, most of us feel a little nervous when someone says, "Next week, you will be tested on . . ." or "It's time to assess your skill level in . . ." or even "Demonstrate how well you've mastered the goal of. . . ." Why? Because evaluation is the major way we receive information about our levels of competency and skill—and that information may reveal some of our inadequacies. In a commercialized world that constantly promotes perfection, being shown that you have more to learn is about as much fun as a two-hour root canal procedure.

If evaluation is that unpleasant, why bother with it? Although many students may think that tests are created merely as a way for teachers to inflict pain and suffering, in most cases there are good reasons for their use. Those reasons center around the *feedback* they provide. By obtaining feedback about your current level of performance, you can make the changes needed to reach your specific goal. Reread the title of this section: "Ensuring Successful Technology-Enhanced Learning Experiences." Evaluation is a key step in making sure that success is achieved.

When individuals realize the value of feedback, evaluation becomes a desirable tool for facilitating improvement. Think about an experience you may have had with someone who is an expert at something (e.g., cooking, teaching, managing people, art). In all cases (at least all that we can think of), those experts have mastered the art of self-evaluation. Their goal is to change or eliminate small imperfections early on, so they do not become big problems later. This is the true essence of evaluation—helping learners to assess where they are and then envisioning what their next steps might be.

In Chapter 12 the focus is on evaluation as a tool for improvement. It looks at evaluating both students and instructional materials. In both cases we discuss various instruments you can use to supply feedback *as* learning is occurring (or supposed to be occurring) as well as *after* learning has occurred. Additionally, you will see how the computer can be an important assistant in your evaluation process.

12

Evaluation of Students and Materials

CHAPTER OBJECTIVES

After reading and studying this chapter, you will be able to:

◗ Describe the purposes of evaluating student learning and the effectiveness of instruction before, during, and after a learning experience.
◗ Identify and describe a variety of techniques for evaluating both students and instruction and describe their advantages and limitations.
◗ Use a list of developmental guidelines to construct and/or assess a set of evaluation instruments.

INTRODUCTION

Evaluation is a common activity. As an example, recall the last time that you took a shower. Did you just take off your clothes, step in, turn on the water, lather up, rinse off, and step out? Probably not. Most of us have learned not to stand in front of a shower and then turn it on. Instead, we first stand off to the side, run the water for a moment, and then check its temperature with our hand or foot. If the water is too hot or too cold, we adjust it until it feels "just right." Likewise, during the shower, we monitor the temperature and adjust it whenever it feels too hot or too cold. During a typical shower we may also find ourselves thinking about whether we have rinsed all the soap off, left enough hot water for the next person in the family, and stayed in the shower long enough to wake up, sing, and think about the day's activities.

This example illustrates the basic purpose of evaluation: to make sure that we are getting what we want and, if not, to figure out what we can do so that we can get what we want in the near future.

In this chapter, we describe evaluation in terms of *what* it is, *why* you should do it, and *how* it should be done. As shown in Figure 12–1, evaluation of both learners and the instructional materials is a key piece in the jigsaw puzzle of planning and delivering valuable learning experiences. Recall (see Chapter 1) that the vision of this text is to provide the foundations for enhanced learning experiences. Through the process of evaluation we help to ensure that those learning experiences are of the quality that will lead to the greatest levels of learning.

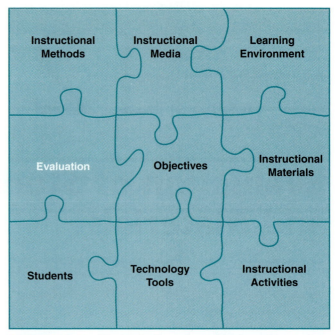

FIGURE 12–1 "Evaluation" as a key piece in understanding the full design, development, and implementation procedures.

WHAT IS EVALUATION?

Evaluation is the process of gathering information about the worth or quality of something as a way of making decisions designed to increase its worth or quality.

Within education, evaluation is an ongoing process. Recall again your most recent shower, described in the introduction. Note that evaluation in this case did not occur at a single point in time. Evaluation occurred before, during, and after the shower. This is typical of good evaluation, in the classroom as well as the bathroom.

In Chapter 1, we described evaluation as a time to reflect on both successes and problems, resulting in information you can use to improve the quality of instruction. Seen in this way, a thorough evaluation considers all instructional components—objectives, activities, methods, media, and materials—as well as the way you combine and present them to students to help them learn. This reflection can occur at any point in the learning process. This translates into a **cycle of continuous improvement**, represented graphically in Figure 12–2.

There are three important characteristics of this cycle. First, evaluation is an integral part of planning and implementing instruction, rather than something that simply gets tacked on to the end of the process. Evaluation is an important part of "reflection in action" (Schön, 1983), in which instructional experts continually monitor their efforts to help their students learn, looking for and incorporating ways to better match instruction to the students.

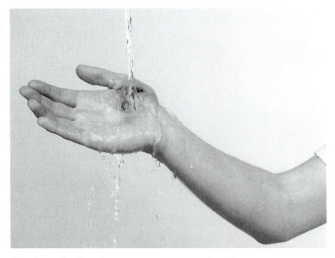

Just as evaluating the water temperature in a shower ensures a comfortable, safe, and reliable experience, so too the evaluation of instructional materials ensures a successful learning experience.

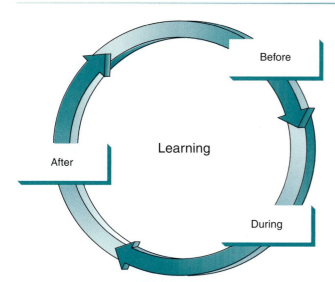

FIGURE 12–2 The cycle of continuous improvement.

Second, evaluation allows you to make adjustments as you move from one part of the learning process to the next. You can use the information as the input for the next part of the process, following it with more evaluation and adjustment. This cycle repeats throughout the instructional process. Naturally, evaluation takes a somewhat different form at different points in the cycle. Evaluation *before* instruction has a future orientation: How will it work? This encourages *pre*planning by providing a framework for making conscious estimates about the effectiveness, efficiency, and appeal of instruction. Evaluation *during* instruction has a present orientation: How is it working? Continuing the evaluation during the lesson allows you to revise instruction in time to benefit current students. Evaluation *after* the instruction has a past orientation: How did it work? This encourages conscious reflection about the effectiveness, efficiency, and appeal of the instruction so you can improve it for the next time.

Third, evaluation can focus on both the students and the instruction. We commonly think of teachers evaluating their students in order to give them a grade. But teachers also naturally evaluate their own instruction. As a result, evaluation can focus on determining both how well students have learned the desired material and how effectively the instruction helped them learn.

WHY EVALUATE?

This is not always as simple a question as it seems. Sometimes, evaluations indicate that "all is well." However, evaluations often point out problems and weaknesses, and indicate the time and effort that you must devote to making changes. This isn't always something to look forward to.

So, if evaluation often points out your weaknesses and increases your workload, why would you want to

do it? The answer lies in the fact that evaluation provides information you can use to guide your efforts to improve. In addition, the amount of information increases as you repeat the cycle. Throughout the cycle, the consistent purpose of the evaluation is to increase the amount of student learning that takes place by continually evaluating the instruction in terms of its effectiveness (does it lead students to their learning goals?), efficiency (does it make good use of available time and resources?), and appeal (does it hold students' interest and maintain their motivation?). As you repeat the cycle, your evaluation gains power, like the proverbial snowball rolling downhill. It should come as no surprise that instruction that has been used (and evaluated) several times often works better than instruction being used for the first time. Through repeated evaluation, information accumulates and trends—both positive and negative—become identifiable. Based on emerging trends, you can update content; revise methods, media, activities, and materials; and add new ones. Thorough and continuous evaluation contributes to this in the following ways:

▶ Identifying areas of the content that are unclear, confusing, or otherwise not helpful
▶ Identifying areas of the content that have the highest priority for revision because they (1) are the most critical aspects, (2) are the most difficult to learn, or (3) are likely to have the greatest impact on learning
▶ Providing a rationale and evidence in support of making specific revisions

Thinking like an evaluator, therefore, means that you view evaluation as a way to improve and that you seek, rather than avoid, opportunities to evaluate your efforts.

Evaluation takes on slightly different purposes depending on whether the focus is on the students or the instruction. We focus first on student learning.

Evaluating the Students

During a recent parent-teacher conference, Ms. Sara Powley, the ninth-grade English teacher at McCutcheon High School, explained some of the assignments and tests her students had completed. Her comments focused on the first essay examination. She explained that, for many students, this was the first exam they had taken that relied entirely on essay questions. She described how well the students had done and to what extent they had achieved the intended objectives. This particular evaluation method, Ms. Powley explained, had been helpful in a number of different ways. First, she thought that it had served as a great motivator. It gave students a reason to think about what they had discussed in class and to assimilate information from many different topics.

Second, it provided information about how well students were able to recall, analyze, and integrate critical information. Third, students' answers provided an indication of their writing skills. Fourth, the exam gave students the chance to determine how well their study habits were working. By comparing *how* they had studied with *what* had been asked on the exam, they could judge if their efforts had been successful. Finally, the exam provided Ms. Powley with a way to give students useful feedback. Her extensive comments on the essays highlighted strengths and weaknesses of students' work.

Before instruction, evaluation (often called a **pretest**) can serve the following purposes:

▶ Identify students' preinstructional knowledge and skill levels. This indicates (1) whether students have the prerequisite knowledge and skills and (2) whether they already know the lesson content.

▶ Focus learners' attention on the important topics you will cover. In this way, the students are primed to notice those important topics when they come up during the instruction (Fleming, 1987).

▶ Establish a point of comparison with postinstruction knowledge and skills. One word of caution: Tell your students that you predict lower scores on a pretest since they are taking it prior to the lesson. Be sure they understand that you are not holding them responsible for content you have not yet taught them.

For example, our English teacher, Ms. Powley, could have given her English class an essay pretest as a way of identifying the students' prerequisite knowledge and showing the students what they would be expected to learn. For those students who had already mastered the content, Ms. Powley could have provided some enrichment activities.

During instruction, evaluation (often called an **embedded test**) serves the following purposes:

▶ Determine what students have learned to that point. Both teachers and students can use this information to determine if new content can be introduced or if additional practice is needed to master the previous content.

▶ Supply feedback as the learning process occurs. This feedback can both increase students' confidence by indicating that they have mastered content to that point and correct problems *before* they become thoroughly ingrained.

▶ Identify when and what type of additional practice may be needed. As students progress, evaluation ensures that they are integrating the new knowledge and skills with previously learned information and that they can apply this learning when needed.

▶ Refocus students' attention. In the event that students lose sight of their goals and objectives, a formative evaluation can be an effective tool for refocusing their attention.

For example, Ms. Powley evaluated how well students were learning new information throughout the course. Her formative evaluations often consisted of asking students to write a paragraph or two summarizing a new topic. As Ms. Powley pointed out, her reasons for evaluation during instruction were to (1) find out how well students were assimilating the information and (2) encourage the students to monitor their own learning.

After instruction, evaluation (often called a **posttest**) serves the following purposes:

▶ Measure what students have learned. This is the most frequent use of formal evaluation. Along with demonstrating their learning, a posttest gives students the opportunity to think about and synthesize what they have learned.

▶ Make specific decisions about grades, accreditation, advancement, or remediation.

▶ Review important knowledge and skills and **transfer** them to new and different situations. The value of new knowledge and skills increases when it can be used in a variety of contexts and a summative evaluation can facilitate this transfer.

For example, Ms. Powley used the essay exam to determine how well her students could perform following instruction. The exam indicated how much improvement they had made and whether they could advance to the next unit of instruction.

Evaluating the Instruction

Each semester, Mrs. Singleton teachers a 12th grade U.S. history course to about 25 students. One of the units in the course focuses on the broad impact of various social issues that took shape during the 1960s, including desegregation and civil rights, the Cold War, poverty and the Great Society, and the space race. As part of her research, Mrs. Singleton previewed the *American History* CD-ROM produced by the Instructional Resources Corporation. The CD contains a collection of photographs and short video, and audio clips that can be randomly accessed and placed within presentation programs such as a *PowerPoint* presentation. The photographs and video clips are arranged chronologically and described in an accompanying catalog. Mrs. Singleton thinks the images on the CD will help make her presentation of the events of the 1960s less abstract and will stimulate discussion among her students.

Before the lesson (often called a **pilot test**), Mrs. Singleton discusses the visual images she has selected with Ms. Fellows, who also teachers history at the school. They discuss which issues might be most interesting to students, which are most likely to be confusing to students, and what possible directions students might take in their discussion of the issues. Based on this conversation, Mrs. Singleton decides to add a few images to her initial presentation and to identify a second set of images that matches the directions students are likely to take in their discussion.

During the lesson (often called **formative evaluation**), Mrs. Singleton begins by showing a few selected images related to each issue, briefly describing each image. She begins the discussion by asking, "Which of these events had the greatest impact on American society during the 1960s?" Mrs. Singleton closely monitors the discussion as it progresses. She uses images from the CD, including the second set she had selected, to focus the discussion when it gets off track, to provide additional information when students request it, and to provide visual support to students making critical points.

After the lesson (often called **summative evaluation**), Mrs. Singleton assigns students the task of selecting one of the issues presented in class and writing an essay about the breadth and depth of its impact. As she reads the essays, she notes that, in general, they are thoughtful and insightful and that they include more specific references to people, places, and events than had been the case when she had taught the lesson without the CD. She determines from this that the presentation is worth trying again, and she decides to expand its use. She considers using the CD in American history to

link the social issues of the 1960s and the 1930s to encourage students to compare the two periods. She makes notes on her lesson plan about the issues and questions that generated a lot of discussion, the types of images that might help bridge the two periods, and possible adaptations to the essay assignment.

Before she teaches the lesson during the next year, Mrs. Singleton reviews her notes and incorporates them into a revised instructional plan, emphasizing the link between the 1960s and the 1930s. She selects a new set of photographs and video clips to show to students, revises the question she will ask to begin the discussion, and modifies the essay assignment.

Table 12–1 summarizes the key questions that you should consider when evaluating both students and the instruction before, during, and after the instruction.

HOW TO EVALUATE

Now that you understand what evaluation is and why you should do it, we look at specific techniques you can use to conduct the actual evaluation. There are three basic principles to keep in mind as you select and use these techniques. First, continuous improvement requires continuous information. Recall that the purpose of evaluation is to increase the amount of student learning through ongoing self-renewal. This kind of continuous improvement depends on a steady stream of

---

TABLE 12–1   *Key Questions for Evaluating Learning and Instruction*

	Evaluating Learning	Evaluating Instruction
Before instruction	Do students have the prerequisite knowledge and skills? Do students already know the content they are slated to learn? What is the students' current level of performance (baseline)?	How well is the instruction likely to work? Will the instruction hold student interest? Is there an alternative way to organize the instruction to make better use of available time and resources?
During instruction	Are students ready for new content or is additional practice and feedback needed? In what specific areas do students need additional practice and feedback? What types of remediation or enrichment activities may be necessary for students?	What obstacles are students encountering and how can they be overcome? What can be done to maintain student motivation? How can these students be helped to better progress through the instruction?
After instruction	Have students learned what was intended? Can students be accredited or "passed"? What will be needed to help students generalize what they have learned and transfer it to new situations?	What improvements could be made in the instruction for future use? What revisions have the highest priority? Did students find the instruction interesting, valuable, and meaningful? Were the selected instructional methods, media, and materials effective in helping students learn?

information flowing before, during, and after every period of instruction. Over time this information may become increasingly detailed and the refinements in the instruction may become increasingly small, but these small refinements are no less important to student learning than the earlier, larger refinements (for a full discussion, see Stiggins, 2005).

Second, encourage and teach students how to evaluate for themselves. We most often think of evaluation as being done by the teacher. Teachers, as instructional experts, are responsible for evaluation. However, throughout the evaluation cycle, students can often evaluate their own learning and the instruction implemented to help them learn. They may need help in identifying the best techniques to use and guidance in how to use those techniques, but they can often be effective evaluators.

Before the lesson, students can ask, "What will work best for me?" This will encourage them to think strategically, identifying the instructional methods, media, activities, and materials that are most likely to help them achieve the learning goals. *During* the lesson, students can ask, "Is this working for me?" This will encourage them to think about what they are learning and what they are having trouble with, thus helping to identify where they need additional information and/or different study techniques. *After* the lesson, students can ask, "Did this work for me?" This will encourage them to think about their own skills as learners and about the learning strategies they use. They can then make a conscious effort to add to their repertoire of learning strategies and become more effective learners. Finally, *before* the next lesson, students can ask, "What will work best for me now?" This will encourage them to think ahead about their newly developed learning skills and strategies, identifying ways the instructional methods, media, activities, and materials can be matched to their particular skills and strategies.

Third, information will carry more weight when it has been "triangulated" (Morrison, Ross, & Kemp, 2004). **Triangulation** refers to the process of obtaining information from multiple techniques or sources. All information is useful. However, information is strengthened when supported by information from other techniques or sources. Similarly, information is weakened when contradicted by information from other techniques or sources. Therefore, rather than relying on a single source of information, when possible gather information from several different sources.

Techniques to Evaluate Student Learning

It would be wonderful if all learners could be plugged into a machine that would tell us when learning had occurred. Although it isn't quite that easy, there are means that you can use to help identify when, and to what degree, learning has occurred.

This section will give you an overview of different techniques you can use to evaluate student learning, some of their advantages and limitations, and some guidelines for their selection and use. The first group of techniques will focus on traditional means of gathering evaluation data (e.g., multiple-choice, essay, and true-false items), and the second will be devoted to alternative evaluation techniques (e.g., portfolios, logs, journals). We have included both types for a very important reason: Different techniques will provide different types of information. Just as we have shown the need for you to know a variety of instructional methods and media to ensure the appropriate learning of individual students, you need to know different forms of evaluation to be able to determine which will deliver the best possible information. You must understand the types from which to choose and under which conditions each is most appropriate. For example, many educators feel that standard evaluation techniques (e.g., multiple-choice or true-false items) will not always produce the best information about student learning during the learning process. In some cases, then, alternative techniques (e.g., portfolios, journals) may prove more beneficial. Again, you must understand the students, the situation, and the type of information that you want before you can choose a proper evaluation technique. In all cases, however, you are in a much better position when you know the different techniques and their individual strengths and limitations.

Standard Evaluation Techniques

True-False. This technique consists of statements in which a choice is made between two alternatives—generally either true or false, agree or disagree, or yes or no. Examples:

▶ Slavery was the main cause of the American Civil War.
▶ In the sentence, "The old woman and her husband walked slowly up the stairs," the word *slowly* is an adjective.

Advantages of true-false items:

▶ These items and their answers tend to be short, so you can ask more items within a given time period.
▶ Scoring is relatively easy and straightforward.

Limitations of true-false items:

▶ There is no real way to know why a student selected the incorrect answer; thus it is difficult to review students' responses and diagnose learning problems.
▶ There is a tendency to emphasize rote memorization. It is difficult to design true-false items that measure comprehension, synthesis, or application.

Matching. In this type of evaluation, students are asked to associate an item in one column with a number of alternatives in another column. Example:

Match the following wars with their main causes.

Wars

    _____ 1. American Revolutionary War
    _____ 2. American Civil War
    _____ 3. Spanish-American War

Main Causes

a. Failure of the British to sign commercial agreements favorable to the United States.
b. Use of yellow journalism to sway public opinion about the need for humanitarian intervention and the annexation of Cuba by the United States.
c. The Nullification Controversy, in which South Carolina declared the U.S. tariff laws null and void.
d. Imposition of taxation without proper representation of those being taxed.

Advantages of matching items:

▶ Matching items are well suited for measuring students' understanding of the association between pairs of items.
▶ Students can respond rapidly, thus allowing for more content coverage.

Limitations of matching instruments:

▶ They are frequently used to associate trivial information.
▶ They measure students' ability to recognize, rather than recall, the correct answer.

Completion/Short Answer. This type of item asks students to recall a particular short answer or phrase. Completion and short-answer items are similar. A completion item requires students to finish a sentence with a word or short phrase; a short-answer item poses a question they can answer in a word or phrase. Examples:

▶ A major cause of the American Civil War was the _____.

▶ The Nullification Controversy was a major cause of which American war? _____

Advantages of completion and short-answer items:

▶ These items work well when students are expected to recall specific facts such as names, dates, places, events, and definitions.
▶ The possibility of guessing a correct answer is eliminated.
▶ More items can be used because this type of item usually takes less time to read and answer than other types. This allows you to cover a larger amount of content.

Limitations of completion and short-answer items:

▶ It is difficult to develop items that measure higher-level cognitive skills.
▶ They can be difficult to score. For example, which is the correct answer for the following item? Abraham Lincoln was born in _____ (Kentucky, a bed, a log cabin, 1809).

Multiple Choice. The multiple-choice item is one of the most frequently used evaluation techniques. Each item is made up of two parts: a stem and a number of options or alternatives. The **stem** sets forth a problem, and the list of options contains one alternative that is the correct or "best" solution. All incorrect or less appropriate alternatives are called **distractors,** or **foils.** Examples:

▶ Which of the following was a major cause of the American Civil War?
  a. Failure of the British to sign commercial agreements favorable to the United States.
  b. Use of yellow journalism to sway public opinion about the need for humanitarian intervention and the annexation of Cuba by the United States.
  c. The Nullification Controversy, in which South Carolina declared the U.S. tariff laws null and void.
  d. Imposition of taxation without proper representation of those being taxed.
▶ If one frequently raises the cover of a container in which a liquid is being heated, the liquid takes longer to boil because
  a. boiling occurs at a higher temperature if the pressure is increased.
  b. escaping vapor carries heat away from the liquid.
  c. permitting the vapor to escape decreases the volume of the liquid.
  d. the temperature of a vapor is proportional to its volume at constant temperature.
  e. permitting more air to enter results in increased pressure on the liquid.

Advantages of multiple-choice items:

▶ You can use them with objectives ranging from simple memorization tasks to complex cognitive manipulations.
▶ You can use them to diagnose student learning problems if incorrect alternatives are designed to detect common errors.
▶ You can construct them to require students to select among alternatives that vary in degree of correctness. Thus, students are allowed to select the "best" alternative and aren't left to the absolutes required by true-false or matching instruments.

Limitations of multiple-choice items:

▶ They are often difficult and time-consuming to write. Determining three or four plausible distractors is often the most arduous part of the task.
▶ Students may feel there is more than one defensible alternative. This may lead to complaints of the answer being too discriminating or "picky."

Essay. The essay item asks students to write a response to one or more questions. For elementary students an answer may consist of a single sentence. For older students the responses may range from a couple of sentences to several pages. Essay items can be used to compare, justify, contrast, compile, interpret, or formulate valid conclusions—all of which are higher-level cognitive skills. Example:

▶ Why does the single issue of slavery fail to explain the cause of the American Civil War?

Advantages of essay items:

▶ You can use them to measure desired competency at a greater depth and in greater detail than with most other items.

▶ They give students the freedom to respond within broad limits. This can encourage originality, creativity, and divergent thinking.
▶ They effectively measure students' ability to express themselves.

Limitations of essay items:

▶ They are difficult and time-consuming to score, and scoring can be biased, unreliable, and inconsistent.
▶ They may be difficult for students who misunderstand the main point of the question, who tend to go off on tangents, or who have language and/or writing difficulties.
▶ They provide more opportunity for bluffing.

Figure 12–3 presents guidelines for developing these standard types of evaluation items.

Alternative Evaluation Techniques

Alternatives are available to the traditional evaluation techniques described previously. In particular, the performance and portfolio techniques have gained popularity in recent years. Here we outline their purpose,

---

Addressing the Standards

NETS Connection

According to the NETS IV (Assessment and Evaluation) for teachers, you should be able to *integrate technology-based assessment strategies to facilitate the evaluation of learning activities.* Reflect on the various ways that technology could be used to monitor, record, analyze, and report evaluation/assessment data. For example, think about the value of video cameras to provide visual assessment feedback for specific psychomotor learning performances (e.g., diving, dancing, public speaking). The table below lists a number of learning activities. In the opposite column, identify different types of technologies that may be used to facilitate the evaluation of those activities in some way.

Learning activities involving	Technology to assist in evaluation
Public speaking	Use of video to provide visual feedback on voice quality, body language, audience reaction
Website development	
Identification of art sculptures	
Math word problems involving two variables	
Newspaper editing techniques	
Use of adjectives and adverbs	
Food preparation	
Accounting	
Discrimination of symptoms of major diseases in cattle	
Overgeneralization and undergeneralization of the concept of color	

General guidelines	❑ Relate all items to an objective.
	❑ Provide clear, unambiguous directions.
	❑ Make sure all options appear on the same page.
	❑ Make sure the vocabulary is suitable for students.
	❑ Avoid lifting statements verbatim from the instructional materials.
True-false	❑ Select items that are unequivocally true or false. Avoid words such as *always, all,* and *never.*
	❑ Avoid multiple negatives (e.g., "It was not undesirable for the First Continental Congress to meet in response to the Intolerable Acts of the British Parliament").
	❑ Make sure the evaluation has approximately the same number of true and false answers.
Matching	❑ Explain to students the basis for matching and whether options may be used more than once or if more than one option is given for any of the questions.
	❑ Provide extra alternatives in the answer column to avoid selection by elimination.
	❑ Provide between six and eight associations within a single question.
	❑ Arrange the answer choices in a logical manner (alphabetical, chronological, etc.).
Multiple choice	❑ Avoid opinion items.
	❑ Include graphics, charts, and tables within items whenever possible.
	❑ Present one problem or question in the stem, and make sure it presents the purpose of the item in a clear and concise fashion.
	❑ Make sure the stem contains as much of the question or problem as possible. Do not repeat words in each option that you could state once in the stem.
	❑ Use negatives sparingly. If the word *not* is used in the stem, highlight it to make sure students do not overlook it.
	❑ Provide only one correct or clearly best answer.
	❑ All alternatives should be homogeneous in content and length and grammatically consistent with the stem.
	❑ Provide three to five alternatives for each item.
	❑ Write alternatives on separate lines beginning at the same point on the page.
	❑ Ensure that all alternatives are plausible.
	❑ Compose incorrect alternatives by including common misconceptions.
Completion and short answer	❑ Write the item specifically enough that there is only one correct answer.
	❑ Omit only key words from completion items.
	❑ Put the blanks near the end of the statement rather than at the beginning.
	❑ Avoid writing items with too many blanks.
	❑ Require a one-word response or at most a short phrase of closely related words.
	❑ Use blanks of the same length to avoid providing clues as to the length of the correct response.
Essay	❑ Phrase each question so students clearly understand what you expect. For example, include specific directions using terms such as *compare, contrast, define, discuss,* or *formulate.*
	❑ Provide as many essay items as students can comfortably respond to within the time allowed.
	❑ Avoid using items that focus on opinion and attitudes—unless the learning goal is to formulate and express opinions or attitudes.
	❑ Begin, when possible, with a relatively easy and straightforward essay item.
	❑ Minimize scoring subjectivity by preparing a list of key points, assigning weights to each concept, scoring all papers anonymously, and scoring the same question on all papers before moving on to the next question.

FIGURE 12–3 Development guidelines for standard evaluation items.

advantages and limitations, and some guidelines for their use. Following this we describe additional techniques: interviews, journals, writing samples, open-ended experiences, and long-term projects. (See Stiggins, 2005, for more on all of these alternatives.)

Performance. The purpose of a performance evaluation is to measure skills (usually psychomotor or physical) needed to accomplish a specific task. Within a performance situation, students are required to perform some feat or demonstrate some skill they have learned,

Check It Out

Automated Testing

All types of assessments and evaluations take time. Often one of the leading reasons why they are not completed has to do with the time that is involved in the process. Individuals are constantly examining methods that could be used to obtain the needed evaluation and assessment information and feedback, but make the process as reliable, valid, and efficient as possible. Technology has been viewed as one possibility for helping in the area of efficiency. For example, testing (especially of large numbers of test takers) can be impacted in a number of ways: the production of the test, the distribution of the test, the monitoring of the testing, the manner in which the test is taken, how the test is collected, analyzed, and the results are distributed. To get a small idea of the impact of technology in this area do the following:

1. Go to a website that offers online testing. For example www.4tests.com is a website that offers all types of short tests that can cover a wide variety of topics.
2. Select one of the provided tests. Examine the types of questions used (e.g., true-false or multiple-choice questions).
3. Complete the short test and submit it.
4. Examine the feedback that is provided.
5. Reflect on the following questions:
   a. What advantages and limitations do you think this kind of assessment has for the instructor? For the student?
   b. How might you use this kind of assessment in a class that you're taking now?

---

such as delivering a persuasive speech, calculating an arithmetic average, performing a successful ceiling shot in racquetball, or parallel parking a car. Unlike the previous techniques, learners in this situation must demonstrate not only that they know *what* to do but also that they know *how* to do it. Regarding the Civil War topic previously presented, for example, you may ask a student to present a persuasive speech explaining why the Southern states were justified in seceding from the Union. Figure 12–4 shows a performance checklist used by water safety instructors to evaluate swimming performance.

Advantages of performance assessment:

▶ This technique allows for the objective evaluation of a performance or product, particularly when using a checklist.

▶ Students actually get to demonstrate, rather than simply describe, the desired performance.

▶ With the use of a performance checklist, students can practice the performance before the test and receive reliable feedback from other students, parents, teachers, or themselves.

Limitations of performance assessment:

▶ This format can be time-consuming to administer (usually one student at a time).

▶ It may require several individuals or judges (e.g., skating and diving competitions) to assess the abilities of the performers.

▶ Increased setup time with specialized equipment at a specialized location is often required.

FIGURE 12–4   Performance checklist for evaluating the front crawl swimming stroke. *Source: Courtesy of the American Red Cross. All rights reserved in all countries.*

Swimming stroke: **Front Crawl**	
Component	Level V
Body Position	❑ Body inclined less than 15°
Arms	❑ Elbow high during recovery ❑ Hand enters index finger first ❑ Arm fully extended at finish of pull ❑ Arms pull in "S" pattern
Kick	❑ Emphasis on downbeat ❑ Relaxed feet with floppy ankles
Breathing/Timing	❑ Head lift not acceptable during breathing ❑ Continuous arm motion in time with breathing

Portfolio. Arter and Spandel (1992) define the student **portfolio** as "a purposeful collection of student work that tells the story of the student's efforts, progress, or achievement" (p. 36). The portfolio is a rich collection of work that demonstrates what students know and can do. For years, artists have used portfolios to highlight the depth and breadth of their abilities. Similarly, students may use portfolios to illustrate their unique problem-solving or critical-thinking skills, as well as their creative talents (e.g., writing, drawing, design). Additionally, portfolios can be used to demonstrate the evolution students went through to achieve their current performance level. Unlike the end-of-the-unit objective evaluation, the portfolio is designed to capture a greater range of students' capabilities and to indicate how those capabilities developed and grew over time. Not only does the portfolio convey to others the students' progression, but it also serves as a vehicle for students to gauge their own development and to envision what additional things they might learn. In our discussion of constructivist theory in Chapter 2, we explained that this theory deals with the creation of meaning and understanding by the student. Portfolios (as well as journals, logs, long-term projects, etc.) can effectively show how and to what degree that meaning and understanding have developed. Moreover, the portfolio itself offers a means by which learners can reflect and gain greater insights as they think about what they have accomplished and what additional things they can do.

As suggested by D'Aoust (1992), portfolios may be structured around the exemplary "products" of students' work (i.e., including only those of the best quality) or around the "process" by which students arrived at current levels of performance (i.e., pieces from the beginning, middle, and end of the course that show the progression of students' abilities), or they could include a mixture of both. In either case, a major benefit comes from actually putting it together. "Students cannot assemble a portfolio without using clearly defined targets (criteria) in a systematic way to paint a picture of their own efforts, growth, and achievement. This is the essence of assessment. Thus, portfolios used in this manner provide an example of how assessment can be used to improve achievement and not merely monitor achievement" (Arter & Spandel, 1992, p. 37).

Within the classroom setting, the portfolio is becoming more and more accepted as a means of student assessment. Some states, such as Vermont, now have a mandated statewide portfolio assessment program. Other states, such as Indiana, will invoke similar programs in the near future.

Advantages of portfolio assessment:

▶ It provides a broad picture of what students know and can do.
▶ It can portray both the process and the products of student work, as well as demonstrate student growth.

▶ It actively involves students in assessing their own learning and actively promotes reflection on their work and abilities.

Limitations of portfolio assessment:

▶ The work in the portfolio may not be totally representative of what students know and can do.
▶ The criteria used to critique the product may not reflect the most relevant or useful dimensions of the task.
▶ The conclusions drawn from the portfolio can be heavily influenced by the person doing the evaluation.

Figure 12–5 presents a set of guidelines to consider when developing either performance or portfolio evaluation instruments.

There are many advantages for using portfolios. The problems that often occur, however, have to do with two basic questions. First, is the portfolio constructed in a manner that is usable and valuable for student assessment? Second, once it is assembled, how is it stored so that it can be expanded and used whenever needed?

Today several software programs are available to assist in the development of **electronic portfolios** (Baron, 2004; Bullock & Hawk, 2005). Scholastic's *Electronic Portfolio,* for example, is a program to develop an electronic cumulative record that can be used for each student every year, from prekindergarten through grade 12. Within programs such as this, you or your students can build the portfolio from within the program itself or import work from other programs or through scanned images. Once stored, the portfolio can be searched and sorted based on a table of contents, by subject, project, or theme.

With this program, you can include images and photographs of the student and sample work, include videos of the student as well as videos produced by the student, and record all of the information that is standard in a cumulative record. This capacity enables you to capture and monitor both the learning process and samples of work within the same portfolio. The electronic portfolio provides teachers, students, and parents with access to rapid evaluation of student progress and comprehensive capacities for reporting and monitoring student performance. The program provides you with the ability to transfer selected pieces or entire portfolios onto VHS videotape for presentation in the classroom, to pass on to next year's teachers, or to be viewed at home.

As shown in Figure 12–6 a popular portfolio software program for preservice teachers is *TaskStream: Tools for Engagement.* This software not only facilitates the development of portfolios, but also provides website development software, design tools to create lesson plans, **assessment rubrics,** standards integration wizards, and communication tools that provide e-mail, discussion boards, and so on.

Performance test guidelines	❏ Specify exactly what learners are to do (through a demonstration and/or explanation), the equipment and materials that will be needed, and how performances will be assessed.
	❏ Develop and use a checklist based on acceptable performance standards. In most cases, the checklist should include some type of scoring system.
	❏ Make sure the checklist outlines all the critical behaviors that should be observed. List behaviors that should *not* be observed on a separate part of the checklist.
	❏ Be sure that, if a sequence of behaviors is needed to complete a task successfully, it is highlighted in some way.
	❏ Keep the scoring system as simple as possible.
	❏ Give a copy of the checklist and scoring system to students before they begin to practice the skill. Have them refer to it as they are learning the skill.
	❏ Use video- and/or audiotape to record performances. This may be extremely helpful when behaviors occur very quickly or in rapid succession. The tapes are also an effective means for supplying feedback to students.
Portfolio guidelines	❏ Many different skills and techniques are needed to produce an effective portfolio. Students need models of finished portfolios as well as examples of how others develop and reflect on them.
	❏ Students should be involved in selecting the pieces to be included in their portfolios. This promotes reflection on the part of students.
	❏ A portfolio should convey the following: *rationale* (purpose for forming the portfolio), *intents* (its goals), *contents* (the actual displays), *standards* (what are good and not-so-good performances), and *judgments* (what the contents tell us).
	❏ Portfolios should contain examples that illustrate growth.
	❏ Student self-reflection and self-evaluation can be promoted by having students ask, What makes this my best work? How did I go about creating it? What problems did I encounter? What makes my best piece different from my weakest piece?
	❏ All pieces should be dated so that progress can be noted over time.
	❏ Students should regularly be given time to read and reorganize their portfolios.
	❏ The portfolio should be organized, inviting, and manageable. Plan a storage system that is convenient for both you and your students.
	❏ Students should be aware of the criteria used for evaluating the portfolio.

FIGURE 12–5   Development guidelines for performance and portfolio evaluation.

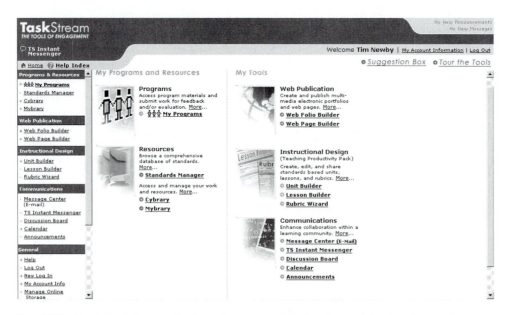

FIGURE 12–6   *TaskStream: Tools of Engagement* electronic portfolio development software.

Reprinted with permission from TaskStream, LLC. © TaskStream, LLC 2004. All rights reserved.

Today, storage of the portfolio has also become more simplified. Where once you had to create folders of materials for each student and store them in some file drawer or closet, much of the information can now be stored electronically on CD-ROM. In particular, the CD-R (CD-Recordable) and CD-RW (CD-Rewritable) formats are capable of storing huge amounts of information. Unlike the standard prerecorded CD-ROM, a CD-R allows the user to select information and "burn" or write it on the CD. A CD-RW permits information to be written, erased, and rewritten. CD-R and CD-RW recorders are now found as standard equipment on most computers. This technology allows you to record huge amounts of written text, scanned pictures, other digital images, and even videos. With this amount of storage space, it is possible for you to place on a single CD-ROM the entire school portfolio of a student from kindergarten to 12th grade. Recordable DVD formats also are available. These provide even greater storage capacity. So, storage capacity is no longer a barrier to maintaining student portfolios.

Interviews and Oral Evaluations.

Interviews and oral evaluations are generally conducted face-to-face, with one person asking questions and the other responding. To conduct an interview or oral evaluation, first design a set of questions covering a specific set of objectives. The questions may be very structured (i.e., requiring a specific response) or fairly unstructured (i.e., open-ended questions that allow for lengthy, detailed answers). As with the questions for an essay evaluation, the person conducting the interview or oral evaluation (normally you, the teacher) asks a question and allows the student to respond. For purposes of clarification, students may take (or be asked to take) the opportunity to explain their answers in more depth and detail. You may record the response on video- or audiotape, or transcribe the main points. Because this form of evaluation is conducted orally between two or more individuals, you can also conduct it over the telephone. As our expertise with e-mail increases, adaptations that incorporate this technology will become prevalent. Interviews allow for more in-depth, on-the-spot questioning if needed. However, they can take a lot of time to complete and they may be somewhat unreliable.

Logs and Journals.

Logs and journals are written records that students keep as they work through a long-term experience. For example, students in a discussion group might take time at the end of each session to write out their thoughts and experiences about what happened in the group. How well was the topic covered? What feelings did the discussion provoke? There is value in organizing one's thoughts and presenting them logically in writing. There is also value in rereading the journal later and reflecting. Just as students can reflect on their experiences, you can use the journal or log as a means to evaluate what they experienced. This is a good instrument to use during the formative stages of learning.

Writing Samples.

This evaluation technique is frequently combined with the portfolio. It generally consists of the student selecting one or more samples from

---

Addressing the Standards

NETS Connection

The National Educational Technology Standard IV (Assessment and Evaluation) for teachers emphasizes one's need to be able to *develop a portfolio of technology-based products from one's coursework.* One way to address this standard would be to actually create an electronic portfolio. This would entail selecting representative digital documents. Think of the possibilities by considering the following:

▶ Refer to Teacher Resource A on page 297 and read each of the NETS for teachers and the accompanying performance indicators.

▶ Identify a number of artifacts you have developed that could be shown to demonstrate skills with one or more of those standards.

▶ Review the electronic journal entries that were discussed throughout this text within the NETS Connection sections. These could form the basis of narratives of how specific products illustrate and address the standards.

▶ Create a simple flowchart that identifies, organizes, and lists the standards, your selected artifacts, and your narratives. The flowchart should illustrate how the items could be linked together.

▶ Finally, consider the various types of software that could be used to create your portfolio. For example, what would be the advantages and the challenges of using Web editing software to develop web pages for the various standards and associated artifacts? Could you use database software? What about word processing, presentation (e.g., *PowerPoint*), or even spreadsheet software?

Oral interviews and evaluations allow for in-depth as well as spontaneous information to be collected.

different writing assignments and submitting them for evaluation. The samples may be selected as the student's "best work" as a means to demonstrate the progression that has occurred over a specific period of time. This technique is frequently used by businesses and by graduate school selection committees.

Open-Ended Experiences. This type of evaluation technique generally is not focused on a single "correct" answer. Here students are placed in a novel situation that requires a performance, and that performance is judged by how they respond and react. Many results from a continuum of possible "correct" outcomes may be produced. Examples include mock trials, debates, and different types of simulated experiences.

Long-Term Projects. Term papers, science fair projects, and unit activities (e.g., mini-societies, dramatic reenactments, trade fairs) are all examples of long-term projects. They can require extended research and library work and often involve the use of cooperative groups. As stated by Blumenfeld et al. (1991), "Within this framework, students pursue solutions to nontrivial problems by asking and refining questions, debating ideas, making predictions, designing plans and/or experiments, collecting and analyzing data, drawing conclusions, communicating their ideas and findings to others, asking new questions, and creating artifacts" (p. 371). This technique generally requires the use of checklists with important attributes that must be exhibited within the project. Frequently, the effectiveness of this project is enhanced through the use of journals or logs.

Table 12–2 gives application examples of this and other alternative evaluation instruments.

Planning Evaluation

After considering different types of evaluation instruments, we are ready to plan evaluation. Think back to the instructional plan described in Chapter 5. Evaluation is an integral part of that plan. In Chapter 4, we emphasized the importance of planning so that your final instructional materials accomplish the desired learning goals. Likewise, forethought and planning are required to properly measure learning. The following suggestions outline important considerations for planning and implementing an evaluation. Do not interpret the following to be a "cut-in-stone" prescription of exact steps to follow. These are guidelines, proven helpful in the past, that you can adapt to your specific situation.

1. Ask yourself the following question: What is it that students are supposed to have learned? The easiest and quickest way to answer this question is to refer to the objectives. As explained in Chapter 4, objectives, instruction, and evaluations should all be parallel. This means that the evaluation instruments should measure what you taught during your instruction and that instruction should be developed from the objectives.
2. Determine the relative importance of each objective. Make decisions on how many questions to ask related to the different objectives and how much time you will need to evaluate each one. In most cases, those decisions are closely aligned with the relative importance of each objective.
3. Based on the objectives, select the most relevant evaluation technique(s) and construct the evaluation items. These items should reflect the principles of good evaluation item construction discussed earlier. It is critical that the conditions and the behaviors mentioned in the objectives match those within the evaluation item. Be sure to consider other techniques you could use to evaluate the given objective.
4. Assemble the complete evaluation. As you bring together all of the individual items, it is important to consider the following:
   a. Group questions according to item type (e.g., multiple-choice, true-false) so students don't have to continuously shift response patterns.
   b. Do not arrange items randomly. Try to list items in the order the content was covered or in order of difficulty. When possible, place easier questions first to give students confidence at the outset of the test.
   c. Avoid using a series of interdependent questions in which the answer to one item depends on knowing the correct answer to another item.

TABLE 12–2   *Examples of the Application of Different Alternative Evaluation Instruments*

Alternative Evaluation Instrument	Application Examples
Portfolio	Evaluate the improvement of writing skills over the course of a semester by having 11th-grade English students create a portfolio of their best writing samples at the end of the first week, at the end of the first 9 weeks, and at the end of the semester.
	Have student teachers compile a portfolio of their teaching philosophy with accompanying documents and examples to illustrate the implementation of their philosophy during the semester of classroom teaching.
Interviews and Oral Examinations	Interview third-year Spanish students about different cultural aspects of Mexico. All questions and responses are to be given in Spanish.
	Ask preschool children to complete a sorting task and then explain how they actually accomplished the task.
Logs and Journals	Have students within a fifth-grade "Conflict Resolution" program keep a journal about what they learned in class and how they used the techniques with their family and friends.
	Have students in a high school psychology class keep a daily journal of interactions between themselves and their friends, including descriptions of the "most significant interaction to happen each day" and thoughts on why it was important.
Writing Samples	Evaluate potential graduate student applicants' writing and organizational skills by having them submit three or four papers from their undergraduate classes.
	Assess the abilities of candidates for the school newspaper by having them submit short articles about recent school events.
Open-Ended Experiences	Evaluate students on their ability to research and then debate the pros and cons of corporal punishment (e.g., spankings) used within the school systems of other countries.
	Assess student understanding of the concept of supply and demand by having them set up a classroom store and demonstrate what would happen given different conditions (e.g., competition from other classes, lack of product, increased costs of product).
Long-Term Projects	In a project on the Native American tribes of Indiana, group students into tribes of Miami, Potowatami, and Delaware Indians and have them develop reports and skits on the village life of their tribe. This could include designing a model of the village, preparing food similar to what their tribe would eat, and dressing in authentic attire.
	After a science unit on sound, have students in a fourth-grade class develop different ways in which the principles of frequency and pitch can be demonstrated.

    d. Reread the examination and make sure items do not provide clues or answers to other items.

5. Construct the directions for the complete evaluation and any subparts. Make sure you include the full directions on the type of response required. You may also wish to include information regarding the value of each item or subpart of the evaluation. This is useful to students as they determine how much emphasis they should place on any one item.

6. If possible, have a content expert or another teacher check the items to be sure they are accurate and valid. This is helpful with both the items and the directions.

7. If possible, try out the exam on a few students who are similar to the ones you are actually evaluating. This tryout will ensure that the directions are clear, that the vocabulary is at the correct level, that the test length is appropriate, and that the scoring system is adequate.

8. Finally, consider what will occur after the evaluation is over. Evaluate the evaluation. Ask yourself the following questions: How well did the students do? Were there any particular problems? What should I change before using this evaluation again? How should this evaluation and the suggested changes be filed and retrieved when I need it in the future?

Summary of Student Evaluation Techniques

We have suggested a number of different techniques that you can use to evaluate what your students have learned. It is important, however, to realize that in most cases this information is most effectively used by the learners themselves. For the cycle of continuous improvement to function appropriately, students must know how well they are performing and what adjustments they need to make in order to achieve your learning objectives. These evaluation techniques will help learners gain that information if they are constructed and delivered in the proper manner, at the proper time, and coupled with timely feedback about the results.

Techniques to Evaluate Instruction

In this section we describe a collection of techniques that you can use to generate information in order to evaluate your instruction.

Tests

We use the term *test* here in a generic sense to refer to any of the variety of standard and alternative evaluation techniques you can use to assess students' knowledge and skills. As noted, evaluation techniques can identify what students know before beginning instruction, assess their growing knowledge and skills during instruction, and measure what they have learned at the end of instruction. Since evaluation techniques focus primarily on student learning, which is invariably the purpose of instruction, they provide a direct measure of a lesson's effectiveness. As a result, it is usually beneficial to use test results as a part of evaluating your own teaching.

As an example, Ms. Estes has her fourth-grade students play the computer game *Where in the World is Carmen Sandiego?* At the beginning of the lesson, Ms. Estes gives students a pretest, an assortment of matching, multiple-choice, and short-answer items, to find out how much they already know about geography. Then, at the end of the lesson, when everyone has completed the game, she gives them a posttest to find out how much their knowledge of geography has grown. Ms. Estes finds that virtually all students score much higher on the posttest than on the pretest. She determines from this that the game has been a valuable addition to her students' learning experience and decides to make it a permanent part of the lesson.

Student Tryout

A **student tryout** refers to having a "test run" of some instructional activity, method, media, or material with a small group of students before using it on a large scale. In a sense, a tryout is a rehearsal or practice runthrough intended to identify any problems that might come up when you actually teach using the particular lesson. A

tryout has two distinct advantages. First, it is an opportunity to test your assumptions about the usefulness of the materials. Second, it helps you find any problems in the materials so you can "fix" them before using the materials in the "real" classroom.

Mr. Hughes has developed a board game to use in his eighth-grade social studies class. However, before he uses the game in the class, he decides to try it out. He enlists the help of his 14-year-old daughter and several of her friends, asking them to play the game as though they were his students. He notices from this that the rules of the game are clear and that the game seems to engage their interest. However, he also notices that his tryout learners seem to become bored with the game if it slows down for any reason. He determines from this that the game is potentially useful as long as sessions are kept brief, so he decides to use it as a relatively short review activity.

Direct Observation

As may be clear from the term, **direct observation** refers to watching students as they go through some part or parts of the lesson, often when group activities are involved. The primary advantage of observing students is that you gain information about the process of your instruction as well as the products of their learning. With careful observation, you will learn how students actually use materials and how they respond to different parts of the lesson, and can identify places where you may need to give them more information or guidance.

Students in Mr. Lockwood's high school art appreciation class are learning about the different forms of creative art through a cooperative learning activity. Mr. Lockwood has divided the students into groups. Each group contains a student who plays a musical instrument, a student who paints, and a student who sculpts. The students' task is to use research, as well as their own experience, to identify the similarities and differences among these art forms. From this, they are to identify the essential characteristics of the concept "art." Much of their research occurs outside of class, but the groups meet during the class period to discuss what they have found. Mr. Lockwood routinely listens as they talk, making sure that he spends time with each group. For the most part, he lets the students do their own work. However, because individual students have different experiences, each group is examining somewhat different issues and coming to different conclusions. As a result, Mr. Lockwood is modifying the activity "on the fly" and pushing the groups in somewhat different ways. He challenges some groups to incorporate a broader range of creative arts to test their emerging definition. He helps other groups narrow their focus on the important similarities among the arts as a way of developing a definition.

Talking with Students

Talking with students may take a variety of forms. It may involve a relatively formal discussion with a student or group of students, or it may consist of a relatively informal chat with them. Whether formal or informal, talking with students has the advantage of going straight to the source to find out what they think about instruction. As a result, it is an excellent source of information about the appeal of particular materials. You can learn a great deal, from the students' perspective, about how well the materials worked and how interesting they were. This encourages students to reflect on their own learning and to think about what helps them learn. It also helps communicate to your students your interest in them. Students get the message that you are committed to helping them learn.

The fifth-grade Ecology Club is taking a field trip to a creek near the school, and the club's advisor decides to ask club members to research the source of oil floating in the water and to determine what may be done about it. Each member of the group is given a specific task to perform. After completing the research, preparing a report, and delivering it to the public health department, the advisor decides to spend a club meeting discussing the project. He asks members specific questions to identify which parts of the project were easy and challenging, fun and boring, and informative and uninformative. Based on the discussion, the advisor determines that the project is a useful learning experience for students and decides that the club should do similar projects on a regular basis.

Peer Review

Peer review refers to asking a colleague or colleagues to examine all or part of the materials for a lesson, to comment on their usefulness, and to suggest ways to improve the lesson. This is a little like getting a second opinion before having surgery. The idea is to have another set of eyes look at the materials. This has two distinct advantages. First, it helps identify trouble spots that you may miss. Sometimes, when a lesson is relatively new, you aren't sure what to look for. On the other hand, sometimes you are so familiar with a lesson that you look past existing problems, just as you can sometimes read past your own spelling errors. In either case, you may overlook inaccuracies, inconsistencies, and other potential problems. Second, a review by a colleague will provide a fresh perspective on the materials, offering new insights on student responses to the lesson, ways to update the content, and so on.

Mr. Crawford has developed a *PowerPoint* presentation for his fifth- and sixth-grade Spanish class. He included the pictures he took during his trip to Spain, and has added Spanish music and his own audio narration clips describing the various people, places, and activities he photographed. Before showing the presentation to his class, Mr. Crawford invites Mrs. Rivera, who also teaches Spanish, to review the presentation. Mr. Crawford is particularly interested in whether he has created slides that will be interesting to students, whether he has adequately matched the pictures and his narration, and whether the technical quality of the presentation is sufficient. Mrs. Rivera agrees that the slides add a personal touch to the lesson, which will increase its relevance to the students. However, in some parts she feels the students will become confused by the lack of explanation about locations and landmarks. Based on this review, Mr. Crawford decides to rearrange the presentation slides and to add more narration clips at several points.

Classroom Observation

Classroom observation refers to inviting a colleague into the classroom to watch the lesson in process, comment on how well the materials and activities work, and suggest improvements. Like peer review, classroom observation provides another set of eyes that can offer a different perspective and help find problems in the implementation of the instruction that you may otherwise overlook.

Nancy Borelli uses a presentation with a larger-than-life model to teach her vocational school students how an automobile carburetor works. Because this is a relatively new part of the lesson, Nancy is interested in getting some feedback, so she asks Ted Morrison to observe her presentation. Ted, who teaches construction methods, frequently uses models in his classes, and Nancy is particularly interested in how effectively she uses the model carburetor during her presentation. After observing Nancy's class, Ted makes a number of suggestions that allow Nancy to improve this specific presentation and her use of models in general.

Teacher Preview

Regardless of the content area, a variety of instructional materials may already be available from several different sources. Some have been produced commercially, some have been produced by teachers and published in professional journals or on the Internet, and some you may have produced yourself during previous terms. **Previewing** materials refers to the process of reading or working through specific instructional materials to appraise their quality and usefulness prior to their actual classroom implementation (Smaldino, Russell, Heinich, & Molenda, 2005). In Chapter 8, we described the instructional materials acquisition process, noting that your students, content, instructional method, and instructional setting are all important considerations when selecting materials. A thorough preview is the necessary first step in determining how well specific materials match these considerations and, therefore, in deciding whether to use the materials as they are, use a part or parts of them, use them with some modifications or adaptations, or not use them at all.

Mr. McCormick has found a piece of computer software titled *Discover—A Science Experiment,* which he thinks would be useful in his first-year high school biology class. However, before he makes a final decision, he previews the software by working through the entire program himself. As he works through the exercises in the program, he makes notes on a preview form for computer software. See the text's accompanying CD **(Chapter info and Activities >>>Chapter 7>>> Media Preview Forms)**. He is particularly interested in how well the program matches the objectives he has for the lesson, encourages collaborative hypothesis testing, and presents realistically complex problems, as well as how likely it is to hold his students' interest. Based on his preview, Mr. McCormick determines that the exercises in the software match his learning objectives and are engaging, interesting, and reasonably complex. He decides to use it in class, adding only his own introduction to the lesson and the software.

Reflection

In many cases, experience is the best gauge of whether something worked. As described in Chapter 1, *reflection* refers to the process of thinking back over what happened during a lesson, using your own experience and expertise to identify the parts of the lesson that did and did not work.

For example, in her middle school U.S. history class, Mrs. Chan uses a debate as part of a lesson. She selects two teams of students and asks them to debate the question, "Were the causes of the Civil War primarily economic or political?" The rest of the class observes the debate, evaluates the two teams on their presentation of facts and arguments, and selects a "winner." Later in the term, Mrs. Chan reflects on this activity. She reviews the notes she had made on her lesson plan, specifically considering the clarity and scope of the debate topic, the time allotted to the debate, and the amount of participation of students who were not on one of the debate teams. From her reflection, Mrs. Chan determines that, while it had been interesting, there had been too many students in the class not involved in the debate. She concludes that this activity is not a good match for the large classes she often teaches, so she decides to save the activity for a time when she has a smaller class.

Figure 12–7 presents guidelines to consider when using these evaluation techniques.

Summary of Techniques to Evaluate Instruction

We have suggested a number of techniques you can use to evaluate how well your instruction has helped students learn. Your students, too, can use these techniques.

Addressing the Standards

NETS Connection

The National Educational Technology Standard IV (Assessment and Evaluation) for teachers indicates the need to be able *to discuss assessment and evaluation strategies that are technology based.* In Chapter 1 of this text, we discussed several advantages of technology integration including effectiveness, efficiency, transfer, impact, and appeal (see Figure 1–1, page 7). Looking specifically at technology-based assessment strategies (e.g., electronic portfolio), consider in what ways those strategies and methods could positively impact evaluation and assessment. To do this, develop a table similar to the one below that includes a list of the various types of assessment strategies and a description of their potential impact.

Examples of technology-based assessment strategies	Potential impact on effectiveness, efficiency, etc.
Electronic portfolio	

Guidelines for direct observation of students	❏ Prior to the observation, identify anything that is of particular interest in your evaluation of the materials. You'll want to pay particular attention to these aspects of the materials during the observation.
	❏ Observe a range of students. Although it's relatively easy to observe students who ask for help, or who are particularly active, it's important to observe as many different types of students as is practical.
	❏ Be as unobtrusive as possible; avoid letting your observation interfere with students' use of the materials.
	❏ Rather than trust your memory, make notes about what seems to work well, what doesn't seem to work well, and for what types of students it seems to work or not work.
Guidelines for talking with students	❏ Prior to talking with students, identify anything of particular interest in your evaluation of the materials. You'll want to pay particular attention to these aspects of the materials during the discussion.
	❏ Talk with a range of students. Although it's relatively easy to talk with students who express themselves easily or who are opinionated, it's important to talk with as many different types of students as is practical.
	❏ Keep the discussion short and focused. To keep the discussion on track, ask about specific aspects of the materials.
	❏ Use your listening skills. Try to avoid being defensive about the instruction. Remember that you're trying to find out what students think. Use open-ended questions, paraphrasing, and other active listening techniques to encourage students to talk. Clarify their comments when necessary.
Guidelines for peer review	❏ Prior to asking a colleague to review your materials, identify anything of particular interest in your evaluation. Give this information to your colleague; you'll want him or her to pay particular attention to these aspects of the materials during the review.
	❏ Ask colleagues who are familiar with the topic, the students, and/or the methods or media in the lesson.
	❏ Try to get a perspective that is different than your own by (1) asking more than one colleague to review the materials, when practical; (2) asking someone who is likely to hold a view of the content, the students, instructional methods, and so on, that is different than yours; and (3) asking the colleague(s) to make a conscious effort to look at the materials in different ways.
	❏ Use your listening skills. Explain your rationale, when necessary, but try to avoid being defensive about the materials. Remember that you're trying to get a second opinion. Use open-ended questions, paraphrasing, and other active listening techniques to encourage your colleague(s) to talk. Ask for clarification when necessary.
Guidelines for classroom observation	❏ Prior to asking a colleague to observe your classroom, identify anything of particular interest in your evaluation. Give this information to your colleague; you'll want him or her to pay particular attention to these aspects of the materials during the observation.
	❏ Ask colleagues who are familiar with the topic, the students, and/or the methods or media used in the lesson.
	❏ Arrange to talk with the observer after the lesson. Make this conversation unhurried.
	❏ Encourage the observer to use a "good news–bad news" format to make it easy to consider both the strengths of the lesson and the areas where you could improve it.

FIGURE 12–7   Guidelines for evaluating the effectiveness of instructional materials.

Check It Out

Previewing Instructional Materials

A key skill that one needs is the ability to evaluate instructional materials. It is important for both teacher and student to be able to determine the quality of target learning materials. To practice this skill, do the following:

1. Go to the CD of this textbook and launch the *PowerPoint* presentation titled "Cellular Division" (**Chapter info and Activities >>> Chapter 12 >>> Evaluation of a Student Biology Project**).
2. Work through the short instructional unit there.
3. Using the preview form found on the same CD (**Chapter info and Activities >>> Chapter 7 >>> Media Preview Forms),** evaluate this instruction for use in a high school biology class (for example).

Planning	❑ Was the planning of the instructional materials effective and efficient?
	❑ How could you have planned the instructional experience in a better/more efficient/effective manner?
Implementation	❑ How well was the instructional experience carried out?
	❑ Did the feedback from students indicate that they were motivated by the materials?
	❑ Did students achieve the desired results?
Evaluation	❑ How could you have improved the instructional materials?
	❑ Were the materials evaluated properly?
	❑ Were the correct criteria for evaluation used?

FIGURE 12–8   Evaluation of instruction within the PIE model.

Review the information found in Figure 12–8, relating evaluation of the instruction to our PIE model. What needs to occur during planning, implementation, and actual evaluation? These questions are focused on the instruction and what you can do to improve it.

TECHNOLOGY COORDINATOR'S CORNER

Anne Ramirez was worried about the quality of information that some of her sixth-grade students were obtaining for their recent English research papers. For the most part, it sounded good, but she knew that most of it was coming from various Internet websites and that her students really didn't know how to determine if the information was reliable or not—they simply accepted what they found. What brought it to the forefront was that two of her students found conflicting information about a similar topic they were investigating. They had come to her to determine which source "was right."

In a conversation with Jan Ingrahm, the technology coordinator for her building, Jan had indicated that this is a question that many students are now facing—whether the students realize it or not. Many had been schooled over the years to trust the information they found in their textbooks and other written reference materials. Learning now to question Internet website information was not an easy task for them to accept and they quickly found out that it was more work to question a source than it was to just accept it as fact.

Jan suggested that Anne invest some time in teaching her students the skills needed to effectively evaluate materials they find on the Internet (see discussion in Chapter 10). She suggested that they start with five traditional evaluation criteria suggested by Alexander and Tate (1999) in their book *Web Wisdom: How to Evaluate and Create Information Quality on the Web*. When Jan returned to her office, she e-mailed Anne a short synopsis of the key things she had gleaned from *Web Wisdom* that may serve as a foundation on what could be taught to

Anne's students about learning to evaluate websites. Her e-mail included:

▶ **Accuracy** (Is the information reliable and free from error?)
▶ **Authority** (Who actually produced the material on the website? Do they identify themselves and do they have the background and qualifications to provide reliable information?)
▶ **Objectivity** (Is the information presented in an unbiased fashion or is there an attempt to convey a specific point of view?)
▶ **Currency** (How old is the material? Has a publication date as well as revision dates been printed on the website? Has the website been updated in the last few days, weeks, or months?)
▶ **Coverage** (To what degree is the subject explored? Is there some depth to the topic being presented?)

As a final note, Jan also suggested that she could develop a short presentation on this topic that would help the students understand the need to develop their website evaluation skills. She suggested that one way to catch their attention would be to expose them to one of the many hoax sites on the Internet (for a listing of hoax sites, one can visit www.museumofhoaxes.com) and have them use their evaluation skills to determine why such information should be examined closely before accepting it as fact.

SUMMARY

In this chapter we described evaluation as a "cycle of continuous improvement" in which you can use a variety of evaluation techniques before, during, and after a learning experience. We discussed different techniques to evaluate both how much students have learned (including both standard and alternative evaluation techniques) and how effective your instruction is. For each technique, we described its advantages and offered a set of practical guidelines for its use.

SUGGESTED RESOURCES

CD Resources

To increase retention and transfer of this information, review the *Reflective Questions and Activities* located in the Chapter 12 section (**Chapter info and activities >>>Chapter 12>>> Reflective Questions and Activities**) of the text's accompanying CD.

In addition, examine the given example projects and portfolio. Practice evaluating the materials with the use of the provided preview forms. Moreover, in this section of the CD you can access relevant Internet websites, NETS Connection exercises, and direct e-mail access to the text's authors.

Website Resources

Access the text's website (**www.prenhall.com/newby**), navigate to Chapter 12, and review the Question and Answer section for relevant questions that have been generated by students and answered by the authors. You may also submit your own questions directly to the authors.

In addition, you can access presentations by the authors about this chapter and gain insights directly from them about the topics that have been presented.

Printed Resources

Blumenfeld, P. C., Soloway, E., Marx, R. W., Krajcik, J. S., Guzdial, M., & Palinscar, A. (1991). Motivating project-based learning: Sustaining the doing, supporting the learning. *Educational Psychologist, 26,* 369–398.

McMillan, J. H. (1997). *Classroom assessment: Principles and practices for effective instruction.* Boston: Allyn & Bacon.

Montgomery, K., & Wiley, D. (2004). *Creating e-portfolios using PowerPoint.* Thousand Oaks, CA: Sage Publications.

Stiggins, R. J. (2005). *Student-involved assessment FOR learning* (4th ed.). Upper Saddle River, NJ: Merrill/ Prentice Hall.

Worthen, B. R., White, K. R., Fan, X., & Sudweeks, R. R. (1999). *Measurement and assessment in schools* (2nd ed.). New York: Longman.

V

TECHNOLOGY AND LEARNING TODAY AND TOMORROW

Throughout this textbook we have discussed how you can use educational technology to identify principles and processes, as well as hardware products that both you and your students can use to increase learning effectiveness, efficiency, transfer, impact, and appeal. We have attempted to demonstrate the importance of such tools for both you and your learners. When considering the individual differences in learners, the varying content, environment, and constraints in today's world, learning is an ever increasingly complex activity. As we progress into the twenty-first century, that complexity will not diminish. Individuals will require skills with advanced instructional tools and techniques to succeed, to be able to function and solve the complex problems of an advanced society.

Where are we going? What skills and tools will you need to be successful in the future? To be prepared, it is important that you have a vision of the future. We conclude the text with a look at the past, present, and future of educational technology. The highlights of the past help to illustrate how we have progressed to our current position, but even more importantly, they help us predict what will be the challenges and needs of the future. Although predicting exactly what the future will

bring is not a simple task, of this you can rest assured: Change will be a constant, and you will be continually learning.

New problems and issues will confront us as we go about teaching and learning now and in the future; likewise new tools and techniques will be introduced. It is up to us to develop the mindset and skills needed to confront the challenges, make the needed changes, and find creative solutions. Educational technology will play a vital role in providing tools and techniques to facilitate learning so that we can solve all upcoming problems no matter how complex.

Chapter 13 focuses on the current issues that are increasingly confronted as we learn to integrate technology within our classrooms. Although not all answers are available, suggestions and guidance are provided in order to help us in our quest for answers and our attempts to not repeat problems of the past. Chapter 14 concludes the text with a look at the past, present, and future of educational technology. The highlights of the past help to illustrate how we have progressed to this point, but even more important, they help us to project the changes that are on the horizon. This is a great asset as we envision and plan for the future.

13

Issues in Integrating Technology

KEY WORDS AND CONCEPTS

Technology integration plan
Technology integration vision
Library/media specialist
Technology coordinator
Digital divide
Hackers
Computer virus
Plagiarism Detection Services

CHAPTER OBJECTIVES

After reading and studying this chapter, you will be able to:

▶ Describe the need for a technology plan and the role and value of the vision within the plan.
▶ Describe the process involved in creating a school or district technology plan, including who should be involved and the steps that should be included.
▶ Identify the barriers that commonly inhibit the integration of technology and describe how the technology integration plan, training, and support address those barriers.
▶ Identify other issues (e.g., equity, privacy, security, plagiarism, isolationism) that have been produced or enhanced because of the integration of technology and describe how these issues can be effectively addressed.
▶ Explain the key benefits of investing time, energy, and money for the integration of technology within the classroom and other learning environments.

Previous chapters of this text have highlighted various forms of technology and how they could potentially impact learners. For the most part, technology has been shown as a means to accomplish the desired end of enhanced levels of learning. Just as a boat that glides across a still lake leaves a wake of disturbance behind it, the use of technology changes the environment in which it is implemented. These changes may be necessary in some cases, but they may also create problems and challenges to address and solve. Within this chapter we will discuss several issues created by the integration of technology within the learning environment.

INTRODUCTION

On a recent hiking/camping experience with a group of young 11-year-olds, an adult leader noticed that one young man had quickly fallen behind the main group of hikers as they moved up the high mountain trail. When asked about his slow progress, the young hiker complained about the work involved in "all the walking." At the first opportunity to take a break, the leader asked what he was carrying in his large backpack. The boy responded that he had included just the normal list of required camping gear and a "couple of other things." Upon examination—besides the needed sleeping gear, cover, eating utensils, and food—the leader found several extra pounds of candy, two heavy cans of pork and beans (the boy's favorite), three rolls of toilet paper, a giant flashlight with extra batteries, an extra pair of hiking boots, as well as a pair of tennis shoes, three school textbooks (in case he had extra time to get some homework done), and a handheld electronic game (with extra batteries). His oversized pack was weighed down by an extra 15 to 20 pounds of those "other things." While each item may have seemed like a good idea to include, their combined weight actually inhibited the boy from being able to adequately participate in the hike. Instead of learning about the joy of hiking and camping, he was learning only about how painful such an experience could be. Those extras needed to be removed from his backpack so that he could focus on the goals of the hiking experience.

Similar to this hiker, many of us today find the use of technology has created a number of issues. These issues are often considered as "extra things" that are continually added to our daily load. At times they may come to overburden us to the point that they inhibit our performance. In fact, if not careful, we may lose sight of our purpose for using the technology. With better initial planning and by identifying and removing (or at least redistributing) the heavy weight of these "extra things," we should be able to address issues and obstacles created by the technology so that we can experience the benefits of its use.

Just as planning can help ensure a successful hiking experience, it also ensures productive and enjoyable technology integration.

Teachers in typical schools of today face many challenges as they attempt to enhance their students' learning through the integration of technology. What types of issues do schools face as they attempt to integrate instructional technology? Here are some key questions to consider.

1. How can the integration of technology be effectively accomplished?
2. What barriers to integration of technology may be encountered?
3. How can we address and overcome the barriers to integration?
4. What additional issues will the integration of technology create?
5. Why invest the time, energy, and cost in the integration of technology?

The remaining sections of this chapter address each of these questions in detail. Although perfect solutions have not been found in every case, these discussions should help you identify ways that solutions may be uncovered for your specific situation.

HOW CAN THE INTEGRATION OF TECHNOLOGY BE EFFECTIVELY ACCOMPLISHED?

First and foremost, planning for the integration and use of technology is essential. Throughout this text, we have stressed the importance of planning. When it comes to the integration of technology, planning is no less important for schools and school districts than it is for individual educators. How should schools plan for instructional technology? Figure 13–1 provides an overview.

1. Create a technology committee with representation from all school constituents.

2. Develop a vision of education and articulate a role for technology in that vision.

3. Assess ongoing technology implementation efforts.

4. Identify general goals and plan how to achieve them over 3 to 5 years.

5. Develop specific objectives and have teachers create implementation plans.

FIGURE 13–1   Important steps in school technology planning.

In addition, view Table 13–1. Various organizations have created Internet sites to help create and implement **technology integration plans.**

An initial step in the technology planning process focuses on the creation of a district-level or building-level technology committee. The committee should have representation from all of the constituent groups: teachers representative of various grade levels, disciplines, and schools; administrators; parents; the community; the school board; and even students, assuming an adequate level of understanding and maturity.

The first task of any school's technology committee is to develop a vision of education and to articulate a role for technology in that vision. What separates model schools from the typical schools of today is not just access to instructional technologies but a *vision* for their use. The technology committee should identify the school's general educational goals for all students and how technology can facilitate the achievement of those goals. The vision statement will begin to drive the plan for the integration of instructional technologies. Review "Toolbox Techniques. Creating the Technology Integration Vision" to understand the importance of the vision within the planning process.

The technology committee should then evaluate the school or district's ongoing implementation efforts—including cataloging hardware and software resources, identifying current uses of technology, assessing faculty and staff proficiencies, and evaluating students' uses of technology. Then, the committee can get more specific about what sorts of technology should be implemented, at what grade levels, in what curricular areas, and how. Table 13–2 on page 261 highlights various types of tools available that can be used to assess the current level of technology training, hardware and software inventories, and so on, within a single school or an entire school district.

TABLE 13–1   *Websites for Technology Integration Planning (adapted from Solomon, 2004)*

Organizations supporting technology integration planning efforts:

▶ National Center for Technology Planning (www.nctp.com)

▶ SouthEast Initiatives Regional Technology in Education Consortium (www.seirtec.org/techplan.html)

▶ NetDayCompass (www.netdaycompass.org)

▶ North Central Regional Technology in Education Consortium (NCRTEC) (www.ncrtec.org/pe/index.html)

▶ North Central Regional Educational Laboratory (www.ncrel.org)

Comprehensive technology planning guides:

Technology Planning Guide (www.apple.com/education/planning)

This is a complete planning guide developed by Apple Computer that walks you through a six-step planning process. In addition, resources and case studies are provided.

Guidebook for Developing an Effective Instructional Technology Plan (www.nctp.com/downloads/guidebook.pdf)

This guidebook was assembled by Dr. Larry Anderson and his graduate students at Mississippi State University. It describes in detail all of the individual elements of a technology plan and how those elements are created, evaluated, and distributed.

Learning Through Technology: A Planning and Implementation Guide (http://www.ncrel.org/tandl/homepg.htm)

This guide for technology planning was created by the North Central Regional Educational Laboratory. It consists of articles and links that explain the different processes involved in creating a technology plan.

Technology Planning Tools (http://www.nsba.org/sbot/toolkit/tpt.html)

This is a list of very practical tools that were created by the National School Board Association. These tools walk you through each of the steps involved in the technology planning process.

Web search key words: Using Google or other Web search engines, use of the following search terms should generate updated, relevant websites: *technology integration planning guides*

TOOLBOX

TECHNIQUES

Creating the Technology Integration Vision

What is a technology integration vision?	A **technology integration vision** is a broad statement that expresses your thoughts about how technology should be used now and in the future. If created properly, it tells you "where you want to go and exactly what you would like to accomplish." (Technology Planning Guide, Apple, www.apple.com/education/planning/envision/index.html)
What purpose does the vision serve?	• It provides a focus and a common direction for all concerned individuals (e.g., teachers, administrators, students, parents).
	• As a reference point of common values, it facilitates collaboration and group decision making.
	• It motivates individuals to see and work toward higher levels of achievement and performance.
How is it created?	Several steps are generally included to ensure the generation of an acceptable vision:
	• Generate a list of potential items that should be reflected within the vision.
	• Gather ideas and examples from other individuals, schools, or organizations.
	• Develop a draft statement.
	• Review and revise the draft based on input from all significant stakeholders.
Key questions to ask and consider as the vision is developed	• How do we want our students to perform in the future?
	• What will teaching and learning encompass in the future?
	• How can technology be integrated and used to facilitate and extend learning?
	• What long-term needs for teaching and learning may be addressed by the integration of technology?
	For additional questions, see http://www.nsba.org/sbot/toolkit/vft.html.
Example technology integration vision statements	"Technology will be integrated into the curriculum to make learning more efficient and productive in order to improve student achievement." (Crawfordsville IN, Community Schools)
	"Through rigorous academic standards, high expectations, and an integrated curriculum, the Harlingen Consolidated Independent School District, in partnership with our community, will graduate students with the knowledge and skills necessary to excel in higher education and careers with the confidence not only to dream, but to determine their futures."
	"As we advance into the 21st century, the challenge we face is to create an environment, which prepares all of our students to successfully participate in a highly competitive global society. We will cultivate an environment where technology is a part of the

academic culture empowering students to meet state academic standards in all content areas using traditional and innovative technologies. We will expand the school community beyond the physical campus benefiting from local and global resources. We will develop independent life-long critical thinkers and learners who can communicate effectively, work collaboratively, and solve problems efficiently by setting high expectations and fostering an awareness of cultural diversity and gender equity."
(Harlingen Consolidated Independent School District, http://www2.harlingen.isd.tenet.edu/4yrplan/ HCISD2002_2005TechnologyPlan.PDF)

TABLE 13–2 *Tools to Use During the Gathering Data Stage of the Planning Process*

Type of Data Collection Instrument	Example Assessment Instrument

Student Technology Skills and Attitudes
Often this consists of a self-report survey that examines perceived levels of comfort, confidence, desire, and overall skill in selecting and using various forms of technology.
	http://images.apple.com/education/planning/pdf/form2c.pdf
	Example instrument items from this form:
	• I use computers to complete school projects.
	  (always—frequently—sometimes—never)
	• Computers help me do research.
	  (strongly agree—agree—disagree—strongly disagree)

Teacher Technology Skills and Attitudes Frequently quite similar to the student technology survey, the focus is to measure teacher perceived levels of comfort, confidence, desire, and overall skill in selecting and using various forms of technology.	http://images.apple.com/education/planning/pdf/form2a.pdf *Example instrument items from this form:* • Which of the following most adequately defines the types of activities you engage in with the technologies in the school? —I don't use the computers. —I use the computer for basic computing skills such as drill and practice. —I use the computer for improving writing skills. —I integrate the computers across the curriculum. —I guide the class in creative explorations of multidisciplinary problem-solving activities. • Finding time to engage in staff development activities is a challenge for me. (strongly agree—agree—disagree—strongly disagree)
Hardware Inventory Checklist or other mechanism used to tabulate what hardware is currently available, the number, brand, type, size, date purchased, date put into service, upgrades made, and so on of all items.	http://images.apple.com/education/planning/pdf/form5a.pdf
Software Inventory Checklist that lists all titles of software, license agreements, purchase price, vendors, machine compatibility, evaluation data, and so on that are currently accessible to teachers, students, and administrators	http://images.apple.com/education/planning/pdf/form5c.pdf

Note: For a general overview of these various tools, review the Technology Planning Guide (www.apple.com/education/planning/assess/index2.html).

Check It Out

The Review of Technology Integration Plans

To fully understand the process and effort involved in the development of a technology integration plan, it is important to review examples of such plans that have been developed and that are currently being used by various schools and school corporations. Complete a Web search for a selected school district (e.g., one that you or your children have attended, one within which you currently live or work). From the search, identify if a current technology plan has been completed and posted on the website. Once you have located the technology plan, review its content and then generate responses to the following questions:

▶ What steps were taken to create a representative committee to develop the plan?
▶ What procedures were used to gather and analyze data, and report the current technology capabilities of the administrators, teachers, and students, as well as the current level of hardware and software inventories?
▶ Is the vision of the plan clearly presented?
▶ Is it possible to see how the goals and objectives relate directly to the plan's vision?
▶ Are the goals and objectives of the plan clearly defined? Do they appear to be attainable with the proper effort, funding, and time?
▶ What specific questions would you like to ask the technology planning committee that are not addressed within the current plan?

If you have difficulty finding a current technology plan on the Web, here are a few that we have identified that could be used for your review.

Sample technology plans:

Harlingen Consolidated Independent School District
http://www2.harlingen.isd.tenet.edu/4yrplan/HCISD2002 2005TechnologyPlan.PDF

Tippecanoe School Corporation
http://tsc.k12.in.us/techdept/techplan/Total%20Plan%20for%20Web%20Publication.pdf

Federal Way Public Schools
http://www.fwps.org/dept/tech/techplan/index.html

In addition, a full technology plan from the Crawfordsville School Corporation can be found on the accompanying CD (**Chapter info and activities >>> Chapter 13 >>> Technology plan**).

The committee then should begin the process of planning for the future. It should identify general goals and plan for how to achieve them. Technology implementation efforts should be planned over a reasonable, short-term period. In most cases, a three- to five-year plan is desirable. This looks far enough into the future to provide useful guidance, but not so far that conditions are likely to change dramatically because of changes in the technology. To ensure that the plan stays on course, however, it is important to have clearly achievable objectives for each year of the multiyear plan. Observable progress is key to the plan's success.

In the end, specific technology objectives must be associated with the general goals outlined by the committee. Actual implementation of particular objectives is best left to the discretion of local committees of teachers. Teachers have a tremendous amount of autonomy in their classrooms—their own ways of doing things. A decentralized approach that emphasizes shared leadership in achieving technology goals and objectives generates a sense of ownership and involvement across a broad base of faculty. At this point, we are back to the planning issues we discussed in Chapters 4 and 5. Individual teachers must make specific lesson plans to help students accomplish the learning goals and objectives.

WHAT BARRIERS TO INTEGRATION OF TECHNOLOGY MAY BE ENCOUNTERED?

Effective planning helps to identify needs as well as to establish goals and means whereby school administrators, teachers, and individual students can come to reliably achieve desired levels of technology integration. However, along the journey to integration, barriers that inhibit, and at times stop, progression with integration are often encountered. A key issue within educational technology is being able to know and understand the ramifications of these barriers. Some may be quickly addressed through the acquisition of specific tools, while others may require extensive training, time, and experience to overcome.

Barriers to technology integration have been categorized in a number of ways (Ertmer, 1999). One type relates to problems created by such things as equipment difficulties, time restrictions, or inadequate training, support, and funding. These are frequently found to be outside, or external to, the teacher's control. A different category of barrier is that which is viewed as more internally oriented for the teacher. These barriers are "typically rooted in teachers' underlying beliefs about teaching and learning" (Ertmer, 1999, p. 51). They are often produced when the use of technology conflicts in some way with an individual's teaching philosophy. A teacher, for example, who frequently utilizes a classroom discussion method may find it a challenge to integrate certain types of computer Web searches and tutorials that can require a more individualized approach to learning.

In order to better understand these barriers and ways to address them, we discuss several of the key issues that underlie each.

What Are the Costs Involved?

As pointed out by Tiene and Ingram (2001), several categories of cost are incurred when attempting to integrate technology. No longer can we just consider the hardware costs and leave it at that. As shown in Table 13–3, the integration of technology requires one to consider all potential costs.

Cost estimates for technology expenses in order to reach a target level of one computer for every five students "would require an annual investment of somewhere between $10 and $20 billion for an unspecified period of time" (Healy, 1998, p. 80). Questions have been and will continue to be raised about those expenses and if that money would see greater utility in other areas. Although computers are becoming more available and are being utilized to a greater degree, indications are that those gains may come at the expense of other programs (e.g., art, music, physical education). A significant question should be, Can we afford the technology when it comes at a cost to these other important areas of study?

A second area of cost that also must be considered is the additional time involved in planning, implementing, and evaluating the effectiveness of the integration of technology within an instructional unit or lesson (Chuang, Thompson, & Schmidt, 2003a). This cost of time can be viewed from three different perspectives. First, those developing the instructional experience need to understand when and why specific technology can and should be used. Understanding what various types of technology have to offer, the benefits and challenges of each, and how to make a proper selection all require time to determine. Second, expertise in using the technology for both the teacher and the student requires time to develop. Training and practice are often needed in order to gain the needed skill to use the technology to the desired level of effectiveness and reliability. Finally, time also must be invested in the management of the technology. There is always time needed to schedule and access the equipment and facilities, make certain that all technology will work properly, and that everything is stored correctly following the lesson. To illustrate, imagine teaching a group of students how to creatively write and report a personal autobiography. If the assignment allowed for the creation of a video autobiography, additional time would be needed by the students to plan the project, determine the types of software and hardware to use, as well as learn how the

TABLE 13–3	*Costs of Educational Technology (adapted from Tiene & Ingram, 2001, p. 124)*
Hardware	Computers, Monitors, Projectors, Scanners, Digital Cameras, etc.
Software	Programs used to run on the computers and other hardware. These programs may include productivity software such as Microsoft *Office*, but may also include all instructional software used for student learning and exercises.
Infrastructure	May include things such as the rooms and furniture used to house and support the technology. In addition, networks and wiring also are considered part of this cost category.
Maintenance	It is often necessary to repair and periodically update hardware and software. Upkeep of the technology requires time, skill, as well as money.
Personnel	With the complexity and quantity of computer systems being used within school systems, it is now important to have individuals who understand the hardware and the software to ensure its proper implementation and maintenance. Moreover, individuals to secure and staff computer labs may be needed to ensure their availability and proper care.
Materials	With all hardware, there are always a number of ancillary items that need to be purchased in order to make sure the hardware functions properly. These would include storage devices (e.g., CDs, diskettes), cables, printer supplies (e.g., ink cartridges, paper), technical manuals, and so forth.
Training	Without an understanding of the technology and how that technology should/could be integrated within the classroom, the technology will not be viewed as a benefit. In fact, without proper training, individual teachers can come to view technology as a major waste of time, money, and effort.
Services and Utilities	Electricity service, as well as Internet service provider fees, room fees, and so on are all expenditures that have to be considered when operating technology as a learning tool.

technology works. There will also be time required to ensure that the video works and that schedules will be allowed for it to be delivered at the proper time and in the desired manner.

The following is a sample list of time commitments that should be considered as one attempts to integrate technology within a learning experience:

Time is needed to:

▶ Analyze what is needed by the learner
▶ Plan
▶ Reflect and imagine how the technology may be used with the learner to produce a potential learning experience
▶ Learn the technology's capabilities and what it has to offer
▶ Develop needed skills to use the technology appropriately

▶ Prepare the lesson
▶ Implement the lesson
▶ Evaluate the integration
▶ Try out to see if it works

Table 13–4 outlines the different elements of planning, implementing, and evaluating an instructional learning experience. For each of these elements, we have included several "time-oriented" questions about the integration and use of technology that should be considered.

Tables 13–3 and 13–4 reveal a number of different issues and barriers that one must overcome in order to effectively integrate technology. In addition, other types of barriers may be encountered by the classroom teacher. For example, some individuals may feel that their teaching is just as (or even more) effective without the

---

TABLE 13–4 *PIE Model, Steps Involved and Technology Integration Considerations*

Planning for instruction

Analyze the learners

Will students be able to use all technology that is required within the designed learning experience?

What additional prerequisite skills/knowledge will they need?

Will training be required?

Determine the learning environment

Will a computer lab be needed?

What preparations for use of the learning environment will be needed (e.g., scheduling)?

Will special equipment be needed in order to effectively run the technology (e.g., earphones for the computers), and if so, who will make those arrangements and when must the arrangement be completed?

Establish the lesson objectives

Will the technology impact the learning in such a way that the objectives should be altered, enhanced, focused, or changed in some way?

Will the performance, conditions, or criteria of the objectives be altered due to the integration of technology?

Determine the instructional activities

In what ways could each of the instructional activities within a lesson be impacted by the integration of technology?

Would additional planning time be required?

Select and include the media and methods

How will the addition of various types of technology impact the methods that are selected to be used within the instruction?

What types of preparation will be needed in order for selected media to be used properly?

Assemble, adapt, and/or create the instructional materials

Will training be needed in order for the teacher/instructor/lesson developer to understand how to use technology in order to properly select, adapt, and/or produce the instructional materials?

Implementing the instruction

How will the scheduling of technology for the delivery of the lesson be accomplished?

What preparation/setup time will be required?

Will practice time need to be included?

Evaluation

What training will be needed in order to use technology to evaluate the instructional experience?

What training will be needed in order to analyze and report the data derived from the evaluation?

problems associated with the addition of technology. Reflect back on the chapter involving the various instructional methods (Chapter 6) or the one that described the various media (Chapter 7). In both cases, we presented a list of various methods and media, all of which are effective some of the time—but few of which are optimally effective all of the time. The same type of selection and integration philosophy applies to the use of the computer or other technology within a specific lesson experience that you desire for your students. We want you to understand not only how integration occurs but, more important, when and why it should occur. There will be times in all learning when the integration of computers or other technology may not be the optimal thing to do. By understanding the strengths and limitations, the benefits and the costs, a proper selection can be made.

Some educators (both new and experienced) may be reluctant to integrate technology because it is new and different. Change increases anxiety and allows for mistakes and other problems to occur. Again, we would suggest that you look closely at your audience, your objectives, the content, and the environment to help determine if it would be advantageous to integrate technology. Here are several questions that you could reflect on when determining if the integration of technology may be worth the effort and time. Ask yourself if the integration would help your students:

- Understand the material to a greater degree?
- Gain the needed understanding in a faster, more efficient manner?
- Transfer the new information to a greater degree?
- Gain increased levels of insight (see things not previously seen, be more open to new ideas, etc.) about the material?
- Experience the material through different means that will perhaps help them grasp it in a more memorable fashion?

- Be motivated by increasing their curiosity, levels of confidence, excitement, and/or interest in the content?

Once an opportunity for integration, as well as any potential barriers, has been identified, several specific tactics may be utilized to facilitate the potential integration effort. Ertmer (1999, pp. 55–56) suggests, "(a) talking to others at the same grade level, or in the same content area, to share ideas about how and when to use technology, (b) developing creative ways to address logistical and technical problems during early stages of use (e.g., team teaching; soliciting parent volunteers as classroom helpers; grouping students to include a more knowledgeable student in each group), (c) starting small—incorporating technology into the curriculum, one lesson at a time, and (d) working with others at the school, district, and state levels to incorporate technology competencies into existing curriculum guidelines."

We need to emphasize several of these points. First, as suggested above, start small. You and your students need to see success early on, and that can readily be achieved through a small integration experience. Once experience with the smaller project has been accomplished, then it will be possible to move to other more complex integration efforts. In addition, the small efforts will help you begin to see the possibilities (and the potential barriers) that will help facilitate the success of the larger integration efforts. Second, if at all possible, get help from others. Those individuals who have worked in your school's computer labs and who have attempted projects in the past should have relevant information about the integration process that is specific to your situation. It is always helpful to know what works and what doesn't within your own setting. These individuals can serve as (a) guides to point you in the right direction, providing examples and ideas; (b) watchdogs to warn you of potential problems; (c) motivators to give you insights and encouragement; and (d) valued resources for

Check It Out

Teachers Integrating Technology

VisionQuest is a Web-based multimedia tool that illustrates the integration process experienced by six K–12 teachers. It is a tool that will help you reflect on how and why technology can be used within your classroom. It addresses the incentives and the barriers that one faces as this integration is attempted. Most important, using exemplary technology using teachers, it helps you envision how technology can be integrated in a way that meaningfully enhances the learning experience within your classroom.

Review *VisionQuest* at http://tcct.soe.purdue.edu/visionquest/index.htm (this can also be accessed via the text's CD (**Chapter info and activities** >>> **Chapter 13** >>> **VisionQuest**)). Note within the "Road Map" section the various challenges and barriers that were encountered by the various teachers. In addition, note within the "Path" section how the vision of technology integration was translated into classroom practice. How could you use these examples to formulate your own vision of technology integration, overcome presented barriers, and instigate the needed changes in order to achieve the desired level of classroom technology use?

A school technology specialist, a library/media specialist, or technology coordinator helps teachers and students effectively use instructional technology.

the solution of problems. In the next section, we will expand our view of individuals who specialize in training and supporting integration activities.

HOW CAN WE ADDRESS AND OVERCOME THE BARRIERS TO INTEGRATION?

Successful schools have technology specialists who can help teachers with the process of implementing instructional technology. Until recently, most of the specialized work related to instructional media in the schools was performed by **library/media specialists.** Library/media specialists help students and teachers become effective users of ideas and information by providing access to materials, providing instruction to develop users' interest as well as competence in finding and using information and ideas, and working with teachers to design learning strategies to meet the needs of individual students.

Over the past decade or so, a new category of specialist has emerged in the schools—the computer or technology coordinator. The **technology coordinator** is a specialist and resource person who handles computers and related technologies for a school building or district. In some school districts, the position of technology coordinator is a full-time post. Indeed, some larger school districts employ a technology support staff of several individuals. Many schools today also support building-level coordinators. At the building level, and at the district level in smaller school districts, it is common for the technology coordinator to be a teacher who has expertise in the use of computers and who assumes these duties on a part-time basis. Part-time coordinators usually receive some release time and/or extra compensation for their activities. Perhaps you will find yourself serving as a part-time coordinator one day.

The job of a technology coordinator varies considerably from school to school. In some cases, responsibilities are distributed among a number of persons, while in other cases one person does it all. It is common for a technology coordinator to do any or all of the following:

▸ Work with administrators and the district's technology committee to develop and implement a technology plan
▸ Work with teachers to support and promote technology integration
▸ Plan and oversee hardware and software purchases and installations
▸ Install and maintain the school's computer network
▸ Maintain up-to-date records of the school's hardware and software
▸ Arrange for, or conduct, repairs of equipment
▸ Assemble and disseminate information about instructional technologies
▸ Write grants to seek support for the school's technology activities
▸ Provide in-service training for faculty and staff

Although typical schools today devote only a small portion of their technology budgets to faculty and staff training, regular in-service education is needed to keep teachers up to date in educational technology. In-service training should be considered as part of overall technology planning. It should be regular and ongoing. It should derive from the school's technology plan. It should help teachers to utilize technology effectively within the framework of both the plan and their own classroom goals and objectives.

Several approaches to in-service education for instructional technology are common. Single, focused presentations or workshops on a topic (sometimes referred to as "one-shot" in-service sessions) can be useful for raising faculty awareness and stimulating interest, but they are unlikely to have a long-term impact without follow-up activities. More successful programs involve a series of activities, with opportunities for guided practice, exploration, and feedback. Better in-service training experiences use local computer experts and teachers, provide hands-on experience, are conducted in a non-threatening environment and at convenient times for teachers, present information in steps with opportunities for practice and mastery, and provide follow-up support and feedback. Good in-service education is a key component of successful implementation of instructional technology in schools today. In addition, positive results have been shown for the establishment of groups of individuals (teachers and students) into learning communities where the focus is on mentoring each other through the integration process (Chuang, Thompson, & Schmidt 2003b).

Training, planning, and support are all critical issues that have to be addressed by anyone attempting to

integrate technology. Ignoring these issues will lead to increased levels of frustration by the teacher and students, as well as lower levels of accomplishment. In addition, when future efforts at integration are required or even suggested, apprehension based on these earlier frustrations can develop into another issue that could taint and inhibit that future success.

Other issues have also been created and/or heightened, extended, and so on by the integration of technology. Several of these have been discussed in earlier chapters. One example would be the issue dealing with copyright (see Chapter 8). As technology has made it easier to duplicate and produce instructional materials, the need to understand copyright has come to the forefront. In the next section we highlight several additional key issues that should be considered by the classroom teacher, administrator, parent, and student.

WHAT ADDITIONAL ISSUES MAY THE INTEGRATION OF TECHNOLOGY CREATE?

Equity and Other Issues of Access

Equity is another key issue for all schools planning for instructional technology. It seems likely that access to technology and opportunity to learn to use it appropriately will be a key factor for individual students' economic success both now and in the future. Unfortunately, socioeconomic differences have the potential to create a serious gap when it comes to technology. This "gap"

between those who have access to technology and those who don't is often referred to as the "**digital divide.**" While students from wealthier households are likely to have access to a computer at home today, this is not as true for students from poorer households. Schools have a responsibility to help remedy this problem by providing access to all students.

As reflected in Table 13–5, the situation in U.S. schools mirrors that of society as a whole. Poorer school districts and those with higher percentages of minority students have fewer computers per capita and are less likely to have Internet connections than wealthier districts. Fortunately, the ratio of students to computers continues to improve, and efforts to bring the Internet to every school in the United States have been very successful. Of course, this is a problem that schools cannot solve alone. Government, communities, and businesses must help schools provide needed access to technology.

However, even when access is not an issue, there are concerns about equity within schools. Less wealthy and less able students are more likely to experience computers as a tool for things such as remediation and drill and practice over basic skills, while more affluent and more capable students tend to have more opportunities to use computers in creative and open-ended ways. Schools and teachers need to avoid the stereotype that certain students can't use technology in creative ways. *All* students can benefit from such applications.

In the past there have also been reported gender inequities with regard to technology. Boys tended to be more involved with computers, both in school and out,

TABLE 13–5   *Percentage of Children and Adolescents Who Use Computers and the Internet by Child and Family/Household Characteristics (DeBell & Chapman, 2003).*

Characteristics	Using Computers (%)	Using the Internet (%)
Total (persons age 5–17)	89.5	58.5
Child characteristics		
Sex		
Female	90.0	58.6
Male	89.1	58.3
Race		
White	93.4	66.7
Black	85.0	45.3
Hispanic	78.7	37.2
Asian	89.7	64.6
American Indian	89.8	53.5
Family & household characteristics		
Family income		
Under $20,000	80.1	36.5
$20,000–$34,999	86.3	48.8
$35,000–$49,999	92.0	62.8
$50,000–$74,999	93.6	67.1
$75,000 or more	96.2	75.4

than girls, and girls tended to exhibit less confidence with computers than boys. There is some evidence (refer to Table 13–5) that these tendencies have been ameliorated through the involvement of girls with computers at an early age and through the maintaining of that involvement throughout the school curriculum. Schools need to plan their curricula so that both girls and boys have opportunities to be involved with instructional technology throughout their schooling.

Schools and teachers also need to guard against other biases in access to technology. In some schools, available computers are monopolized by a minority of users. This may result from preferential laboratory scheduling for certain classes, historical patterns of use, or other reasons. To some extent, this is natural. But when prioritizing access to available equipment, schools should make an effort to encourage a spectrum of users. Teachers, too, sometimes unconsciously stack the deck against certain students. Some teachers, for example, may provide access to a classroom computer as a reward for students getting their work done early. While this may occasionally be all right, it can create a pattern where the same speedier students are rewarded time after time, and other students are left out. Teachers must take care to provide equitable access to all students.

Legal, Ethical, and Security Issues

Schools and teachers must also be concerned with a range of potential legal and ethical issues associated with instructional technologies. For example, in Chapters 8, 9, and 11 we discussed one of these—copyright—and how it affects teachers and schools. Schools should have a clearly stated policy regarding copyright, and this policy should be made known to every teacher and student. Schools and teachers have a responsibility to model proper use of instructional technology within the confines of copyright law. This includes the use of copyrighted materials and application of fair use guidelines. Certainly, an important part of this modeling also includes a stance of zero tolerance for software piracy, the illegal copying of computer software. Teachers have often been guilty of illegally copying software, often rationalizing that limited school budgets and high software costs make it justified. It does not! Illegal copying of software is theft. Teachers must not do it, and they must educate their students about illegal software copying.

Teachers must also help students learn to use computers and other technologies in proper ways. This can sometimes be difficult when the computer culture itself glorifies questionable behavior. **Hackers,** individuals who gain access to computer systems without authorization, usually for the intellectual challenge and thrill,

Addressing the Standards

NETS Connection

Standard VI (Social, Ethical, Legal, and Human Issues) of the National Educational Technology Standards (see Teacher Resource A on page 297 for a full listing of the standard and its performance indicators) for teachers indicates the need *to identify and understand issues dealing with equitable access to technology.* Read and ponder the following situation in terms of accessibility issues.

In a recent interview, a professor from Kabul University in Afghanistan expressed that one of the key problems facing the faculty and students of that university was access to textbooks. In many cases, after years of wars and the rule of the Taliban, the only textbook for a course was the one owned by the faculty member. Therefore, in such situations, classroom lectures for the course often consisted of the professor slowly reading large portions of the text while the students wrote word for word what was being read. These notes were their only access to the course information.

How does this limited access to information and instructional materials limit the type of learning experience that the students can have?

Although most teachers in the modern world will not find the access to basic information to be this restricted, what kinds of problems are created by limited access to technology (i.e., computer hardware and software, the Internet, etc.)?

In a journal entry:

▶ Describe some of the problems that may restrict access to technology and how this may limit learning. Make sure you consider issues from school, community, and home environments.

▶ Identify possible means to address some of the key problems of access.

---

are viewed as heroes—sort of latter-day Robin Hoods—by many members of the computing community. While hackers are often not malicious, they can create problems on accessed computer systems, either intentionally or unintentionally. In addition, it is a small step from hacking into a computer for fun to hacking into one for the purpose of stealing information or committing some other type of computer crime. Schools and teachers need to help students understand that this type of activity is wrong.

Computer viruses represent another threat in the school computer environment. While school age students are rarely responsible for creating viruses, they can certainly be responsible for infecting school computers. Viruses are easily spread from infected disks to school computers, and they can often unknowingly be downloaded from sites on the Internet. To avoid virus problems, both schools and individuals should use antivirus software. For more information on viruses and virus protection, see "Toolbox Tips: Computer Viruses."

Plagiarism

When an individual copies an original idea or piece of work and attempts to pass it off as his or her own, a problem known as plagiarism occurs. Plagiarism is wrong because it robs the work's originator of the acknowledgment that he/she deserves for its production.

It is dishonest because those who plagiarize misrepresent something as their original creation when it is not.

Technology has played an interesting role in the world of plagiarism. First, plariarism generally involves the copying of something. In today's digital world, the copy feature found in almost all software allows for exact duplicates to be created in fast, efficient, and extremely cost-effective ways. Second, plagiarism requires access to original items and works. Again, in today's information age, access to all types of digital information via the Internet has allowed individuals unprecedented access to sources of information. Coupling these elements together, you have a means to access and copy huge amounts of information, figures, video, music, and so on. This has produced an environment that easily allows individuals to copy and paste information. When used appropriately, these elements can facilitate the learning experience; when used inappropriately, they may lead to individuals finding ways to misrepresent original work.

What can be done to help address the problems of plagiarism? Here is a list based upon the work of Mc-Cullen (2002):

1. Educate students about the concepts of *intellectual property, plagiarism,* and the problems associated with plagiarism.
2. Show examples of intentional and unintentional plagiarism.

Computer Viruses

Computer viruses can create significant problems both for individual users and in school laboratories. In the biological realm, viruses are tiny particles that infect organisms; they can be benign or disease causing. A virus invades a cell, taking it over to make more viruses, and releasing the copies to start a new cycle of infection. In the computer world, the term *virus* refers to a computer program that functions in a manner similar to a biological virus. A computer virus invades software, usually without any overt sign, and directs the computer to copy the virus and pass it on. Like natural viruses, computer viruses can have effects ranging from fairly benign (e.g., a prankish message appears on the infected computer's screen) to quite serious (e.g., the contents of the computer's hard disk are damaged or erased). Computer viruses have become a common problem for computer users in many settings, including schools.

Take the following precautions to reduce problems due to computer viruses:

▶ Use antivirus software (e.g., *Norton Internet Security, PC-cillin Internet Security Suite, NOD32 Antivirus System, McAfee VirusScan*) on personal and school computers to check for and eliminate known viruses and spyware, as well as provide a firewall, filter spam, and even provide parental controls. Regularly update this software, because antivirus programs have limited effectiveness against new or unknown viruses.

▶ Avoid downloading software from bulletin boards and Internet sites that may not be trustworthy; this is a common source of infection. If you do download software, scan the downloaded files with antivirus software before use.

▶ In schools, establish practices that reduce the spread of viruses. Discourage or prohibit students from bringing their own software to school. Restart each computer between users, and set up your antivirus software to perform a scan automatically when the computer starts up or when a diskette is inserted.

Many viruses pose real threats to computer data. However, there are also many reports of viruses, often circulated on the Internet, that are groundless. These virus hoaxes warn of catastrophic results often from just reading an e-mail message with a particular subject heading (e.g., Good Times, Penpal Greetings). While some security problems with popular e-mail programs have been reported, manufacturers have patched many of these potential security holes, and there have been few reports of viruses that can infect a computer through the simple act of reading an e-mail message. E-mail attachments, on the other hand, can contain executable programs, and these can be infected by a virus, such as the Code Red and Code Red II virus of 2001, which had a massive corrupting effect on personal, educational, and corporate computers in the United States and many other countries. It was estimated that over two billion dollars was spent repairing the damage from these two viruses alone (DeLong, 2001). It is good practice to scan e-mail attachments with antivirus software before use. For more information about real viruses and virus hoaxes, visit the Computer Incident Advisory Capability Website, operated by the U.S. Department of Energy (http://ciac.llnl.gov/).

3. Highlight why plagiarism cannot be tolerated and indicate what your expectations and policies are.

4. Teach how to utilize one or more note-taking techniques (e.g., Cornell method) that help to ensure students use only their own original work and proper citations are given to the work of others.

5. Provide students examples of proper citation methods.

6. Develop activities where the students can practice gathering information, taking notes, developing drafts, and creating proper citations.

7. Demonstrate for the students how you will use electronic means to monitor their use of improperly cited references and works (see "Toolbox Tools: Electronic Plagiarism Detection Tools").

For more information on plagiarism and techniques that can help students overcome associated problems, a multitude of websites can readily be found on the Internet using key words such as "plagiarism" in regular search engines (e.g., Google). One such site that has information on this topic and other writing subject matter is the Purdue University Online Writing Lab (OWL) http://owl.english.purdue.edu/handouts/print/research/r_plagiar.html.

In addition to problems created by plagiarism, where someone accesses and steals the work of others, educators are now faced with students accessing services that for a price will sell work to students. Imagine a student faced with a social studies paper that requires 10 pages of writing about a topic that the student doesn't have the time and/or motivation to complete. Instead of

TOOLBOX TOOLS

Electronic Plagiarism Detection Tools

Although plagiarism has never been a difficult task, technology has made it even easier (e.g., through efficient access, copying, and pasting of information). Electronic tools, however, have now been developed to help identify and document when plagiarism has taken place. These tools are used to compare the submitted document with documents from huge electronic databases and the Internet. In fractions of seconds, millions of comparisons can be made and matches can be identified, highlighted, and cited. For teachers that means that suspicious work can be quickly and efficiently scanned and a documented report generated showing if proper citations have been attributed; likewise, for students such scanning can help identify places within their work where potential problems may exist and what they need to do to ensure that no plagiarism has transpired.

TYPES OF DETECTION TOOLS

Simple Detection

A very simple form of this tool would involve the use of a common Internet search engine (e.g., Google). Simply copy a suspect phrase, sentence, or paragraph and place it within quotation marks within the search window of the search engine. The search should highlight Web documents with similar statements that are found on the Internet.

Advanced Detection Services

Several commercial **plagiarism detection services** are now available (generally for a small fee; however, there are some free services available) where a suspected document can be submitted and within a short period of time, a report will be generated about the document (see Figure 13–2) that highlights suspect plagiarized areas of the paper and gives citation of similar works. Examples of companies that provide such tools include:

▶ Turnitin.com (www.turnitin.com)
▶ MyDropBox.com (www.mydropbox.com)
▶ EVE2 (www.canexus.com/eve/index.shtml).

In most cases, free sample searches or free trial days are offered by these services. A free service (WCopyfind) is offered at http://plagiarism.phys.virginia.edu/.

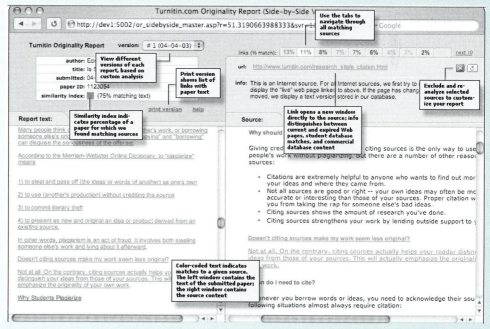

FIGURE 13–2 Screen shot of a sample page from a commercial plagiarism detection service.

Reprinted with permission from Melissa Lipscomb, co-founder and vice president of iParadigms, LLC.

(continued)

TOOLBOX TOOLS (continued)

Benefits and Challenges of the Use of Detection Tools

Benefits include:

▶ Fast, efficient identification of work that has been plagiarized. Evidence can be shown to the student in an efficient manner so that appropriate actions can be taken.

▶ Educating students about such tools and then indicating that they will be used often has the effect of students taking extra effort to ensure that plagiarism is held to a minimum.

▶ It allows writers to use the tool with their own work to mark potential problems that may have been inserted unintentionally.

Challenges include:

▶ Cost of the service may be prohibitive to individual teachers.

▶ In some cases (e.g., turnitin.com) the submitted student papers are kept in a database by the detection service and used as reference for later comparisons. Questions about copyright infringement have been raised.

▶ All material that is found matching other sources is highlighted in many cases—even sources that are properly cited.

▶ The search may be limited so plagiarized materials are not detected.

▶ Trust between student and teacher may suffer because of the feeling that all work is suspect and thus must be examined.

ADDITIONAL REFERENCES RELEVANT TO PLAGIARISM DETECTION

Current Issues and Resources. Center for Intellectual Property. Retrieved November 5, 2004, from University of Maryland University College website:

http://www.umuc.edu/distance/odell/cip/links.html.

failing the assignment, students have now found it possible to access websites that will provide access to databases of previously completed work that may be similar to the student's assignment. For a price, papers within the database can be obtained. Examples of such services include Thousands of Papers (www.termpapers-on-file.com) and School Sucks (www.schoolsucks.com). Frequently these services are advertised as research assistance for students, where papers on various topics and subjects can be purchased to be used as research and help for the student's own work. However, educators complain that, frequently, these papers are used in their entirety with only a name change being completed. To overcome these problems, instructors can again inform students of their policies, use plagiarism detection services, and have students turn in various drafts of their work to monitor the students' progression through the development process.

Security

Schools must address issues related to privacy and security. Certainly, one concern that has been around for a number of years is security of student data. Schools and teachers often keep grades and other student records on the computer. These should not be accessible to students. But perhaps a bigger concern today is the access to personal information that is possible through the Internet. Many Internet sites collect personal information; this is of such concern that lawmakers have drafted legislation to make it illegal for websites to collect information

from children. Individuals bent on exploitation may try to gather information from young people in chat rooms or online forums. Finally, schools that post information about students on the school website may inadvertently allow pedophiles or others to locate the students. Care must be exercised. Students should be educated about the risks of giving out information on the Internet and taught to use precautions. Schools and teachers should not post student information or products to a website without first getting the approval of both the students and their parents/guardians. Inadvertently, information about a student may be obtained by individuals who could use that for other purposes. For example, cases have occurred where student health information was transmitted via an unsecured e-mail transmission, which was unknowingly electronically monitored and filtered by a third party. Later, health insurance services were denied to the student's family because of information gained via that e-mail. When it comes to protecting privacy, it is best to err on the side of caution. For additional information (e.g., lesson plans, activities) on security issues that pertain to parents, teachers, and technology coordinators, see the Center for Education and Research in Information Assurance and Security (http://www.cerias.purdue.edu/K-12).

Finally, schools today must also be concerned with how students access information and what information they access on school computers. Probably the most important example today is the Internet. As we pointed out in Chapter 10, there is much on the Internet that is

NETS Connection

Within several National Educational Technology Standards (see NETS V and VI—refer to Teacher Resource A on page 297 for a full listing of the standards with their accompanying performance indicators), the need for teachers to *develop classroom procedures to implement safe and responsible use of technology* is emphasized. Although most of us have come to understand the need to be wary about giving out personal information through unsecured communications, other issues dealing with safety and security should also be considered. Go to one or more of the Internet sites listed below and/or complete your own Internet search (simple search terms such as "Internet safety" should reveal appropriate sites to visit). After you have reviewed the ideas that they give, create your own list of actions you should model within your classroom that would teach safe and responsible use of the Internet.

http://www.4teachers.org/4teachers/inttech/aupis.php
(Long list of Internet safety-related sites from the 4teachers.org University of Kansas website)

http://www.ou.edu/oupd/kidsafe/start.htm
(From University of Oklahoma's Department of Public Safety, The Police Notebook's Kid Safety on the Internet)

http://www.indianapolis.in.us/home/child.htm ("Child Safety on the Internet" tips)
In addition, download "A Teacher's Guide to Internet Safety" (http://www.netalert.net.au/ schools/NetAlert Guide a4.pdf) and review its content for additional safety ideas and suggested actions.

Check It Out

Other Issues of Technology Integration

Within this chapter (and throughout other sections of this text) we have touched on several issues involving technology that will have an impact on not only how technology is integrated but also how that technology will impact our daily lives. In some cases those changes are important and beneficial; however, they also frequently produce impacts that may not be viewed as desired. For example, the advent of central air conditioning for most people who live in warmer climates is seen as a great benefit. However, for many individuals that invention negated the need for people to sit outside or take walks in the cooler evening to escape the heat of the house. This has impacted the degree to which individuals have come to interact with their neighbors and their overall feelings of community. The technology changed more than just the temperature of the house interior.

Listed below are a number of different topics that identify various technological changes that have occurred in recent years. Each topic has several reflective questions for you to consider. Select one or more of the topics, consider the questions that are associated with that topic, and then complete library and/or Internet searches to identify a minimum of two different perspectives for one or more of the topics. Review the questions being asked and respond to the authors of the text.

▶ *Information access on the Internet.* What is the impact on students who now have access to the vast quantities of information available on the Internet? Is there a problem for students having access to information that may or may not be correct? Should the freedom of expression be limited in some way on the Internet? Should filters be used to stop students from accessing certain types of information?

▶ *Cross-cultural comparisons.* In what ways can technology facilitate cross-cultural comparisons? Will this type of comparison increase levels of understanding or could it highlight differences and subsequently increase levels of animosity?

▶ *Isolationism.* If we can shop, get educated, be entertained, and complete our job assignments all from the confines of our own home, is there a need for us to ever go out? Are we missing anything by not shopping at the store, interacting with classmates in a school class, or working with coworkers in real time at a central work location?

Check It Out

Other Issues of Technology Integration, continued

▶ *Communications*. Is technology allowing us to develop and use new ways of effectively communicating with others? Are we learning ways that enhance the quality of person-to-person communication? In what ways have social norms been impacted by technology and how has the technology impacted the quality of our interactions?

▶ *Research methodology*. In what ways has technology allowed for new research methodologies to be developed and used? For example, can access to a wider variety of individuals (e.g., via the Internet) be helpful or does it cause problems for researchers?

▶ *Technology dependency*. Are there times that we can become so dependent on technology that we begin to lose or not develop needed skills? For example, are spell checkers helping our ability to spell words correctly or hindering our development of good spelling techniques? Similarly, are calculators helping us develop basic math skills or inhibiting our math development?

▶ *"Staying up with the Jones."* Is there a need to always have the latest and greatest technology? Is it possible (and possibly desirable) to skip certain generations of new machines and software?

▶ *Quantity versus quality*. If the technology allows us to produce more efficiently and/or effectively, why do individuals still seem to not have enough time to get things done? Is the technology helping to make our lives "better" or just more demanding?

▶ *Spurning technology*. Are there times when the use of technology should not be used? Under what situations should we begin to think about eliminating technology or at least inhibiting its integration?

---

unsuitable for school children and has much potential for misuse. As a result, it is incumbent upon schools to educate students and to develop and implement acceptable use policies regarding the Internet.

WHY INVEST THE TIME, ENERGY, AND COST INTO THE INTEGRATION OF TECHNOLOGY?

This is a critical question for many individuals. With billions of dollars being spent on technology and technology integration and maintenance within our schools each year, a strong, convincing rationale needs to be given. A recent report from the U.S. Department of Education, Office of Educational Technology (Culp, Honey, & Mandinach, 2003) presented findings about why the investment is justified.

Technology as a Means to Address Difficulties in Teaching and Learning

As pointed out in Chapter 1 of this text, the demands placed on learners over the past century have shifted dramatically. Development of technology in some ways has produced and intensified some of these demands and at the same time has come to provide a means for accomplishing needed learning. For example, in a world demanding greater levels of problem-solving skills within complex learning environments,

technology offers students a variety of ways to access, analyze, synthesize, and communicate their methods and potential solutions. Moreover, technology can be used to enhance the learning experience in order to help the learner grasp the problem, practice needed skills, present relevant answers, and assess the quality of the learning. In other situations, technology can increase the effectiveness of instruction by reaching those students who may have been previously inhibited geographically, physically, or even socially. Finally, technology tools offer a way to add greater levels of diversity. Through advanced communications, students can now more readily access timely information from a multitude of relevant sources (e.g., content experts, professional organizations, other students, teachers, and administrators from around the world) who may offer a more expansive view of specific learning situations.

Technology as a Change Agent

Another rationale for the value of technology integration is the impact it has on how teachers design and carry out their instructional lessons. Assimilating technology in a learning situation often triggers "changes away from lecture-driven instruction and toward constructivist, inquiry-oriented classrooms" (Culp et al., 2003, p. 5). That is, teachers who integrate and utilize technology effectively often find the need to first make their lessons "more flexible, more engaging, and more challenging for students" (Culp et al. 2003, p. 5). In this role, the integration of technology facilitates how learning is viewed and subsequently how the optimal learning experience is designed and implemented.

Technology as a Means to Maintain Economic Competitiveness

Rapid shifts in the world economy have dictated the need for many individuals to obtain, maintain, and enhance their skills with technology. For example, within the manufacturing industry, technology is central to being able to increase productivity while decreasing the time and costs involved with that production. As labor and material costs increase, ways of using technology to reduce expensive person-hours and material scrap are constantly being sought. This continuous implementation and adaptation of technology requires a workforce that understands the need to constantly learn and upgrade their skills. Likewise, within education, technology

Check It Out

Impact of Technology Integration

The CEO Forum on Education and Technology was a five-year project that began in 1996 to assess how well America's schools were teaching essential technological, critical-thinking, and communication skills. At the completion of the project a final report with research and recommendations was submitted. The "School Technology and Readiness Report" highlights research on how well schools were integrating technology and the impact of what had been accomplished. This report can be downloaded at http://www.ceoforum.org/downloads/report4.pdf. It is also available at the ISTE website (http://www.iste.org/starchart/pdf/ceo-forum-star-report.pdf).

Part 1: Go online and access this report. Read through the report's Executive Summary and then analyze various sections within the full report. Finally, based upon the information within the report, create a table similar to that shown here and fill in the benefits of technology and the current challenges that have been highlighted.

Benefits of Technology Integration	Challenges to the Integration and Use of Technology in the Classroom

Part 2: A major contribution of the CEO Forum was the development of the School Technology and Readiness (STaR) chart. This is a self-assessment tool that helps show where a school is in regard to technology integration (on a continuum from an "Early Tech" school where little technology is used, to a "Target Tech" school that is a model of technology integration and implementation). The STaR chart can be accessed in either paper or online interactive format.

For this portion of the "Check It Out," imagine that you are currently a technology coordinator or a teacher at a school of your choice (choose one that you recently attended, worked within, or have some knowledge of). Go to the following website and answer the multiple-choice questions about the current status of the school. Based on the feedback provided within the assessment, determine what types of improvements could be needed and how the planning process could be successfully completed.

The Interactive STaR chart self-assessment tool can be located at http://www.iste.org/starchart/.

For additional sites that will access the STaR chart, use the following key words in your Internet search engine (e.g., Google): CEO Forum STaR Chart.

impacts how, when, and why we learn. That doesn't mean that you will no longer be able to learn without the use of some form of technology; however, technology can provide for greater access to information, broader and more realistic learning experiences, increased quantity and quality of practice, or even greater levels of in-depth feedback that produce more efficient and effective learning. Learners may find that the use of technology allows them to ask questions, see novel perspectives, explore and discover solutions to more complex problems, and be able to adapt more readily to change. All of these qualities are fundamental to the success of living and learning within an information society.

"These three rationales for investing in educational technology surface again and again throughout the last twenty years. They are also highly interconnected. At their core, each of these rationales is based on recognition that technology is the embodiment and the means of much of the social and economic change of the past century. There is also an acknowledgement that integrating technologies into the instructional fabric of teaching and learning in our society requires commitment, focus, and resources from multiple stakeholders" (Culp et al., 2003, p. 6)

TECHNOLOGY COORDINATOR'S CORNER

Lisa Bristol had been ecstatic about her new position as the technology coordinator at Neil Armstrong Middle School. Armstrong is still under construction and will not be finished for another year.

In recent days, however, Lisa has begun to receive several warning signs that have increased her level of anxiety about her new job. First, building cost overruns have the district administrators looking for ways to cut costs. Eliminating some of the planned technology within the building is being considered. Second, the electrical contractors are asking for specifics on how many computers, peripherals, and Internet connections will be needed in each classroom. She realizes those decisions could impact the school for years to come and, thus, they should not be made haphazardly. Third, several of the teachers who will transfer into the new school have a history of not using technology and do not show any desire to begin using it. Some are suggesting administrators should divert part of the current technology budget to other programs within the new school. Finally, there have been some comments at recent school board meetings that Armstrong students will be receiving all of the new technology while other students attending the older schools will have many fewer opportunities. A warning of potential inequalities between those within and those outside of the new school is being raised.

Frustrated with the complexity of addressing many of these challenges, Lisa decided to visit John Randolf, the technology coordinator for her school district. John had been a friend for several years and Lisa had come to depend on his practical advice. After listening to Lisa's explanation of her frustration, John smiled and said that Lisa really needed to know three key things: (a) where they were (in terms of technology capabilities); (b) where they needed to be; and (c) how to get from (a) to (b). He emphasized that each of these is a major element within a well-constructed technology plan.

John encouraged Lisa to form a technology planning committee to develop a plan based on these three elements. The first element would concentrate on examining the current capabilities of future Armstrong teachers, administrators, and students. From it, Lisa would know the level of technology capabilities and what could be expected from those at that current level. In addition, future educational development programs could be identified based upon this information. The second element really focuses on the vision of how technology should be used within the school. This element provides the direction for one's efforts. It helps teachers and administrators see the importance of their integration efforts. Finally, the gap between the current state and the desired state is the tough one—it is where the majority of work will be directed. These are the short-term goals and objectives that help one to achieve the needed steps in order to realize/attain the desired vision.

With John's advice and the examples that he gave from his own technology planning committee. Lisa took the needed steps to organize a committee, gather the needed information, and develop and structure a plan that she could use to guide the integration of technology within her new school setting. In the end, the plan gave the direction that Lisa sought and it gave her the confidence to be able to make decisions in how to best use her resources to accomplish the needed goals.

SUMMARY

This chapter suggests that there are several important benefits that can be gained through the integration of technology. In particular, technology integration within education was viewed as a means to address and overcome specific challenges faced by learners; as a way to help teachers design, develop, and implement learning experiences that engage learners to a greater degree and create more complex, realistic learning experiences for their learners; as well as a means to help individual learners be productive and competitive in a rapidly shifting world economy.

Although the integration of technology has been important to accomplish, that integration has also introduced several issues. For example, the importance of planning for the use of technology comes to the forefront. Planning helps to address several critical barriers that are often encountered by teachers. Those barriers include the monetary cost of the technology, the time needed to invest in learning the skill and implementing the technology within lessons, and how to address the changes that have to be made in how one designs the learning experience. The technology planning process helps school districts, schools, and teachers see the possible impact of technology, identify goals, set objectives, and outline the directions needed to achieve the desired end.

Other significant issues created by the integration of technology were also discussed. For instance, (a) the ramifications for learners who come from different socioeconomic backgrounds and cultures and their varying levels of technology access; (b) the increased need to identify and implement privacy and security measures; and (c) the implications of legal and ethical issues such as heightened levels of plagiarism or even the purchase of completed projects and assignments.

SUGGESTED RESOURCES

CD Resources

To increase retention and transfer of this information, review the *Reflective Questions and Activities* located in the Chapter 13 section **(Chapter info and activities >>>Chapter 13>>> Reflective Questions and Activities)** of the text's accompanying CD.

In addition, you can access relevant school technology example plans, VisionQuest, Internet websites, NETS Connection exercises, and direct e-mail access to the text's authors.

Website Resources

Access the text's website **(www.prenhall.com/newby)**, navigate to Chapter 13, and review the Question and Answer section for relevant questions that have been generated by students and answered by the authors. You may also submit your own questions directly to the authors. In addition, you can access presentations by the authors about this chapter and gain insights directly from them about the topics that have been presented.

Print Resources

Frazier, M., & Bailey, G. (2004). *The technology coordinator's handbook.* Eugene, OR: International Society for Technology in Education.

Solomon, G. (2004). Drafting a customized tech plan. *Technology & Learning, 24*(7), 34–35.

Tiene, D., & Ingram, A. (2001). *Exploring current issues in educational technology.* Boston: McGraw Hill.

Tomei, L. A. (2002). *The technology façade: Overcoming barriers to effective instructional technology.* Boston: Allyn & Bacon.

Electronic Resources

http://nationaledtechplan.org
National Educational Technology Plan. U.S. Department of Education. Retrieved March 11, 2005.

http://nces.ed.gov/pubs2003/tech schools/.
Technology in schools: Suggestions, tools, guidelines for assessing technology in elementary and secondary education. National Center for Education Statistics. U.S. Department of Education: Washington, D.C. Retrieved December 15, 2004.

www.apple.com/education/planning
Technology planning guide. Retrieved November 6, 2004.

14

Trends in Educational Technology

CHAPTER OBJECTIVES

After reading and studying this chapter, you will be able to:

▶ Discuss the evolution of the fields of instructional design, educational media, and educational computing, and describe the contributions of prominent individuals or projects to the development of those fields.

▶ Describe the status of educational technology and its role in education today.

▶ Identify significant trends in educational technology and speculate about their impact in the future.

▶ Describe at least three "horizon technologies," those that are emerging in importance, and discuss how they might impact education.

▶ Describe a vision for education and schooling in the future, based on the changes now occurring in technology.

In the preceding chapters of this text, we have introduced you to educational technology and to a systematic approach to planning, implementing, and evaluating the integration of educational technology in the classroom. Throughout the book, we have focused a great deal of attention on the personal computer, because it is a powerful tool that teachers can use throughout the instructional process and that learners can use as a tool for constructing understanding and for communicating with others. In this final chapter, we look back on educational technology in the past to get some perspectives on where we are today. We use these perspectives to identify important trends in the field. Finally, we look to the future and try to envision what teaching and learning with technology will be like in the years to come.

INTRODUCTION

One of the most enduring legends of the Old West is that of the Pony Express. Most of us have images of daring young Pony Express riders, braving the elements and the constant threat of attack, racing across the plains to deliver the mail. Leaping from exhausted horses to fresh ones along the trail, the riders battled time and their own exhaustion to carry the mail from Missouri to California in a record-breaking 6 to 10 days. The Pony Express was truly a marvel of its day.

Did you know that the Pony Express actually operated for only 18 months? Why did this legendary mail service exist for such a short time? To understand what happened to the Pony Express, we need a little historical perspective. Prior to its creation, communication between the east and west coasts of North America was slow indeed. Ships had to travel the long route around South America or transport materials overland across Panama (the canal was not yet built) to another waiting ship. Stagecoaches, though faster than ships, still required 20 days to carry mail from Missouri to California. The Pony Express, with its relays of riders, was a much faster way to deliver the mail. For a time, at least, it fulfilled a need. But, in 1861, the whole concept of communication was radically altered; overland telegraph connections across America were completed. In a flash, technology transformed life. Communication was achieved in a whole new way, and the Pony Express faded into memory.

Just as a historical perspective helps us understand what happened to the Pony Express, a historical perspective allows us to better understand technology and its role in education. The saga of the Pony Express underscores the importance of knowing where we are and where we might be going. Had the owners of the Pony Express realized that the critical issue for their business was really communication (not just mail delivery), they might have predicted the impact of the telegraph on that business and taken steps to adapt. We are in the business of teaching and learning. Today, new technologies have the potential

The lesson of the Pony Express can give us perspective in understanding educational technology today.

to transform that business. If we are to avoid going the way of the Pony Express, we need to understand what is happening in order to prepare for the future.

As with almost any field of study, there is a tendency for students new to the field to view the discipline in static terms—as an established body of knowledge, practices, rules, and procedures. Of course, no discipline, including educational technology, is static. As with any other field, what we know today has accumulated over many years as the result of the dedicated work of many individuals. Like any other field, it is growing and evolving. Undoubtedly, educational technology will be different in the future than it is today. We need to understand this continuum from past to present to future.

We begin this chapter with a historical perspective of educational technology. We examine the roots of instructional design, educational media, and educational computing. We then turn our attention to the present and beyond. What is the status of educational technology today? Can we identify trends and/or new directions? Can we extrapolate to the future? What changes might we reasonably expect, and how might these changes affect education and schooling in the future?

EDUCATIONAL TECHNOLOGY IN THE PAST

The roots of educational technology run deep, and a complete exposition of the history of the field is well beyond the scope of this text. For the historical account that follows, the authors are indebted to the work of Anglin (1991), Gagné (1987), Shelly and Cashman (1984), and particularly Saettler (1990). Interested readers are encouraged to consult these references for more information.

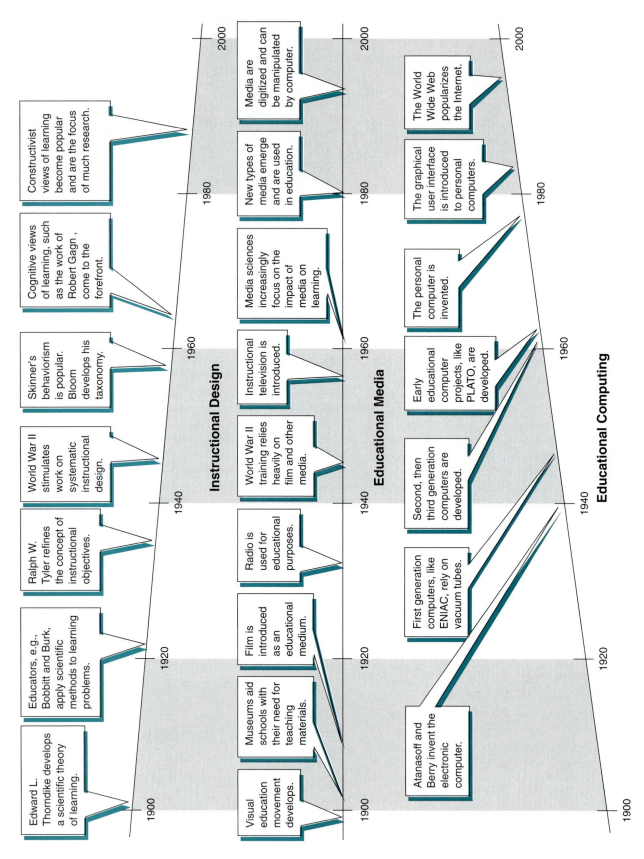

FIGURE 14—1 Converging time lines of developments in instructional design, educational media, and educational computing.

Instructional Design

Edward L. Thorndike develops a scientific theory of learning.

Educators, e.g., Bobbitt and Burk, apply scientific methods to learning problems.

Ralph W. Tyler refines the concept of instructional objectives.

World War II stimulates work on systematic instructional design.

Skinner's behaviorism is popular. Bloom develops his taxonomy.

Cognitive views of learning, such as the work of Robert Gagn, come to the forefront.

Constructivist views of learning become popular and are the focus of much research.

Educational Media

Visual education movement develops.

Museums aid schools with their need for teaching materials.

Film is introduced as an educational medium.

Radio is used for educational purposes.

World War II training relies heavily on film and other media.

Instructional television is introduced.

Media sciences increasingly focus on the impact of media on learning.

New types of media emerge and are used in education.

Media are digitized and can be manipulated by computer.

Educational Computing

Atanasoff and Berry invent the electronic computer.

First generation computers, like ENIAC, rely on vacuum tubes.

Second, then third generation computers are developed.

Early educational computer projects, like PLATO, are developed.

The personal computer is invented.

The graphical user interface is introduced to personal computers.

The World Wide Web popularizes the Internet.

280

The beginnings of educational technology can be traced back as far as the ancient Greeks. Indeed, the word *technology* comes from the Greek *technologia,* meaning systematic treatment or craft. The Sophists, from whom we derive the term *sophisticated,* were a group of Greek teachers who were known for their clever arguments and oratorical style. Sophists often tutored groups of youths using a formal rhetorical style and, thus, can probably lay claim to being the first educational technologists. Sophist teachings influenced the likes of Socrates, Plato, and Aristotle and, as a result, helped to form the basic philosophical foundations of Western thought.

While we can see the bases for educational technology in the ideas of the ancient Greeks, the modern history of the field is one that falls largely within the twentieth century. Figure 14–1 presents an overview of developments in instructional design, educational media, and educational computing in the twentieth century. We begin here by looking briefly at the foundations of each of these three component disciplines.

Instructional Design Roots

One of the single most influential figures in the early history of the instructional design field was Edward L. Thorndike, who joined the faculty of Teachers College of Columbia University in 1899. Thorndike conducted scientific investigations of learning, first on animals and then on humans, and developed what is considered by many to be the first scientific theory of learning. Thorndike's view of learning was founded on the basic notion that organisms establish a connection between stimulus and response. Every action has a consequence, and that consequence influences whether or not the action will be repeated. In a nutshell, when a particular action yields a satisfying result, it is more likely to be repeated in similar circumstances. When an action leads to a dissatisfying

Edward L. Thorndike (left) developed one of the first scientifically based theories of learning and is often viewed as the "father of instructional technology."

or unpleasant consequence, repetition is less likely. From an educational standpoint, Thorndike's work suggested that teachers needed to make explicit appropriate connections (e.g., between the stimulus 2 + 2 and the response 4), reward students for making the proper connections, and discourage inappropriate connections. These concepts are evident in classrooms even today. Refer to the discussion of behavioral learning theory in Chapter 2.

John Dewey, among the most influential thinkers in the history of education, was also at Teachers College Columbia in the early part of the twentieth century. Dewey's view of learning in many ways contrasted with that of Thorndike. Whereas Thorndike focused on stimulus and response, a somewhat mechanistic view of learning, Dewey believed that organisms consciously interact with their environments through self-guided activity. He viewed experience, interaction, and reflection as central to the learning process. While some of Dewey's progressive ideas fell out of favor during the mid-twentieth century, his emphasis on learning-by-doing has enjoyed a rebirth today, and many of Dewey's ideas are considered foundational to the constructivist view of learning that is popular today.

In the 1920s, Thorndike's idea of applying empirical methods to educational problems was expanded. Franklin Bobbitt, an advocate of schooling for practical ends, suggested that the goals of schooling should be based on analysis of the skills necessary for successful living. This laid the foundation for the practice of analyzing tasks in order to design better instruction and established the link between instructional outcomes and instructional practices. The early part of the century also gave rise to efforts to individualize instruction. Frederic Burk and his associates developed individualized instruction programs that laid the foundations for later work.

In the 1930s, Ralph W. Tyler focused on the use of objectives to describe what students were expected to learn. He found that schools often failed to specify objectives or specified them poorly. Resolving to address this problem, he refined the process of writing instructional objectives. Tyler established that instructional objectives could be clearly stated in terms of student behaviors and that the use of clearly specified objectives made it possible to formatively evaluate instructional materials.

World War II gave a big boost to the field of instructional design. The need to rapidly train tens of thousands of new military personnel created a heightened interest in applying educational research in a systematic way. Many educational researchers participated in the war training effort, and this helped to advance systematic efforts to design instruction.

After World War II, there was intense activity in the emerging field of instructional design. In 1956 Benjamin Bloom and his colleagues published the *Taxonomy of Educational Objectives,* a hierarchical scheme for categorizing educational objectives that is now familiar to most students of education. Initially, behavioral perspectives such as B. F. Skinner's theory of operant conditioning dominated instructional design. In the 1960s, the work of cognitive scientists, such as Robert Gagné gained more attention. Researchers and developers began to focus on instructional systems, and instructional design emerged as a discipline in its own right.

The decades after the 1960s gave rise to refinements and expansions of the field. Cognitive theories of learning, and later constructivist perspectives, came to the forefront of the field. Increased attention was given to student-centered perspectives of learning including discovery learning (e.g., Jerome Bruner), situated cognition (e.g., Brown, Collins, and Duguid), and social learning (e.g., Albert Bandura, Lev Vygotsky). Instructional design proliferated in military and business training, and its influence began to be felt in K–12 classrooms. At the beginning of the twenty-first century, instructional design is a recognized field of endeavor with widespread applications, an active research community, and evolving perspectives.

Educational Media Roots

Educational media and instructional design developed along separate but converging pathways. Although the use of real objects, drawings, and other media has been a part of instruction at least since the dawn of civilization, the history of educational media, like that of instructional design, is mostly confined to the twentieth century. In North America, museums had a significant early influence on educational media. In 1905 the St. Louis Educational Museum became the first school museum to open in the United States. A forerunner of what is now called a media center, the museum housed collections of art objects, models, photographs, charts, real objects, and other instructional materials gathered from collections around the world. These materials were placed at the disposal of teachers in the St. Louis schools. Weekly deliveries of instructional materials to the schools were first accomplished by horse and wagon and later by truck. Teachers could request specific materials from a catalog. In 1943 the museum was renamed the Division of Audio-Visual Education for the St. Louis schools.

Late in the nineteenth century, there was widespread interest in what was then called visual instruction or visual education, based on the idea that pictures could better represent real objects than words. Magic lanterns that projected slides, and stereopticons, early 3-D visual display devices, were popular means of illustrating public lectures and could be found in schools early in the twentieth century. These were the first of many forms of media and new media technologies that were appropriated for educational use. Films came into classrooms early in the twentieth century. Radio was the focus of a number of educational experiments from the 1920s through 1930s. In the 1950s, television took center stage as an important new medium on the educational

Training of U.S. military personnel during World War II made extensive use of media such as film.

scene. Later came overhead projectors, VCRs, videodisc players, and, of course, personal computers.

During World War II, educational films and other media became an integral part of the training effort for the war. The rapid deployment of large quantities of mediated instruction influenced the field and contributed to the perception that media can be very useful for education and training. After the war, the educational media field began to focus increasingly on the role of media in schools. Systematic studies were undertaken to establish how the attributes or features of various media affected learning. A convergence of audiovisual sciences, communication theories, learning theories, and instructional design began. This marked the beginnings of educational technology as we have defined it in this book.

Educational Computing Roots

The first all-electronic digital computer was invented in 1939 by John Atanasoff and Clifford Berry at Iowa State University. The first large-scale, general-purpose electronic digital computer, called ENIAC, was put into service by John W. Mauchly and J. Presper Eckert at the University of Pennsylvania in 1946. First-generation computers, like ENIAC, relied on vacuum tube technology. The second generation, which emerged in the late 1950s and early 1960s, was based on transistors. The third generation followed rapidly on the heels of the second in the 1960s; it used solid-state technology or integrated circuits (ICs) that replaced discrete transistors and other electrical components with circuits etched onto tiny wafers of silicon called *chips*. The fourth generation, which arrived

ENIAC was the first large-scale, general-purpose electronic digital computer.

in the 1970s, relied on large-scale integration and very large-scale integration such as the *microprocessor,* a single silicon chip that included all of the key functions of a computer, first developed by engineers at Intel Corporation. This development made possible the invention of the personal computer in the late 1970s and early 1980s.

The first efforts to use computers for education date to the 1960s. At Stanford University, Patrick Suppes and his associates initiated a computer-assisted instruction (CAI) project. The PLATO (Programmed Logic for Automatic Teaching Operation) project, the largest CAI effort in history, was initiated at the University of Illinois.

Much of the courseware originally developed for PLATO was ultimately adapted for personal computers, and the authoring language originally used with PLATO, called TUTOR, was used as the basis for subsequent personal computer authoring packages.

In the 1970s, other developments occurred. TICCIT (Time-Shared Interactive Computer Controlled Information Television) was another major CAI system begun at the University of Texas and then developed at Brigham Young University; TICCIT was used to teach concepts and principles using a rule and example instructional approach. Also in the 1970s, Seymour Papert and his associates at MIT began work on the Logo computer language, which brought powerful computing ideas to young learners and for a time became very popular in schools. The Minnesota Educational Computing Consortium (MECC), one of the first large-scale state initiatives involving educational uses of computers, was launched. Then, the personal computer emerged in the late 1970s with the emergence of ready-to-run models from Apple, Commodore, and Tandy/Radio Shack. The personal computer quickly became the focus of educational efforts involving computers.

The 1980s saw a dramatic rise in the number of computers in U.S. schools. Initially, there were few productivity tools and little educational software, so much early educational use focused on programming and learning about computers. The concept of computer literacy, analogous to reading and writing literacy, was put forth. As the use of

Check It Out

Discovering the Roots of Educational Technology

Learn more about key theorists and researchers in the history of educational technology. What were the important contributions of some of the major figures from the history of educational technology such as Albert Bandura, Jerome Bruner, John Dewey, Robert Gagné, Seymour Papert, Patrick Suppes, Edward L. Thorndike, and Lev Vygotsky? Use the following websites to learn more about these influential figures in educational technology.

Site	URL
The Psi Cafe, a resource site for theories and theorists in psychology	http://www.psy.pdx.edu/PsiCafe/KeyTheorists/
Classics in the History of Psychology, York University	http://psychclassics.yorku.ca
The Encyclopedia of Informal Education, Learning Theory	http://www.infed.org/biblio/b-learn.htm
Theory into Practice Database by Greg Kearsley	http://tip.psychology.org/
T.H.E. Journal, Computers in Education: A Brief History (June 1997)	http://www.thejournal.com/magazine/vault/A1681.cfm

What were the seminal ideas from each of these important figures in the history of educational technology? In what ways are these ideas important in education today? What additional resources can you locate on the Internet that provide information about these individuals and others who have made important contributions to the field of educational technology?

computers proliferated and their capabilities grew, more software became available. CAI programs in various subject areas appeared, and productivity applications such as word processors, electronic spreadsheets, and database managers were developed. By the end of the 1980s, most experts in educational computing had abandoned the idea of computer literacy as a separate field of study and instead had adopted a more comprehensive view of curricular integration that included the use of computers and computer tools in authentic subject-area contexts. Today, computers are viewed as just one educational tool, albeit one with capabilities and flexibility never before seen.

EDUCATIONAL TECHNOLOGY TODAY

Instructional design, educational media, and educational computing began as largely separate disciplines, and each has been around as a field of study for a century or less. Yet, each has a history, and that history helps us to see where we are today. So, we now shift our focus to the present. Where is educational technology today?

Educational Technology Status

Educational technology continues to grow and evolve. Today we can see a number of trends that will help us to project where the field might be headed in the future.

▶ *Discipline convergence.* The disciplines of instructional design, educational media, and educational computing are merging into a single discipline that we call *educational technology.* You can see the seeds of convergence in the historical record, such as the World War II training effort that made use of mass-mediated instruction including training films. Today, educational technology is a composite of its component disciplines. See Figure 14–2.

▶ *Evolution of learning perspectives.* In Chapter 2, we introduced you to some of the basic theoretical perspectives of learning and their implications for instruction. The field was founded on the works of Edward L. Thorndike and B. F. Skinner, researchers who took a behavioral approach to learning. However, beginning in the 1960s and 1970s, cognitive theories of learning, such as the information processing perspective, began to hold sway. Today, constructivism is the focus of much research. Although the application of the constructivist perspective to the practice of designing, implementing, and evaluating instruction is not always clear, there is a shift today from a more teacher-centered perspective to a more learner-centered perspective.

▶ *Media convergence.* Where once media developed separately—each with its own technological basis, vocabulary, and experts—today all media are converging in the computer. Media are going digital! The advantages of this development are considerable. Digital media can be reproduced flawlessly. They can be recorded on computer-readable media such as diskettes, CD-ROMs, and DVDs. They can be sent anywhere in the world by computers over the Internet without loss of information. Additionally, computers can be used to process, transform, or otherwise manipulate the media in myriad ways.

▶ *Increasing computing power with decreasing size and cost.* Continuing developments in computing are affecting more than just media. Moore's Law, which predicts a doubling of microchip power about every 18 months, has remained in effect since the birth of the microprocessor. This has allowed personal computers to become more powerful, more compact, and less expensive over time. Microchips are powering a host of new educational

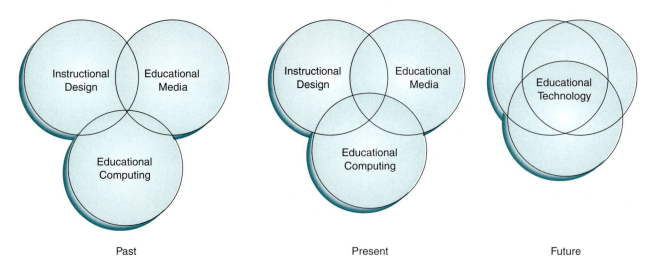

Past   Present   Future

FIGURE 14–2   Intersections of instructional design, educational media, and educational computing in the past, present, and future.

devices in addition to computers such as calculators and PDAs (personal digital assistants), which are already providing new educational opportunities. In addition, advances in related technologies continue to expand opportunities. For example, storage capacities are increasing, and wireless technologies are making it possible for people to use computers and the Internet without being tethered to a wired connection.

▸ *The growth of the Internet.* The emergence of the Internet as the Information Superhighway is another key trend of today. While personal computers were once isolated desktop machines, networking is common today and increasing globally at a phenomenal rate. It is as though our planet is growing its own nervous system. The Internet brings unprecedented opportunities for teaching and learning. It brings up-to-the-minute multimedia resources into classrooms, it provides a vehicle for communication among schools and between schools and their communities, and it provides a forum for students to publish their work. Computers

and the Internet are bringing tremendous new educational opportunities.

Today, educational technology is the focus of great attention. A number of professional organizations are devoted strictly to the issues and concerns that confront educational technology (Table 14–1). In the military and business training settings, the systematic design and implementation of instruction has been widely embraced, and the interconnectedness of the disciplines is evident in the widespread use of mediated instruction delivered via video, multimedia computer software, intranets, and the Internet. Schools are investing millions of dollars in the "nuts and bolts" of educational technology—computers and allied technologies. But the influence of educational technology on K–12 education remains an open question. Are we getting a return on our investment? Some schools are moving forward with innovative programs, but others seem mired in nineteenth-century approaches. We now turn our attention to the schools. What is the status of educational technology in schools today?

TABLE 14–1 *Professional Organizations in the Field of Educational Technology*

Organization	Publications	Web Address
AACE (Association for the Advancement of Computing in Education)	• *AACE Journal* • *International Journal on E-Learning* • *Journal of Computers in Mathematics and Science Teaching* • *Journal of Educational Multimedia and Hypermedia* • *Journal of Interactive Learning Research* • *Journal of Technology and Teacher Education* • *Information Technology in Childhood Education Annual*	http://www.aace.org/
AECT (Association for Educational Communications and Technology)	• *Tech Trends* • *Educational Technology Research and Development*	http://www.aect.org/
ALA (American Library Association)	• *American Library Association Archives*	http://www.ala.org/
ASTD (American Society for Training and Development)	• *Training & Development Magazine* • *Technical Training Magazine*	http://www.astd.org/
ISPI (International Society for Performance Improvement)	• *Performance Improvement Journal* • *Performance Improvement Quarterly*	http://www.ispi.org/
ISTE (International Society for Technology in Education)	• *Learning & Leading with Technology* • *Journal of Research on Computing in Education*	http://www.iste.org/
ITEA (International Technology Education Association)	• *The Technology Teacher* • *Technology and Children* • *The Journal of Technology Education*	http://www.iteawww.org

NETS Connection

How does one develop *positive attitudes toward using technology to support lifelong learning?* This is an area of emphasis within two of the National Educational Technology Standards (see NETS V and VI—refer to Teacher Resource A on page 297 for a full listing of the standards with their accompanying performance indicators) for teachers. What can be done to impact the technology attitude of you or someone you know? Ponder about this for a few minutes and then do the following:

▶ Think of someone you know who has little to do with computers and related technology.
▶ Based on the table provided below, what types of experiences could you provide to this individual that may influence his or her perception of the utility of specific technology?
▶ Do you think that a number of positive experiences with the technology and the outcomes of its use will have a long-term impact on the attitude of this individual for the use of technology? Why or why not?

Use of Technology	Type of Experience You Could Provide for Someone Who Is Not a High User of Technology
Technology that allows one to communicate in some faster, cheaper, enhanced fashion.	
Technology that allows one to access information, learning experiences, and so on at an efficient rate of speed and expense.	
Technology that allows one to create materials—whether it is digital materials, web pages, word-processed documents, analyzed reports, and so on.	

Educational Technology in the Schools of Today

Educational technology is evident in schools today as never before. Of course, the instructional process has always been there. Teachers have always been instructional experts, even if many in the past may not have viewed the process from a perspective such as the PIE model. However, in days past, the tools available to teachers were few. Today, computers and other educational technologies are on the increase in schools. Using data from national reports (National Center for Education Statistics, 2000, 2002; Market Data Retrieval, 2003) what follows is what you might find in a "typical" school today. We follow this section with a discussion about model schools that have embraced technology as a central feature of reform.

In the "typical" school of today, you will find one computer for about every three or four students or so on average; the ratio is a little worse in schools with greater numbers of poor and minority students. Computers capable of running modern multimedia applications are somewhat less common, perhaps only one for every five or six

students. About seven out of every ten computers belong to the Windows/Intel family from various vendors; Apple computers, mostly Macintosh brand, make up the balance. Many of the computers are likely to be found concentrated in labs, although having one or more computers in the classroom is now the norm rather than the exception.

Our "typical" school is likely to have a relatively fast, dedicated connection to the Internet, and network connectivity extends to nine out of ten instructional rooms on average. There is one Internet-connected computer available for about every five students. Video technologies are also evident. You are almost certain to find one or more VCRs in the school, and cable TV is common. You might find some evidence of newer DVD-video and perhaps satellite video access, though that is less common. Access to instructional technologies in the typical school of today is much better than it was in the past, but it is still a long way from ideal. Teachers continue to cite the lack of computers as one of the major barriers to technology use in the schools.

Having access to certain technologies, of course, does not guarantee their use. Whereas almost all teachers with access to computers now report using them for administration purposes, only about half to three-quarters of teachers report using computers for instruction to a moderate or large extent. When they do use computers, the most common instructional applications include word processing, Internet research, drill and practice on basic skills such as mathematics facts, and problem solving/data analysis. Multimedia projects, CD-ROM research, graphical presentations, and demonstrations/simulations are also fairly common. Two-thirds to three-quarters of students use computers and the Internet at least an hour per week. While this is encouraging, it can also be argued that as little as one hour per week is inadequate to truly develop students' knowledge and skills.

The availability and use of technology in the "typical" school has improved greatly in the past decade. However, given the wide variety of applications available for teaching and learning that we have introduced in this book, the picture of the typical school of today remains somewhat disappointing. A lot of the potential of educational technologies is going untapped. However, some schools are trying to change all that.

One of the longest-running efforts involving educational technology in the schools is Apple's Classrooms of Tomorrow (ACOT) project. First initiated in 1985, the basic goal of the ACOT project is to investigate what happens to students and teachers when they have access to technology whenever they need it. Since its inception, the project has involved a number of schools across the country, and a number of findings have emerged from the ACOT school environments.

In the technology-rich ACOT classrooms, students tend to work collaboratively more than in traditional classrooms. They are comfortable with technology and use it for creating and communicating. Social skills improve. The technology tools afford students the opportunity to represent information in multiple ways and to analyze that information. Students tend to become independent learners, and they often become recognized for their own areas of expertise within the classroom. Teachers, too, are influenced by the ready access to technology. They tend to move through stages from learning about the technology, to adopting technology to support traditional teaching, to adapting it to classroom practices, to appropriating it for project-based and cooperative student work, to inventing new uses for it. In the process, teachers tend to become more collaborative and guiding in their teaching. And, because both teachers and students are learning and doing new things, less-traditional forms of assessment, such as portfolios, tend to be used. In the ACOT classrooms, a transformation of teaching and learning occurs with educational technology serving as a catalyst.

Similar themes emerge from other model school projects. For example, Peakview Elementary School in Aurora, Colorado, which opened in 1991, is an example of a technology-focused model school. Students, who progress through the school in multi-grade teams, have access to networked multimedia computers in every classroom. They use technology extensively as a tool for such work as research and writing, and they collaboratively create projects using technologies such as multimedia authoring packages, video, and digital cameras. Using the Internet, they have created a Community Learning Center on the school's website that serves to link the community to ongoing school projects. Assessment is performance-based. Teachers use the technology to adapt to individual students' interests and needs. They also use the computer as a productivity tool and report increased time devoted to teaching, greater effectiveness, and increased satisfaction. Teachers function as collaborators and guides as students take significant responsibility for their own learning.

A number of schools, such as the Cincinnati (Ohio) Country Day School, have experimented with equipping students with laptop or, more recently, tablet computers. Providing such a high level of computer access to students has shown a number of benefits. Students who have access to portable computing devices consistently use their computers and access the Internet more frequently than their counterparts who do not have such technology, even when availability of desktop computers is the same. Students using laptops spend more time on homework and use computers at home for a wider array of subjects and tasks than their peers. There is at least some evidence that they write better. Teachers in schools with laptop programs increase their use of computers for specific academic purposes, shift toward more use of student-led inquiry and collaborative work, and decrease their reliance on direct instruction. These results mirror those found in other model technology projects.

What can we learn from these examples? In these settings, the barrier of lack of access to educational technology was removed, and the results were strikingly similar. The process of teaching and learning itself became

Portable computers are increasingly common in schools today.

Technology-Using Schools of Today

Learn more about model technology-using schools of today. Visit the websites of schools or school-based projects that have been recognized as being exemplary users of technology. Some examples are provided in the table below. Feel free to seek other examples on the Web.

School	URL
Cincinnati Country Day School (Cincinnati, Ohio)	http://www.countryday.net/
Generation Yes Project (Olympia, Washington)	http://www.genyes.org/
Napa New Technology High School (Napa, California)	http://newtechhigh.com
Newsome Park Elementary School (Newport News, Virginia)	http://npes.nn.k12.va.us/
Peakview Elementary School (Aurora, Colorado)	http://peakview.ccsd.k12.co.us/index.htm
Project-Based Learning with Multimedia (San Mateo County, California)	http://pblmm.k12.ca.us

What uses of technology are featured in these exemplary technology-using schools/projects? How do these projects tend to view the role of technology in teaching and learning? What do you think we can learn from schools like these?

transformed. These model school technology projects have the following in common:

- Technology is used as a tool for creative expression, information access, communication, and collaboration.
- Teachers are models, guides, collaborators, and sometimes learners.
- Students are active and collaborative learners, and sometimes teach others.
- Assessments are performance-based (e.g., projects, portfolios).

As access to technology continues to expand, and schools take advantage of technology, we can probably expect to see these characteristics in more classrooms in the future.

EDUCATIONAL TECHNOLOGY IN THE FUTURE

Predicting the future is always a risky business. Conditions change, new developments occur, and old patterns fail to hold true. Nonetheless, developments in educational technology over the past 100 years certainly do suggest some trends. We noted some of these above: discipline convergence, new perspectives on learning, media convergence, continuing computer developments, and growth of the Internet. If we assume that these trends will continue, then we are able to make some predictions. The implications of these trends may not always be clear, but it is possible, at least in some cases, to see the direction in which we are headed. And knowing which way we are going helps us to chart our course.

Horizon Technologies

A number of technologies are emerging in importance today. Many of these technologies are not yet fully functional or widely implemented. But the nature of these technologies suggests that they could become increasingly important to teaching and learning. We call these *horizon technologies,* because, like the horizon, we can see them in the distance but we are not altogether sure what they will look like when we get closer. We examine some of these horizon technologies here.

- **Artificial intelligence (AI).** AI is a branch of computer science concerned with the design of computers and software that are capable of responding in ways that mimic human thinking. While AI has been around as a field of study for some time now, the early promise of "intelligent" machines that can truly think like people has not been realized. However, the field has borne fruit, and we expect to see further developments in the future. One successful result of AI research has been the development of *expert systems,* programs that embody the knowledge and skills of an expert in a particular discipline. They have already proven to be successful in fields as diverse as oil exploration and medical diagnosis. In education, the concept of the expert system has led to the development of **intelligent tutoring systems,** sometimes called *intelligent computer-assisted instruction* (ICAI). These programs have been developed in mathematics, geography, and computer science, to name just a few subjects. For example, *Cognitive Tutor* is intelligent tutoring software in secondary mathematics from Carnegie Learning **(http://www.carnegielearning.com),** an outgrowth of AI research at Carnegie Mellon University, that is now used in a number of school districts across the country. Intelligent tutoring systems usually combine detailed information about the subject area and a database of common student mistakes with a model of student performance to diagnose a given student's level of understanding and provide instruction designed to meet that student's specific needs. They embody the expertise of a tutor within a particular content domain. We may see more of these programs in the future as well as the adaptation of techniques from these programs to more common instructional software.

▶ **Speech and handwriting recognition.** Another outgrowth of AI research has been developments in speech and handwriting recognition. **Speech recognition** systems translate speech into text that the computer can manipulate, and some support basic computer commands (e.g., opening or closing applications) issued by voice. Several speech recognition systems are on the market now. Examples include ScanSoft's *Dragon Naturally Speaking* and *RealSpeak* as well as IBM's *ViaVoice.* Microsoft includes a speech recognition and speech synthesis engine in *Windows,* and Apple's *Plain Talk* speech recognition and synthesis software is part of the *MacOS.* In addition to these, several vendors produce speech recognition products for telephony applications and access to the World Wide Web via spoken commands. As developments continue, the day when we can routinely communicate with our computers via spoken language, just like on *Star Trek* or *2001: A Space Odyssey,* may not be far off. Handwriting recognition software is now part of the operating system on Tablet PCs and personal digital assistants (PDAs). This software translates handwritten notes into text that can be saved and edited on the computer. Speech and handwriting recognition technologies are

Tablet PCs support basic handwriting recognition.

beginning to change the ways that we enter information into and work with our computers.

▶ **Wireless computing.** A recent trend that has rapidly become important to schools and businesses alike is wireless forms of connectivity. A widespread standard for wireless LANs, IEEE 802.11b, supports computer-to-network connectivity with a fairly substantial range (up to hundreds of feet) and reasonably fast connections (up to 11 Mbs). Faster wireless connectivity is supported by newer standards, IEEE 802.11a and IEEE 802.11g (the latter being backwards compatible with IEEE 802.11b), which promise to become more widespread in the near future. The emergence of these wireless networking standards and equipment that supports them means that many older schools can be outfitted for networking without the significant expense of running wires to every computer workstation. Another wireless networking standard called *Bluetooth* supports short-range connectivity between computers and a variety of peripheral devices, such as printers. Wireless networking gives schools and teachers more flexibility in using computing resources because it removes the necessity to always be tethered to a wire.

▶ **Broadband network connectivity.** In the context of the Internet, broadband generally refers to a fast connection that can support rapid transmission of large amounts of information. The term is often used to describe cable modem and DSL (digital subscriber line) connectivity, which is much faster than typical dial-up services. Information intensive applications such as video and audio require larger bandwidth for optimal use. Broadband provides that. While most schools already possess high-speed connections to the Internet, broadband is bringing fast Internet connectivity to an increasing number of homes as well.

▶ **New Web technologies.** In addition to new ways of connecting to the Internet, several new Web technologies are under development today. New ways of defining Web pages, such as cascading style sheets (CSS) and dynamic HTML (DHTML), are becoming more prominent. XML (Extensible Markup Language), a superset of HTML, is becoming an important tool for data exchange between different computer systems on the Web. These developments promise to make web pages more interactive and flexible. In addition, **Java,** a computer language designed for making platform-independent applications that can be distributed over the Web, is emerging as one of the most important computer languages in use today. Java is also the language that underlies JSP (Java Server Pages), a technology for linking databases with web pages to produce dynamic, database-driven Web content. Other technologies for linking databases and web pages include Microsoft's ASP (active server pages) technology and ColdFusion, a markup language for developing database-linked Web applications. Web pages that connect to databases can be more dynamic and customized than standard web pages, because they draw content from the database in response to choices made by the individual user. As these technologies mature, the Web promises to become an even more exciting place than it is today.

▶ **Handheld devices.** Since their inception, computing devices have grown steadily more compact. Today, many schools are moving away from desktop computers and toward laptops and tablet PCs. The next generation of computing devices promises to be even smaller. Graphing calculators are already a staple in many mathematics classes. Now, a new generation of **personal digital assistants (PDAs),** running operating systems such as the Palm OS or Windows CE, are finding their way into classrooms as multipurpose tools. They can be used for data entry, note taking, calculations, Web browsing, and a host of other functions. As they continue to grow more capable, handheld devices promise to become essential educational tools that in many cases may replace larger and more expensive computers.

▶ **Virtual reality.** Another emerging area of computer development is virtual reality. **Virtual reality (VR)** refers to a computer-generated, three-dimensional, visual representation of an environment that responds to the user's motion within it. Today, VR systems usually consist of a computer linked to special headgear and bodysuits or gloves worn by the user. The headgear projects the image of a three-dimensional world before the user and senses the motion of the user's head so that as the head turns, the image the user sees also turns appropriately. With a sensor-equipped glove, the user can reach out and touch or grab objects in the virtual environment. For example, a student studying organic chemistry might be able to reach and rotate an organic molecule in three dimensions to better understand its structure and function. While VR technology is fairly crude now, it has already gained popularity as an arcade attraction, and developments are continuing rapidly. For example, newer stereo projection systems allow for similar imaging without the special headgear. As VR technology improves, we can envision a variety of educational applications. It may be possible for students to take virtual field trips—re-creations of historical events, travel to faraway places, or

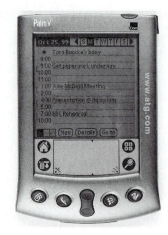

Personal Digital Assistants (PDAs) put computing power in a handheld form.

One day, virtual reality gear like this may allow students to take virtual field trips.

journeys inside the human body. In addition, students may be able to perform virtual tasks such as mixing dangerous chemicals or learning how to perform an operation without the risk and expense of the real thing. Virtual reality could make simulations incredibly lifelike. The possibilities are truly exciting.

▸ **Ubiquitous computing.** Ubiquitous computing, sometimes called pervasive computing or distributed intelligence, refers to situations in which computer processing power is embedded, often invisibly, in objects in the everyday environment. The idea, which was originally developed by researchers at the Xerox Palo Alto Research Center, is in some ways the opposite of virtual reality. Whereas virtual reality puts the user in a computer-generated environment, in ubiquitous computing the environment itself is imbued with computer processing power. Given the low cost and widespread availability of powerful processors today, it is not a stretch to envision a day when many devices will contain "smart" computer chips. Cars, microwave ovens, and other consumer appliances already contain processors. In the future, we might imagine computer chips in our clothing that alert us to excess exposure to harmful ultraviolet radiation, a sensor in a wristwatch that continuously monitors glucose levels in a diabetic individual, or chips embedded in the walls of a

house that sense the presence of people in a room and automatically adjust temperature and lighting. Educational applications might include "smart" museum exhibits that automatically provide customized content when visitors approach. As ubiquitous computing grows, computing power will increasingly fade into the background, invisibly playing an important role in our work and our lives.

Schooling and Education in the Future

How will these predicted changes affect education and schooling in the future? This is the most difficult question of all to answer; our crystal ball is growing cloudy! The difficulty lies in the fact that education is a complex so-cial, cultural, and political phenomenon. While it is rela-tively simple to predict that present technological trends will one day result in a computer capable of responding to human vocal commands, it is far less certain how, if at all, such a development may impact the educational en-terprise. It may help to remember that we are all about the business of learning. As we noted at the beginning of this chapter, if the owners of the Pony Express had rec-ognized that their business was communication rather than simply mail delivery, they might have recognized the potential impact of the telegraph and been able to adapt. We must always bear in mind that our business is learning, and technology has the potential to impact that

Check It Out

Exploring Horizon Technologies

Information about emerging technologies is available from a number of sources on the Internet. You can use these sources to research future developments in computing that may impact education. Use the following websites to explore trends in emerging technologies.

Site	URL
CIO, a magazine and accompanying website for chief information officers	http://www.cio.com/research/current/
EDUCAUSE Forum for the Future of Higher Education	http://www.educause.edu/forum/
ITtoolbox Emerging Technologies, a website about information technology	http://emergingtech.ittoolbox.com/
MIT's Media Lab at the Massachusetts Institute of Technology	http://www.media.mit.edu
Xerox Palo Alto Research Center	http://www.parc.com/
Ziff Davis net, a website supporting a number of information technology topics	http://www.zdnet.com/

What emerging technologies are commonly mentioned across the various sites? Which ones seem likely to have an impact in the next few years or in the next few decades? Which ones do you foresee having a significant impact on education? Why?

business just as it impacted the Pony Express. If we stay focused on our business, it may help us to recognize how technology developments may impact what we and our students do. So, with trepidation, let us forge ahead.

In many ways, public education in the United States has been a tremendous success. Yet despite this success—or perhaps because of it—the history of education and schooling shows remarkable resistance to change. If you have ever seen a picture of a nineteenth-century classroom, you probably noticed a teacher in the front of the room, students with books at neat rows of benches and worktables, and a potbellied stove in the corner. Except for the use of individual desks and more modern heating systems, not a lot has changed in many present-day classrooms. Most classrooms today still look like and to a large extent function as they did over one hundred years ago. Even the summer vacation common to most school calendars is a vestige of a bygone era when children were needed during the summer to work on the family farm. Do schools today prepare students for the Information Age that is upon us?

Over the years, many educational innovations with promises of dramatic change have come and gone. Instructional television is certainly a case in point. During the 1950s, advocates of instructional television envisioned a radical change in education and schooling as a result of this innovation. Although instructional television did not disappear, it never lived up to the expectations created by early advocates. Today, some people think that the computer and related technologies represent a similar "flash in the pan" for schools. Critics

charge that despite investments of huge sums of money, computers have not delivered the expected educational improvements. Clifford Stoll, author of *Silicon Snake Oil* (1996) and *High-Tech Heretic* (2000), has argued that computers detract from the most important things in education, including students' interactions with teachers and peers, and so should be used only minimally in schools. It may be that Stoll is correct, and computers have been oversold as a benefit to education. If so, computers may simply fade into a minor role in the classroom, as did instructional television. Education and schooling will continue unaffected. This is one extreme position.

Yet it would be foolish to deny that technology is bringing dramatic changes to society. The Information Age is here now. Computers have brought about significant changes in the workplace, and they are becoming more common in homes. Media convergence is well under way, and there is no denying that major corporations are investing significant sums of money to get on and make use of the Information Superhighway. Major changes *are* occurring!

Lewis Perelman, the author of the controversial book *School's Out* (1992), made a strong case for educational transformation. He suggested that schools and education today are already obsolete and that the only way to proceed is to scrap the current system altogether. With computers, he argued, knowledge acquisition is no longer something that happens only in school; now it occurs everywhere and is lifelong. Further, with the growth of hypermedia and networking, learning is something that can happen anytime and anywhere. To put it simply, according to Perelman, schools are no longer needed, and, to make matters worse, they are getting in the way of the truly necessary changes. This is another extreme position.

So it seems that we have two extreme possibilities before us for education and schooling in the future. On one hand, perhaps the status quo will continue; little or nothing will change. On the other hand, changes may be so dramatic that they completely alter what we think of as education and schooling today. What will happen?

While either of the extremes described here might come to pass, we envision a more moderate course. It is clear that individual learning is already developing into a lifelong commitment. The days when a person could expect to get a high school diploma, go to work for the local company, and retire 45 years later without ever having cracked a book again are long gone. It is also clear that the tools are here now, or will be here soon, to free learning from the confines of the school building. Soon the world's knowledge may be traveling into every household via a thin fiber-optic cable or through the airways. Will this mark the demise of schooling and education as we have known it? While it could, the social and political ramifications of such an eventuality would be considerable. Alternatively, this may provide the

Classrooms of today do not look much different from this classroom of the nineteenth century.

impetus needed to truly change schools to become centers of lifelong learning for the Information Age.

We envision a future between the two extremes. We envision a future where teachers and learners embrace and integrate educational technology and use it to improve both teaching and learning. To be sure, this will mean that there must be some important changes in education. The following are possible outcomes of this process of change:

▶ Multimedia learning resources, available via information networks, will proliferate and become an essential feature of education.

▶ Learners and teachers alike will have access to powerful, portable computing devices that will be wirelessly connected to network resources.

▶ Learning increasingly will take place in authentic contexts and focus on authentic tasks. Students will work on real problems, finding their own answers. Technology will be one tool in that process.

▶ Students will become active learners, collaborating with one another and with more experienced members of society, to seek out information and gain knowledge.

▶ Teachers' roles will tend to shift from "the sage on the stage" to the "guide on the side." Instead of conveying information, they will help learners make use of new information tools to find, analyze, and synthesize information; to solve problems; to think creatively; and to construct their own understandings.

▶ Education will become a lifelong process, important and accessible to all, and schools will become centers of learning—not just for children, but for all members of the community.

What do you think the future holds?

Addressing the Standards

NETS Connection

Based on several National Educational Technology Standards (see NETS I, III, IV, and V—refer to Teacher Resource A on page 297 for a full listing of the standards with their accompanying performance indicators) for teachers, one should have the ability to *evaluate new technological innovations and information sources to determine their appropriateness for specific learning tasks.* New technologies, adaptations, and upgrades seem to bombard us each and every day. Often we may find ourselves asking questions such as, How is one able to keep up with all of it—or should I even try? When will we be able to tell if it is time for a needed upgrade or change? Each of these questions has to do with one's ability to evaluate. Evaluation of your needs, as well as the evaluation of the potential costs and benefits of a new innovation, is a critical skill for all teachers to have. The desire by most is to find ways to stay current and provide the best possible learning experience, but at the same time not fall victim to useless and unimportant "bells and whistles" of new gadgets that prove ineffective and/or too costly.

From your own perspective (e.g., the classes you teach [or wish to teach], the time you have to design learning materials, the hardware accessibility that you have, etc.) in what way would you evaluate new technologies to determine if they would be helpful in your teaching? Create a list of questions you would want answers to in order to determine if you should invest the needed time, effort, and funds to integrate the new technology. We have listed several questions to get you started—but tailor these and add to them to help you in your specific situation.

EVALUATION QUESTIONS FOR NEW TECHNOLOGY DECISION MAKING

▶ Is this new technology practical?
▶ Does this new technology add something we don't already have?
▶ What is the time it will take to learn and effectively use this new technology?
▶ Can we afford it (both in terms of time to learn and in terms of initial cost and upkeep)?

- The artificial divisions of grade levels will disappear. Education will focus increasingly on authentic performance-based forms of assessment. Students will be judged by their ability to find and use information to solve genuine problems.
- The boundaries separating schools from each other and from the community will blur or disappear. Using distance learning technologies, including the Internet, students will learn from teachers at other locations and collaborate with students at other locations. Teachers will learn alongside students. Students will learn from other students or from members of the community. Communities themselves will change as technology enables collaboration over distances.

This is a future that is not just about educational technology. Education and schooling are bigger than that. However, without educational technology, it will be very hard for us to get where we need to go. We see a future that is *enabled* by educational technology.

TECHNOLOGY COORDINATOR'S CORNER

Not long ago, Donna Owens, a middle school math teacher, stopped by the office of her district's computer coordinator, Maria Cavazos. Donna and Maria chatted about the future of technology in education, a topic that came up because Donna had read an article that predicted future developments including continuous network connectivity, virtual environments, and computers in eyeglasses.

Maria pointed out that these developments, while seeming somewhat far-fetched, were evident in the trends of today. She noted that the district had installed wireless access points throughout Donna's school the year before last, students liked to play a virtual reality game at the arcade in the local shopping mall, and PDAs, while not small enough to fit in eyeglasses, packed the power that was once in desktop computers into a very small package. Maria remarked that it was not hard to imagine these trends continuing and leading to exciting new developments.

Donna agreed that the new developments in technology were exciting, but she also found them to be a little intimidating. She commented to Maria that technology, unlike the curriculum in her math classroom, seemed to change every year. Technology, she noted, seemed to require that she learn something new all of the time, and she found it difficult to keep up. She asked Maria for advice on how to learn about new developments in the field.

Maria explained that there was not any secret to it. She told Donna to approach learning about technologies the way she approached learning anything. Here's what she suggested. Spend time gathering information about new developments. Look for opportunities to try out new technologies to see what they might have to offer. Think about how new technologies replace, build upon, or go beyond what has been available in the past. Reflect on how any new technology might be applied to teaching and learning. Additional specific suggestions include the following:

- Read about new developments in technology. Magazine articles often provide a nice overview of trends, and articles in professional journals are a good source of ideas for integrating technology into teaching practice. You can also find a lot of useful information about new developments on the Internet.
- Take workshops or courses. Having someone else lead you through learning about a new technology can be one of the quickest ways to gain some expertise.
- Attend professional conferences in your discipline. Presentations at conferences are where you are apt to hear the most up-to-date ideas about using technology in the classroom. On top of that, technology vendors often display their products at professional conferences. That's a great place to try out things that you think you might want to use in the classroom. For a real technology experience, go to a conference that focuses on technology in education such as the National Educational Computing Conference (NECC).
- When you get new software or other new technology in the classroom, take advantage of the tutorials, online support, and other forms of help that often come with it. You might not remember how to do something such as a mail merge using an Excel data file if you don't do it all the time, but the built-in help files can walk you through the process.
- Talk to other teachers. You can learn a lot about new developments by talking to other teachers or school technology coordinators.
- Finally, don't be afraid to learn from your students. Students have a lot of time to explore computers and other new technologies, and they seem to pick it up very quickly. Make students your resident technology experts in the classroom, and let them teach you. You'll benefit, and they will get a feeling of pride and accomplishment from being acknowledged as experts in the class.

Maria concluded by advising Donna that she should not feel like she needed to become knowledgeable about every new development. There will always be new developments in technology, and no one can be an expert in all of them. She suggested that Donna just try to keep up with the developments in her own field, learn the things she would need in order to do her job productively, and find ways to integrate technology in her classroom that complement her personal teaching style. For any teacher learning about new technologies, that's good advice.

SUMMARY

In this chapter we examined the past, present, and future of educational technology. The modern era of instructional design and media began near the start of the twentieth century with the work of pioneers such as Edward Thorndike and with the school museum movement. Because of the need for effective and efficient training of military personnel during World War II, the fields received a major boost. Following the war, instructional design and media became established fields of study. Educational computing began with early computer-assisted instruction experiments on mainframe computers, such as the PLATO project. Computers proliferated in education following the development of the personal computer in the late 1970s.

Today, instructional design, educational media, and educational computing are all established disciplines and are converging through the capabilities of the computer. Media are becoming digital, and the computer offers new capabilities for planning, implementing, and evaluating instruction. While the typical school of today has a fair amount of technology, it may not be used fully. Model schools suggest how things might change if all schools made better use of available technology. As schools move toward the future, we see trends that are likely to continue in the future. There will be even greater convergence of instructional design, media, and computing. Computer networking will expand, and computer capabilities will grow. While education and schooling may ultimately either ignore these innovations or become totally transformed by them, we see a middle course in which instructional technology empowers both teachers and learners.

SUGGESTED RESOURCES

CD Resources

To increase retention and transfer of this information, review the *Reflective Questions and Activities* located in the Chapter 14 section (**Chapter info and activities >>>Chapter 14>>> Reflective Questions and Activities**) of the text's accompanying CD.

In addition, you can access Internet websites, NETS Connection exercises, and direct e-mail access to the text's authors.

Website Resources

Access the text's website (**www.prenhall.com/newby**), navigate to Chapter 14, and review the Question and Answer section for relevant questions that have been generated by students and answered by the authors. You may also submit your own questions directly to the authors. In addition, you can access presentations by the authors about this chapter and gain insights directly from them about the topics that have been presented.

Print Resources

Anglin, G. J. (Ed.). (1991). *Instructional technology: Past, present, and future.* Englewood, CO: Libraries Unlimited.

Dwyer, D. C., Ringstaff, C., & Sandholz, J. H. (1990). Teacher beliefs and practices. Part I: Patterns of change. The evolution of teachers' instructional beliefs and practices in high-access-to-technology classrooms first–fourth year findings. ACOT Report #8. Cupertino, CA: Apple Computer, Inc. Available on the World Wide Web: **http://www.apple.com/education/k12/leadership/acot/pdf/rpt08.pdf.**

Gagné, R. M. (Ed.). (1987). *Instructional technology: Foundations.* Hillsdale, NJ: Lawrence Erlbaum Associates.

Market Data Retrieval. (2003). *Technology in education 2003.* Shelton, CT: Author.

National Center for Education Statistics. (2000, September). *Teachers' tools for the 21st century.* Washington, DC: U.S. Department of Education. Available on the World Wide Web: **http://nces.ed.gov/.**

National Center for Education Statistics. (2002, September). *Internet access in U.S. public schools and classrooms: 1994–2001.* Washington, DC: U.S. Department of Education. Available on the World Wide Web: **http://nces.ed.gov/.**

Perelman, L. J. (1992). *School's out.* New York: Avon.

Saettler, P. (1990). *The evolution of American educational technology.* Englewood, CO: Libraries Unlimited.

Senge, P. M. (2000). *Schools that learn: A fifth discipline fieldbook for educators, parents, and everyone who cares about education.* New York: Doubleday.

Shelly, G. B., & Cashman, T. J. (1984). *Computer fundamentals for an information age.* Brea, CA: Anaheim.

Stoll, C. (1996). *Silicon snake oil: Second thoughts on the information highway.* New York: Doubleday.

Stoll, C. (2000). *High tech heretic: Why computers don't belong in the classroom and other reflections by a computer contrarian.* New York: Doubleday.

Electronic Resources

http://www.infed.org/biblio/b-learn.htm.
Smith, M. K. (1999). *Learning theory, The encyclopedia of informal education.* Available on the World Wide Web. Last update: May 31, 2004.

http://www.psy.pdx.edu/PsiCafe/ KeyTheorists/
The Psi Café

http://psychclassics.yorku.ca
Classics in the History of Psychology (York University)

http://tip.psychology.org/
Theory into Practice Database (Greg Kearsley)

**http://www.thejournal.com/
magazine/vault/A1681.cfm**
T.H.E. Journal, Computers in Education: A Brief
History (June 1997)

http://www.cio.com/research/current/
CIO

http://www.educause.edu/forum/
EDUCAUSE Forum for the Future of Higher Education

http://emergingtech.ittoolbox.com/
ITtoolbox Emerging Technologies

http://www.media.mit.edu
MIT's Media Lab

http://www.parc.com/
Xerox Palo Alto Research Center

http://www.zdnet.com/
Ziff Davis net

Teacher Resource

A

National Educational Technology Standards (NETS) for Teachers

http://cnets.iste.org/teachers/t_stands.html

Educational Technology Standards and Performance Indicators for All Teachers*

Building on the ISTE NETS for Students, the ISTE NETS for Teachers (NETS*T), which focus on preservice teacher education, define the fundamental concepts, knowledge, skills, and attitudes for applying technology in educational settings. All candidates seeking certification or endorsements in teacher preparation should meet these educational technology standards. It is the responsibility of faculty across the university and at cooperating schools to provide opportunities for teacher candidates to meet these standards.

The six standards areas with performance indicators listed below are designed to be general enough to be customized to fit state, university, or district guidelines and yet specific enough to define the scope of the topic. Performance indicators for each standard provide specific outcomes to be measured when developing a set of assessment tools. The standards and the performance indicators also provide guidelines for teachers currently in the classroom.

I Technology operations and concepts.

Teachers demonstrate a sound understanding of technology operations and concepts. Teachers:

- demonstrate introductory knowledge, skills, and understanding of concepts related to technology (as described in the ISTE National Education Technology Standards for Students).
- demonstrate continual growth in technology knowledge and skills to stay abreast of current and emerging technologies.

II   Planning and designing learning environments and experiences.

Teachers plan and design effective learning environments and experiences supported by technology. Teachers:

- design developmentally appropriate learning opportunities that apply technology-enhanced instructional strategies to support the diverse needs of learners.
- apply current research on teaching and learning with technology when planning learning environments and experiences.
- identify and locate technology resources and evaluate them for accuracy and suitability.
- plan for the management of technology resources within the context of learning activities.
- plan strategies to manage student learning in a technology-enhanced environment.

III   Teaching, learning, and the curriculum.

Teachers implement curriculum plans that include methods and strategies for applying technology to maximize student learning. Teachers:

- facilitate technology-enhanced experiences that address content standards and student technology standards.
- use technology to support learner-centered strategies that address the diverse needs of students.
- apply technology to develop students' higher-order skills and creativity.
- manage student learning activities in a technology-enhanced environment.

IV   Assessment and evaluation.

Teachers apply technology to facilitate a variety of effective assessment and evaluation strategies. Teachers:

- apply technology in assessing student learning of subject matter using a variety of assessment techniques.

- use technology resources to collect and analyze data, interpret results, and communicate findings to improve instructional practice and maximize student learning.
- apply multiple methods of evaluation to determine students' appropriate use of technology resources for learning, communication, and productivity.

V   Productivity and professional practice.

Teachers use technology to enhance their productivity and professional practice. Teachers:

- use technology resources to engage in ongoing professional development and lifelong learning.
- continually evaluate and reflect on professional practice to make informed decisions regarding the use of technology in support of student learning.
- apply technology to increase productivity.
- use technology to communicate and collaborate with peers, parents, and the larger community in order to nurture student learning.

VI   Social, ethical, legal, and human issues.

Teachers understand the social, ethical, legal, and human issues surrounding the use of technology in PK–12 schools and apply those principles in practice. Teachers:

- model and teach legal and ethical practice related to technology use.
- apply technology resources to enable and empower learners with diverse backgrounds, characteristics, and abilities.
- identify and use technology resources that affirm diversity.
- promote safe and healthy use of technology resources.
- facilitate equitable access to technology resources for all students.

Teacher Resource
B

Kevin Spencer's Sample Lesson Plan (Civil War Unit)

Created by Anne Ottenbreit-Leftwich, Purdue University

BACKGROUND INFORMATION
(required for planning, but not included in the plan itself)

Students

23 sixth-graders in a suburban public school in a predominantly blue-collar neighborhood

Gender—13 boys and 10 girls

Ethnicity—10 white, 6 African American, 2 Asian, and 5 Hispanic

SES—7 students qualify for free or reduced price lunch (definition of low SES)

Learning preferences—16 primarily visual, 5 primarily auditory, and 2 primarily kinesthetic

Special needs—1 visually impaired student; 1 student with epilepsy, controlled by medication; and 1 student who works with a reading teacher 1 hour a week

Technology literacy—Students are all able to use MS Word, PowerPoint, and Internet Explorer

Learning Environment

A traditional classroom with 25 movable student desks, arranged in 5 rows of 5 with a teacher's desk at the front of the room.

A teacher's computer, at the front of the room, is connected to a data projector.

Against the back wall are 4 computers with broadband Internet connections.

Along one side of the room is a bank of windows with book shelves underneath. Along the opposite side is a bulletin board covering the wall. A chalkboard covers the wall behind the teacher's desk. Two pull-down maps are located above one side of the chalkboard. A pull-down screen is located above the center of the chalkboard.

THE LESSON PLAN

Grade—6th grade social studies
Topic—US Civil War
Time frame—10 days

Standards—from NCHS Era 5: Civil War and Reconstruction (1850–1877)

Standard 2:   The course and character of the Civil War and its effects on the American people.

Standard 2A: The student understands how the resources of the Union and Confederacy affected the course of the war.

Standard 2B: The student understands the social experience of the war on the battlefield and homefront.

Objectives

1. Given a WebQuest containing information about the Civil War, students will be able to create a journal that (1) is written in the first person from the perspective of the assigned character, (2) uses historically accurate language, and (3) refers to historically important events.

2. Given a WebQuest containing information about the Civil War and working with a small group of peers, students will be able to create either a story-telling PowerPoint presentation or a script for a play that (1) is at least 5 minutes long, (2) tells a story from the perspective of the assigned character, (3) uses historically accurate language, and (4) refers to historically important events.

Instructional activities
Introduction (motivation/orientation activity)
Allotted time—10 minutes

Method—discussion
Media—Internet; projected visuals
Equipment and materials required—computer with Internet access and a data projector.

1. Show a short series of photographs of people from the Civil War era, one at a time. Possible source—http://www.civilwarphotos.net
   Vary the pictures as much as possible: man-woman-child; black-white; city-rural; military-civilian.

2. With each photograph, briefly identify the person and ask the students—What do you think life was like for this person? How do you think the war affected him/her? In what ways do you think life was different than for the previous person?

3. Explain that this lesson will explore what life was like for various people during the Civil War.

Outline the objectives, emphasizing that the students will use the story-telling presentation to teach the rest of the class about how the war affected various people. This will help create a transition to the next activity.

Digital video presentation
Allotted time—10 minutes

Method—presentation
Media—computer; projected visuals
Equipment and materials required—computer connected to a data projector

1. Briefly introduce a sample story-telling presentation. Explain that this is an example of what the students will be creating in this lesson. Point out 2 or 3 things that they should pay particular attention to as they watch the presentation.

2. Show a digital story-telling presentation created by a previous group of students (if available) or the teacher.

3. Briefly discuss the presentation by asking the students about the things you pointed out in your introduction.

Development of a KWL chart (orientation activity)
Allotted time—15 minutes

Method—discussion
Media—projected visuals
Equipment and materials required—data projector; KWL chart template
This new lesson should build on what the students already know. Create a starting point for the lesson by asking the students to develop a know-want-learn (KWL) chart, based on previous Civil War lessons.

1. Show a blank KWL chart and explain what information should be put in each column.

2. Ask the students to provide information for the K column, describing what they know about the Civil War. Enter the information from the students into the blank chart. The entries in the chart can be short bullet points, but make sure that each entry is accurate and that everyone understands it.

3. Ask the students to provide information for the W column, describing what they would most like to learn about the Civil War. Enter this information into the blank chart. Again, the entries can be short bullet points, but make sure that everyone understands each entry.

4. Close the discussion by pointing out the still blank L column and saying that we'll fill that column in at the end of the lesson.

Overview of important events (information activity)
Allotted time—10 minutes

Method—presentation
Media—projected visuals
Equipment and materials required—data projector; time-line handouts

The purpose of this activity isn't to provide a lengthy description of these events, but to provide an overview of the time period to help students organize the information that they may gather from the WebQuest.

1. Show a timeline of key events that took place during the Civil War—include events from both the battlefield and the homefront.
2. Briefly describe each key event. One thing to emphasize during this presentation is the chronological relationships among the events. For example, point out any events that take place at the same time or that follow one another in time.

Introduction to WebQuest search (orientation activity)
Allotted time—20 minutes

Method—presentation
Media—Internet
Equipment and materials required—computer with Internet access and a data projector; scoring rubric on handouts (attached)

1. Use the following list and ask the students to pick the character they would most like to learn about. Students may choose a character that is not on the list, with teacher approval.

Southern farmer	Northern farmer
Southern plantation owner	Northern storekeeper
Southern belle	Northern woman
Southern newspaper reporter	Northern newspaper reporter
Female African American slave	African American freeman
Confederate infantry soldier	Union infantry soldier
Southern abolitionist	Northern railroad engineer

2. Introduce the WebQuest and demonstrate how to access it.
3. Describe the expectations for the journal assignment. Explain that this assignment is intended to help the students learn what it was like to live during the Civil War. They are to gather as much information as possible about their character and to write in their journals as though they were that person. They can also include drawings in their journals. Remind the students of the key events included in the timeline discussed previously and suggest that they look at these events from their character's point of view—how did it affect that character, what did it mean to that character.

4. Present the scoring rubric and explain it. Emphasize that the journals must use historically accurate language and historically accurate descriptions of events. Each day in the classroom will be one month during the Civil War.

WebQuest search (information activity)
Allotted time—30 minutes a day

Method—discovery
Media—computer
Equipment and materials required—computers with Internet access

1. Provide students with time during each class period to search the WebQuest and write in their journals.
2. During the search periods, meet with individual students to answer questions and help them make sense of the information they're finding.

Preparation of student presentations (application activity)
Allotted time—30 minutes a day

Method—collaborative learning
Media—computers
Equipment and materials required—computers loaded with Microsoft Word and PowerPoint

1. Assign students to groups of 3 or 4. You can group common roles together to provide more depth to one viewpoint, or include a variety of characters in a group to provide more breadth.
2. Describe the expectations for the assignment. The primary sources of information for the assignment are the students' journals. Remind them that they have two options—a PowerPoint presentation or a play script. Each must be at least 5 minutes long.
3. Present the scoring rubric and explain it. Emphasize that the journals must use historically accurate language and historically accurate descriptions of events.
4. Provide the students with time during each class session to meet with their groups and prepare their presentations. The main message that each presentation should convey is what life was like for that character. Emphasize that the presentations must use historically accurate

language and historically accurate descriptions of events.

5. Throughout the preparation, meet with each group to answer questions, correct any misconceptions, and provide guidance.

Student presentations (application/evaluation activity)
Allotted time—60 minutes

Method—presentation; discussion
Media—computer, projected visuals
Equipment and materials required—computers loaded with Microsoft Word and PowerPoint and connected to a data projector; scoring rubric on handouts (attached)

1. Briefly remind the students of the assignment.
2. Ask the groups of students to give their presentations.
3. Briefly discuss the presentations, when they are all done. Ask the students questions such as:
   ▶ What did you learn about your character from the other presentations?
   ▶ Based on what you saw in the presentations, how did the _____ (insert one of the key events from the timeline activity) affect your character?

▶ What events had the biggest effect on the most people?
▶ What other characters were affected most by the war and how were they affected?

4. Evaluate each presentation, using the scoring rubric for this assignment.

Summary (information/orientation activity)
Allotted time—10 minutes

Method—discussion
Media—projected visuals
Equipment and materials required—data projector; KWL chart from the earlier activity

1. Show the KWL chart from the earlier activity and briefly review the K and W columns.
2. Ask the students to provide information for the L column, describing what they learned about the Civil War from this lesson. Enter this information into the chart. The entries can be short bullet points, but make sure that everyone understands each entry.
3. Close the lesson by briefly describing the subject of the next lesson.

Rubric for WebQuest Journaling Assignment

	4	3	2	1
Ideas	Ideas were expressed in a clear and organized fashion. The writer showed thoughtful interpretation of characters.	Ideas were expressed in a clear manner, but the interpretation of the characters could have been better.	Ideas were somewhat organized, but were not very clear. It took more than one reading to figure out what the character was feeling.	The journal seemed to be a collection of unrelated sentences. It was very difficult to figure out what the character was thinking.
Content accuracy	The journal entry contains at least 5 accurate facts about the topic.	The journal entry contains 3–4 accurate facts about the topic.	The journal entry contains 1–2 accurate facts about the topic.	The journal entry contains no accurate facts about the topic.
Historical language	Historically accurate language was used.	Some historically accurate language was used.	Little historically accurate language was used.	Historically accurate language was not used.
Grammar	There were no spelling or grammar mistakes.	There were 1–3 spelling or grammar mistakes.	There were 4–6 spelling or grammar mistakes.	There were more than 6 spelling or grammar mistakes.
Total	_____/16 = _____ %			
Comments				

Rubric for Digital Storytelling Assignment

	4	3	2	1
Historical accuracy	The story and images contain historically accurate information and create an accurate portrayal of life during the Civil War according to the specific character.	The story and images contain historically accurate information, although some incorrect interpretations are presented. The final product is a somewhat accurate portrayal of life during the Civil War according to the specific character.	The story and images contain historically accurate information, although many incorrect interpretations are presented. The final product is not a very accurate portrayal of life during the Civil War according to the specific character.	The story and images did not contain historically accurate information and the final product did not present an accurate portrayal of life during the Civil War according to the specific character.
Detail	The story is told with perfect detail. It does not seem too short or too long.	The story is good, though it seems to drag or it needs more detail.	The story is satisfactory, but it is too long or too short in more than one section.	The story needs work. It is too long or too short to be interesting.
Images	Images are chosen to match different parts of the story. There was a specific purpose for each picture.	Some images are chosen to match different parts of the story. There was a purpose for almost every picture.	Few images are chosen to match different parts of the story. There was no purpose for some of the pictures.	No images are chosen to match different parts of the story. There was no purpose for some of the pictures.
Point of view	Establishes an idea and maintains a focus throughout.	Establishes an idea early on and maintains focus for a majority of the presentation.	There are a few parts which lack focus, but the idea is fairly clear.	It is difficult to distinguish the idea behind the presentation.
Voice	Voice is audible and the narration makes sense.	Voice is audible throughout a majority of the presentation and the narration makes sense.	Voice is audible throughout some of the presentation and most of the narration makes sense.	Voice is audible throughout some of the presentation and some of the narration makes sense.
Length	The presentation was at least 5 minutes long.	The presentation was at least 4 minutes long.	The presentation was at least 3 minutes long.	The presentation was less than 2 minutes long.
Total	_____ /24 = _____ %			
Comments				

GLOSSARY

Acceptable use policy   An agreement signed by all participants defining proper Internet usage guidelines.

Acronym   A type of mnemonic in which a single word is made up of the first letters of a group of words.

Acrostic   A type of mnemonic in which letters in the new information are used as the first letters of the words in a sentence or phrase.

Advance organizer   An outline, preview, or other such preinstructional cue used to promote retention of content to be learned.

Algorithm   A series of steps needed to solve a particular problem or perform a particular task.

Analogy   A statement that likens something new to something familiar. Analogies are typically used either to make abstract information more concrete or to organize complex information.

Antecedent   An event, object, or circumstance that prompts a behavior.

Application activity   A type of instructional activity that provides students with an opportunity to practice using what they are learning.

Applications   Software programs designed to perform a specific function for the user, such as processing text, performing calculations, and presenting content lessons.

Artificial intelligence (AI)   A branch of computer science concerned with the design of computers and software that are capable of responding in ways that mimic human thinking.

ASCII format   American Standard Code for Information Interchange; the standard way of representing text, which allows different computer brands to "talk" to one another. Sometimes referred to as plain text or unformatted text.

Assessment rubric   A set of guidelines used to reliably appraise or judge products or performances.

Assistive technology   Computer hardware and software that supports students with special needs.

Asynchronous   Not occurring at the same time.

Attachments   E-mail additions; may be either documents, graphics, or software.

Attention   The process of selectively receiving information from the environment.

Attitudes   A type of learning that refers to feelings, beliefs, and values that lead individuals to make consistent choices when given the opportunity.

Audio   Spoken words or sounds, either live or recorded.

Audio teleconferencing   A distance education technology that uses a speakerphone to extend a basic telephone call and permits instruction and interaction between individuals or groups at two or more locations.

Audiographics   The use of audio teleconferencing accompanied by the transmission of still pictures and graphics via slow-scan video, fax, or an electronic graphics tablet.

Audiotape   Acetate on which sounds are recorded using magnetic signals, usually stored in a cassette case.

Authoring systems   Computer programs that permit the development of interactive, computer-based applications without a need for programming knowledge.

Backbone   The set of high-speed data lines connecting the major networks that make up the Internet.

Baud rate   The communication speed between a computer and a device (such as a modem), roughly equivalent to bits per second.

Behavior   A response made by an individual.

Bit   The smallest amount of information that the CPU can deal with; a single binary digit.

Bitmapped graphics   Sometimes called paint or raster graphics, in which each pixel directly corresponds to a spot on the display screen. When scaled to larger sizes, this type of graphic looks jagged.

Bookmark   A way to store addresses of frequently used websites on your computer.

Browser   A computer application for accessing the World Wide Web.

Bulletin board system   A computer network software tool that allows individuals to "post" messages and to read messages posted by others.

Byte   A collection of eight bits, equivalent to one alphanumeric character.

Case study   A type of problem solving that requires students to actively participate in real or hypothetical problem situations that reflect the types of experiences actually encountered in the discipline under study.

CD   See Compact disc.

CD-ROM (Compact disc–read-only memory)   Digitally encoded information permanently recorded on a compact disc.

Cell   A single block in a spreadsheet grid, formed by the intersection of a row and a column.

Chat room   On computer networks, a location for person-to-person real-time (synchronous) interaction by typing messages.

Classroom observation   A form of evaluation that involves having a knowledgeable person come into the classroom to watch a lesson in process, to comment on how well the materials and activities work, and to make suggestions for improvements.

Clip art   Previously created graphics designed to be added to word processing or desktop publishing documents or to computer-based instruction.

Cognitive overload   Inhibited functioning created by excessive demands being placed on memory and/or other cognitive processes.

Compact disc (CD)   A 4.72-inch-diameter disc on which a laser has digitally recorded information such as audio, video, or computer data.

Computer   A machine that processes information according to a set of instructions.

Computer conferencing   An asynchronous communication medium in which two or more individuals exchange messages using personal computers connected via a network or telephone lines.

Computer gradebook   A computer database program that can store and manipulate students' grades.

Computer program   A set of instructions that tells the computer how to do something.

Computer software   See Software.

Computer system   A collection of components that includes the computer and all of the devices used with it.

Computer virus   See Virus.

Computer-assisted instruction (CAI)   See Computer-based instruction.

Computer-assisted learning (CAL)   See Computer-based instruction.

Computer-based instruction (CBI)   The use of the computer in the delivery of instruction.

Computer-managed instruction (CMI)   The use of the computer in the management of instruction, including applications such as student recordkeeping, performance assessment, and monitoring students' progress.

Computer-mediated communication (CMC)   The use of the computer as a device for mediating communication between teacher and students and among students, often over distances. Electronic mail and computer conferencing are two types of application software commonly used in CMC.

Concept map   A graphical representation of interrelated concepts that students can use as a learning aid or that teachers can use as an aid in content organization.

Conditional information   A type of information that describes the potential usefulness of facts, concepts, and principles.

Conditions   A portion of the instructional objective that indicates under what circumstances students are expected to perform.

Consequence   An event, object, or circumstance that comes after a behavior and is attributable to the behavior.

Contingencies   The environmental conditions that shape an individual's behavior.

Cooperative learning   An instructional method that involves small heterogeneous groups of students working toward a common academic goal or task. Its use promotes positive interdependence, individual accountability, collaborative/social skills, and group processing skills.

Copyright   The legal rights to an original work produced in any tangible medium of expression, including written works, works of art, music, photographs, and computer software.

Corrective feedback   Feedback that tells students specifically what they can do to correct their performance.

CPU   The central processing unit, or brain, of the computer, which controls the functions of the rest of the system and performs all numeric calculations.

Criteria   A portion of the instructional objective that indicates the standards that define acceptable performance.

CRT   Television-like display screen that uses a cathode ray tube.

Culture   Refers to the attitudes, values, customs, and behavior patterns that characterize a social group (Banks, 1997).

Cursor   A highlighted position indicator used on the computer screen.

Cursor control   The use of directional movement keys or a mouse to position the cursor anywhere within a document for the purposes of editing.

Cycle of continuous improvement   The continuous evaluation of instruction before, during, and after implementation, which leads to continual revision and modification in order to increase student learning.

Database   An organized collection of information, often stored on the computer.

Database management system (DBMS)   Software that enables the user to enter, edit, store, retrieve, sort, and search through computer databases.

Datafile   The collection of all related records in a database.

Declarative information   A type of information that includes facts, concepts, principles, and the relationships among them.

Demonstration   An instructional method that involves showing how to do a task as well as describing why, when, and where it is done. Provides a real or lifelike example of the skill or procedure to be learned.

Designing instruction   The process of "translating principles of learning and instruction into plans for instructional materials" and activities (Smith & Ragan, 1999, p. 2).

Desktop publishing (DTP)   Computer application software that gives users a high degree of control over the composition and layout of material on a printed page, including both text and graphics.

Digital camera   A camera that stores pictures in computer-compatible digital format rather than on film.

Digital divide   A term used to describe the gap between those individuals who have access to technology such as computer software, the Internet, and so on and those who do not.

Digital Versatile Disc (DVD)   See Digital video disc.

Digital Video Disc (DVD)   A compact disc format for storing motion video and computer data.

Digitizer   A device that allows audio as well as still or motion video to be captured in a form that the computer can use.

Direct observation   A form of evaluation that involves watching students as they work through some part(s) of the lesson.

Discovery   An instructional method that uses an inductive, or inquiry, method to encourage students to find "answers" for themselves through the use of trial-and-error problem-solving strategies.

Discussion A dynamic instructional method in which individuals talk together, share information, and work cooperatively toward a solution or consensus. This method encourages classroom rapport and actively involves students in learning.

Display boards Classroom surfaces used for writing and displaying information, including chalkboards, multipurpose boards, bulletin boards, magnetic boards, and flip charts.

Displayed visuals Category of visuals that are generally exhibited on display boards (e.g., multipurpose boards, bulletin boards) and are not projected.

Distance education An organized instructional program in which the teacher and learners are physically separated by time or by geography.

Distractors The incorrect or less appropriate alternative answers for a given multiple-choice question. Also called *foils*.

Domain A major category of locations on the Internet. Major domains include com (company), edu (educational institution), gov (government), mil (military), net (network), and org (organization).

Downloading Receiving information over a network from another computer.

Drill and practice A series of practice exercises designed to increase fluency in a new skill or to refresh an existing one. Use of this approach assumes that learners have previously received some instruction on the concept, principle, or procedure to be practiced.

Drop Point of actual physical connection between a computer and external network access lines.

DVD See Digital video disc.

Educational technology The "application of technological processes and tools which can be used to solve problems of instruction and learning" (Seels & Richey, 1994, p. 4).

Electronic mail (e-mail) Electronically transmitted private messages that can be sent from individuals to other individuals or groups.

E-mail See Electronic mail.

E-mail address A unique electronic address for an individual or organization, analogous to a postal address.

Emoticons Combinations of type characters that resemble human faces when turned sideways. Used to indicate emotion or intent on e-mail or in chat rooms.

Encoding The process of translating information into some meaningful form that can be remembered.

Ergonomics A field of study focusing on the design of technology systems that align with human characteristics, needs, and capabilities.

Ethnicity The manner in which individuals identify themselves based on their (or their ancestors') country of origin.

Evaluation The third phase in the Plan, Implement, Evaluate model. Focus is on assessment techniques used to determine the level of learning learners have achieved and/or the effectiveness of the instructional materials.

Evaluation activity A type of instructional activity designed to determine how well students have mastered lesson objectives.

Event driven Computer actions or programs, such as hypermedia software, that respond to events in the environment; for example, a mouse action event that occurs when the user clicks on a button.

Fair Use "A policy established by the courts interpreting copyright law that allows parts of a copyrighted work to be used free of charge by educators, under certain very specific conditions having largely to do with the amount of the work used and the degree to which this use would financially penalize the copyright owner" (Tiene & Ingram, 2001, p. 310).

FAQ Acronym for "frequently asked questions." Used on the Internet to disseminate basic information and to reduce repetitive queries.

Feedback Information provided to students regarding how well they are doing during practice.

Field Each individual category of information recorded in a database.

File server A computer dedicated to managing a computer network and providing resources to other computers on the network (the clients). The file server is usually faster and has larger storage capabilities than the client machines.

Fixed disk See Hard disk.

Flat filer A type of DBMS that works with a single datafile at a time.

Floppy disk/diskette A magnetic storage medium for computer data that allows users to randomly access information.

Flowcharting A graphical means of illustrating the logical flow of a computer program.

Focusing question A question typically used at the beginning of a lesson to direct students' attention to particularly important aspects of the new information.

Foils See Distractors.

Font The appearance of the text itself, which can be altered through the selection of various typefaces and sizes of type. These include many typefaces common to the printing field, such as Times, Helvetica, Geneva, and Courier.

Formative evaluation A form of assessment that indicates whether or not students have learned what they must know before progressing to the next portion of the instruction.

Formula A mathematical expression that directs an electronic spreadsheet to perform various kinds of calculations on the numbers entered in it.

ftp (file transfer protocol) The standard method for sending or retrieving electronic files on the Internet.

Game An activity in which participants follow prescribed rules as they strive to attain a goal.

Grammar checker Ancillary feature of word processors that identifies a range of grammatical and format errors such as improper capitalization, lack of subject-verb agreement, split infinitives, and so on.

Graphic Any pictorial representation of information such as charts, graphs, animated figures, or photographic reproductions.

Graphical user interface (GUI) The use of graphical symbols instead of text commands to control common computer functions such as copying programs and disks.

Graphics tablet A computer input device that permits the development of graphic images by translating drawing on the tablet into onscreen images.

Hacker   An individual who gains access to computer systems without authorization.

Hard copy   A printed copy of computer output.

Hard disk   A large-capacity magnetic storage medium for computer data. Also called a *fixed disk,* it remains sealed within the case of most computers to protect it from dust, smoke, and other contaminants.

Hardware   The physical components of the computer system.

Heuristic   A rule of thumb or flexible guideline that can be adapted to fit each instructional situation.

High-level language   A computer language that contains instructions that resemble natural language and that does not require knowledge of the inner workings of the computer to use successfully.

Highlighting   Various techniques designed to direct attention to certain aspects of information, including the use of **bold,** underlined, or *italicized* print; color, labels, and arrows for pictorial information; and speaking more loudly or more slowly to highlight verbal information.

Home page   The preliminary or main web page of a particular website.

HTML   See Hypertext Markup Language.

Hybrid courses   Instructional format that combines elements of face-to-face teaching and learning with elements of distance education.

Hypermedia   A system of information representation in which the information—text, graphics, animation, audio, and/or video—is stored in interlinked nodes.

Hypertext   An associational information-processing system in the text domain. In a hypertext system, text information is stored in nodes, and nodes are interconnected to other nodes of related information.

Hypertext Markup Language (HTML)   The authoring "language" used to define web pages.

I/O device   Any computer input or output device.

Icon   A small pictorial or graphical representation of a computer hardware function or component, or a computer software program, commonly associated with a graphical user interface.

IM   See Instant Messaging.

Image capture   The software capability to copy images from web pages or computer applications and store them on your own computer.

Imagery   A type of mnemonic in which mental pictures are used to represent new information.

Implementation   The second phase of the Plan, Implement, Evaluate model. Focus is on the use of instructional materials and activities designed to help students achieve the outcomes specified in the instructional plan.

Individualized education program (IEP)   An instructional plan for an individual student (usually one with special needs) that describes the student's current level of proficiency and also establishes short- and long-term goals for future focus. An IEP is typically developed through a conference with the student's teachers and parents and other appropriate individuals.

Information activity   A type of instructional activity designed to help students understand, remember, and apply new information.

Inkjet printer   A type of printer that forms letters on the page by shooting tiny electrically charged droplets of ink.

Input   Information entered into the computer for processing.

Input device   Hardware such as a keyboard, mouse, or joystick through which the user sends instructions to the computer.

Instant Messaging (IM)   Generally one-to-one synchronous or real-time interaction using computers in which individuals interact by typing messages back and forth to one another.

Instruction   The selection and arrangement of information, activities, methods, and media to help students meet predetermined learning goals.

Instructional activity   Something done during a lesson to help students learn. There are five types of instructional activities: motivation, orientation, information, application, and evaluation activities.

Instructional appeal   The interest, or value, that instructional materials or activities have for the learner.

Instructional computing   The use of the computer in the design, development, delivery, and evaluation of instruction.

Instructional design   "The systematic process of translating principles of learning and instruction into plans for instructional materials and activities" (Smith & Ragan, 1999, p. 2).

Instructional effectiveness   A measure of the difference between what learners know before and after instruction; for example, Posttest − Pretest = Achievement.

Instructional efficiency   A measure of how much learners achieve per unit of time or dollar spent; for example, (Posttest − Pretest)/Time, or (Posttest − Pretest)/Cost.

Instructional game   An instructional approach that provides an appealing environment in which learners invest effort to follow prescribed rules in order to attain a challenging goal.

Instructional materials   The specific items used in a lesson and delivered through various media formats, such as video, audio, print, and so on.

Instructional media   Channels of communication that carry messages with an instructional purpose; the different ways and means by which information can be delivered to or experienced by a learner.

Instructional method   A procedure of instruction selected to help learners achieve objectives or understand the content or message of instruction (e.g., presentation, simulation, drill and practice, cooperative learning).

Instructional plan   A blueprint for instructional lessons based on analyses of the learners, the context, and the task to be learned. Planning involves "the process of deciding what methods of instruction are best for bringing about desired changes in student knowledge and skills for a specific course content and a specific student population" (Reigeluth, 1983, p. 7). The instructional plan also includes the selection of appropriate media.

Instructional technology   "Applying scientific knowledge about human learning to the practical tasks of teaching and learning" (Heinich et al., 1993, p. 16).

Integrated learning system (ILS)   A single networked delivery system that combines sophisticated computer-assisted instruction (CAI) with computer-managed instruction (CMI).

Intellectual skills   A type of learning that refers to a variety of thinking skills, including concept learning, rule using, and problem solving.

Intelligence   The adaptive use of previously acquired knowledge to analyze and understand new situations.

Intelligent tutoring system   Combines detailed information about a subject area and common student mistakes with a model of student performance to diagnose a given student's level of understanding. Also provides instruction designed to meet that student's individual needs. Sometimes called intelligent computer-assisted instruction (ICAI).

Interactive media   Media formats that allow or require some level of physical activity from the user, which in some way alters the sequence of presentation.

Interactive multimedia   Multimedia that allows user interactions so that the user can determine the direction of the program or presentation.

Interface   An electronic go-between by which the computer communicates with a peripheral device.

Internal memory   Storage inside the computer. The CPU in a personal computer retrieves and deposits information in the computer's internal memory. Also called *main memory.*

Internet   A network of computer networks that links computers worldwide.

Intrinsic motivation   Motivation in which the act itself is the reward.

Java   A computer language, often associated with the Internet, designed to create applications capable of operating across different hardware platforms.

Keyboard   The most common input device; resembles the key layout of a typewriter.

Key word   A type of mnemonic in which an unfamiliar new word is linked to a similar-sounding familiar word, which is used to create a visual image that incorporates the meaning of the new word.

Knowledge   A type of learning that refers to the ability to recall specific information.

Label   Text used to name parts of an electronic spreadsheet.

Laser printer   A printer that combines laser and photocopying technology to produce very high-quality output, comparable to that produced in typesetting. Laser printers can produce text as well as high-quality graphics and can achieve print densities of up to 1200 dots per inch for very finely detailed images.

LCD projector   A liquid crystal display device used with a computer or VCR for large-group display.

LCD screen   Liquid crystal display screen, commonly used in laptop computers and also in conjunction with display panels and projectors as large-group display devices for computer output.

Learner-centered instruction   "Actively collaborating with learners to determine what learning means and how it can be enhanced within each individual learner" (Wagner & McCombs, 1995, p. 32). An emphasis is placed on drawing on the learner's own unique talents, capacities, and experiences.

Learning   "Learning is a persisting change in human performance or performance potential [brought] about as a result of the learner's interaction with the environment" (Driscoll, 1994, pp. 8–9). To change (or have the capacity to change) one's level of ability or knowledge.

Learning environment   The setting or physical surroundings in which learning takes place, including the classroom, science or computer laboratory, gymnasium, playground, and so on.

Learning in context   The application of knowledge to solve problems or complete tasks that are realistic and meaningful.

Learning style   An individual's preferred ways for "processing and organizing information and for responding to environmental stimuli" (Shuell, 1981, p. 46).

Learning theory   A set of related principles explaining changes in human performance or performance potential in terms of the causes of those changes.

Library/media specialist   A school specialist who helps students and teachers to become effective users of ideas and information by providing access to materials, providing instruction, and working with teachers to design learning strategies to meet the needs of individual students.

Liquid crystal display (LCD)   See LCD screen.

Listserv   Also called a *mail server,* this is the computer or software that operates an e-mail discussion list on the Internet. Interested individuals subscribe to the list and subsequently receive all e-mail that is sent to the listserv.

Local-area network (LAN)   A computer network covering a limited geographical area, such as a single building or even a single room within a building.

Logo   A computer language developed by Seymour Papert and based on the learning theories of Jean Piaget; it is used in schools, particularly at the elementary level.

Macro   A shortcut to encoding a series of actions in a computer program. Provides the means to perform a number of separate steps through a single command.

Mailing list   Software that uses e-mail to deliver topic-specific information to a targeted group of respondents.

Mass storage   Input/output devices that provide for storage and retrieval of programs and other types of data that must be stored over a long period of time. Also referred to as *external* or *auxiliary* memory.

Medium/media   See Instructional media.

Megabyte   Approximately a million bytes, or 1000 kilobytes.

Memory   Within a computer, this is an area that stores instructions (programs) and information that can be readily accessed by the processor.

Methods   See Instructional methods.

Microprocessor   A single silicon chip that contains all of the CPU circuits for a computer system.

Mnemonic   Any practical device used to make information easier to remember, including rhymes, acronyms, and acrostics.

Model   A three-dimensional representation of a real object; it may be larger, smaller, or the same size as the object represented.

Modem   A combination input and output device that allows a computer to communicate with another computer over telephone lines. A modem (short for *modulator-demodulator*) converts digital computer information into sound (and vice versa) for transmission over telephone lines.

Monitor   A video or computer display device. The most common output device for personal computers.

Motivation   An internal state that leads people to choose to work toward certain goals and experiences. Defines what people will do rather than what they can do (Keller, 1983).

Motivation activity   A type of instructional activity that leads students to want to learn and to put in the effort required for learning.

Motor skills   A type of learning that refers to the ability to perform complex physical actions in a smooth, coordinated manner.

Mouse   A pointing device used to select and move information on the computer display screen. When the mouse is moved along a flat surface such as a desktop, an arrow moves across the display screen in the same direction. The mouse typically has one to three buttons that may be used for selecting or entering information.

Multimedia   Sequential or simultaneous use of a variety of media formats in a single presentation or program. Today, this term conveys the notion of a system in which various media (e.g., text, graphics, video, and audio) are integrated into a single delivery system under computer control.

Netiquette   Rules for polite social behavior while communicating over a network.

Newsgroup   On computer networks, a discussion group created by allowing users to post messages and read messages among themselves.

Objective   A statement of what learners will be expected to do when they have completed a specified course of instruction, stated in terms of observable performances.

One-computer classroom   Classroom equipped with a single computer.

Online learning   Course of study or training generally delivered via the Internet

OOPS   Object-oriented programming systems, where each thing that one sees on the computer screen is treated as an object, and each object can have a programming code associated with it.

Operating system (OS)   The master control program for a computer system.

Orientation activity   A type of instructional activity that helps students understand what they have previously learned, what they are currently learning, and what they will be learning in the future.

Output   Information that comes out of the computer.

Output device   The hardware that receives and displays information coming from the computer.

Overhead transparencies   Acetate sheets whose images are projected by means of a device that transmits light through them and onto a screen or wall.

Packet   A chunk of information routed across the Internet.

PDA   See Personal digital assistant.

Peer review   A form of evaluation that involves asking a colleague to examine all or part of an instructional lesson and make suggestions for improvement.

Performance   A portion of the instructional objective that indicates what students will do to demonstrate that they have learned.

Peripheral   Any of various devices that connect to the computer, including input devices, output devices, and mass storage devices.

Personal computer   Members of the third class of computers; these are the smallest, least powerful, and least expensive, intended for use by individuals.

Personal digital assistant (PDA)   A handheld mobile electronic device that provides users access to calendars, e-mail, contact information, and even some applications programs such as word processing and spreadsheets.

PhotoCD   A CD format developed by Kodak that can store high-quality images made from 35-millimeter photographic negatives or slides.

Pilot test   An evaluation of instruction conducted before implementing the instruction.

Pixel   A single dot, or picture element, on the computer screen.

Plagiarism detection services   Companies and organizations (e.g., Turnitin.com) that offer services to help identify if, and to what degree, potential plagiarism has occurred within written documents.

Planning   The first phase of the Plan, Implement, Evaluate model. Focus is on the design of instructional materials based on the learners, content, and context.

Plug-in   Small software program that works with a Web browser to perform tasks that the browser cannot perform on its own.

Portfolio   "A purposeful collection of student work that tells the story of the student's efforts, progress, or achievement" (Arter & Spandel, 1992, p. 36).

PowerPoint   Microsoft Office presentation applications software. Also a common term to refer to a type of projected visual (slide) that is created within presentation software.

Prerequisite   The knowledge and skills students should have at the beginning of a lesson.

Presentation   An instructional method involving a one-way communication controlled by a source that relates, dramatizes, or otherwise disseminates information to learners, and includes no immediate response from, or interaction with, learners (e.g., a lecture or speech).

Presentation software   Computer software designed for the production and display of computer text and images, intended to replace the functions typically associated with the slide projector and overhead projector.

Pretest   Preinstructional evaluation of students' knowledge and/or skills to determine students' level of performance before instruction.

Preview   A form of evaluation that involves reading, viewing, and/or working through specific instructional materials prior to using them (Heinich et al., 1999).

Printed visual   Nonprojected drawings, charts, graphs, posters, and cartoons that are commonly found in printed sources such as textbooks, reference materials, newspapers, and periodicals.

Printer   A device that provides printed output from the computer.

Printer driver   Software that ensures that an application's formatting commands are correctly translated into printer actions. Most operating systems, for example, provide a number of different printer drivers to support different models of printers.

Problem solving   An instructional method in which learners use previously mastered skills to reach resolution of challenging problems. Based on the scientific method of inquiry, it typically involves the following five steps: (1) defining the problem and all major components, (2) formulating hypotheses, (3) collecting and analyzing data, (4) deriving conclusions/solutions, and (5) verifying conclusions/solutions.

Problem-solving software   Computer applications designed to foster students' higher-order thinking skills, such as logical thinking, reasoning, pattern recognition, and use of strategies.

Processor   The "brain" of the computer that controls the functions of the rest of the system and manipulates information in various ways.

Programming   The process of creating a computer program. See Computer program.

Programming language   A set of instructions that can be assembled, according to particular rules and syntax, to create a working computer program.

Projected visual   A drawing, chart, graph, and so on that is presented in a projected fashion (e.g., overhead transparencies, projected PowerPoint slides).

Public Domain   Materials (e.g., book, song, artwork) that are not protected by intellectual property laws (e.g., copyright) and may be freely copied and distributed without first getting permission.

RAM   See Random-access memory.

Random-access memory (RAM)   The computer's working memory. In a personal computer, RAM provides a temporary work space that allows you to change its contents, as needed, to perform different tasks. Common RAM is volatile, which means that its contents disappear as soon as the power is turned off (or otherwise interrupted).

Read-only memory (ROM)   The permanent memory that is built into the computer at the factory, referred to as "read only" because the computer can read the information that is stored there but cannot change that stored information. ROM contains the basic instructions the computer needs to operate.

Real objects   Actual materials, not models or simulations.

Record   A collection of related fields that is treated as a logical unit in a database.

Reinforcing feedback   Feedback used to recognize good performance and encourage continued effort from students. Takes the form of verbal praise or a "pat on the back."

Relational database   A type of computer database that permits the interrelation of information across more than one datafile.

Reliability   "The degree to which a test instrument consistently measures the same group's knowledge level of the same instruction when taking the test over again" (Gentry, 1994, p. 383).

Retrieval   Identifying and recalling information for a particular purpose.

Rhyme   A type of mnemonic that uses words spoken in a rhythm or in verse to help remember information.

ROM   See Read-only memory.

Router   A computer that regulates Internet traffic and assigns data transmission pathways.

Rubric   See Assessment rubric.

Scan converter   A device that converts computer output for display on a television or video monitor.

Scanner   A device that uses technology similar to a photocopying machine to take an image from a printed page and convert it into a form the computer can manipulate.

Search and replace   A common feature of word processors that allows the user to locate the occurrence of any word or phrase within a document and substitute something else.

Search engine   A website that maintains a database of Internet-accessible information that can be searched to locate information of interest.

Server   See File server.

SES   See Socioeconomic status.

Simulation   An instructional method involving a scaled-down approximation of a real-life situation that allows realistic practice without the expense or risks otherwise involved. Similar to problem solving, simulations often include case studies and/or role-plays.

Slides   A small-format (e.g., 35mm) photographic transparency individually mounted for one-at-a-time projection.

Socialization   The process by which we learn the rules, norms, and expectations of the society in which we live.

Socioeconomic status (SES)   One's perceived rank or standing in a society based on a variety of factors, which may include family income, parents' occupations, and the amount of formal education completed.

Software   The programs or instructions that tell the computer what to do, usually stored on diskette or CD-ROM.

Special needs students   Individuals who require special educational services to help them reach their potential.

Speech recognition   Artificial intelligence based computer technology in which oral speech is converted by the computer into text.

Spelling checker   A common ancillary feature of word processors that searches through a document and reports any instances of text that do not match a built-in dictionary.

Spreadsheet   A general-purpose computer calculating tool based on the paper worksheet used by accountants.

Stem   The part of a multiple-choice assessment instrument that sets forth the problem that will be "answered" by one option from a list of alternatives.

Storyboarding   A technique for illustrating, on paper, what the screen displays in a computer program will look like before they are actually programmed.

Structural information   Information that refers to the relationships that exist among ideas and concepts (e.g., it allows one to understand how items are related).

Structured programming   A set of programming conventions designed to result in organized, easy-to-read, and correct programs. It relies on a top-down method, modular program design, a limited set of program constructs, and careful documentation of the program.

Student tryout   A "test run" of an instructional activity, approach, media, or materials with a small group of students before using it on a large scale (Mager, 1997).

Summative evaluation   Assessment that occurs after instruction that measures what students have learned.

Synchronous   Occurring at the same time.

Syntax   Rules for using computer languages.

Systems software   The basic operating software that tells the computer how to perform its fundamental functions.

Tags   Elements of HTML that are used to define properties of web pages; for example, the tags, <B>. and, </B>. denote the beginning and end of boldfaced text.

TCP/IP   Transmission Control Protocol/Internet Protocol—the communication standard used by computers on the Internet.

Technology   "The systematic application of scientific or other organized knowledge to practical tasks" (Galbraith, 1967, p. 12). Technology performs a bridging function between research and theory on one side and professional practice on the other.

Technology coordinator   A specialist and resource person who handles computers and related technologies for a school building or district.

Technology literacy   The ability to understand and use various forms of technology.

Technology plan   Organized set of goals, objectives, and steps that outline how an individual or organization will acquire and maintain specific levels of technology hardware and software (e.g., computers).

Telnet   A standard method for directly connecting to and using the resources of a remote computer on the Internet.

Template   A prepared layout designed to ease the process of creating a product in certain computer applications, for example, a slide design and color scheme for presentation software or a spreadsheet with appropriate labels and formulas but without the data.

Test generator   A computer program used to create assessment instruments.

Text   A combination of alphanumeric characters and numbers used to communicate.

Text justification   The positioning of text in a word-processed document. This includes text that is centered, aligned with respect to the right margin (right justified), and aligned with respect to the left margin (left justified). Left justified, the most common, aligns text flush with the left margin, leaving a "ragged" right margin.

Text selection   The ability to choose portions of a word-processing document for subsequent editing through the use of cursor movement keys or the mouse. Selection is sometimes called *highlighting* because selected text is usually rendered in special colors designed to stand out from surrounding material.

Theory   A set of related principles explaining observed events/relationships. Theories typically make predictions in the form of "If . . . , then . . . " statements that can be tested.

Top-down approach   An approach to problem solving and computer programming that begins by outlining the basic solution at a fairly high level of abstraction and then breaks that outline down into its component parts until they can be coded.

Transfer   The use of prior knowledge in new situations or as it applies to new problems.

Triangulation   The process of obtaining information from more than one technique or source in order to strengthen individual findings.

Tutorial   An instructional method in which a tutor—in the form of a person, computer, or special print materials—presents the content, poses a question or problem, requests learner response, analyzes the response, supplies appropriate feedback, and provides practice until the learner demonstrates a predetermined level of competency.

Two-way interactive video   A distance education technology in which sending and receiving sites are equipped with cameras, microphones, and video monitors and linked via some means of transmission (e.g., satellite, microwave, cable, fiber-optic cable).

Type style   Application of different features to any word-processing font, including **boldface,** *italics,* underline, and others.

Ubiquitous computing   Sometimes called pervasive computing or distributed intelligence, it refers to situations in which computer processing power is embedded, often invisibly, in objects in the everyday environment.

Undo   A software feature that allows the user to recover from an error; for example, if you select and delete the wrong block of text, the undo command restores the text to the document.

Uniform Resource Locator (URL)   The unique address for every Internet site or World Wide Web page, containing the protocol type, the domain, the directory, and the name of the site or page.

Uploading   Sending information over a network to another computer.

URL   See Uniform resource locator.

Vector graphics   Also called *draw graphics,* in which the computer "remembers" the steps involved in creating a particular graphic image on the screen, independent of a particular screen location or the graphic's size.

Video   The display of recorded pictures on a television-like screen. Includes videotapes, videodiscs, and CDs.

Video conferencing   A distance education technology that uses two-way audio and two-way video between sites.

Video digitizer   An add-on device for the computer that takes video from standard video sources and captures it as a computer graphic or motion video.

Videodisc   A video storage medium composed of recorded images and sound, similar to the CD. Depending on format, a videodisc can hold from 30 to 60 minutes of motion video images, up to 54,000 still images, or a combination of motion and still images. As with the CD, the videodisc can be indexed for rapid location of any part of the material.

Videotape   A video storage medium in which video images and sound are recorded on magnetic tape. Popular sizes include one-inch commercial tape, three-quarter-inch U-matic, half-inch VHS or S-VHS, and 8-millimeter.

Virtual reality (VR)   A computer interface that simulates an interactive environment that appears to the observer as another reality. A VR system uses special hardware and software to project a three-dimensional visual representation of an environment and responds to the user's motion within that environment.

Virus   A computer program that infects a computer system, causing damage or mischief. Like a biological virus, it causes the host computer to make copies of the virus, which can then spread to other computers over networks, through online services, or via infected diskettes.

Vision   How one perceives the future could/should be (e.g., technology vision—how technology should be used in the future).

Visual   Combination of graphics and text presented in a two-dimensional format.

Web   See World Wide Web.

Web browser   Application program designed to access the Internet and navigate its nonsequential pathways.

Web page   A hypertext document on the World Wide Web, somewhat analogous to a printed page.

Web server   A computer connected to the Internet that makes web pages and websites available to other computers.

Website   A set of interrelated web pages usually operated by a single entity (e.g., company, school, organization, or individual).

Web use policy   See Acceptable use policy.

Wide-area network (WAN)   A computer network covering a broad geographical area, such as between buildings, campuses, or even across hundreds or thousands of miles. Often involves the interconnection of multiple local-area networks.

Word processing   Using a word processor.

Word processor   A computer program for writing that supports the entry, editing, revising, formatting, storage, retrieval, and printing of text.

Word wrap   A feature of a word processor that automatically shifts the next whole word to the next line of the document when a line of text in a computer document is filled.

World Wide Web (WWW or the Web)   An information retrieval system on the Internet that relies on a point-and-click hypertext navigation system.

WYSIWYG   What You See Is What You Get—a standard for word processor displays where what shows on the computer display is what the document will look like when it is printed.

REFERENCES

Alexander, J. E., & Tate, M. A. (1999). *Web wisdom: How to evaluate and create information quality on the Web*. Mahwah, NJ: Lawrence Erlbaum Associates.

Anglin, G. J. (Ed.). (1991). *Instructional technology: Past, present, and future*. Englewood, CO: Libraries Unlimited.

Arter, J. A., & Spandel, V. (1992). Using portfolios of student work in instruction and assessment. *Educational Measurement: Issues and Practice, 11*(Spring), 36–44.

Asimov, I. (1984). *Asimov's guide to science* (2nd ed.). New York: Basic Books.

Ausubel, D. P., Novak, J. D., & Hanesian, H. (1978). *Educational psychology: A cognitive view*. New York: Holt, Rinehart & Winston.

Ayersman, D. J. (1996). Reviewing the research on hypermedia-based learning. *Journal of Research on Computing in Education, 28*(4), 500–525.

Bangert-Drowns, R. L. (1993). The word processor as an instructional tool: A meta-analysis of word processing in writing instruction. *Review of Educational Research, 63*(1), 69–93.

Banks, J. (1997). Multicultural education: Characteristics and goals. In J. Banks & C. Banks (Eds.), *Multicultural education: Issues and perspectives* (3rd ed.) (pp. 3–32). Boston: Allyn & Bacon.

Barell, J. (1995). *Teaching for thoughtfulness: Classroom strategies to enhance intellectual development*. White Plains, NY: Longman.

Baron, C. L. (2004). *Designing a digital portfolio*. Indianapolis, IN: New Riders.

Bernard, R. M., Abrami, P. C., Lou, Y., Borokhovski, E., Wade, A., Wozney, L., Wallet, P. A., Fiset, M., & Huang, B. (2004). How does distance education compare with classroom instruction? A meta-analysis of the empirical literature. *Review of Educational Research, 74*(3), 379–439.

Bloom, B. S. (1956). *Taxonomy of educational objectives: Book 1, Cognitive domain*. New York: Longman.

Blumenfeld, P. C., Soloway, E., Marx, R. W., Krajcik, J. S., Guzdial, M., & Palinscar, A. (1991). Motivating project-based learning: Sustaining the doing, supporting the learning. *Educational Psychologist, 26,* 369–398.

Borko, H., & Livingston, C. (1992). Cognition and improvisation: Differences in mathematics instruction by expert and novice teachers. *American Educational Research Journal, 26,* 473–498.

Brown, J. S., Collins, A., & Duguid, P. (1989). Situated cognition and the culture of learning. *Educational Researcher, 18*(1), 32–42.

Bruer, J. T. (1993). *Schools for thought: A science of learning in the classroom*. Cambridge, MA: MIT Press.

Bruner, J. S. (1961). The act of discovery. *Harvard Education Review, 31*(1), 21–32.

Brunner, C. & Bennett, D. (1997). Technology and gender: Differences in masculine and feminine views. *NASSP Bulletin, 81*(592):46–51.

Bullock A. A., & Hawk, P. P. (2005). *Developing a teaching portfolio: A guide for preservice and practicing teachers*. Upper Saddle River, NJ: Pearson/Merrill/Prentice Hall.

Chen, P., & McGrath, D. (2003). Moments of joy: Student engagement and conceptual learning in the design of hypermedia documents. *Journal of Research on Technology in Education, 35*(3), 402–422.

Chuang, H., Thompson, A., & Schmidt, D. (March, 2003a). Issues and barriers to advanced faculty use of technology. Paper presented at the *Society for Information Technology and Teacher Education International Conference (SITE),* Albuquerque, NM.

Chuang, H. H., Thompson, A. D., & Schmidt, D. (2003b). Faculty technology mentoring programs: Major trends in the literature. *Journal of Computing in Teacher Education, 19*(4), 101–106.

Cochran-Smith, M. (1991). Word processing and writing in elementary classrooms: A critical review of related literature. *Review of Educational Research, 61*(1), 107–155.

Collins, A., Brown, J. S., & Holum, A. (1991). Cognitive apprenticeship: Making thinking visible. *American Educator, 15*(3), 6–11, 38–46.

Collis, B. (1990). *The best of research windows: Trends and issues in educational computing*. Eugene, OR: International Society for Technology in Education. (ERIC Document Reproduction Service No. ED 323 993).

Crews, K. D. (2003). New copyright law for distance education: The meaning and importance of the TEACH Act. Retrieved December 9, 2004, from http://www.copyright.jupui.edu/teach summary.htm.

Culp, K. M., Honey, M., & Mandinach, E. (2003). A retrospective on twenty years of education technology policy. U.S. Department of Education, Office of Educational Technology: Washington DC. Retrieved November 3, 2004, from www.nationaledtechplan.org/participate/20years.pdf.

Dallmann-Jones, A. S. (1994). *The expert educator: A reference manual of teaching strategies for quality education*. Fond du Lac, WI: Three Blue Herons.

D'Aoust, C. (1992). Portfolios: Process for students and teachers. In K. B. Yancey (Ed.), *Portfolios in the writing classroom* (pp. 39–48). Urbana, IL: National Council of Teachers of English.

Deaux, K. (1984). From individual differences to social categories: Analysis of a decade's research on gender. *American Psychologist, 39,* 105–116.

DeBell, M., & Chapman, C. (2003). Computer and Internet use by children and adolescents in 2001: Statistical analysis report. National Center for Education Statistics. U.S. Department of Education: Washington, D.C. (http://nces.ed.gov/pubs2004/2004014.pdf).

DeLong, D. F. (2001). Code red virus—Most expensive in history of Internet. NewsFactor Network. Retrieved November 2, 2004, from ww.newsfactor.com/perl/story/12668.html#story-start.

deMarrais, K., & LeCompte, M. (1999). *The way schools work* (3rd ed.). New York: Longman.

Derry, S., & Murphy, D. A. (1986). Designing systems that train learning ability: From theory to practice. *Review of Educational Research, 56*(1), 1–39.

Dewey, J. (1897). My pedagogic creed. *School Journal, 54,* 77–80.

Dick, W., & Reiser, R. A. (1996). *Planning effective instruction.* Upper Saddle River, NJ: Prentice Hall.

Driscoll, M. P. (1994). *Psychology of learning for instruction.* Boston: Allyn & Bacon.

Driscoll, M. P. (2005). *Psychology of learning for instruction* (3rd ed.). Boston: Allyn & Bacon.

Duffy, T. M., Lowyck, J., & Jonassen, D. H. (1993). Introduction. In T. M. Duffy, J. Lowyck, & D. H. Jonassen (Eds.), *Designing environments for constructive learning* (pp. 1–5). Berlin: Springer-Verlag.

Eggen, P., & Kauchak, D. (2001). *Educational psychology: Windows on classrooms* (5th ed.). Upper Saddle River, NJ: Merrill.

Ehrman, L., Glenn, A., Johnson, V., & White, C. (1992). Using computer databases in student problem solving: A study of eight social studies teachers' classrooms. *Theory and Research in Social Education, 20*(2), 179–206.

Ertmer, P. A. (1999). Addressing first- and second-order barriers to change: Strategies for technology integration. *Educational Technology Research and Development, 47*(4), 47–61.

Ertmer, P. A., & Newby, T. J. (1993). Behaviorism, cognitivism, constructivism: Comparing critical features from an instructional design perspective. *Performance Improvement Quarterly, 6*(4), 50–72.

Fleming, M. L. (1987). Displays and communication. In R. M. Gagné (Ed.), *Instructional technology: Foundations* (pp. 233–260). Hillsdale, NJ: Lawrence Erlbaum Associates.

. Gagné, R. M. (Ed.). (1987). *Instructional technology: Foundations.* Hillsdale, NJ: Lawrence Erlbaum Associates.

Gagné, R. M., Wager, W. W., Golas, K., & Keller, J. M. (2005). *Principles of instructional design* (5th ed.). Belmont, CA: Wadsworth.

Galbraith, J. K. (1967). *The new industrial state.* Boston: Houghton Mifflin.

Gardner, H. (1985). *The mind's new science: A history of the cognitive revolution.* New York: Basic Books.

Gentry, C. G. (1994). *Introduction to instructional development: Process and technique.* Belmont, CA: Wadsworth.

Gredler, M. E. (2001). *Learning and instruction: Theory into practice.* Upper Saddle River, NJ: Merrill/Prentice Hall.

Hanor, J. H. (1998). Concepts and strategies learned from girls' interactions with computers. *Theory into Practice, 37*(1), 64–71.

Harper, G. K. (2001). The TEACH Act finally becomes law. The UT System Copyright Crash Course. Retrieved December 9, 2004, from http://www.utsystem.edu/OGC/IntellectualProperty-/ teachact.htm.

Healy, J. M. (1998). *Failure to connect: How computers affect our children's minds—for better and worse.* New York: Simon & Schuster.

Heinich, R., Molenda, M., Russell, J. D., & Smaldino, S. (1993). *Instructional media and technologies for learning* (4th ed.). Upper Saddle River, NJ: Merrill/Prentice Hall.

Heinich, R., Molenda, M., Russell, J. D., & Smaldino, S. (1999). *Instructional media and technologies for learning* (6th ed.). Upper Saddle River, NJ: Merrill/Prentice Hall.

Houtz, L. E., & Gupta, U. G. (2001). Nebraska high school students' computer skills and attitudes. *Journal of Research on Computing in Education, 33*(3).

Hunter, M. (1982). *Mastery teaching.* El Segundo, CA: TIP.

Jacobsen, D., Eggen, P., & Kauchak, D. (1993). *Methods for teaching: A skills approach* (4th ed.). Upper Saddle River, NJ: Merrill/Prentice Hall.

Johnson, R. T., Johnson, D. W., & Stanne, M. B. (1985). Effects of cooperative, competitive, and individualistic goal structures on computer-assisted instruction. *Journal of Educational Psychology, 77*(6), 668–677.

Jonassen, D. H. (1991). Evaluating constructivist learning. *Educational Technology, 31*(9), 28–33.

Kauchak, D., & Eggen, P. D. (1989). *Learning and teaching: Research based methods.* Boston: Allyn & Bacon.

Kearny, C., Newby, T., & Stepich, D. (1995). *Building bridges: Creating instructional analogies.* Presentation at the Annual Convention of the National Society for Performance and Instruction, Atlanta, GA, March.

Keller, J. M. (1983). Motivational design of instruction. In C. M. Reigeluth (Ed.), *Instructional design theories and models: An overview of their current status* (pp. 383–434). Hillsdale, NJ: Lawrence Erlbaum Associates.

Keller, J. M. (1987). Development and use of the ARCS model of instructional design. *Journal of Instructional Development, 10*(3), 2–10.

Kleiner, A., & Lewis, L. (2003). *Internet access in U.S. public schools and classrooms: 1994–2002.* Washington, DC: U.S. Department of Education, National Center for Education Statistics.

Kozma, R. (1991). Learning with media. *Review of Educational Research, 61*(2), 179–211.

Kulik, J. A. (2003). *Effects of using instructional technology in elementary and secondary schools: What controlled evaluation studies say.* Arlington, VA: SRI International. Available: http://www.sri.com/policy/csted/reports/ sandt/it.

Kulik, C. C., & Kulik, J. A. (1991). Effectiveness of computer-based instruction: An updated analysis. *Computers in Human Behavior, 7,* 75–94.

Lee, J. (1999). Effectiveness of computer-based instructional simulation: A meta-analysis. *International Journal of Instructional Media, 26,* 71–85.

Leshin, C. B., Pollock, J., & Reigeluth, C. M., (1992). *Instructional design strategies and tactics.* Englewood Cliffs, NJ: Educational Technology.

Lou, Y., Abrami, P. C., & d'Apollonia, S. (2001). Small group and individual learning with technology: A meta-analysis. *Review of Educational Research, 71*(3), 449–521.

Machtmes, K., & Asher, J. W. (2000). A meta-analysis of the effectiveness of telecourses in distance education. *The American Journal of Distance Education, 14*(1), 27–46.

Macionis, J. (1997). *Sociology* (5th ed.). Upper Saddle River, NJ: Prentice Hall.

Mager, R. F. (1997). *Preparing instructional objectives* (3rd ed.). Belmont, CA: Pitman.

Maor, D., & Taylor, P. C. (1995). Teacher epistemology and scientific inquiry in computerized classroom environments. *Journal of Research in Science Teaching, 32*(8), 839–854.

Market Data Retrieval. (2003). *Technology in education 2003*. Shelton, CT: Author.

Mayer, R. E. (2003). *Learning and instruction*. Upper Saddle River, NJ: Merrill/Prentice Hall.

McCullen, C. (2002). Preventing digital plagiarism. *Technology & Learning, 22*(9), 8.

McCutcheon, G. (1980). How do elementary school teachers plan? The nature of planning and influences on it. *Elementary School Journal, 81*(1), 4–23.

McKeachie, W. J. (1994). Why classes should be small, but how to help your students be active learners even in large classes. In W. J. McKeachie (Ed.), *Teaching tips* (pp. 197–210). Lexington, MA: Heath.

Mehlinger, H., & Powers, S. (2002). *Technology and teacher education: A guide for educators and policymakers*. Boston: Houghton-Mifflin.

Milem, J. F. (2003). The educational benefits of diversity: Evidence from multiple sectors. In M. J. Chang, D. Witt, J. Jones, & K. Hokuta (Eds.), *Compelling interest: Examining the evidence on racial dynamics in colleges and universities* (pp. 126–169). Stanford, CA: Stanford University Press.

Moll, O., Amanti, C., Neff, D., & Gonzalez, N. (1992). Funds of knowledge for teaching: Using a qualitative approach to connect homes and classrooms. *Theory into Practice, 31*(2), 132–141.

Morrison, G. R., Ross, S. M., & Kemp, J. E. (2004). *Designing effective instruction*. Hoboken, NJ: John Wiley & Sons.

National Center for Education Statistics. (2000, September). *Teacher's tools for the 21st century*. Washington, DC: U.S. Department of Education. Available on the World Wide Web: http://nces.ed.gov/.

National Center for Education Statistics. (2002, September). *Internet access in U.S. public schools and classrooms: 1994–2001*. Washington, DC: U.S. Department of Education. Available on the World Wide Web: http://nces.ed.gov/.

Neumann, Y., & Shachar, M. (2003, October). Differences between traditional and distance education academic performances: A meta-analytic approach. *International Review of Research in Open and Distance Learning, 4*(2). Available at http://www.irrodl.org/content/v4.2/shachar-neumann.html.

Niemiec, R., & Walberg, H. J. (1987). Comparative effects of computer-assisted instruction: A synthesis of reviews. *Journal of Educational Computing Research, 3*(1), 19–37.

Ogbu, J. (1992). Understanding cultural diversity and learning. *Educational Researcher, 21*(8), 5–14.

Ogbu, J., & Simons, H. (1998). Voluntary and involuntary minorities: A cultural-ecological theory of school performance with some implications for education. *Anthropology & Education Quarterly, 29*(2), 155–188.

Ormrod, J. E. (1995). *Educational psychology: Principles and applications*. Upper Saddle River, NJ: Merrill/Prentice Hall.

Ormrod, J. E. (2004). *Human learning*. Upper Saddle River, NJ: Merrill/Prentice-Hall.

Palinscar, A. S. (1986). Metacognitive strategy instruction. *Exceptional Children, 53*(2), 118–124.

Perelman, L. J. (1992). *School's out*. New York: Avon.

Phillion, J., Johnson, T., & Lehman, J. D. (2004). Using distance education technologies to enhance teacher education through linkages with K–12 schools. *Journal of Computing in Teacher Education, 20*(2), 63–70.

Phillips, D. C. (1995). The good, the bad, and the ugly: The many faces of constructivism. *Educational Researcher, 24*(7), 5–12.

Pintrich, P. R., & Schunk, D. H. (1996). *Motivation in education: Theory, research, and applications*. Englewood Cliffs, NJ: Merrill/Prentice-Hall.

Reigeluth, C. M. (1983). Instructional design: What is it and why is it? In C. M. Reigeluth (Ed.), *Instructional-design theories and models: An overview of their current status* (pp. 3–36). Hillsdale, NJ: Lawrence Erlbaum Associates.

Reigeluth, C. M. (1999). *Instructional design theories and models: A new paradigm of instructional theory, vol. 2*. Hillsdale, NJ: Lawrence Erlbaum Associates.

Reiser, R. A., & Dick, W. (1996). *Instructional planning: A guide for teachers*. Boston: Allyn & Bacon.

Reynolds, A. (1992). What is competent beginning teaching? A review of the literature. *Review of Educational Research, 62*(1), 1–35.

Robinson, P. W. (1981). *Fundamentals of experimental psychology*. Upper Saddle River, NJ: Merrill/Prentice Hall.

Rogoff, B. (1990). *Apprenticeship in thinking: Cognitive development in social context*. New York: Oxford University Press.

Rothwell, W. J., & Kazanas, H. C. (1992). *Mastering the instructional design process: A systematic approach*. San Francisco: Jossey-Bass.

Russell, T. L. (1999). *The no significant difference phenomenon*. Available at http://www.nosignificantdifference.org/.

Saettler, P. (1990). *The evolution of American educational technology*. Englewood, CO: Libraries Unlimited.

Salend, S. J. (2005). *Creating inclusive classrooms: Effective and reflective practices for all students* (5th ed.). Upper Saddle River, NJ: Merrill/Prentice Hall.

Sapon-Shevin, M. (2001). Schools fit for all. *Educational Leadership, 58*(4), 34–39.

Sardo-Brown, D. (1990). Experienced teachers' planning practices: A U.S. survey. *Journal of Education for Teaching, 16*(1), 57–71.

Schmitt, M. S., & Newby, T. J. (1986). Metacognition: Relevance to instructional design. *Journal of Instructional Development, 9*(4), 29–33.

Schön, D. A. (1983). *The reflective practitioner: How professionals think in action*. New York: Basic Books.

Schunk, D. H. (1996). *Learning theories: An educational perspective*. Englewood Cliffs, NJ: Prentice-Hall.

Schunk, D. H., & Zimmerman, B. J. (Eds.) (1998). *Self-regulated learning: From teaching to self-reflective practice*. New York: Guilford Press.

Seels, B. B., & Richey, R. C. (1994). *Instructional technology: The definition and domains of the field*. Washington, DC: Association for Educational Communications and Technology.

Sharan, Shlomo. (Ed.) (1990). *Cooperative learning: Theory and research*. Westport, CT: Praeger.

Shelly, G. B., & Cashman, T. J. (1984). *Computer fundamentals for an information age*. Brea, CA: Anaheim.

Shuell, T. J. (1981). Dimensions of individual differences. In F. H. Farley & N. J. Gordon (Eds.), *Psychology and education: The state of the union* (pp. 32–59). Berkeley, CA: McCutchan.

Skinner, B. F. (1968). *The technology of teaching*. New York: Appleton-Century-Crofts.

Skinner, B. F. (1984). The shame of American education. *American Psychologist, 39,* 947–954.

Smaldino, S. E., Russell, J. D., Heinich, R., & Molenda, M. (2005). *Instructional technology and media for learning* (8th ed.). Upper Saddle River, NJ: Pearson/Merrill/Prentice Hall.

Smith, P. L., & Ragan, T. J. (1999). *Instructional design*. Upper Saddle River, NJ: Merrill/Prentice Hall.

Snow, R., Corno, L., & Jackson, D., III (1996). Individual differences in affective and cognitive functions. In D. Berliner & R. Callee (Eds.), *Handbook of educational psychology* (pp. 243–310). New York: Simon & Schuster Macmillan.

Solomon, G. (2004). Drafting a customized tech plan: An up-to-the-minute design. *Technology & Learning, 24*(7), 34–35.

Stepich, D. A., & Newby, T. J. (1988). Analogical instruction within the information processing paradigm: Effective means to facilitate learning. *Instructional Science, 17,* 129–144.

Stiggins, R. J. (2005). *Student-involved assessment FOR learning* (4th ed.). Upper Saddle River, NJ: Merrill/Prentice Hall.

Stoll, C. (1996). *Silicon snake oil: Second thoughts on the information highway*. New York: Doubleday.

Stoll, C. (2000). *High tech heretic: Why computers don't belong in the classroom and other reflections by a computer contrarian*. New York: Doubleday.

Swain, S. L., & Harvey, D. M. (2002). Single-sex computer classes: An effective alternative. *TechTrends, 46*(6), 17–20.

Taylor, R. P. (Ed.). (1980). *The computer in the school: Tutor, tool, tutee*. New York: Teachers College Press.

Terenzini, P. T., Cabrera, A. F., Colbeck, C. L., Bjorklund, S. A., & Parente, J. M. (2001). Racial and ethnic diversity in the classroom: Does it promote learning. *The Journal of Higher Education, 72*(5).

Tessmer, M. (1990). Environment analysis: A neglected state of instructional design. *Educational Technology, 38*(1), 55–64.

Thorndike, E. L. (1931). *Human learning*. New York: Century.

Tiene, D., & Ingram, A. (2001). *Exploring current issues in educational technology*. Boston: McGraw Hill.

U.S. Department of Commerce. (1998). *Current population survey, 1997*. Washington, DC: Bureau of the census.

U.S. Department of Education. (1996). *Getting America's students ready for the 21st century*. Washington, DC: U.S. Department of Education.

Villegas, A. M., & Lucas, T. (2002). *Educating culturally responsive teachers: A coherent approach*. Albany, NY: State University of New York Press.

Wagner, E. D., & McCombs, B. L. (1995, March–April). Learner centered psychological principles in practice: Designs for distance education. *Educational Technology, 35,* 32–35.

Wasserman, S. (1992). *Asking the right question: The essence of teaching*. Bloomington, IN: Phi Delta Kappa.

Watson, J. B. (1924). *Behaviorism*. New York: Peoples' Institute.

West, C. K., Farmer, J. A., & Wolff, P. M. (1991). *Instructional design: Implications from cognitive science*. Upper Saddle River, NJ: Merrill/Prentice Hall.

Williams, M., & Linn, M. C. (2002). WISE inquiry in fifth grade biology. *Research in Science Education, 32,* 415–436.

Wittrock, M. C. (1990). Generative processes of comprehension. *Educational Psychologist, 24,* 345–376.

Woolfolk, A. E. (1990). Generative processes of comprehension. *Educational psychology* (4th ed.). Upper Saddle River, NJ: Merrill/Prentice Hall.

Woolfolk, A. E. (1995). *Educational psychology* (6th ed.). Boston: Allyn & Bacon.

Woolfolk, A. E. (1998). *Educational psychology* (7th ed.). Boston: Allyn & Bacon.

Yelon, S. L. (1991). Writing and using instructional objectives. In J. L. Briggs, K. L. Gustafson, & M. H. Tillman (Eds.), *Instructional design: Principles and applications* (2nd ed.) (pp. 75–122). Englewood Cliffs, NJ: Educational Technology.

Yelon, S. L. (1996). *Powerful principles of instruction*. White Plains, NY: Longman.

Young, B. (2000). Gender differences in students' attitudes toward computers. *Journal of Research on Computing in Education, 33*(2).

NAME INDEX

SUBJECT INDEX